Changing Uganda

9780852553480

EASTERN AFRICAN STUDIES

Abdul Sheriff
Slaves, Spices & Ivory in Zanzibar
Integration of an East African Commercial Empire
into the World Economy 1770–1873

Abdul Sheriff & Ed Ferguson
Zanzibar under Colonial Rule

Isaria N. Kimambo
Penetration & Protest in Tanzania
The Impact of the World Economy
on the Pare 1860–1960

T.L. Maliyamkono & M.S.D. Bagachwa
The Second Economy in Tanzania

Tabitha Kanogo
Squatters & the Roots of Mau Mau 1905–1963

David W. Throup
Economic and Social Origins of Mau Mau 1945–1953

Frank Furedi
The Mau Mau War in Perspective

David William Cohen & E.S. Atieno Odhiambo
Siaya
The Historical Anthropology of an African Landscape

Bruce Berman & John Lonsdale
Unhappy Valley *
Clan, Class & State in Colonial Kenya

Bruce Berman
Control & Crisis in Colonial Kenya
The Dialectic of Domination

Holger Bernt Hansen & Michael Twaddle
(Editors)
Uganda Now
Between Decay & Development

Bahru Zewde
A History of Modern Ethiopia *
1855–1974

*forthcoming

Changing Uganda

The Dilemmas
of Structural Adjustment
& Revolutionary Change

EDITED BY
HOLGER BERNT HANSEN
& MICHAEL TWADDLE

JAMES CURREY
London

FOUNTAIN PUBLISHERS
Kampala

OHIO UNIVERSITY PRESS
Athens

HEINEMANN KENYA
Nairobi

James Currey Ltd
54b Thornhill Square, Islington
London N1 1 BE
Fountain Publishers
P.O. Box 488
Kampala
Ohio University Press
Scott Quadrangle
Athens, Ohio 45701, USA
Heinemann Kenya
Kijabe Street, P.O. Box 45314
Nairobi, Kenya

British Library Cataloguing in Publication Data

Changing Uganda : the dilemmas of Structural
adjustment and revolutionary change.
I. Hansen, Holger Bernt II. Twaddle, Michael
967.6104
ISBN 9970-02-158-3 (Fountain Paper)
ISBN 0-85255-349-8 (James Currey Cloth)
ISBN 0-85255-348-X (James Currey Paper)

Library of Congress Cataloging-in-Publication Data

Changing Uganda: the dilemmas of structural adjustment & revolutionary
change/edited by Holger Bernt Hansen & Michael Twaddle.
p. cm. — (Eastern African Studies)
Based on a conference sponsored by the Danish Research Council for
Development Research, and others.
Includes bibliographical references and index.
ISBN 0-8214-1004-0. — ISBN 0-8214-1005-9 (pbk.)
1. Uganda — Politics and government — 1979 — Congresses.
2. Uganda — Social conditions — 1979 — Congresses. I. Hansen,
Holger Bernt. II. Twaddle, Michael. III. Forskningsrader for
udviklingsforskning (Denmark) IV. Series: Eastern African studies
(London, England)
DT433.285.C47 1991
967.61—dc20   91-25720
                                                                          CIP

Typeset in 10/11 pt Baskerville
by Colset Pte Ltd., Singapore
Printed in India
by UBS Publishers' Distributors Ltd.
New Delhi

This volume,
and the conference upon which it is based,
were sponsored by
the Danish Council for Development Research,
the Danish International Development Agency (DANIDA),
the Danish Committee for Cultural Cooperation
with Developing Nations,
the Danish Social Science Research Council,
Institute of Commonwealth Studies, University of London,
Carl Bro International
and Danbrew Consult.
Thanks are also given to
the Swedish Agency for Research Cooperation
with Developing Countries
for assistance with travel expenses.
Thanks to the good offices of
the Lutheran World Federation, Kampala,
and Danchurchaid, Copenhagen,
copies are available for sale
in Uganda.

CONTENTS

List of Maps   ix

List of Contributors   xi

1. Introduction Holger Bernt Hansen & Michael Twaddle   1

PART ONE
Structural adjustment on trial

2. *Structural adjustment in Uganda: the initial experience*
    K. Sarwar Lateef   20
3. *Economic adjustment programmes in Uganda, 1985–8*
    E.O. Ochieng   43
4. *IMF conditionality and structural adjustment under the National
    Resistance Movement* Joshua B. Mugyenyi   61

PART TWO
How people cope

5. *The agrarian context of the Ugandan crisis* Vali Jamal   78
6. *Women, children and a 'living wage'* Christine Obbo   98

PART THREE
The health of Ugandans: the social sector under pressure

7. *Living on the edge: changing social structures in the context of AIDS*
    George C. Bond & Joan Vincent   113
8. *Medicines and self-help: the privatization of health care in eastern
    Uganda* Susan Reynolds Whyte   130
9. *The quest for therapy in Moyo district* Tim Allen   149

Contents
PART FOUR

Prophetic resistance, external challenges, and human rights issues

10. *Is Alice Lakwena a witch? The Holy Spirit Movement and its fight against evil in the north* Heike Behrend   162
11. *Uganda and southern Sudan 1986–9: new regimes and peripheral politics* Peter Woodward   178
12. *Kenya's relations with Museveni's Uganda* David Throup   187
13. *Human rights issues in Museveni's Uganda* M. Louise Pirouet   197

PART FIVE

The constitutional bases of revolutionary change

14. *Legal adjustment to revolutionary change* Sam K. Njuba   210
15. *The rule of law and human rights in Uganda: the missing link* E. Khiddu-Makubuya   217
16. *Towards constitutional renovation: some political considerations* A.G.G. Gingyera-Pinycwa   224

PART SIX

Rebuilding political institutions

17. *Institution-building: the case of the NRM and the military 1986–9* Dan Mudoola   230
18. *The Ugandan elections of 1989: power, populism and democratization* Nelson Kasfir   247
19. *Resistance councils and committees: a case study from Makerere* Apolo R. Nsibambi   279
20. *Rebuilding survival structures for the poor: organizational options for reconstruction in the 1990s* E.A. Brett   297

PART SEVEN

Problems of landholding

21. *Institutional dimensions of land tenure reform* W. Kisamba-Mugerwa   311

Contents

PART EIGHT

Revolution in education? Tackling the diploma disease

22. *Educational reform during socio-economic crisis* W. Senteza Kajubi   322

PART NINE

Getting Ugandans to speak a common language

23. *Recent developments in the language situation and prospects for the future* Ruth G. Mukama   334

PART TEN

Problems of gender and inculturation within a wider context

24. *Privatization versus the market: cultural contradictions in structural adjustment* Ali A. Mazrui   351

Bibliography   379

Index   387

LIST OF MAPS

Map 1   Uganda   xii
Source: Uganda Country Profile 1990–91
The Economist Intelligence Unit, London

Map 2   Administrative Divisions of Uganda after 1976   77
Source: *Uganda Now*, Hansen and Twaddle (eds), London, 1988

Map 3   Masaka and Rakai Districts in Western Uganda   114
Source: Dept. of Geography, Makerere University, Kampala, 1991

Map 4   Bunyole County   131
Source: *Uganda Now*, Hansen and Twaddle (eds), London, 1988

Map 5   Northern Uganda   163
Source: Dept. of Geography, Makerere University, Kampala, 1991

CONTRIBUTORS

Tim Allen teaches anthropology at the Open University, UK.

Heike Behrend is an anthropologist at the University of Bayreuth.

George C. Bond teaches anthropology at Columbia University, New York.

Edward A. Brett is a researcher associated with the Institute of Development Studies at the University of Sussex.

A.G.G. Gingyera-Pinycwa is Professor of Political Science at Makerere University.

Holger Bernt Hansen is research professor in religious and political studies at the University of Copenhagen.

Vali Jamal is Senior Research Economist, ILO, Geneva.

W. Senteza Kajubi is a former head of the Institute of Teacher Education and presently Vice-Chancellor of Makerere University.

Nelson Kasfir is Professor of Government at Dartmouth College, New Hampshire.

Edward Khiddu-Makubuya is a lawyer, currently teaching in the Faculty of Law at Makerere University; he is also a member of the Constitutional Commission.

W. Kisamba-Mugerwa is Senior Research Fellow at Makerere Institute of Social Research and also a member of the National Resistance Council.

K. Sarwar Lateef is Lead Economist for the Eastern Africa Department of the World Bank, Washington.

Ali A. Mazrui is Albert Schweitzer Professor in the Humanities, State University of New York at Binghamton.

Dan M. Mudoola is Director of Makerere Institute of Social Research and Vice-Chairman of the Constitutional Commission.

Joshua Mugyenyi is Head of the Secretariat at the Bank of Uganda.

Ruth G. Mukama is Head of the Department of Languages at Makerere University.

The Hon. Sam K. Njuba is Minister of Constitutional Affairs in Uganda.

Apolo R. Nsibambi is Professor of Political Science at Makerere University.

Christine Obbo teaches social anthropology at Wayne State University, Detroit.

Erisa O. Ochieng is attached to the Department of Economics, Makerere University, and is Director of Export Policy Analysis and Development Unit in the Ministry of Planning and Economic Development in Uganda.

M. Louise Pirouet taught at Homerton College, Cambridge.

David Throup teaches politics at the University of Keele.

Michael Twaddle teaches politics and history at the Institute of Commonwealth Studies, University of London.

Joan Vincent is Professor of Anthropology, Barnard College, Columbia University, New York.

Susan Reynolds Whyte is at the University of Copenhagen, where she teaches anthropology.

Peter Woodward teaches political science at the University of Reading.

Uganda

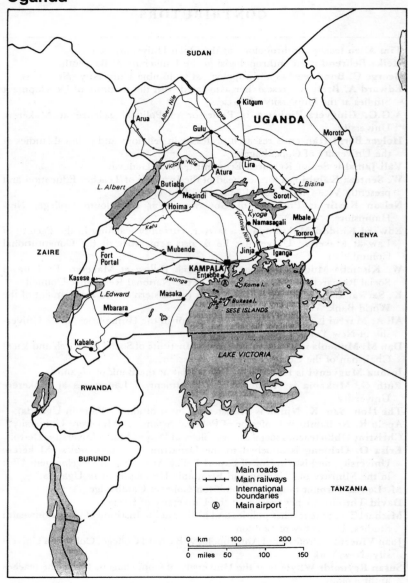

Map 1 *Uganda*

ONE
Introduction

Holger Bernt Hansen & Michael Twaddle

There has been a qualitative change in the character of political leadership in Uganda since the seizure of central powers in January 1986 by guerrillas attached to the National Resistance Movement (NRM) and Army (NRA) led by Yoweri Museveni. According to *The Economist* four years later, Yoweri Museveni and his NRA/NRM government had not only provided the country with its best government since independence from British protectorate rule almost three decades before, but had provided other African states struggling to develop their resources in the best interests of their peoples with a splendidly appropriate role model.[1]

An earlier collection, *Uganda Now: Between Decay and Development* (1988), published a number of studies of developmental problems in the country. These were originally presented to an international conference that we organized at Lyngby Landbrugsskole near Roskilde, Denmark, in September 1985. At that time the NRA was only the most likely successor to a short-lived and northern-led military dictatorship currently and brutally in power; a year later, at Mbale in eastern Uganda, one of us was told repeatedly that the Okellos' atrocities and other infringements of human rights in 1985 were worse than Idi Amin's and Milton Obote's followers' earlier ones combined.[2] However, when *Uganda Now* went to press it was only possible to take account of the first year of the NRM government, and then only provisionally. By the time our second international meeting on Uganda was held at Lyngby Landbrugsskole in September 1989, nearly four years had passed with the NRM in power. By then a much clearer picture had emerged of the NRM's economic and political objectives. There was also a much clearer picture of the actual changes that had been introduced by the new government, and what changes had *not* been introduced; and also a sharper understanding of the principal problems still facing it in common with many other African governments. There was therefore much to write about, to talk about, and to complete more considered contributions about in the light of the further conference discussions made possible at Lyngby Landbrugsskole in September 1989 by the support of DANIDA, other donors and our respective university employers

1

in Copenhagen and London and the contributions of more than 40 delegates. This book is the result.

Inflation in Uganda is inevitably one of its principal concerns. In part because of the very tranquillity that has come to the greater part of Uganda under the NRM government, Ugandans grumble the more about the problems that remain – in particular about the difficulties of raising a decent 'living wage', as Christine Obbo describes it in Chapter 6 with specific reference to women and children. The reduction of inflation has also been one of the principal aims of successive stabilization and reform packages promoted in Uganda by the International Monetary Fund, the World Bank and the two institutions' affiliates since the start of the 1980s. When the NRM came to power in January 1986, its attitudes towards the earliest of these was frankly hostile – basically because of their association with the corruption, inefficiency, and political actions of the second presidency of Milton Obote between 1980 and 1985 (now popularly known as 'Obote 2' in Uganda). Furthermore, there was still a war to be waged away from Kampala against remaining supporters of the Okellos' dictatorship as well as surviving partisans from Obote 2. Only in 1987–8 was the NRM government finally ready to do business with the IMF and the Bank, albeit still only rather half-heartedly, along lines indicated by Sarwar Lateef, E.O. Ochieng and Joshua Mugyenyi in Chapters 2, 3 and 4, respectively.

The principal political energies of the new government meanwhile were directed along lines already made clear in the *10-Point Programme* issued by the NRA during its bush war against Obote 2 and the Okellos' dictatorship. It sought to restore Ugandans' human rights after the horrors of the Luwero triangle; strengthen the resistance committees that had proved so important in winning the bush war against Obote 2; introduce democracy at all levels of decision making in the country; politicize the army into a 'pro-people' rather than an 'anti-people' attitude; and introduce a new constitution for the whole country after adequate consultation.

Respect for freedom of speech and the press had been strongly stressed in the *10-Point Programme*; and this is one area where the NRM government continues to receive praise from left-leaning observers otherwise critical of the NRM's 'capture' by the IMF, such as Mahmood Mamdani,[3] as well as by more specialist commentators such as Louise Pirouet in Chapter 13. Indeed a marked feature of life in Kampala today, in notable contrast to Kenya, is the number of newspapers on sale in the streets highly critical of the government of the day. Since May 1986, too, a human rights commission chaired by Judge Oder has reviewed and adjudicated upon earlier infringements of human rights. And successive reports by International Alert, the Minority Rights Group, and Amnesty International have given the NRM government a generally clean bill of health in the field of human rights in comparison with neighbouring governments such as Burundi, Ethiopia, Kenya, Rwanda, Somalia, Sudan, and Zaire.[4] However, as Pirouet notes in her chapter, there have been unhappy incidents from time to time. Also the most recent Amnesty report on Uganda at the time of writing (December 1990) expresses concern at atrocities by NRA troops in Soroti district while simultaneously (and somewhat paradoxically) criticizing the NRM government for executing rather than imprisoning soldiers found guilty of earlier failings in this field.[5] Surprisingly, the report does not mention the immediate cause of the NRA troops' misbehaviour, which was the beheading of two NRA soldiers by supporters of Peter Otai's Uganda People's Army a few days before.[6] Otai had been one of the ministers of Milton Obote most active in organizing counter-insurgency operations against the NRA during the early 1980s. Nonetheless, the need for improved self-control by troops tackling remaining pockets of anti-NRA insurgency in Uganda seems clear enough, as does greater constitutional backing for human rights in general and of the future role of the Ugandan army as servant of civilian government in particular – all points stressed and elaborated further below by Pirouet, E. Khiddu-Makubuya (Chapter 15) and Dan Mudoola (Chapter 17).

Mudoola argues that the Ugandan military will be domesticated effectively by accepting it as an interest group in its own right rather than by denying it any extra-military role. Hence the desirability of integrating the military into such political institutions as the National Resistance Council and giving it a role in production, particularly farming. These links are seen by Mudoola as part of a wider integrationist process enabling the military, among other things, to act as a positive socializing agency. For this reason he also sees it an advantage for Uganda to have a large army because this makes it less likely that it will foster sectional interests. Integration, however, needs to go hand in hand with domestication, the process whereby the military is subjected to civilian control mechanisms. Thus far Mudoola considers that this has proved broadly successful under the NRA government since January 1986. But he admits that there are still risks in this policy. This is principally because institution building is taking place in Uganda at a time when scarcity of resources is still helping to make corruption rampant. Another danger apparent at the end of 1990 is that the defection of leading NRA personnel to form the Rwandan Patriotic Front and launch an invasion of neighbouring Rwanda (leading to the death of some of them) might ultimately prove the forerunner of further civilian conflict in Uganda along ethnic lines. Inevitably the Ugandan military would be sucked into such a conflict and its command structure would be substantially undermined.[7]

One way of meeting this risk is increased popular participation and responsibility in politics at all levels. The NRA government has attempted to do this by establishing resistance committees throughout the country. These are directly elected in villages, at which level delegates in turn elect indirectly a tier of further committees or councils at progressively higher and wider levels, until the National Resistance Council itself is reached. This was further enlarged in February 1989 to include not only NRM leaders, army personnel, representatives of women, youth and labour unions, but also 160 councillors elected from within the resistance committee and council pyramidal complex.[8]

In Chapter 18 Nelson Kasfir specifically analyses the elections of February 1989. He is concerned to establish the extent to which those elections may be considered democratic, and how far they stemmed forces hostile to democracy in Uganda. He concludes that on balance the elections were democratic, but that their character and the way in which they were conducted made their 'democratic' aspects in certain respects ambiguous. To start with, all elections above village level were indirect, and direct voting at RC1 level was by queueing. Here, however, Kasfir agrees with Sam K. Njuba, Minister for Constitutional Affairs (Chapter 14), in concluding that, given the socio-economic and political situation, and popular memories of the notoriously rigged election of December 1980 that ushered in Obote 2, queueing was not essentially unfair, in marked contrast to recent elections in Kenya. However, it did limit the extent to which the elections of February 1989 could be considered to be a vote of confidence in the NRM government.

Another limiting factor was prohibition of active participation by political parties. Prominent in the *10-Point Programme* was distaste for 'sectarianism' entrenched by politicians earlier associated with Uganda's two veteran political parties, the Democratic Party and the Uganda Peoples Congress. By denying the DP and UPC overt participation in the February 1989 elections, the NRM may have pre-empted a further outburst of 'sectarianism'. It also thereby ensured its own continuance in power at national level, as did direct appointment of a quarter of the membership of the National Resistance Council. Nonetheless, at the heart of the whole electoral exercise at national level there remained ambiguity about whether the NRM government ultimately intended to develop populist democracy in Uganda, with the NRA/NRM itself becoming a mass movement, or whether its eventual aim was multi-party democracy, with open competition between the NRM and the two or three older parties taking place after an interval.

At village level, however, there can be little doubt that Ugandans in general considered the February 1989 elections to have constituted a revolutionary change in politics. All observers speak of great enthusiasm amongst voters and a high turn-out. The electoral framework may not have encouraged major discussion of political alternatives, but for once

4

Introduction

Ugandans had a real chance to decide in whose hands future decisions would be placed, at least at constituency level. Compared with what they had been used to, it was no small change that 14 ministers and deputy ministers were not re-elected and that alternative candidates were actually voted onto the National Resistance Council in their places.

Another innovation in institution building in Uganda since the advent of the NRM government, as already remarked, has been the further establishment and spread of resistance committees and councils throughout the country. In Chapter 19 Apolo Nsibambi presents one of the first detailed accounts of this process. Himself a former chairman of an RC1 at Makerere University, he provides a very lively account of the day-to-day issues with which a resistance committee may be concerned in one highly urbanized area of Uganda. Nsibambi's account speaks for itself, suggesting that the RC system has now established itself firmly even at Uganda's leading university. Comments by other observers suggest that it is also now well established in most other parts of Uganda. Personal experience strengthens this impression. In 1989 when one of us was driving with a Ugandan friend on a minor road in Toro, a cyclist carrying a man with a loaded gun on his passenger seat suddenly appeared in front of the car. We were motioned to a halt and quickly discovered that the two men were local resistance committee members who had just disarmed a soldier who had disobeyed army regulations by bringing a gun home for the weekend. The two RC members were so excited that they were keen to speak of the incident before continuing on their way to inform the RC chairman and arrange for the soldier to be formally arrested. The incident seemed instructive for two reasons: first, the RC members had acted against clearly illegal behaviour; secondly, they had acted decisively against a member of the armed forces in order to demonstrate that law no longer came out of the barrel of a gun.

However, as Nsibambi's and other chapters in this volume indicate, there are also evident weaknesses in the RC system. Its pyramidal organizational pattern seems fairly detailed and effective from village to sub-county level, but above that there appears to be a level of responsibility missing. This hinders further communication and action both upwards and downwards. The roles of RCs *vis-à-vis* other organs of government, too, have not been defined adequately; overlapping jurisdictions and consequent struggles for power are therefore not infrequent. The efficient exercise of RCs' functions is also hampered by a chronic lack of funds, and this may well further explain the relatively poor attendance at RC meetings since the February 1989 elections. The resistance committee and council system presupposes an ambitious degree of popular mobilization, but the more RCs are loaded with administrative functions the more problematical will become the maintenance of popular interest and support for them as truly democratic and local institutions.

5

Introduction

This point was brought home vividly during the same tour in Toro in 1989, when one of us took a photograph of a gravity water pump. A man then appeared to ask if written permission to take the photograph had been obtained from the RC1 chairman. He turned out to be the member of the local resistance committee concerned with security and quickly proved utterly irresponsive to all argument about the innocence of photographing water pumps. Then suddenly the writer's companion in the car, a Ugandan recently graduated from Makerere University, became very angry and told the RC man to stop talking nonsense and instead take a note of the car registration number if he wanted to pursue the matter. We then stopped talking to him and drove off. When asked subsequently why he had become so angry, the writer's companion replied that misuse of authority had been the root of all Uganda's evils and it was sad to see it continuing within the new system. If Uganda were to get anywhere, the old practices had to stop – at the bottom as well as the top.

But where is change to start – at the bottom or at the top? To be successful, policy changes depend at least in part upon accurate information. Information is required from as many levels of political, cultural and economic activity as possible before changes can be introduced in any sphere with a reasonable chance of success. That had been the principal motivation of our September 1985 conference at Lyngby Landbrugsskole and the subsequent publication of *Uganda Now*. That too doubtless explains the kindness of one reviewer in describing *Uganda Now* as 'virtually a mini-encyclopedia of Uganda';[9] or, as another put it: 'In the absence of anything more recent and equally comprehensive, it is the best overview of Uganda's political trauma in the last two decades'.[10] It is principally because of the warmth with which the first book has been received that the present collection has been published. It is concerned with Uganda's continuing developmental and other problems since January 1986 and, political changes apart, information has been specifically solicited for it from workers researching health, education, language and land tenure policy, and the economic difficulties facing women and children.

The health of Uganda is reviewed by George Bond and Joan Vincent (Chapter 7), Susan Reynolds Whyte (Chapter 8) and Tim Allen (Chapter 9); and concern for the health of Ugandans is also never far from the heart of Heike Behrend's study (Chapter 10) on the Holy Spirit Movement of Alice Lakwena in northern Uganda, possibly the most formidable of the popular opposition movements confronted by the NRA government since its coming to power.

First AIDS. As Bond and Vincent see it, AIDS has been deeply debilitating to Ugandans in recent years. First, by crowding into hospitals and clinics in search of a cure that tragically does not yet exist, AIDS sufferers have obstructed access to medical care for people suffering from

6

curable diseases. Secondly, because AIDS in Uganda is currently hitting the parental generation most severely, there has been a great increase in single-parent (and often female-headed) households, with a growing number of children – when they do not simply become orphans – having to live with grandparents. Needless to say, many of these children form a lost educational generation in Uganda in view of increasing school fees and growing dues for parent–teacher associations necessitated by increased cutbacks in government education expenditure. Thanks to the remarkable openness of the current Ugandan government as well as the work of researchers like Bond and Vincent, we now know much more about the effects of AIDS on everyday life at community, family and individual level. From their case study of how AIDS originated in Rakai district (see Map 3) in economic conditions dominated by the black market or *magendo*, and then spread in epidemic manner because of the character of the local extended family system, Bond and Vincent argue that the only effective preventive remedy lies in personal behaviour. In this they are in full accord with President Yoweri Museveni who severely reprimanded his countrymen for their immoral way of life in April 1990.[11] However, here a further problem posed by AIDS must be mentioned. In Rakai, as Bond and Vincent stress, AIDS already represents far too heavy a burden for the existing social support system. Over Uganda as a whole AIDS may well alone be consuming a very large part of the investment the World Bank has proposed for the run-down social sector.

What is to be done? In her case study of Bunyole county in Bukedi district (see Map 4), Whyte describes the explosive expansion in private medical care that has taken place in Uganda during the last ten years. This has taken place essentially because of the breakdown of state medical services, and health officials' attempts to raise a 'living wage' for themselves and their families – at a time when the *magendo* economy was still expanding. Whyte interprets this ten-year trend as a process of privatization, whereby market forces have, as it were, entered Ugandan health care from below, rather than as a consequence of any deliberate World Bank-sponsored policy imposed from above. She suggests that this process has lessons for both the Uganda state and external donor agencies. Privatization from below should be encouraged in public health care, and the state discouraged from re-establishing its former dominance in this sphere. Instead the state should concentrate on training health workers and preventive health in general, leaving a good deal of curative work to the private sector. If accepted and turned into official policy, this approach would constitute a revolutionary change for Uganda and other African countries. It would amount to a planned withdrawal of the postcolonial African state from an area in which it had previously been the principal actor, and its retention of only a reduced (and therefore, it is to be hoped, more manageable) role for itself in health care.

However, there is yet another complication in the Ugandan health field, as both Whyte and Allen make clear. Independently of the Ugandan state during the last ten years, and of the massive privatization of health care discussed by Whyte, indigenous traditional healing and healers have survived with seemingly undiminished popular appeal. Indeed, as Allen makes clear for Moyo district (see Map 5), indigenous medical practices seem to have survived both as a supplement and as an alternative to the modern health care system. Indigenous healers provide additional explanations of misfortune in Moyo district, particularly in cases where it is ascribed principally to impersonal causes. They also cure sicknesses and cope with misfortunes attributed to both ancestors and poisoners alive today. Bond and Vincent, and Allen report increased activity from indigenous medical specialists in AIDS-infected areas during the last five years. All three also report continuing support for traditional healing practices in Moyo and Rakai districts alongside continuing devotion to Roman Catholicism.

It was with a very heady mixture of Christian and indigenous theology that the Holy Spirit Movement of Alice Lakwena simultaneously attempted to cleanse society from sorcery, introduce a new moral order, and overthrow the NRA government during its first years in power. Heike Behrend is one of the first scholars to have studied the Holy Spirit Movement seriously in the field. It undoubtedly posed a very serious threat to the NRM government and represented a utopian attempt to introduce a new moral order in northern Uganda of great appeal both to small farmers and former soldiers. Essentially it failed when it attempted to move southwards into Busoga. Behrend's account of it (Chapter 10) is one of the first attempts to explain the specific factors that informed its particular strategies for healing the social divisions of Ugandan society, both within Acholiland and between Acholiland and the rest of the country.

In introducing *Uganda Now* (p. 23), we noted that 'the distinction between citizens and refugees is a difficult one to draw in Uganda because of the comparative smallness of the country and the sociological complexity of many areas bordering on neighbouring countries.' Uganda's northern frontier with the Sudan is one such area of sociological fluidity. In *Uganda Now*, Peter Woodward explored the possibility of a regional political consciousness emerging there to undermine wider national integration, an analysis he updates here (Chapter 11). He stresses not only the ties between the present NRM government in Uganda and SPLA guerrillas currently establishing themselves in ever larger swathes of southern Sudan, but also the continuing role of the Khartoum government in fighting the SPLA with militias recruited from remnants in Uganda of the armies of Obote 2 and the Okellos' dictatorship as well as with its own northern Sudanese troops. The importance of this for an increase in the NRM's security problems in the far north of Uganda was further demonstrated at the start of 1990, when the Sudanese army chased SPLA guerrillas into northwestern Uganda and laid mines on the main road linking Moyo to the Sudanese border.

Further external complications to Uganda's security problems during the last four years have sprung from the Kenyan government's support for the SPLA and its less than total approval of the NRA government's domestic and foreign policies. The further complications created by recent Kenyan policy towards Uganda, which brought Uganda to the very brink of war with its neighbour in 1986–7, are chronicled by David Throup (Chapter 12).

Zaire, meanwhile, has been in flux since President Mobutu endorsed the need for a move towards a multi-party system of government early in 1990, and the Ruwenzuru secessionist movement in the Mountains of the Moon straddling Uganda's border with Zaire (see Map 1) continues to cause concern to the NRM. But it was undoubtedly the invasion of Rwanda by a Rwandan Patriotic Front recruited in part from – and led wholly by – soldiers from the National Resistance Army in Uganda that must still cause Yoweri Museveni's government most concern about national integration. For this particular adventure poses most dramatically the question: who are, and who are not, Ugandans? Lunyarwanda-speakers have lived legitimately in the eyes of the international community in Uganda since its borders were agreed with Belgium in the early days of the British protectorate.[12] But it was the turmoil and massacre accompanying the ending of Belgian rule over Rwanda between 1959 and 1962 that led the greatest numbers of Lunyarwanda-speakers now living in Uganda – or their parents – to move there.[13] Most Lunyarwanda-speakers currently settled in Uganda are undoubtedly under 25 years of age; and it is from their ranks that personnel for the Rwandan Patriotic Front were principally recruited. In what sense are these younger folk Rwandans rather than Ugandans today? Clearly this is a question open to more than one answer.

It is also a question in which a crucial role is played by language. It is therefore helpful to have the contribution by Ruth Mukama (Chapter 23) on the need for Ugandans to speak a common language. At present language is a source of division rather than commonality in the country. 'Standard Swahili for the army, English for the elitist institutions, pidgin Swahili for group employees and traders, and the indigenous languages for the peasants', she remarks. And the result? A government without adequate means of communication with the governed, and a country whose political, economic and cultural development is hampered by that absence. As Mukama argues, getting Ugandans to speak Swahili more fluently would prove one of the most important ways of strengthening the forces for unity.

But how is this to be done? Currently the language issue is being considered along with others by the constitutional commission touring Uganda (two of whose members, incidentally – E. Khiddu-Makubuya (Chapter 15) and Dan Mudoola (Chapter 17), its vice-chairman – are contributors to this volume) in preparation for the writing of a new constitution. But any official changes in language policy will necessarily involve tackling current practice in Ugandan schools and universities, where English is privileged at the very top of the educational pyramid and a diversity of Ugandan vernacular languages are taught during the first years of schooling and have been so taught since the beginning of British protectorate rule. Change will be expensive, because any modifications of constitutional and educational practice in Uganda will require new textbooks, retraining, and so on, at least in the short term.

Money is also much to the fore in Senteza Kajubi's account (Chapter 22) of the recent educational policy review commission that he chaired in Uganda. This is not surprising given the virtual halving in recent years of the proportion of the government budget devoted to education – now roughly 12.2 per cent. Primary education has taken most cuts. As a result overall educational achievements of Ugandans have fallen drastically at a time when unemployment has also risen dramatically. Nowadays Ugandan parents pay most of the costs of primary education (70–80 per cent in the educational policy review commission's estimation), mainly through PTAs. University education has not suffered quite such drastic cuts. Kajubi essentially sees the tertiary sector of education in Uganda as a charge on taxpayers as a whole rather than on students' parents or students themselves. He notes that the ratio of government spending per capita on tertiary and primary education in Uganda is currently of the order of 300 : 1. This he considers grossly inequitable. 'It can be argued that the free education, food, accomodation and personal allowances [currently accorded to Ugandan university students] are a form of subsidy by the poor to the rich parents [who are able to fund their brighter children through school to university entrance level].' He argues that the balance of advantage in Ugandan education should therefore be altered to favour the primary and vocational sectors. This, Kajubi suggests, can be done by abolishing or at least reducing allowances currently paid to university students and introducing cost-sharing into the tertiary sector. However, initial attempts at reform in these directions in November 1989 provoked considerable opposition at Makerere University and led to its closure for three months; in December 1990 there was further turmoil there resulting in the deaths and wounding of several students, again partly because of further cuts in university finances.

The decreasing proportion of the government budget devoted in

Introduction

recent years to education as well as to curative and preventive health (for which Bond and Vincent suggest that government spending has been even more drastically reduced from about 10 per cent to 3.5 per cent over the last ten years) leads us to wonder how Ugandans cope? This is the question considered by Vali Jamal (Chapter 5) and Christine Obbo (Chapter 6).

Jamal, indeed, remarks that low salaries have not only eroded morale and motivation in the public sector of Uganda but have also pushed wage earners ever more deeply into engagement with the *magendo* economy and the subsistence sector – away from areas previously controlled by the state. This process sharply accelerated after Idi Amin came to power in January 1971 and continued into the 1980s through what Jamal terms 'massive structural shifts in the economy'. An unprecedented fall in real wages during the last two decades has forced the economy into an essentially subsistence mode and prompted substantial growth in the informal sector as well as still greater dependence upon agriculture. Wage earners lost their viability as a group and developed into a 'conglomerate trade-cum-wage-earner-cum-*shamba* group'. Real wages fell to 7 per cent of their 1972 level, and by July 1988 the monthly minimum wage could purchase only five days' supply of *matooke*, the basic banana plantain diet of southern Ugandans. In rural areas there was also a shift from cultivation of export cash crops to food grown for domestic consumption. This was documented by Deryke Belshaw and Michael Whyte in *Uganda Now*. The greatest sufferers from these developments have undoubtedly been urban dwellers on fixed incomes.[14]

Their sufferings are mentioned by a number of contributors to the present volume, but Obbo tackles the problem in greatest detail. Using illustrative case studies she chronicles coping mechanisms that vulnerable groups such as women and children employ in order to enable their immediate families to survive. These fall within the informal sector, and Obbo reckons that most families need two or three income-generating activities to supplement a fixed salary. This is true even of wives of university professors and senior civil servants, who in many instances have interests in businesses on city pavements or market stalls in addition to their primary incomes. Obbo's vivid chapter gives the clear impression that links between declining salaries in the public sector and variable incomes obtained from activities in the informal sector provide the economy of Uganda with much of its contemporary dynamic.

But this dynamism is bought at a high social price. Public sector activities in Uganda are haunted by inefficiency that results from the comparatively short periods of time civil servants can devote to work in their offices. The frequent question: 'My friend, what shall I eat?', legitimates corrupt and uncorrupt additional activities alike. 'It is a collective disease in Uganda,' Obbo points out, 'that most people have problems

11

passing judgement on'. In June 1990 the Ugandan Minister of Finance finally legalized the black market in foreign exchange. Until then it had been illegal to acquire foreign currency outside the official banking system, which did not deter the magazine *Weekly Topic* from routinely publishing black market rates of exchange alongside official ones. It was principally on the black or parallel market that traders imported goods available in Ugandan shops, and it was black market rates that determined their prices – not the official rate with its frequent devaluations.[15] While it lasted, such a practice represented an untenable double system. Nonetheless it came as a surprise when the parallel market was legalized unconditionally. It represented a revolutionary change by wider African standards, and in Ugandan terms marked a further opening of the national economy to market forces and privatization and a retreat by the state from yet another area where it had maintained a monopoly.

What is frankly amazing from Jamal's and Obbo's accounts is the extent to which people succeed in raising a living wage, particularly in the urban areas of Uganda. It is clear, though, that they are unable to pay for services from the social sector to any extent, and under the terms of successive adjustment and stabilization packages agreed between successive Ugandan governments and international financial institutions social spending has been substantially reduced to enable deficits to be reduced and books to be balanced. It remains to be seen whether the World Bank's new poverty-oriented strategies regarding investment in health and education will improve these sectors' situations in the longer term. In the shorter term, Ugandans living under *magendo* conditions have to raise very considerable sums to pay for services from the already semi-privatized health services described by Whyte and schooling through the PTAs discussed by Kajubi. Inevitably the Ugandan poor have been worst hit by cutbacks in social spending. Lateef's reference (Chapter 2) to the PAPSCA programme (Programme for the Alleviation of Poverty and the Social Costs of Adjustment) is an admission that special measures have had to be taken to address their problems. The World Development Report published in July 1990 further underlined the need to address the problems of poverty in countries like Uganda directly. Besides assistance to the most exposed groups it suggested a twofold poverty-oriented strategy for the 1990s – first, making developmental efforts much more labour-intensive; secondly, investing directly in the social sector, especially in health and education. Nonetheless, the effects of such actions to mitigate the social costs of structural adjustment policies in Uganda will only come to fruition over the longer term.

But what happens to the Ugandan poor in the shorter term? E.A. Brett (Chapter 20) takes as his point of departure the institutional decay that he sees as characterizing Uganda since the 1960s. This has meant that service provision has effectively stopped and the role of the state in providing services has been increasingly questioned. In the resulting dominance of parallel markets and the *magendo* economy, institutional responses have been geared primarily to survival. The task now is to rebuild an institutional order that provides a framework for autonomous and self-sustaining growth. Brett stresses that one precondition for a successful rebuilding of institutions to serve the Ugandan poor is that it takes place under democratic control and with direct accountability. This is an argument repeated in a number of contributions to this volume. Brett also stresses the continuing importance of the state in providing social services. We are living at a time when moves from state provision to market competition are considered desirable on many sides and liberalization and privatization are regarded as unquestionable benefits in Europe as well as black Africa. However, as Brett underlines in his chapter, everything cannot be left to market forces, least of all control of scarce resources and the determination of social policy in poor countries. Ali Mazrui (Chapter 24) also stresses that structural adjustment policies in Africa need to be seen within the context of African traditions. Structural adjustment raises cultural as well as economic and political dilemmas that only African states themselves can ultimately resolve.

The cultural dilemmas with which Mazrui is most concerned are those posed by ethnicity, excessive consumption by rulers, and women. If market forces tend to be monopolized by a single ethnic group, he argues, only the state will have the authority to act as referee and prevent ethnic competition resulting in excessively damaging political conflict. The same goes for other social forces that impede rather than advance market forces in Uganda. Here Mazrui is thinking principally of the prestige factor in African politics and the inclination of African rulers to maximize conspicuous consumption in times of shortage rather than to advance productive investment in more modest but effective ways. He is also concerned with women and sees the state as utterly crucial in protecting their interests (as indeed the NRM government has attempted to do by reserving special seats for them on the NRC amongst other things) in the face of structural adjustment policies that otherwise seem steadily to reduce African states' capacities for strategic decision-making.

In one respect structural adjustment policies in Uganda have had a perverse effect – they have increased rather than decreased state patronage and control of the economy. This is because the sheer scale of lending and debt servicing in the initial adjustment packages led to a state takeover of financing hitherto undertaken by commercial banks, marketing boards and cooperatives. The continuing war in the north and the resultant costs of an enlarged army, particularly one incorporating substantial elements of earlier armies (through the policy of 'reconciliation through assimilation' outlined in *Uganda Now*) serve further to enhance the powers of the NRM government in general and of its armed forces in particular. Here lies another issue of concern to several contributors to this volume: control of the army.

During the last four years, remnants of Obote's and Amin's armies have operated intermittently on the Sudanese and Zairean borders with varying success, while further east other groups have from time to time benefited from unofficial links with Kenya. These remnants, small though they have been on the whole and progressively reduced though they have been by the NRM government's policy of amnesty and reconciliation, have inevitably adversely influenced Uganda's political, economic and cultural recovery. By tying down resources of money and manpower, they have delayed economic recovery and made potential external donors much more reluctant to become involved with Uganda. The intermittent war has also delayed constitutional rehabilitation and prevented the RC system from functioning in some northern areas. It has also deepened the north–south division and made it more difficult to deal politically with the cleavage along which so much inter-party and intra-party competition and military conflict has been conducted since independence. Lastly, continuous insurgency in the north has led to the enlargement of Uganda's national army to reportedly more than 100,000 men and has thus still further delayed its transformation into the more modest instrument of a predominantly civilian government envisaged in the earlier *10-Point Programme*.

How, then, is this greatly enlarged and still operational army to be controlled by civilians? Take the issue of human rights. Pirouet (Chapter 13) acknowledges that the NRM has improved Uganda's record in this sphere considerably in recent years. But she expresses concern over human rights abuses in the combat areas and poses two pertinent questions: why are so many violations still committed by the army? and are these violations a reflection of a breakdown of military discipline? She sees these infringements of human rights as indicative of an attempt by the Ugandan army to recover immunities and power possessed under Amin and Obote 2, but as essentially counter-productive in ending continuing insurgency in the north of the country. Unlike Mudoola, Pirouet sees the problem of the military as a consequence of its inadequate domestication, and its large size a problem rather than a solution. Like Khiddu-Makubuya, she argues strongly for tougher general backing for human rights in the new constitution as well as much tighter definition of the army's role as the servant of civilian government.

These are challenges to which Sam Njuba responds (Chapter 14). He outlines constitutional changes already made by the NRM government since January 1986 and discusses the guidelines issued to the constitutional commission appointed to draft a new constitution for Uganda in March 1989. Among these, two seem of particular importance in the current context. One is the proposal that the new constitution should facilitate a democratic system of government guaranteeing fundamental rights and freedoms. The second is that viable political institutions should be created that can ensure both maximum consensus in decision making and an orderly succession to government. Previously, both proposals have been more honoured in the breach than in the observance, but because they are both so indispensable to the working of democracy they deserve the closer examination that E. Khiddu-Makubuya (Chapter 15) attempts to provide.

Khiddu-Makubuya specifies a number of safeguards that he considers should be written into the new constitution. One is a permanent human rights commission. A second is a small, skeletal army of a very different kind from that endorsed by Dan Mudoola; this army would be recruited on a quota basis from reasonably educated people from all districts of Uganda. Intelligence agencies and paramilitary organizations would also come under proper control. Like Pirouet, Khiddu-Makubuya is disturbed at recent high-handedness by the military, particularly their detention of people without trial and their removal to barracks instead of being placed in the custody of court officials. However, though himself a member of the current constitutional commission, Khiddu-Makubuya sees the possible absurdity of legislating against the unlegislatable – does it make sense, he asks, to write into the new constitution provisions against the same constitution's overthrow by the military?

A.G.G. Gingyera-Pinycwa (Chapter 16) is more sceptical about the whole process of constitutional rehabilitation currently under way. He warns that a new constitution cannot be a magic formula solving all extant problems. The political upheavals since 1966 have not been caused by a faulty constitution; rather, they are consequences of diverging ethnic traditions, structural difficulties, and a lack of national unity. These, he argues, are the *real* problems facing Ugandans today – the position of Buganda and its monarchy within a wider Uganda; the uneven pattern of economic and social development, which strengthens centrifugal tendencies; the need to decide upon either a single strong central government or some federal compromise; and the question whether the present pyramidal NRM system of government should continue or be replaced by a multi-party system in which older political parties would also participate. Two particular institutions, however, require, in Gingyera-Pinycwa's opinion, immediate reform: the presidency and the army. Both, he argues, should have their powers cut down drastically to a scale more compatible with the democratic operation of the country's other institutions.

But will this ever happen? The answer partly depends upon what the constitutional commission appointed in March 1989 eventually recommends. Partly it depends upon the NRM government itself continuing

Introduction

in power, since any immediately obvious alternative to it – amongst
its opponents either in northern Uganda or in exile – seems unlikely to
take Gingyera-Pinycwa's minimalist political programme more seriously.
But mostly it will depend upon the most recent adjustment and stabilization packages agreed between the NRM government and the
IMF/World Bank proving far more successful than their predecessors
under Obote 2. For without at least modest economic success few of the
NRM government's best plans can prove enduring.

That, essentially, is why the immediately following chapters are
devoted to discussion of structural adjustment programmes in Uganda
during the early as well as the late 1980s. For in the early 1980s the Obote
2 government was one of the first anywhere in black Africa to accept such
a package. This early start had two implications for the later period.
One, as already pointed out, was that in order to distance itself completely from the policies of Obote 2, the NRM government initially
refused to engage in any structural adjustment policy (SAP). Then, in
the light of the disastrous effects of earlier policies, when it eventually did
accept a SAP in 1987, it did so only with modest commitment to making
it a practical success. That was hardly the most auspicious manner
in which to start, or rather restart, a SAP in the later 1980s. Additionally, Uganda in 1987 still suffered considerable weaknesses in its
institutional capacity to implement any economic reforms decided upon
by the government of the day.

Based on his experience at the World Bank, K. Sarwar Lateef
(Chapter 2) outlines the situation of economic distortion that the NRM
government confronted when it came to power in January 1986 and
its consequent considerable need for a stabilization and recovery programme under IMF/World Bank auspices. Lateef provides a thorough
analysis of the structural adjustment programme eventually adopted and
emphasizes the features in it specifically geared towards dealing with
Ugandan problems.

Working with data principally originating from the Bank of Uganda,
E.O. Ochieng (Chapter 3) tackles the same subject and also concludes
that, haunted by its multifarious dilemmas, the NRM government of
Yoweri Museveni has been half-hearted in its economic policy. Furthermore, Ochieng considers that by following IMF/World Bank guidelines too uncritically, it has overloaded a single policy instrument, the
exchange rate.

But despite their differing perspectives, Lateef and Ochieng broadly
agree that the most recent structural adjustment programme in Uganda
has had mixed results and in certain respects has failed completely.
Ochieng is the more pessimistic of the two. He states outright that
all SAPs adopted by Uganda since 1981 have induced only short-term
positive changes: they have proved incapable of adjusting to unforeseen

16

external shocks and internal upheavals, and are much too dependent upon external funding. However, Ochieng agrees that the alternative policies recommended by the Economic Commission for Africa do not look any more likely to succeed in Uganda and his conclusion is therefore essentially a dismal one: the search for an appropriate economic adjustment programme for the country must continue.

Lateef and Ochieng agree that the rate of inflation is one of the clearest indicators of a SAP's success or failure. However, whereas Lateef sees the most important task for Uganda to lie in controlling inflation as a precondition for successful structural adjustment, Ochieng considers this advice unrealistic because in his view SAPs themselves have inherent inflationary tendencies. It is therefore interesting that Michael Hodd, in a paper presented *in absentia* to the September 1989 conference at Lyngby Landbrugsskole that will be published elsewhere, provides a detailed discussion of the relationship between the exchange rate, money supply and inflation in Uganda. Hodd argues that while the exchange rate has had some influence, expansion in the money supply has been by far the most potent cause of Uganda's frequent bouts of spiralling inflation in recent years.[16] Interestingly, a recent pamphlet by the permanent secretary in the Ugandan ministry of planning and economic development, E. Tumusiime-Mutebile, in responses to criticism of the most recent IMF stabilization programme in the Ugandan press by Mahmood Mamdani, also argues that 'the alleged costs of devaluation in terms of causing inflation are utterly mythical' in Uganda today. What really causes inflation and consequent falls in real wages, he argues, is the printing of money in order to finance government deficits.[17]

Joshua Mugyenyi (Chapter 4) takes the discussion further by examining the context in which SAPs were introduced into Uganda and the way in which the most recent one has been negotiated between the NRM government and the IMF/World Bank. Writing from the receiving end, as it were, Mugyenyi stresses the element of compulsion from the international side implicit in the whole exercise of imposing 'conditionalities' upon Uganda. As a result of what he characterizes as incompetence in negotiating with international financial institutions and also 'home-grown socio-political administrative disabling factors', Mugyenyi describes the NRM government as accepting its particular SAP without enthusiasm or very much prior dialogue with the IMF/World Bank but rather through a process of negotiation surely more accurately to be characterized as the diplomacy of mutual exhaustion. Inevitably, such diplomacy hardly helps the resultant SAP to be geared most sensibly to Uganda's specific situation. On the contrary, it strengthens the voices of those who consider any engagement with the IMF/World Bank to be counter-revolutionary, and obscures the unfortunate fact that structural adjustment in Uganda is unavoidable in today's circumstances.

Introduction

What makes structural adjustment a more delicate matter, however, are the various non-economic factors influencing it. Weaknesses in institutional capacity and the security situation have already been stressed, as have external relations outside the NRM government's immediate control. Prospects for peace in northern Uganda will assuredly be hampered for as long as the Khartoum government employs dissidents from earlier Ugandan governments as militiamen acting against the SPLA on the Sudan/Uganda border, while bad relations with Kenya may further cripple Uganda's economy again in other directions. Even more crucial than relations with neighbours in determining the viability of Uganda's latest SAP will be the level of future international donor support. Lateef suggests that one reason for the mixed results of SAPs in Uganda to date has been inadequate external support from the more important donor countries. One consequence is that Uganda still suffers from a huge foreign debt, which eats up about two-thirds of its current foreign exchange earnings in interest payments. Yet, as Mazrui comments, recent developments in Eastern Europe may well depress still further external donor interest in African countries such as Uganda, while high oil prices as a result of continuing turmoil in the Middle East may well make Uganda's economic situation even more onerous in the immediate future.

If the NRM government's room for manoeuvre seems severely constrained on many sides, there is one area in which it really does have an option for revolutionary change – land reform. In *Uganda Now*, Nelson Kasfir drew attention to changes in land tenure legislation introduced during the Amin dictatorship and the ways in which population pressure had increased commercial pressure upon the landless in Bushenyi and Mbarara districts during the early 1980s. In the present volume W. Kisamba-Mugerwa (Chapter 21) contributes another analysis of this subject. A Member of the National Resistance Council as well as a researcher at the Makerere Institute of Social Research, he rejects totally the leasehold system reconstituted by Amin's land reform decree of 1975 and advocates individual ownership of land throughout Uganda with minimum state control. Reform along these lines would both recognize private property rights and involve less hassle and expense than the present very muddled situation for both central and local government. *Mailo* owners, he suggests, would have freehold titles to lands unoccupied by tenants, while *mailo* tenants would themselves become freeholders on their current tenancies. There should also be safeguards for tenant farmers on public lands who would also have the right to obtain freehold titles.

Whether these proposals are implemented clearly depends upon several unknowns. But if they ever are implemented, the political and economic implications will be enormous and truly revolutionary.

18

Introduction

Denmark's modern experience of democracy and economic development is founded upon the mass conferment of freehold title to land to a multitude of small farmers in the late eighteenth century.[18] Britain's path to democracy and development has been longer, more bloody and considerably more tortuous,[19] but small and middling farmers possessing firm title to their properties also played pioneering parts in both processes. Which of these paths to democracy and development will Uganda tread in the coming years – one mapped by a basic land tenure reform, or one that is longer, more tortuous, and possibly still more bloody than its course thus far? Only time will tell.

Notes

1. *The Economist*, 2 June 1990, p. 15.
2. See especially Twaddle, 1988.
3. See Nkamuhayo and Seidel, 1989; Mamdani, 1990a. Mamdani's criticisms of IMF policy have appeared in Uganda in *New Vision* newspaper (e.g., 21 March 1989) and elsewhere in Mamdani, 1990b.
4. See, for example, International Alert 1987, Hooper and Pirouet 1989, and Amnesty International, 1989.
5. Amnesty International, 1990.
6. This was reported in the BBC magazine *Focus on Africa* 1, 3 (November-December 1990), p. 23.
7. This point was stressed in the London newsletter *Africa Confidential* at the end of 1990.
8. For a fuller discussion of NRM policy on women, see Boyd, 1989; also Mamdani, 1990a, p. 370.
9. Kasozi, 1990, p. 117.
10. Hyden, 1990, p. 155.
11. *New Vision*, 28 April 1990.
12. For fuller discussion, see Clay, 1984.
13. *ibid*.
14. See Belshaw, 1988; Whyte, 1988.
15. For further discussion, see Loxley, 1989; Meagher, 1990.
16. Michael Hodd, 'Prices, money and output: Uganda 1966–1988'.
17. E. Tumusiime-Mutebile, 1990. The version of Mamdani's paper originally appeared in *New Vision*. It is reprinted in slightly revised form as Mamdani, 1990b, but without direct reference to Tumusiime-Mutebile's critique.
18. The best discussion is in Bjoern, 1988, vol. 2.
19. See Moore, 1967 for one of the best discussions.

PART ONE
STRUCTURAL ADJUSTMENT ON TRIAL

TWO
Structural adjustment in Uganda:
the initial experience

K. Sarwar Lateef

'Structural adjustment' may be defined in a variety of ways.[1] For the purpose of this Chapter, I intend to follow its most common current usage, i.e., the *sustained* pursuit of a programme of policy reforms that is designed to reduce economic and financial imbalances arising from domestic or external shocks and to address policy deficiencies that are impeding progress towards accelerated economic growth. In this sense, there was no serious attempt at structural adjustment in Uganda until May 1987 when the National Resistance Movement (NRM) began its current programme of economic recovery. While stabilization and adjustment was attempted in mid-1981, two years after Idi Amin was removed from power, it was quickly engulfed by political instability. With the intensification of the civil war in 1984, the programme was abandoned. The breakdown of fiscal and monetary discipline quickly reversed the initial recovery in production and the reduction in inflation.

I intend to ignore the 'false start' of the early 1980s and focus entirely on the initial experience with the current programme of structural adjustment. I will first describe the economic inheritance of the NRM government, outline the main objectives of the Economic Recovery Programme, describe the policies and programmes in place or under contemplation to achieve these objectives, analyse some of the initial results of the programme, and identify some issues and lessons for Uganda and donors for the 1990s.

THE INHERITANCE
When the NRM assumed power in January 1986, it inherited a nation shattered by years of gross misrule, civil war, political instability, and ethnic and religious strife. The economy was characterized by high inflation and intense balance of payments pressures resulting from severe macro-economic imbalances. A once impressive economic and social infrastructure lay devastated by war and lack of maintenance. Farms and industrial enterprises lay abandoned as farmers, workers and managers fled in search of safety. The more experienced and skilled personnel in

the civil service, terrorized by successive repressive regimes, had fled to safer pastures. Those who were forced by personal circumstances to stay behind were deeply demoralized by physical insecurity, the collapse of discipline and management systems, and declining real incomes.

The economic and social cost of this long period of darkness, and the relative decline in Uganda's economic situation vis-à-vis other developing countries is easily documented. Table 2.1 compares a set of economic and social indicators for Uganda with those for low-income sub-Saharan Africa (LISSA) other than Nigeria, and with those for *all* low-income developing countries (LIDC) other than China and India over the 1965–87 period. The data clearly demonstrate that Uganda's economic and social performance and level of development in the 1965–73 period compared very favourably with that of LISSA but that it deteriorated markedly in relative terms in the 1973–87 period.

Economic growth

Per capita GNP in Uganda grew at roughly the same rate as in LISSA in the 1965–73 period. However, in the 1973–80 period, Uganda's per capita GNP fell at an annual rate of – 6.2 per cent, as against – 0.6 per cent for LISSA. In the 1980–7 period, it fell by – 2.4 per cent per annum, somewhat faster than the decline experienced more generally in sub-Saharan Africa. In the 1965–87 period, smaller low-income developing countries as a whole experienced structural transformation, i.e., a declining share of agriculture in GDP and a rising share of industry. Low-income sub-Saharan Africa experienced no such transformation, with stagnation in the sectoral shares of its aggregate GDP. In the case of Uganda, however, structural transformation was reversed. The share of agriculture actually rose from 52 per cent of 1965 GDP to 70 per cent of 1986/87 GDP, while the share of industry declined from 13 per cent of 1965 GDP to 8 per cent of 1986/87 GDP. This dependence on agriculture in Uganda was mirrored in the structure of exports, where agriculture accounted for 96 per cent of 1987 exports as against 54 per cent for LISSA and 27 per cent for LIDC.

Inflation

Inflation in Uganda in the 1965–73 period averaged a modest 5.6 per cent. In the 1973–80 period, inflation had risen to 45 per cent per annum, accelerating to 95 per cent per annum in the 1980–7 period reflecting severe macro-economic imbalances, and in particular rapid monetary expansion. By contrast, inflation in LISSA averaged 19 per cent per annum in 1973–80 and 28 per cent per annum in 1980–7, while all LIDCs fared much better.

Table 2.1 Uganda: relative economic performance

	1965-73			1973-80			1980-87		
	Uganda	Low-income SSA (a)	All small low-income countries (b)	Uganda	Low-income SSA (a)	All small low-income countries (b)	Uganda	Low-income SSA (a)	All small low-income countries (b)
GNP per capita									
Average annual growth rate	0.7	0.8	3.0	-6.2	-0.6	1.8	-2.4	-2.2	-1.1
Growth of production (average annual %)									
Gross domestic product	3.6	3.3	5.9	-2.7	1.9	4.3	0.4	1.4	1.7
Agriculture	3.6	..	2.7	-2.3	1.7	1.4	-0.5	5.0	1.9
Industry	3.0	..	13.4	-11.9	8.0	5.6	1.4	1.6	0.2
Services	3.8	..	4.7	-1.1	2.9	6.0	3.0	1.3	2.9
Growth of consumption and investment (average annual %)									
Private consumption	4.0	2.5	4.4	-3.1	2.5	4.1	..	1.8	2.4
Investment	2.1	6.3	9.3	-9.8	1.6	7.1	..	-3.5	-1.9
Population growth (average annual %)	3.4	2.6	2.6	2.6	2.8	2.6	3.1	3.0	2.8
of which: urban	8.4	5.7	4.8	3.8	5.9	4.8	5.0	5.9	5.6
Broad money									
Average annual nominal growth rate	14.6	..	..	29.3	..	..	77.8	..	..
Inflation									
Average annual rate	5.6	6.7	22.1	45.4	19.3	17.1	95.2	27.5	13.3
Growth of merchandise trade (Average annual growth rate)									
Exports	3.0	4.8	12.3	-9.5	0.6	0.8	2.7	-1.1	-0.1
Imports	-4.1	2.9	1.5	-2.9	1.4	8.2	3.0	-2.5	-3.9
Commercial Energy (Average annual growth rate)									
Energy production	3.7	15.0	20.3	-4.5	14.4	3.4	2.7	-3.8	-0.3
Energy consumption	8.4	8.2	5.0	-7.4	0.9	5.7	4.4	-0.3	4.0

External Trade

	1965		1980		1987	
Terms of Trade	..	..	100	100	84	84
Share of primary products in exports	100	93	100	94	92	75
of which: agricultural	86	54	97	50	54	27
Official development assistance						
Per capita dollars	..	..	9	24	18	31
Bilateral (% of total)	..	..	39	66	32	63
Grants as % of net ODA: Total	..	..	73	70	55	66
Technical assistance as % of net ODA	..	..	18	27	20	25

External debt

	1970		1980		1987	
Debt Service as % of: GNP	1	2	3	2	4	5
Exports of goods & services	7	6	11	7	18	22
Public debt outstanding and disbursed as % of GNP:	18	16	40	35	86	69

	1965		1980		1987	
Demography and fertility						
Crude birth rate (per '000)	49	48	50	47	48	41
Crude death rate (per '000)	19	23	19	19	16	13
Total fertility rate	6.9	6.5	6.9	6.6	6.0	4.7
Life expectancy at birth	45	..	..	..	50	54
Infant mortality (per '000 births)	121	160	113	149	115	103
Education						
% of age group enrolled:						
Primary	67	39	50	69	60	78
Male	83	50	56	78	68	86
Female	50	28	43	59	53	69

continued on page 24 overleaf

Table 2.1 (*cont'd*)

	1965			1984			1986		
	Uganda	Low-income SSA (a)	All small low-income countries (b)	Uganda	Low-income SSA (a)	All small low-income countries (b)	Uganda	Low-income SSA (a)	All small low-income countries (b)
Health and nutrition									
Population per physician	11,110	37,430	28,190	21,900	32,340	13,550	..	..	..
Population per nurse	3,130	5,520	10,170	2,060	2,760	3,130	..	..	..
Daily calorie supply per capita	2,360	2,045	1,976	2,151	2,087	2,166	2,344	2,052	2,227

Source: Sub-Saharan Africa – From Crisis to Sustainable Growth, World Bank, 1989.
(a) Low-income sub-Saharan African countries excluding Nigeria.
(b) Low-income developing countries other than China and India.

Structural adjustment in Uganda: the initial experience

Balance of payments

Uganda's export volumes fell precipitously in the 1973–80 period (averaging − 9.5 per cent per annum) as against a marginal increase for most low-income developing countries. While there was some recovery from this low base, by 1987 Uganda's export earnings totalled a mere $320 million or $20 per capita, as against $32 per capita for LISSA and $46 per capita for LIDC. This in part reflected the sharper deterioration in Uganda's terms of trade than for other developing countries (33 per cent between 1980 and 1987 as against 16 per cent). With aid flows to Uganda also much below the average ($18 per capita in 1987 as against $31 for LISSA), import capacity was significantly lower ($31 per capita in 1987 as against close to $50 for other developing countries). Although Uganda's debt-service ratio was close to the average for LISSA in 1987, reflecting weak export performance, the debt service expressed as a percentage of GNP was only half that of LISSA, reflecting its low past creditworthiness and hence the relatively low level of outstanding and disbursed public debt.

Social Indicators

The collapse of social infrastructure in Uganda can be measured by the relative decline in primary school enrolment between 1965 and 1980 (as against sharply rising trends in the rest of SSA), the near doubling by 1984 in the ratio of population per physician from the 1965 level when Uganda was well ahead of other low-income countries, in contrast to the modest decline in this ratio for LISSA (and the halving of this ratio for LIDC). Similarly, in 1965, the infant mortality rate (IMR) was substantially lower in Uganda than in other developing countries, but it fell much faster in other countries. The IMR nevertheless declined in Uganda, probably reflecting success in maintaining per capita food supply throughout this period at levels above those for other low-income countries. This success is owed to the return to subsistence agriculture in a period of extreme political and economic uncertainty. (For an excellent discussion of the factors that lay behind the buoyancy of food production in 'the lost decade', see Vali Jamal's 'Coping under crisis in Uganda', *International Labour Review*, 127(6), 1988.) Overall, therefore, while Uganda's social indicators in the 1960s were for the most part much better than those of other low-income countries, today they are similar to LISSA, with high birth and death rates, high fertility rates and low life expectancy at birth.

THE ECONOMIC RECOVERY PROGRAMME

In sum, Uganda's once privileged status in the African community had given way over a decade and a half to that of a least developed country.

Structural adjustment on trial

The NRM thus faced an enormous challenge on assuming power. It had to move simultaneously on several fronts in order to rebuild a shattered nation, and to restore to health its polity, its economy and society. To its credit, the new government rose to the task with remarkable courage, persistence and energy. Its first priority was to restore law and order, re-establish civil liberties, and overcome the remaining insurgencies in the north and east. Early successes in establishing a broad-based government and electing a parliament, in reducing the area under insurgencies, in improving the security situation and restoring civil liberties, all helped to shift the attention of policy makers to the economy. After some initial hesitations and false starts, the government developed a bold and sweeping programme of reforms.

Launched in May 1987, the Economic Recovery Programme was aimed at restoring economic stability, establishing more realistic relative prices, and initiating the rehabilitation of the country's productive and social infrastructure. The new policies, now in their fourth year of implementation, were initially supported by an IMF Structural Adjustment Facility (SAF) which was approved by the Fund's Board in June 1987, and by an IDA Economic Recovery Credit, approved by IDA's Executive Directors in September 1987. The SAF was replaced in April 1989 by an Enhanced Structural Adjustment Facility (ESAF) following the government's decision to deepen and accelerate the pace of reforms. IDA extended a second Economic Recovery Credit to Uganda in January 1990. Uganda has also been eligible since January 1988 to draw resources from the World Bank-sponsored Special Programme of Assistance, a facility for enhanced concessional aid flows to debt-distressed low-income Sub-Saharan Africa countries pursuing adjustment programmes.

Objectives and policy framework

The Economic Recovery Programme's key objectives have been to bring about rapid economic recovery while reducing inflation and moving towards increased viability in the balance of payments. A related objective has been to rehabilitate and revitalize the economic and social infrastructure. More specifically, the programme aims at an annual growth rate of GDP in excess of 5 per cent (to permit per capita income to grow by at least 2 per cent per annum); reducing inflation from over 200 per cent in 1986/87 to a single digit level by 1991/92; and to strengthen the balance of payments sufficiently to permit a substantial improvement in net international reserves and to nearly eliminate external arrears.

To attain these objectives the government has begun to put in place a range of mutually reinforcing measures. To *foster economic growth and strengthen the balance of payments*, the government has taken action in the following areas:

26

Structural adjustment in Uganda: the initial experience

Incentive framework The primary strategy in this area has been to establish more realistic relative prices, and the principal instrument has been the exchange rate. Since May 1987, the Ugandan shilling was devalued from UShs14 to UShs440 to the US dollar by June 1990, a nominal depreciation in foreign currency terms of 97 per cent and a real effective depreciation of over 40 per cent. The very large nominal depreciation was necessitated by the substantial (217 per cent) appreciation of the real effective exchange rate during the first year of the programme (1987/88) because of the failure to control inflation in that year. The ratio of the official to the parallel market exchange rate has risen steadily from an average of 21 per cent in 1987/88 to 41 per cent in 1989/90 and an end-June 1990 level of 70 per cent. A significant development with respect to exchange rate policy is that all non-coffee exporters are entitled to retain 100 per cent of their export earnings to finance approved imports. They thus effectively realize an exchange rate close to the parallel market rate. Tax and tariff reforms being implemented will lower and rationalize effective protection. Price and distribution controls have been dismantled (with the exception of petroleum products and sugar). Petroleum prices were promptly adjusted to reflect changes in the exchange rate, and there are no budgetary subsidies on petroleum. Virtually all parastatal marketing monopolies have been abolished; the role of parastatals in agricultural marketing has been substantially reduced, and is now confined to coffee, tea, cocoa and cotton. Consequently, for all other crops, producer prices are market determined. Steps are also being taken to liberalize coffee marketing by permitting competition in the export trade.

Savings and investment The programme calls for a significant increase in domestic savings in support of higher levels of investment. This is to be achieved through positive real interest rates accompanied by other measures designed to strengthen the financial sector and increase private sector confidence. Domestic resource mobilization measures are intended to raise revenues from their current low levels (see below). Together with containment of non-essential recurrent expenditures, the public saving effort is to be improved, although it will remain negative in the medium term. The increase in investment levels will be largely financed from foreign savings, reflecting increased donor support for Uganda's adjustment programme. Public investment will focus on rehabilitating the country's economic and social infrastructure while private investment will be encouraged in the productive sectors.

Sectoral policies Recognizing the importance of agriculture to economic recovery, the programme focuses on alleviating the scarcity of foreign exchange for agricultural inputs, improvement in transport and access to markets, elimination of inefficiencies in processing and marketing

27

and the strengthening of support systems (research, extension, seed distribution and credit). In the industrial sector, the emphasis is on increasing capacity utilization, particularly for industries that are important to government revenue, by reducing the foreign exchange constraints on importation of raw materials and spares, and through the removal of price and distribution controls. The government intends to divest itself of selected public enterprises and to encourage the private sector to play a leading role in efficient production for the domestic and external markets. Transport sector policies are intended to support economic recovery by intensifying road rehabilitation and restoration of the capacity to manage and maintain highway and rural road systems. The railways are being strengthened, particularly to handle long-haul bulk cargo. Increased foreign exchange provision for trucks and spares and improved road conditions have already greatly improved transport availability.

Control of demand and inflation To contain aggregate demand and lower inflation the government has been attempting to follow a consistent set of fiscal, monetary and exchange rate policies. Fiscal policy is aimed at increasing revenues from their very low level (5–7 per cent of GDP), maintaining strict expenditure control and reducing significantly the government's liabilities to the banking system. To strengthen domestic resource mobilization while ensuring appropriate incentives, the government's programme is aimed at lowering the dependence on trade taxes, and in particular on coffee taxation, widening the tax base and rationalizing the tax structure. Increased taxation of petroleum and other commodities is being used as a major source of revenue diversification. Important steps have been taken towards the establishment of a broad-based system of indirect taxes on goods and services accompanied by a rationalized and simplified customs tariff structure intended to provide a moderate and relatively uniform level of effective protection. On the expenditure side, a recovery of expenditures from their present low levels in line with improved resource mobilization would permit much needed increases in real wages for the civil service, higher allocations for operations and maintenance, and rationalization of development expenditure, focusing priorities towards economic and social infrastructure. For the fiscal reforms to go through would require improved tax administration and a more efficient and streamlined civil service. Technical assistance is being focused to respond to this need.

The objective of monetary policy has been to curb monetary expansion while ensuring an adequate growth of credit to the private sector within a framework that requires some improvement in net foreign assets. This has meant policies aimed at reducing the government's liabilities to the banking system while containing the expansion of crop finance by reducing inefficiency in coffee marketing and discouraging the diversion of crop-finance credit for other purposes. The attainment of positive real interest rates has been a goal of the programme, although this is only just being realized. Exchange rate policy has been seen as an important instrument for reducing the demand for imports while offsetting the negative effects on the government's revenues from coffee arising from lower than anticipated export volumes and prices.

Long-term development issues   The programme places considerable emphasis on longer-term development issues. In the education sector, the emphasis is on increasing quality (by providing textbooks and instructional materials, and strengthening school inspections, curricula and examination services) and strengthening management capacity. The government also intends to reduce expenditures on non-instructional activity (boarding costs and allowances) and pass on these costs to parents. In the health sector, resources are currently devoted primarily to hospital-based curative services. With the resurgence of preventable diseases for both children and adults, and the rapid spread of AIDS, the sector is facing a severe crisis. The goverment proposes to increase resources allocated to the sector and budget sufficient domestic and foreign exchange funds for essential health supplies, and to partly finance this increase through cost recovery measures carefully designed to protect the poor. At the same time, the government intends to shift resources within the sector towards primary care while enhancing cooperation with NGOs to improve delivery systems.

The government also attaches considerable importance to the environment. A new Institute of Environment and Natural Resources at Makerere University is to carry out environmental assessments of development projects. Deforestation is the major environmental issue in Uganda and this is being addressed through a forestry project and through more rigorous regulations of the timber trade.

Institutional reforms   Reforms of the nature described above would pose demands on management that would test most governments. Recognizing the threat that weak implementation capacity poses to the success of its reform programme, the government has instituted a number of measures to strengthen its denuded management skills and to restore discipline and accountability in the civil service. These include efforts to strengthen the key functions of the central economic ministries and institutions such as the Ministry of Finance, the Ministry of Planning and Economic Development, the Coffee Marketing Board and the Bank of Uganda, and to strengthen planning and monitoring capabilities in key sectoral ministries. Functional reviews are being carried out in all ministries. Computerization of the payroll is leading to the elimination of ghost workers. These are initial steps towards streamlining of the civil

29

service, where overstaffing combined with the low revenue base prevents government from increasing average wages that are currently well below a living wage.

Poverty and the social costs of adjustment   The restoration of economic growth and the lowering of the rate of inflation will have strong beneficial effects on the weaker sections of society. However, the government has been concerned that large numbers of poor people who were the main victims of years of economic decline and civil strife may not benefit directly in the short run from the reform programme. Deteriorating health conditions, including the devastating impact of AIDS and the resurgence of a number of preventable childhood diseases, and the high cost of primary education are significant problems facing these groups. To address the problems of the vulnerable, the government, with the assistance of donors, has developed a Programme for the Alleviation of Poverty and the Social Costs of Adjustment (PAPSCA). The US$106 million programme aims at addressing over the 1990–3 period Uganda's most pressing concerns through interventions aimed at children (rehabilitation of primary schools and supply of educational materials, assistance to orphans), women (assistance to women NGOs, women in agriculture and war widows), the disabled (community based rehabilitation, training for the handicapped, a prosthetics programme), strengthening delivery of essential services in the most disadvantaged districts (primary health care, water and sanitation, rural housing materials, rehabilitation of small-scale infrastructure), the urban poor (low cost housing and sanitation) and displaced civil servants (assistance to resettle those who are laid off). PAPSCA also incorporates the joint UNDP–World Bank Social Dimensions of Adjustment Project which includes programmes to improve collection and analysis of social indicators, and to strengthen government's capacity for social policy planning and in the design and monitoring of poverty alleviation policies and programmes. As this capacity is strengthened, some of these special interventions will become better integrated into the government's own public expenditure programme. A unique feature of the PAPSCA programme is its heavy reliance on NGOs and community-based rural organizations (the resistance councils) which are well placed to supplement the government's capacity to implement projects directed at the poor.

PERFORMANCE UNDER
THE ECONOMIC RECOVERY PROGRAMME

Uganda's reform programme has been in place for just over three years. The results to date (Table 2.2) have been mixed. The data and physical evidence suggest an impressive, recovery in the economy, with sustained GDP growth of 6–7 per cent per annum over the period. Inflation substantially exceeded targets in the first two years of the programme reflecting slippage in monetary and fiscal performance and external shocks, but it decelerated sharply in 1989/90, and the target for the year has been met. However, progress on fiscal and monetary reforms has been slow.

A large part of the credit for the strong recovery of the economy since 1987 must go to the restoration of peace and security over much of the country. This has facilitated the delivery of inputs and essential services and the rehabilitation of the country's crippled infrastructure. These two factors have enabled farmers and workers to return to their farms and factories. This, combined with good weather, the availability of donor-provided foreign exchange for key inputs in the productive sectors, and an improved incentive framework, has helped to demonstrate once again the resilience of the Ugandan economy. Agricultural growth in the three years ending FY90 has averaged 5.4 per cent while industrial growth has averaged an impressive 13.7 per cent. Despite declining world prices and falling real producer prices, coffee exports over the three years rose by 20 per cent in volume terms, although they declined substantially in dollar values. Non-coffee exports have risen sharply (albeit from a low base of US$6 million in FY89 to US$18 million in FY90) reflecting the policy of permitting 100 per cent export retentions. With increased donor funds as well as private sector imports financed from own foreign exchange (the so-called 'no-forex' scheme), the availability of goods in the market has improved although many producers, especially in the industrial sector, continue to face inadequate supply of industrial inputs.

Data on savings and investment are unreliable. Public savings have been negative, while private savings have been adversely affected by negative real interest rates. Investment levels appear to have been rising. The government has made good progress in the rehabilitation of the highway infrastructure and donor-financed projects are under way to deal with the rehabilitation needs of other infrastructure. This in turn seems to have stimulated a strong private sector response, at least in the area of transport and agriculture, and reawakened some interest in the rehabilitation of industrial enterprises.

These achievements would have seemed more impressive had progress been faster in the area of stabilization. In this respect, however, the programme got off to a bad start, with inflation in 1987/88 reaching a massive 243 per cent (as against a targeted 30 per cent), due in the main to a 212 per cent expansion in broad money. The slippage was due in large part to a series of exogenous shocks that destroyed the initial assumptions on which the programme was based. These included:

- the decline in world coffee prices below programme forecasts and the reimposition of coffee quotas by the ICO in late 1987;

Table 2.2 Uganda: key macro-economic indicators

Indicator	Unit	1983/84	1984/85	1985/86	1986/87	1987/88	1988/89	1989/90(a)
Output								
GDP at constant factor cost	% change at 1987/88 prices	..	−3.3	1.2	3.3	6.8	7.0	6.3
Agriculture	"	..	−4.1	1.5	3.0	5.6	5.6	5.0
Industry	"	..	−3.6	−5.4	4.9	15.7	13.9	11.6
Services	"	..	−0.5	3.1	3.7	6.7	7.9	7.6
Agriculture	% of GDP at current factor cost	63.0	66.2	70.1	70.3	67.9	67.0	66.4
Industry	"	7.5	6.4	6.8	8.3	10.0	10.1	11.2
Services	"	29.5	27.4	23.1	21.4	22.1	22.9	22.4
Coffee exports	'000 tonnes	155.0	127.7	153.1	134.7	154.2	162.1	162.0
Fiscal performance								
Revenues	% of GDP at current market prices	12.4	9.9	7.4	5.0	7.1	5.5	5.9
Expenditures (b)	"	15.3	14.7	12.2	9.4	12.0	10.0	11.6
Recurrent	"	9.2	9.6	9.1	5.9	7.0	6.8	7.8
Capital	"	1.7	2.1	3.1	3.5	4.9	3.0	3.8
Overall deficit (commitment)	"	−3.0	−4.8	−4.9	−4.4	−4.9	−4.5	−5.7
Overall deficit (cash) (c)	"	−4.1	−4.4	−4.9	−4.7	−6.2	−5.3	−6.3
Foreign financing (net) (d)	"	1.0	1.1	2.4	0.8	4.1	3.7	7.3
Domestic financing (net)	"	3.1	3.3	2.5	3.9	2.1	1.5	−1.0
Monetary trends								
Broad money (stocks) as % of GDP	at current market prices	10.1	11.1	11.7	7.3	7.6	7.7	6.1
Broad money growth (stocks)	annual % change	..	139.5	148.4	90.3	212.0	124.3	49.6
Net credit to government	"	..	131.0	58.8	166.2	191.0	121.3	−67.1
Crop financing	"	..	147.6	117.3	32.7	202.0	329.8	−1.5
Net credit to private sector (e)	"	..	109.1	67.4	237.7	198.5	191.1	104.2
Sources of broad money growth:								
Net domestic credit	Flows as a % of GDP at current market prices	..	6.7	3.9	4.1	4.6	5.7	0.4
Credit to government	"	..	3.4	1.5	2.2	2.2	1.9	−1.2
Crop financing	"	..	1.9	1.6	0.3	0.9	1.9	0.0
Credit to private sector (e)	"	..	1.5	0.8	1.6	1.5	1.6	1.6
Inflation								
Consumer prices (annual average)	% change	16.2	155.5	153.1	233.2	243.1	86.2	28.7
GDP deflator	% change	..	128.6	139.4	201.9	177.1	108.8	76.1
Balance of Payments								
Exports of goods and NFS	US $ million	403	408	390	406	324	322	222
Imports of goods and NFS	US $ million	450	484	446	600	682	762	706
Resource balance	US $ million	−47	−76	−56	−194	−358	−440	−484

Table 2.2 *(cont'd)*

Indicator	Unit	1983/84	1984/85	1985/86	1986/87	1987/88	1988/89	1989/90(a)
Net factor income	US $ million	-47	-53	-44	-47	-57	-66	-64
Net current private transfers	US $ million	26	40	101	100	120	118	99
Current account balance (excl grants)	US $ million	-68	-89	1	-141	-295	-388	-449
Current account balance (excl grants)	% of GDP at current market prices	-2.11	-2.76	0.03	-2.38	-5.04	-8.46	-9.79
Terms of trade index	1987/88 = 100	182.2	191.0	164.2	141.1	100.0	94.2	51.1
Gross reserves	Months of imports	..	1.9	2.0	0.7	0.8	0.6	0.4
Official development assistance								
Gross disbursements	US $ million	139.5	247.0	209.0	322.4	336.0	447.1	517.7
Grants	"	71.0	64.0	25.0	40.0	92.0	165.0	190.0
Long-term debt	"	0.0	183.0	178.0	225.0	210.0	188.0	286.0
IMF purchases	"	68.5	0.0	0.0	57.4	34.0	94.1	41.7
Principal repayments	"	111.6	135.2	157.5	170.4	150.0	172.2	134.5
Long-term debt	"	86.0	77.0	76.0	90.0	85.0	86.0	88.0
IMF repurchases	"	25.6	58.2	81.5	80.4	65.0	86.2	46.6
Net flows	"	27.9	111.8	51.5	152.0	186.0	274.9	383.2
Interest payments	"	47.0	56.0	45.4	41.5	48.9	44.8	44.3
Long-term debt	"	21.0	20.8	15.0	18.9	28.6	25.6	31.4
IMF charges	"	26.0	33.9	30.0	22.4	19.3	18.1	11.2
Short-term debt	"	..	1.2	0.5	0.2	1.1	1.2	1.7
Net transfers	"	-19.1	55.8	6.1	110.5	137.1	230.1	338.9
Total debt service	"	158.6	189.9	202.5	211.6	197.8	215.9	177.1
Long-term debt	"	107.0	97.8	91.0	108.9	113.6	111.6	119.4
IMF	"	51.6	92.1	111.5	102.8	84.3	104.3	57.8
Debt service								
As % of exports of goods and NFS		39.4	46.5	51.9	52.1	61.0	67.0	79.8
As % of GNP		5.0	6.0	5.7	3.6	3.4	4.8	3.9

Source: Government of Uganda and June 1991 Bank staff estimates.

(a) Preliminary data.
(b) Including unallocated expenditure and net lending.
(c) Including change in expenditure (related arrears).
(d) Includes debt relief (about 1% of GDP in 1989/90).
(e) Excluding crop financing.

- delays in the arrival of external assistance;
- tension on the Uganda–Kenya border, which disrupted coffee exports and essential imports; and
- a slower than assumed normalization of the security situation, which caused increased defence expenditures and disrupted food supplies to Kampala.

These developments had a severe adverse impact on the government's budgetary position: both revenues and external assistance were below budget estimates while expenditures substantially exceeded the ceiling. Credit for crop financing (for coffee in particular) also substantially exceeded the government's targets, in part to finance higher than anticipated coffee stocks, reflecting aggressive procurement of coffee, improved transportation that increased coffee marketing, and lower than anticipated export volumes. These two elements, combined with a failure to limit credit expansion to the private sector, contributed to the large monetary expansion.

Two further factors account for the substantial slippage on the inflation front in 1987/88. First, given past high inflation and lack of confidence in the banking system, the velocity of circulation in Uganda was extremely high: the ratio of broad money to GDP at the end of 1986/87 was as low as 7.3 per cent. This meant that even a small slippage in fiscal and monetary management resulted in substantial increases in money supply. The continuing high and rising levels of the velocity of circulation has been a constraining factor in demand management in Uganda. Second, in 1987/88, an inexperienced and poorly staffed government failed to respond promptly to the deterioration in the fiscal and monetary situation and delayed corrective action, exacerbating inflationary expectations. This failure partly reflected lack of capacity to monitor performance, and partly the lack of consensus on remedial measures such as exchange rate policy.

The high inflation experienced in 1987/88 caused the real effective exchange rate to appreciate substantially and resulted in highly negative real interest rates. Corrective action was called for and was taken during 1988/89 with a large upfront devaluation (from UShs60 to UShs150 per US dollar). This partly reversed the real appreciation experienced in the previous year. This was accompanied by revenue-raising measures including increased petroleum prices, a contractionary budget and efforts to monitor performance more systematically. Tight expenditure controls helped ease inflationary pressures in the first half of 1988/89. Encouraged by this development and by the supply response to the new policies, the government moved aggressively in March 1989 to broaden and deepen the reform programme. The measures introduced then included a more dynamic and flexible exchange rate policy,

34

increases in commercial bank lending and deposit rates, increases in petroleum duties, and an extension of the 100 per cent export retention scheme for all non-coffee exporters. These measures were accompanied by a number of structural measures, including initial steps towards trade liberalization, civil service reform, coffee sector reforms and parastatal restructuring. A more ambitious three-year programme of structural adjustment was drawn up and this triggered a switch by the IMF from the SAF to an ESAF programme that implied larger access for Uganda to Fund resources.

As the new measures began to bite, monetary expansion slowed and inflation decelerated, enabling a reduction in inflation to 86 per cent; this, however, was still well above the targeted inflation rate of 55 per cent. In 1989/90, monetary expansion decelerated sharply, and inflation fell below 30 per cent.

The slower than anticipated progress on inflation is partly attributable to continuing structural weaknesses in four areas: the budget, the coffee sector, the financial sector and civil service. But in part it reflects the continuing underfunding of the Uganda adjustment programme by donors, particularly in the context of declining coffee prices.

In the first three years of the programme, not only did budgetary slippage contribute to the larger than planned monetary expansion, but also fiscal policy has not played the role expected of it in the adjustment process. The weak revenue performance has been at the heart of this failure. Revenues as a percentage of GDP have stagnated at around 5–7 per cent, roughly half the levels prevailing in 1983/84. This is due in part to weak international coffee prices that have depressed coffee revenues. Despite an impressive effort to raise new revenues, however, the government has failed to capture the rents arising from extreme shortages of goods and foreign exchange. Weak tax administration is a key obstacle to the recovery programme. While this is being addressed through technical assistance, progress in this area has been slow.

The low revenue base has greatly restricted the government's freedom on the expenditure side. As a result, civil service wages remain extremely inadequate, leading to low morale and encouraging corruption. Operations and maintenance expenditure is grossly inadequate and tend to be crowded out by defence expenditure which has proved difficult to predict and contain. Development expenditure, which is primarily donor-financed, is also low in relation to needs (3–5 per cent of GDP), and is probably supporting too wide a range of activities, resulting in inadequate investments in key economic and social infrastructure. The overall deficit, at 5–6 per cent of GDP is not particularly high in absolute terms, but given the resources available from concessional foreign financing, these levels have meant an excessive resort to domestic bank financing and have prevented the government from realizing its objective of lowering its liabilities with the banking system. Given the low ratio of broad money to GDP even the modest levels of domestic financing contributed substantially to monetary expansion. To address these issues, the government, jointly with the World Bank, has recently conducted a public expenditure review that addresses the issues underlying resource mobilization and the level and composition of expenditure. This will result in an action programme that will be incorporated in the government's adjustment programme.

Demand management has been further complicated by policies relating to crop financing for coffee. For various reasons such financing has tended to greatly exceed targets set. The original assumptions underlying the projected credit requirements have tended to be overtaken by events: export prices have inevitably been lower than projected, while stocks and procurement have been higher than planned. In addition, inefficiencies in the Coffee Marketing Board and in the cooperative unions that handle some of the domestic marketing of coffee, and the diversion of funds by these unions for purposes other than coffee procurement and storage, have contributed to increased credit requirements. A further problem has arisen from the practice of bartering coffee for imports. The failure of line ministries that enter into barter agreements to pay the Coffee Marketing Board promptly for bartered coffee has added to credit requirements. A programme of remedial measures has been drawn up and is now under implementation. In the short term, the most important components include firm restraints on barter agreements and prompt payments for barter shipments and the institution of a coffee sector budget as a device to monitor financial performance of the sector and trigger corrective action. Medium-term measures include the decision to remove the Coffee Marketing Board's monopoly in the export of coffee and to commercialize its operations with a view to enabling it to compete efficiently with the private sector.

The financial sector in Uganda has not been immune to the general deterioration in institutions in the country. In particular, the portfolio of state-owned commercial banks has been adversely affected by the country's economic circumstances and by the failure of these banks to adapt to the changing economic environment. Lack of discipline in lending policies and the absence of adequate supervision and regulatory capacity in the Bank of Uganda have compounded the problem. High inflation made it difficult for the government to maintain its stated policy of positive interest rates. But with the recent deceleration in inflation, interest rates have turned positive and government policy continues to be the maintenance of positive real rates. Recognizing the importance of the financial sector to the reform programme, an action plan for the sector is being drawn up for implementation in the coming years.

Poor demand management has been an important contributor to slow

Structural adjustment in Uganda: the initial experience

progress on inflation. However, the situation has been greatly exacerbated by external shocks. Uganda's terms of trade have deteriorated by 64 per cent in the three years since the programme was launched. The primary factor here has been the fall in the price of coffee (see Figure 2.1). If Uganda's average export price had stayed at the level prevailing in 1986/87, coffee exports alone would have totalled close to $390 million in 1989/90; the actual figure was US$167 million. As against this, gross official aid (excluding the IMF) rose by US$211 million to US$476 million in 1989/90 over the very low levels prevailing in 1986/87, not even fully compensating Uganda for the decline in coffee prices, let alone financing additional imports in support of the adjustment programme. In fact, imports have stagnated in real terms over the first three years of the programme. The story is the same if one looks at the net transfer of resources from all sources (including Paris Club debt rescheduling), which rose from US$111 million in 1986/87 to US$339 million in 1989/90. A large part of the problem arises from the substantial borrowing from the IMF by the Obote 2 regime in the early 1980s under the Fund's regular and highly non-concessional facilities. Use of Fund credit rose to US$377 million in the three years ending in 1983. By the start of the SAF programme (June 1987) this had been brought down to a still substantial US$270 million. As a result, over the three years of the programme, on a net basis, i.e., including repurchases and Fund charges, the Fund pulled out of Uganda some US$64 million.

With the decline in coffee prices, nearly four-fifths of Uganda's foreign exchange earnings go to meet debt-service obligations. The balance is insufficient to cover even petroleum and other essential imports, leaving the authorities facing a perpetual cash-flow problem. Uganda's difficulties have been recognized by donors in the context of the Special Programme of Assistance to Africa, and there is some evidence that donors are prepared to provide additional aid. However, as has been the experience with other structural adjustment programmes, countries that have spent a long time in the wilderness have found it difficult to attract new donor support. Most donors operate on the basis of countries of concentration; once a country is off that list it becomes difficult to get on it again, given tight aid budgets.

LESSONS FOR THE 1990s

As Uganda enters a new decade, there remains a substantial unfinished agenda that must be addressed. In the short term, stabilization remains a key concern, and will require stronger demand management, improved resource mobilization efforts and a substantial liberalization of the exchange and trade regime. In the medium to long term, the key focus must be on sustainable growth and rising living standards, made possible by a conducive business environment and an improved

37

economic and social infrastructure: communications, health and education facilities. Most important of all, the government must strengthen its institutional capacity and streamline the civil service. It is a formidable agenda, and one that will test the skills of government and the patience of the populace.

The questions the government's internal and external critics have been posing are: Is there adequate commitment to the programme? Is the programme so preoccupied with stabilization that it is imposing too high a cost on growth and the social sectors? Is the programme too short-term in focus? Does it have the right balance between reliance on markets and reliance on the state? What are the main lessons from the initial experience with reforms?

Three years is a short time in which to judge an adjustment programme, especially one in which the initial conditions were so unpromising. Any conclusions drawn here must therefore be necessarily preliminary and tentative. In my view there are three broad lessons. The

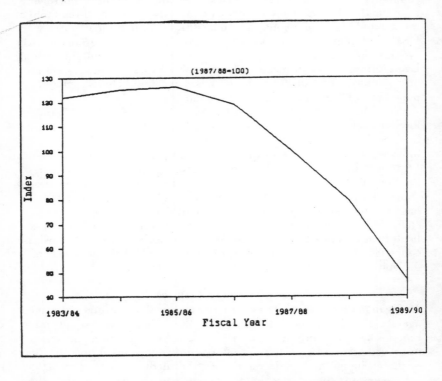

Figure 2.1   Uganda: unit value of coffee exports, 1983/84–1989/90

38

first relates to the issue of commitment. Commitment is difficult to measure, and must be largely a judgmental issue. At the highest level of government there is undoubtedly a strong commitment to the programme. This arises from a larger commitment to restore Uganda to its former glory in all walks of life: the underlying vision and direction have been clearly articulated by President Museveni and others and need no elaboration here. The very fact that so much effort has been made to stay the course despite the exogenous shocks and the relatively slow response of donors is evidence of the seriousness with which the reform programme has been pursued. Experience of other countries also suggests that as the economy begins to pick up, inflationary pressures ease, and as donor response improves, there is increasing self-confidence among policy makers, which results in greater commitment to the programme.

Having said this, however, such a commitment is heavily compromised by weaknesses in institutional capacity to design and implement the programme. Even where such capacity exists, low salaries erode morale and motivation. While external technical assistance fills some of the gaps, ownership of policies and programmes that depend on such assistance is bound to be weak. To overcome this, the government has been encouraging the use of joint government–donor working groups to develop and thrash out policies at the technical level. This is then followed by extensive deliberations at the higher policy levels. While this has slowed decision making, it has improved understanding of policies and resulted in greater ownership. The government has also been encouraging donors to use Ugandan consultants for policy work. However, there is no substitute for internalizing the process of policy formulation and implementation. High priority must be given to strengthening the key institutions (finance, planning, the central bank and the President's office). This must be accompanied by an accelerated effort to streamline the civil service and increase public sector wages. A greater effort is needed to develop a broader consensus within government around the reform programme outside the narrow circle of policy makers. Given the crisis situation facing Uganda, the key policy makers have been preoccupied with fire-fighting. As the crisis lessens, they also need to strengthen current efforts to reach out to academics, journalists, the private sector and professionals, trade unions and farmers to explain the programme and to reflect on the concerns they hear so that the programme can be suitably redesigned. Accelerated implementation of the underfunded PAPSCA would also broaden the reform constituency.

The second issue relates to potential conflicts between stabilization and structural adjustment. It is true that in some cases stabilization programmes can stifle growth and deprive social sectors of much-needed resources. In Uganda, growth has been encouraging. Donor-funded pro-grammes have begun to support social expenditures. Nevertheless, pre-cisely because of high inflation and the collapse of the official economy, the public sector resource base has been eroded and expenditure on social services remains very low. High inflation has other economic and social costs: it redistributes income regressively, distorts the incentive structure by making trading more profitable than production, and shifts asset preferences towards real estate and foreign currency. Thus, the most important lesson for Uganda is that controlling inflation is a pre-condition for structural adjustment. Once the severe macro-economic imbalances are reduced, the government's resource position will improve and provide the resources needed for structural adjustment and to meet the government's social objectives. Given the present low revenue and expenditure base, adjustment in Uganda implies *increasing* rather than lowering the level of government expenditure.

The appropriate level of government expenditure in Uganda must in turn depend on the role the state envisages for itself. In the early years of the NRM administration, the resources of government have been spread thin over a wide range of functions. The government has found itself dealing with a difficult internal security situation, the re-establishment of a legal system, restoration and protection of human rights, restoration of civil service discipline, and containment of the crisis in education and health while simultaneously undertaking a broad-based programme of structural adjustment. Given the severe weaknesses in implementation capacity, and the large number of ineffective facilities and services inherited from the past, it is not suprising that the govern-ment has encountered difficulties in implementing such a broad agenda. Indeed the pace of adjustment envisaged when the recovery programme was launched has proved too ambitious. The third main lesson for the 1990s is that the state will need to withdraw gradually from areas where it is least competent at present: i.e., production, marketing and distribution responsibilities and from the extensive regulation of the private sector, while concentrating its energies on creating the enabling environment: political stability, human rights, a sound policy framework aimed at strengthening the working of markets, and rehabilitation of the economic and social infrastructure needed for development. It is often argued that markets are weak in Africa and that the state must perforce intervene. The underlying assumption that the state has the capacity to intervene efficiently and at costs lower than the costs to the eco-nomy of weak markets may not hold in the case of Uganda where it is already severely stretched in maintaining law and order, ensuring internal security and providing basic services.

This is not to imply that the state should play a passive role in economic development. On the contrary, much of the vision and

40

direction for the future will only come from it as also will the underlying policy environment and the rehabilitation and maintenance of devastated but critical economic and social infrastructure without which the private sector cannot succeed.

Nor should one minimize the constraints facing an adequate private sector response. While the informal sectors of the economy, including agriculture, have demonstrated their capacity to survive the most extreme situations, and can therefore be expected to respond strongly to an appropriate set of policies and public expenditures, the organized private sector has suffered badly and its confidence is thoroughly shaken. It will take time to rebuild that confidence. Foreign investors may prove equally wary of stepping into the breach. Even if the organized private sector proves responsive, it will face some of the same difficulties that public enterprises face in finding skilled people or raising finance for working capital and investment. Given the large present uncertainties, including major changes in relative prices, some in the private sector may wish to sit it out until they have a better sense of the incentive framework. A major focus of the government's efforts will need to be directed towards rebuilding private sector confidence and providing a strong and unambiguous incentive regime.

Finally, while the primary burden of structural adjustment in Uganda lies with the government, its success will depend heavily on sustained external assistance. The weak initial donor response has been a major factor in the relatively slow start to Uganda's programme of reforms. Higher resource flows accompanied by well-designed technical assistance will enable stronger reform measures and greatly ease the costs associated with adjustment. At the same time, donors must not expect an early reduction in aid dependence. Given the high concentration of one commodity in exports and the large imbalance between exports and imports (exports currently cover only 31 per cent of imports), even rapid progress in export diversification will still leave substantial external financing needs, particularly given the large rehabilitation needs of the economy.

Notes

1. The author is Chief of the International Economic Relations Division in the External Affairs Department of the World Bank. However at the time of writing, he was Lead Economist for the Eastern Africa Department. This chapter draws on the analysis contained in the World Bank report No. 7439-UG dated 26 September 1988, entitled 'Uganda: Towards Stabilization and Economic Recovery', and on subsequent analysis and reports by Bank staff through September 1990. Data have been updated through June 1991. The author is grateful to Emmanuel Ablo, Kapil Kapoor, Sanjay Pradhan, and Anne Vaughn for their comments on an earlier draft, and to Mimi Klutstein-Meyer for statistical assistance. However, the findings, interpretations and conclusions are the author's own. They should not be attributed to the World Bank, its Board of Directors, its management or any of its member countries.

THREE
Economic adjustment programmes in Uganda 1985-9

When a country is experiencing balance of payments difficulties, uncontrolled inflation and unemployment, general shortages of goods and services, and widespread bottlenecks disrupting production then there is macro-economic disequilibria. In such circumstances, a programme of adjustment is called for. This implies an improvement in the balances between supply and demand in the economy aimed at moderating inflationary pressures, increasing production and strengthening the balance of payments position.

Adjustment of whatever type is painful, costly, difficult and gradual and requires some sacrifices. It is like surgery to remove a malignant tumor without the use of an anaesthetic. Countries would therefore want to select the method that minimizes the cost (sacrifice) of adjustment. Because of the unpleasantness of adjustment programmes many governments are hesitant to effectuate the operation in time, and then the adjustment becomes even more painful.

Before 1971, Uganda had a very healthy economy in all respects but the socio-economic and political policies during the 1970–80 period quickly led to the deepest depression the country had experienced. There were acute shortages of goods and services, rampant unemployment, galloping inflation, acute balance of payments difficulties, huge external debts, widespread smuggling and black-marketeering, and ever increasing government deficits.

Since 1981 there have been several economic adjustment programmes in Uganda. These may be grouped into two distinct periods: the Obote era (1981–4), and the Museveni period (1986 to date). This chapter focuses on economic adjustments during the Museveni period because the earlier period has already been dealt with by many writers.[1] The next section gives a summary of the adjustment programmes in the period 1981–4. This is followed by discussions of the period of transition and debate (1985–6) and of the subsequent adjustment programmes of the Museveni period from 1987 to date. A final section gives some concluding remarks.

43

Structural adjustment on trial

When the Obote government took over power in December 1980 it inherited a shattered economy that was in macro-economic disequilibria in all the four markets: the goods market, the money market, the labour market and the foreign exchange market. Uganda does not have a bonds market. It was apparent that something had to be done to prevent a bad situation from growing worse.

In 1981 the government instituted programmes of economic stabilization with the guidance and assistance of the International Monetary Fund (IMF). The major objectives were to halt the deterioration of the economy, revive production, restore confidence in the Uganda shilling, eliminate price distortions, improve fiscal and monetary displine, and lay a firm foundation for sustained recovery. Specific measures adopted by government included:

(1) Realignment of the external value of the Uganda shilling, which resulted in the depreciation of its external value by 41 times in only three years.
(2) Provision of incentives through upward adjustment and realignment of producer prices.
(3) The dismantling of price controls.
(4) Rationalization of the internal distribution system and the machinery for importation.
(5) Improving the budgetary performance of government borrowing and curtailing subsidies to inefficient public enterprises.
(6) Introduction of policies to encourage foreign investment and return to private ownership and control companies that were nationalized during the military regime.
(7) Progressively increasing interest rates with a view to mobilizing more savings and achieving greater efficiency in resource allocation.

Overall, the economy responded positively to these measures and GDP growth rates were transformed from negatives to positives for the period 1981–3. In 1982 and 1983 all the sectors had positive growth rates except electricity (1982) and agricultural primary processing (1983). After 1983, the economy had negative growth rates for the years 1984 and 1985 (Table 3.1).

In agriculture the area planted and production of all food crops increased between 1980 and 1983 and declined between 1983 and 1985. For cash crops the area of perennial crops planted did not change but production showed some increase between 1980 and 1983. From 1984 onwards it seems that the recovery of momentum in the sector had waned, and the sector was registering negative growth rates.

The industrial sector also showed temporary signs of revival but most

44

Table 3.1 Selected economic data, 1980-8

	1980	1981	1982	1983	1984	1985	1986	1987	1988
GDP (at 1966 prices million shs)	6115	6351	6873	7171	6787	6715	6532	6827	
CPI (Low-income group 1981 = 100)	97	100	155	152	213	787	4576	10342	24434
CPI (Middle-income group 1981 = 100)			201	249		1093	4691	12338	27004
Government deficit as % of total expenditure	75	35	23	19	27	34	49	28	
Money and Credit (billions of Shs)									
Domestic credit	21	43	58	80	132	257	545	1176	2704
Claims on government	15	32	37	57	86	143	247	351	1168
Broad money (M2)	19	35	39	54	116	262	724	1854	3944
Balance of Payments (millions of US$)									
Total exports	336	246	347	368	408	379	408	334	273
Total imports	564	−415	−428	−422	−342	−264	−476	−635	−626
Trade balance	−228	−169	−75	−60	66	115	−68	−301	−353
Current a/c balance	−7	−171	−70	−70	107	77	8	−170	−194
Overall balance	−288	−187	−33	−36	−59	+67	127	−9	−9
Annual % changes									
GDP	−9.7	+3.9	+8.2	+4.3	−5.4	+1.1	−2.7	+4.5	+7.2
CPI (low income)		3.1	15.0	32.2	40.2	1690	153.0	198.2	197.6
Domestic credit	61	96	36	37	60	114	112	115	130
Claim on government		109	17	41	64	115	73	42	113
Broad money (M²)	32	77	25	41	114	192	177	156	113

* Revised

Source: (1) Ministry of Planning and Economic Development, Background to the Budget, 1981-2 and 1986-7.

**Table 3.2 Gross domestic product by main-sector at factor cost
1981–6 (% change from previous year)**

	1981	1982	1983	1984	1985	1986
Monetary economy	0	7.4	2.6	– 1.2	2.6	– 1.3
Agriculture	– 0.9	13.8	1.1	– 5.7	4.0	– 8.2
Industry	– 2.5	35.1	– 4.0	0	– 2.1	0
Non-monetary economy	10.3	6.9	7.0	– 11.6	– 7.0	– 5.4
Gross domestic product	3.9	8.2	4.3	– 5.4	– 1.1	– 2.7
GDP per capita (Shs)	1.0	5.4	1.4	– 7.1	– 3.8	– 5.3

Source: Bank of Uganda, QER, October–December 1988, Vol. 10/88
(Appendix XIV)

**Table 3.3 Agricultural production of major cash crops
1985–8 (tons) (% change from previous year)**

	1985	1986	1987	1988
Coffee	11.8	– 7.6	11.9	– 6.7
Cotton lint	33.6	– 72.4	– 40.0	– 37.9
Tobacco	– 20.0	– 44.8	44.4	92.3
Tea	7.7	– 42.9	9.4	– 5.7
Sugar	– 66.7	– 100.0	–	–
Maize	22.1	– 18.4	17.9	54.3
Soya beans	– 11.2	25.0	– 30	75
Beans (mixed)	0.8	0	1.9	17.7
Groundnuts	– 28.8	40.5	– 33.9	107.1
Sim-sim	– 15.4	6.1	– 5.8	36

Source: Bank of Uganda, QER, October–December 1988, Vol. 10/1988
(Appendix XV)

industries did not increase their capacity utilization appreciably. Only
soft drinks and cigarette manufacture seem to have maintained the revival momentum and were in 1985 operating at 40 per cent and 75 per cent
capacity respectively; other industries were operating at less than 20 per
cent capacity utilization.

The rates of increase of the consumer price index for the low
income group between 1980 and 1983 were on the average below the
rates during the period 1972–80, but from 1984 onwards the rate of
increase was explosive for both low-income and middle-income groups.
In other words the rate of inflation seems to have been moderated during
the period 1981–83 but thereafter it got out of hand again.

Government deficits were reduced from 75 per cent of government

Economic adjustment programmes in Uganda 1985–9
Table 3.4 Production of manufactured commodities
1985–8 (% change from previous year)

	1985	1986	1987	1988
Beer	– 44.4	– 17.9	144.9	27.2
Uganda waragi	382.1	– 24.2	36.5	– 1.3
Cigarettes	46.6	0.3	1.0	14.1
Textiles	– 0.1	– 6.3	10.3	21.8
Hoes	124.3	24.3	23.1	19.0
Blankets	– 69.5	60.7	263.0	– 66.7
Soap	– 20.0	312.5	378.8	14.5
Matches	–	166.7	– 50	1.9
Steel ingots	78.6	– 64.0	0	21.5
Corrugated iron sheets	20.0	– 54.2	– 45.5	12.6
Cement	– 53.0	553.0	– 79.2	– 10.3
Points	9.8	– 50.6	– 21.3	– 4.8
Edible oil	0	– 50.0		
Footwear	– 48.7	– 6.2	21.4	– 38.2
Fishnets	– 53.0	17.3	43.4	10.6
Bicycle tyres & tubes	– 15.8	– 20.6	– 63.6	97.3

Sources: (1) Bank of Uganda, QER October–December 1988, vol 10/1988
(Appendix XVI)
(2) MPED, Background to the Budget, 1989–1990, July 1989
(Appendix Table 54)

Table 3.5 Summary of government budgetary and financial operations
1982–8 – (billion shs)

	1982–3	1983–4	1984–5	1985–6	1986–7	1987–8*
Total revenue	52.8	94.8	169.9	322.8	585.8	27.7
Total expenditure	69.3	116.9	233.1	486.6	1141.5	36.2
Overall deficit	16.5	– 22.1	– 63.1	– 163.8	– 555.7	– 10.1
Financing:						
External	3.6	3.0	13.4	47.4	136.2	5.9
Domestic	12.9	19.1	49.6	116.4	419.5	4.2
Bank	11.4	– 6.9	53.9	77.5	218.2	3.9
Non-bank	1.5	26.1	– 4.3	38.9	201.3	0.3
Deficit as % of total expenditure	24	19	27	34	49	28
Bank financed deficit as % of total expenditure	19	16	21	24	37	12

* Estimates in New Uganda shillings
Source: Bank of Uganda, QER, October–December 1988, Vol. 10/88 (Appendix XIII)

expenditure in 1980/81 to 19 per cent in 1983/84, but began to rise again to over 30 per cent in 1985/86. They were kept within the overall ceilings set by the IMF up to 1984.

The annual rate of increase of domestic credit and money supply fell from 96 per cent and 77 per cent respectively in 1981 to levels of less than 40 per cent for the years 1982 and 1983. However, they rose again thereafter, so that in 1985 alone they increased by 114 per cent and 192 per cent respectively.

Total exports increased from US$336 million in 1980 to US$408 million in 1984 and then declined to US$379 million in 1985. Total imports declined throughout the period from US$564 million in 1980 to US$264 million in 1985. The balance of trade improved throughout the period from a deficit of US$228 million in 1980 to positive figures in 1984 and 1985, but this was due to a drastic reduction of the import bill from US$428 million in 1983 to US$342 million and US$264 million in 1984 and 1985 respectively. The current account balance also became positive in 1984 and 1985. The overall balance of payments position also improved from a deficit of US$288 million in 1980 to one of US$33 million in 1982 and US$36 million in 1983. In 1985 it was actually positive at US$67 million.

Parallel market activities in goods were wiped out through the abolition of price controls, and smuggling was greatly reduced. The ratio between the parallel market foreign exchange rates and the official rates were reduced from 4 : 1 to 1 : 1 in June 1984 but then the ratio began to rise again.

In summary we can say that the adjustment programme instituted in 1981 attained short-term success in reviving the economy. It revived production in the agricultural and industrial sectors, moderated inflation, reduced parallel market activities and smuggling, and improved the balance of payments position. These positive trends were not sustained beyond the third quarter of 1984 and there are several competing explanations for this, some of which are:

(1) that the programme was not fully implemented and was actually abandoned after June 1984;

(2) that the programme depended for its success on a continued inflow of foreign finance and not enough of it was obtained on a continuous basis;

(3) that the programme failed for non-economic reasons, especially the civil war;

(4) that the programme was altogether misplaced and overloaded a single policy instrument – the exchange rate – to correct a wide range of distortions, some of which had little to do with the foreign sector.

48

Economic adjustment programmes in Uganda 1985-9

Each of these explanations has an element of truth but their evaluation is beyond the scope of this chapter.

THE PERIOD OF TRANSITION, DEBATE AND EXPERIMENT (1985-6)

The Obote regime ended abruptly with a military coup in 1985. The civil war that had continued in parts of the country throughout his tenure erupted with increased violence as Museveni's National Resistance Army (NRA), the military wing of National Resistance Movement (NRM), consolidated power in the south and demanded a role in the administration.

The NRA/NRM conquered Kampala in January 1986 and assumed centre control. The negative economic trends that had began in 1984 continued to accelerate and eroded most of the positive gains of the period 1982 to 1983. When the (NRM/NRA) took power it soon realized that economic conditions were deteriorating fast and that the problems that faced the economy in 1980 had reappeared with greater voracity and were reinforcing themselves, i.e., low and declining production; shortages of goods, services and foreign exchange; uncontrolled government deficits and excessive monetary expansion; galloping inflation; widespread parallel markets and smuggling; balance of payments problems and high level of insecurity, including civil war.[2]

The civil war had ransacked the rural areas and laid many parts of the country to waste. For the first time in the history of conflicts in Uganda, the economic base of the country had been disturbed because of dependence on rural production. Earlier conflicts had been restricted to urban areas and the rural production base had been left intact.

The NRM approached these economic problems with philosophies and approaches that were fundamentally different from those followed by Obote's regime. At that time they were against the spirit of the previous IMF-sponsored programmes. The NRM was anti-IMF, anti-devaluation, and anti-wholesale *laissez-faire*.

The 1986 budget was a reflection of this stand. It abolished the dual exchange rate introduced earlier and fixed the exchange rate at UShs1400 to the US dollar, and increased salaries by 50 per cent. It doubled the budget outlays over the previous year, and increased deficit on a commitment basis with most financing to come from the banking sector. It introduced price controls and extended its monopoly control over internal and external trading. It gave monopolies to some of its parastatals for some commodities: for example it gave the Produce Marketing Board a monopoly for the internal and external marketing of maize, beans, soyabeans, groundnuts and sim-sim; and the Uganda Hardwares was given a monopoly for timber, hides and skins.

Unfortunately, the economic conditions continued to deteriorate

49

(Table 3.1). There was a fall in coffee revenue and tax and Uganda was unable to gain from the coffee boom and suspension of the ICO quota. Non-traditional exports came to a standstill (Table 3.11). The marketed output of food fell and prices rose. Attempts at price control merely led to shortages and a flourishing black market for essential goods. The balance of payments remained critical. The fixed norminal exchange rate severely penalized producers and dramatically reduced revenue from export duty. To finance the resultant deficit, the government accumulated new arrears and borrowed from the banks. Credit to government increased by 72.7 per cent, total domestic credit by 112.5 per cent and money supply (M2) by 176.6 per cent in 1986 (Table 3.6). The inflationary pressures were therefore increased, with the cost of living index for low-income group increasing by 481 per cent and that for the middle-income group by 329 per cent in 1986, compared with 220 per cent and 103 per cent respectively in 1985 (Table 3.7).

The worsening economic conditions made it clear that a major revision of economic policies was urgently required. A relentless debate about what was to be done next was waged. From the point of view of the government, the causes of the problems were mainly historical, such as the distortions in the pattern of economic activity created by the colonialists; Amin's and Obote's economic mismanagement and wars of 'Liberation'; and external factors such as the deterioration in the terms of trade. The IMF however was steadfast in maintaining that the problems were caused or perpetuated by lack of incentives to producers, monetary and fiscal indiscipline, and excessive interference in the market mechanism in the form of administrative controls.

The debate revolved around several points of controversy, including the nature of economic incentives; free-market mechanisms vs administrative controls; devaluation vs no devaluation; fixed vs flexible exchange rates; private enterprise vs public enterprise; and subsidies vs no subsidies.

Considering the level of foreign exchange needed for the NRM government's four-year Rehabilitation and Development Plan[3] of US$2420.5 million (84.4 per cent of total Plan expenditure) and knowing that such finances could not be generated locally through exports, it was clear that the finances had to come from foreign sources. Also, considering the fact that foreign financiers now require the IMF stamp of approval before they release their money, it was easy to predict with certainty the outcome of the debate in the short run. In the medium and long run, however, it continues. As long as one continues to depend on external sources of finance, it will be difficult to have an independent economic policy devoid of the external financier's input.

The economic programme that was finally agreed upon reflected heavily the IMF diagnosis and approach. Producers had to be given

Table 3.6 Monetary survey, 1985-8 (billions of shillings)

Year	1985				1986				1987				1988			
Month	3	6	9	12	3	6	9	12	3	6	9	12	3	6	9	12
Foreign assets (net)	-140	-131	-148	-232	-350	-251	-218	-266	-270	-9.24	-13.69	-11.52	-11.7	-11.83	-23.56	-30.10
Domestic credit	183	195	219	257	337	317	359	546	612	8.27	8.64	11.76	20.17	21.16	23.50	27.04
To government	96	97	108	143	166	154	151	247	278	4.62	2.84	3.51	9.08	8.87	9.86	11.68
To private sector	87	98	110	115	170	162	207	298	333	3.65	5.80	8.25	11.09	12.29	13.64	15.36
Broad money (M2)	161	182	215	262	378	452	573	724	848	8.82	12.34	18.54	23.55	26.83	33.32	39.44
Other items (net)	-118	-118	-237	-237	-391	-386	-433	-445	-504	9.80	-17.36	-18.30	-14.55	-17.50	-33.37	-42.50
Percentage (%) Change from Previous Quarter																
Domestic credit	52.7	6.6	12.3	17.4	31.1	-5.9	13.2	52.1	12.1	35.1	4.5	36.1	71.5	4.9	11.1	15.1
To government	45.5	1.0	11.3	32.4	16.1	-7.2	-9.2	63.6	12.6	66.2	-38.5	23.6	158.7	-2.3	11.2	18.5
To private sector	22.7	2.6	12.2	4.5	47.8	-4.7	27.8	44.0	11.7	9.2	58.9	42.2	34.4	10.8	11.0	12.6
Broad money (M2)	27.3	13.0	18.1	21.9	44.3	19.6	26.8	26.4	17.1	4.0	39.9	50.2	27.0	13.9	24.2	18.4

Sources: (1) Bank of Uganda, Annual Report 1985 (p. 106)
(2) Bank of Uganda, Quarterly Economic Report, October–December 1988, volume 10/1988 (Appendix 11)
(3) MPED, Background to the Budget 1989-1990, July 1989 (Appendix Table 15)

51

Table 3.7 Kampala cost of living index (Low and middle-income groups)
1985–8

| | Low-income group | | Middle-income group | |
| | April 1980 = 100 | | | |
	Index	% change from previous quarter	Index	% change from previous quarter
1985				
March	452	84	656	22
June	558	23	752	14
September	632	13	866	15
December	787	25	1093	26
1986				
March	1423	81	1467	34
June	2026	42	1902	30
September	2223	10	2356	24
December	4576	106	4691	99
1987				
March	4874	7	5217	11
June	5295	9	6339	22
September	7116	34	8909	41
December	10342	45	12338	39
1988				
March	13626	32	14218	15
June	18190	33	21749	53
September	22125	22	25932	19
December	24434	10	27004	4

Sources: (1) Ministry of Planning and Economic Development, Background to the Budget 1987–8, Kampala (Appendix Table 18)
(2) Bank of Uganda, Annual Report 1985, (p. 25)
(3) Bank of Uganda, Quarterly Economic Report, July 1987, (p. 55)
(4) Bank of Uganda, Quarterly Economic Report, July–September 1988 vol. 09/1988 (Appendix VII)
(5) Bank of Uganda, Quarterly Economic Report, October–December 1988, vol. 10/1988 (Appendix VI and VII)

sufficient incentives in the form of increased prices. There had to be monetary discipline in the form of a reduction in government deficits and monetary expansion. Price controls of most commodities had to be dismantled, the fixed exchange rate regime had to be replaced with a more flexible exchange rate system and there had to be massive devaluation. Finally, there was strong pressure for divestment from public enterprises.

Table 3.8 Structure of nominal interest rates 1985–8 (annual %)

	December 1985	December 1986	December 1987	December 1988
Rediscount to commercial banks	24	36	31	45
Treasury bills (90 days)	22	35	28	38
Government stocks (10 years)	26	45	32	42
Commercial banks savings deposit	18	28	18	28
Commercial time deposit (one year)	22	35	22	32
Lending rates				
Agriculture and manufacturing	24	38	22–25	32–35
Commerce	25	40	40	40

Source: Bank of Uganda, Quarterly Economic Report, October–December 1988 vol. 10/1988.

Table 3.9 Structure of real interest rates 1985 – March 1989 (annual %)

	December 1985	December 1986	December 1987	December 1988
Rediscount to commercial banks	– 37	– 68	– 50	– 43
Treasury bills (90 days)	– 38	– 68	– 51	– 37
Government stocks (10 years)	– 36	– 65	– 50	– 35
Commercial banks savings deposit	– 40	– 68	– 55	– 42
Commercial banks time deposit (one year)	– 38	– 68	– 54	– 40
Lending rates				
Agriculture and manufacturing	– 37	– 67	(– 54) + 0(– 52);	(– 40)t(– 38)
Commerce	– 37	– 67	– 47	– 36

Source: Bank of Uganda.

THE RECOVERY PROGRAMMES 1987-8

The major objective of the recovery programme announced on 15 May 1987[4] was economic stabilization, i.e, the reduction of inflation and stimulation of short-run supply responses. Its main elements were:

(1) the demonetization of the Uganda shilling by a factor of 100;
(2) the application of a conversion tax of 30 per cent on all cash holdings, deposits and treasury bills during the currency exchange to syphon off excess liquidity;

Table 3.10 Quarterly average exchange rates

Period	Official exchange rates	
	UShs per US $	% change from previous quarter
1985		
March	549	6.8
June	598	8.9
September	600	0.3
December	942	57.0
1986		
March	1470	56.1
June	1447	– 1.6
September	1400	– 3.2
December	1400	0
1987		
March	1400	0
June	1400	0
September	60	328.6
December	60	0
1988		
March	60	0
June	60	0
September	150	150
December	165	10

Table 3.11. Composition of exports (FOB) 1984–1988 (value) (% of total)

	1984	1985	1986	1987	1988
Coffee	88.0	93.4	97.5	95.0	96.8
Cotton	3.0	4.1	1.3	1.3	1.1
Tea	0.8	0.3	0.8	0.6	0.3
Tobacco	0.4	0.1	–	–	0.2
Maize & beans	2.5	0.8	0.3	–	0.1
Others	5.3	1.3	0.1	3.1	1.1
	100.0	100.0	100.0	100.0	100.0

Sources: MPED, Background to the Budget 1989–1990, July 1989 (Appendix Table 4)

Table 3.12 Balance of payments 1982–88 (million US$)

	1982	1983	1984	1985	1986	1987	1988
Current account	−69.9	−72.3	107.1	77.0	6.9	−169.9	−194.0
Trade balance	−74.9	−60.4	65.7	114.9	−68.5	−300.8	−353.0
Exports	347.1	367.7	407.9	379.0	407.5	333.7	272.9
Imports	−422.0	−428.1	−342.2	−264.1	−476.1	−634.5	−626.1
Capital account	14.6	27.7	−88.3	−27.4	75.6	142.3	59.5
Net change in arrears	22.4	8.3	−77.3	17.3	44.3	19.1	142.1
Overall balance	−32.9	−36.2	−58.5	66.9	127.1	19.1	142.1
Financing	32.9	36.2	58.5	−66.9	−127.1	−8.5	7.6
Change in cross reserves	34.2	−28.2	56.2	29.6	0.8	8.5	7.6
IMF (Net)	82.3	85.4	−10.2	−89.5	−108.4	−19.0	−1.6
Others (Net)	−15.1	−20.9	12.2	−7.2	−19.5	−6.8	5.5
						34.3	−11.5

Sources: (1) Bank of Uganda, Quarterly Economic Review, October–December 1988, Vol. 10 (Appendix XVII)
(2) MFED: Background to the Budget 1989–1990, July 1989 (Appendix Table 3)

(3) a 76.7 per cent devaluation of the Uganda shilling or, in other words, an increase by 328.6 in the price of the US dollar;
(4) increases in producer prices of traditional export crops by a factor of between three and five;
(5) establishment of a revolving fund credit facility to be on-lent to commercial banks for provision of short-term credit to priority importers;
(6) an increase in the prices of petroleum products to eliminate subsidies;

These policies were reinforced by other policies announced during the Budget speech on 24 July 1987 and other occasions that included:[5]

(1) tight fiscal and monetary policies and reduction of government indebtedness to the banking system;
(2) the introduction of the open general licensing (OGL) system under which importers would obtain import licences and foreign exchange immediately upon request;
(3) the reduction of interest rates by about 20 per cent;
(4) the establishment of a Central Purchasing Agency to reduce fraud;
(5) the requirement that all parastatals present audited accounts and pay dividends to the government;
(6) the reactivation and revamping of the verification committee to find a lasting solution to the Departed Asians' Property;
(7) the introduction of barter trade arrangements to reduce foreign exchange requirements;
(8) the reaffirmation of the significant role to be played by the private sector;

The programme was supported by a Structural Adjustment Facility (SAF) of the IMF and a Paris Club rescheduling of bilateral debt, arrears and current obligations for 1986/87 amounting to US$185 million; an IDA economic recovery credit and other foreign assistance of US$200 million. Exports were projected to increase by 17 per cent in volume and 13 per cent in value.

The supply response was therefore expected to be rapid because a greater availability of resources was expected, there were more efficient price incentives and there was an improvement in marketing. The gap between supply and demand would narrow and inflation would therefore be moderated.

The initial results of the Economic Recovery Programme have been mixed. Real output increased but the economy remained severely destabilized. Gross domestic product rose by 4.5 per cent in 1987, thereby reversing the three-year trend of declining real production. The industrial sector grew by around 15 per cent in 1987. Good weather and improved producer prices for coffee and other key crops enabled the agricultural sector to increase production by 8.5 per cent. The output response was facilitated by improvements in infrastructure and transport. (Table 3.1)

Much less was achieved in the stabilization effort. After an initial decline and relative stability between June and August, inflation exploded in September 1987 and it remained high, at an annual average rate of about 24 per cent. Several factors fuelled inflation. These included unforeseen external shocks, a shortfall in external receipts, disruption of the trade route through Kenya, internal distribution problems, and a massive expansion of broad money (M2) by 156 per cent in 1987. Moreover, fiscal performance fell considerably short of objectives because of unbudgeted local capital outlay for the PTA conference, increased relief necessities, and increasing unbudgeted costs of military expenditures. The barrier to exports created by the reimposition of an ICO quota system also had a fiscal impact. Finally, there was a big jump in private sector credit (by 177 per cent) in 1987 because of crop-financing requirements.

The results on the external front were also disappointing because of the fall in exports by 18 per cent in 1987. This was a result of a lower volume of coffee sales, delays in donor assistance and delays in adjusting the exchange rate.

In summary the economy failed to adjust because of a failure to respond promptly to the domestic consequences of the external shocks, an expansionist fiscal and monetary stance, the internal and external security threat, poor budgeting and a weak institutional administrative capacity.

By the end of the 1987/88 programme, the economy was again severely destabilized. The challenge to government was therefore to achieve short-term stabilization while stimulating growth. Following the spirit of the previous programmes, it seems the government had to make three critical adjustments: to fiscal policy, the foreign exchange market and the supply side. In addition there was a need for an adequate inflow of external assistance.

In other words a new programme should seek to reduce financial imbalances and inflationary pressures, increase output, and rehabilitate the productive and social infrastructure. This would again call for controlled government expenditures, increased government revenues, a non-accommodating monetary policy, periodic adjustment of the exchange rate, provision of incentives, better system for monitoring to prevent slippage and facilitate adjustments to external shocks, increased external financing and institutional improvements.

But this is exactly what the government had failed to do so far. Attempts so far have been half-hearted, always being haunted by the following dilemmas:

(1) devaluation vs reduction in inflation and output expansion,
(2) credit contraction vs capacity utilization, investment and growth,
(3) trade liberalization vs increase in public tax revenues and reduction in balance of payment deficits.
(4) subsidies vs reduction in public deficits and income distribution;
(5) financial liberalization vs output expansion investment and growth.

The second stabilization attempt was launched in July 1988.[6] Apparently the government was now even more prone to IMF-type programmes than Obote's regime, although the failure of the first stabilization attempt had evoked political resistance and scepticism. The main objectives of the 1988 programme were to sustain the level of growth of the economy and to reduce inflation.

Budget strategies included a balanced budget; retiring part of its debt to the central bank; increasing taxes; divestment; suspension or minimization of expenditure on new vehicles, construction of houses, and subsidies to parastatals; involving community participation in development projects; and encouraging small-scale industries.

Specifically the government proposed to increase agricultural producer prices by a factor of between 1.33 and 3.00; increase the wage bill by 120 per cent; expand the open general licence (OGL) system; devalue the Uganda Shilling by a factor of 2.5; raise interest rates to between 28 per cent and 40 per cent; increase borrowing from the public; and increase tax revenue. The budget also planned a deficit of over 32 per cent of planned expenditure. This incidently contradicted the strategy of having a balanced budget and containing inflation. The programme had both supply side and demand side components.

The supply side policies included producer incentives, reform of the marketing system, widening of the OGL system to give producers access to foreign exchange and improvement of infrastructure, especially roads and divestiture. On the demand side it hoped to exercise strict fiscal and monetary discipline and to apply a more flexible exchanges rate system.

The 'Background to the Budget 1989–1990[7] reports astronomical growth rates of the real GDP of 7.2 per cent per annum (1987/88), the highest in sub-Saharan Africa. Only electricity reported a negative growth rate of – 23.3 per cent. Other sectors had very high positive growth rates including industry, 25.1 per cent, monetary agriculture 8.5 per cent, agricultural processing 40 per cent, forestry, fishing and hunting 39.2 per cent, manufacture of foods 31.3 per cent, miscellaneous manufacture 22.4 per cent, Construction 19.6 per cent and non-monetary economy 5.2 per cent.

But the economy still remained distabilized. The cost of living index for low-income and middle-income groups grew by an annual average rate of 197.6 per cent and 189.0 per cent respectively in 1988. Domestic credit grew by 130 per cent, credit to government by 233 per cent and money supply (M2) by 113 per cent. The deficits on recurrent and development budget were 22 per cent and 62 per cent respectively of expenditures. Total exports continued to decline from US$333.7 million in 1987 to US$272.9 million in 1988, a fall of 18.2 per cent. The trade balance worsened from a deficit of US$300.8 million to one of US$353.2 million and the current account balance also worsened by 12.5 per cent in the same period. The overall balance, however, improved from a deficit of US$8.5 million in 1987 to one of US$7.6 million in 1988 because of disbursements and rescheduling of arrears.

While monetary statistics are fairly accurate, production statistics are highly suspect, especially those for agriculture. There has not been an agricultural census for more than 20 years and agricultural extension service broke down long ago so that the figures are guesses. Since most of the GDP is derived from agriculture, the GDP figures are not firm. We should therefore treat them with a pinch of salt.

CONCLUSION

An examination of the adjustment programmes implemented in Uganda since 1981 indicates the following:

(1) They are only capable of producing temporary bouts of positive change.
(2) They have been incapable of stimulating exports to produce enough foreign exchange to fill the gap temporarily being filled by IMF and World Bank funding such that whenever such funding dries up or threatens to dry up, the whole programme collapses.
(3) The programmes depend entirely on external funding for their success, and the constant flow of these resources is not guaranteed.
(4) The programmes seem to have inbuilt inflationary pressures because the constant devaluations automatically increase domestic prices in a foreign trade oriented economy like Uganda's. The programmes cannot therefore 'stabilize' the economy.
(5) Because of political considerations most measures seem to be half-hearted.
(6) The economy is incapable of adjusting quickly to unforeseen external shocks.
(7) Internal upheavals reduce further the chances of the programmes succeeding.

The United Nations Economic Commission for Africa in the publication 'African Alternative Framework to Structural Adjustment Programmes for Socio-Economic Recovery and Transformation' (AAF-SAP)[8] contends that the programmes are altogether misplaced. They claim that adjustment for African economies calls for a different approach, since they are characterized by the predominance of the subsistence and informal sectors, or narrow production bases, environmental degradation, lopsided development, and fragmented, dependent and open economies.

The essential differences between what they propose and the IMF type policies include a sectoral allocation of credit, use of selective nominal interest rates, use of multiple exchange rates, selective trade controls, selective subsidies, a limitation of debt service ratios to manageable levels, regional cooperation, an emphasis on the agricultural sector (20–25 per cent of budget) and the social services sector (30 per cent), a reduction of military expenditure, an emphasis on small-scale industries, and structural transformation. The Uganda programmes have tried most of these policies but the results seemed to have been worse (the period 1985–6). The search for an appropriate adjustment programme must therefore continue.

Notes

---

1. See Ochieng, 1985 and Edmonds, 1988.
2. Y.K. Museveni, 'An Address to the Nation on Uganda's Economic Policy Package for Reconstruction and Development at A Special Session of the National Resistance Council on Friday 15th May, 1987', Government Printer, Entebbe.
3. Ministry of Planning and Economic Development, 'National Rehabilitation and Development Plan 1988–1991'.
4. Museveni, Address.
5. C.W.C.B. Kiyonga, 'Budget Speech 24th July 1987', Government Printer, Entebbe, 1988.
6. C.W.C.B. Kiyonga, 'Budget Speech 1st July 1988', Government Printer, Entebbe, 1988.
7. Ministry of Planning and Economic Development, 'Background to the Budget 1989–1990', Government Printer, Entebbe, July 1989.
8. UN-ECA, 'African Alternative Framework to Structural Adjustment Programmes for Socio-Economic Recovery and Transformation', E/ECA/CM.15/6/Rev.3.

FOUR
IMF conditionality and structural adjustment under the National Resistance Movement
Joshua B. Mugyenyi

When the National Resistance Movement (NRM) began organizing for armed struggle against the Obote 2 regime in 1981, many observers, including the then incumbent regime, dismissed it as a reckless youthful aberration.[1] It was a minor lunatic fringe with no more than a nuisance value that would quickly assume its place in the dustbin of history, as many previous attempts had done. Indeed, history seemed to be on the side of sceptics: apart from Chad, no sitting government in post-independence Africa had been dislodged from power by an indigenous guerrilla movement. This scepticism was shared by the bulk of world opinion. Many countries, including those that had intimate knowledge of the brutalities committed by both the Amin and Obote 2 regimes, treated the NRM with, at best, polite disregard. Meanwhile, through meticulous political and military planning, the NRM grew from the initial 27 guerrillas to a huge citizen army which, on 26 January 1986, took control of state power.

By so assuming power in Uganda, the NRM created a crucial precedent in Africa. For the first time a guerrilla movement was able to hold its own with a minimum of external help, and defeat an incumbent regime through an outright military victory. During the excruciating guerrilla war, the NRM was able to bring together groups, that had previously belonged to diverse, even antagonistic, political and religious persuasions; this involved patient and sustained consensus-building and broad-based politics. Necessarily, the NRM also learnt and disseminated the virtues of self-reliance. Many of these attributes still characterize the *modus operandi* of NRM government.

On assumption of power in 1986 the NRM's main policy positions were embodied in a short document, the *10-Point Programme*. If the NRM still harboured a leftist political philosophy, as many observers all along assumed, such predispositions were not evident in its policy framework.

The *10-Point Programme* enunciated an economic policy that aimed at an independent, integrated and self-sustaining economy. As it transpired, this policy framework was a pragmatic reaffirmation of

61

the virtues of a mixed economy, with a thrust towards improved management and a drive against corruption in public affairs.

This carefully woven libertarian economic policy reflected, among other things, the complexity, sensibilities, and expectations of the political rainbow coalition that the NRM was not only able to put together during its long march to Kampala but was also hoping to consolidate into a firm broad-based political foundation. While the NRM's capacity to restore order and civil liberties was as astonishing as it was disarming, even to its harshest adversaries and cynics, its economic policies and programmes, while pragmatic, enthusiastic and open-minded, were somewhat hesitant, episodic and occasionally inconsistent. This was not unexpected. Other competing urgent priorities as well as an understandable lack of experience of economic management on the part of young NRM functionaries, fresh from the bush, contributed to the initial hesitancy.

In time, however, the overriding goal of the NRM to enlarge its political base by incorporating in government former adversaries as well as other diverse but important political groupings has ensured lively heterogeneity, broad-based political accomodation, and increased space for political, economic, and administrative experimentation. As would be expected, efforts towards building an enduring pluralistic mosaic have also tended, in the short run, to translate themselves into vigorous paralysis, particularly in the field of economic management.

THE NRM's INITIAL ATTITUDES TOWARDS THE IMF

The NRM inherited an economy in shambles. The infrastructure was in a sorry state of disrepair and the new administration had urgent rehabilitation and emergency relief work to do; considerable resources were obviously needed to clear the backlog. That notwithstanding, NRM's philosophical attitude towards the IMF, a potential source of funding, was a lot more focused than its domestic economic policy initiatives. The NRM's disposition towards the IMF was one of studied caution, even avoidance. The new leadership, and certainly President Museveni, believed that once order had prevailed in the country economic recovery would be initiated and sustained without necessarily involving the IMF. This view was consistent with the notion of self-reliance that the new leaders espoused in the bush.

In June 1986, President Museveni formally engaged the services of the International Development Research Council of Canada (IDRC), together with local economists and planners, to advise the government on an economic recovery programme. In his address at the launching of the study, the President's pragmatism, which some of his colleagues in the expanded administration were anxious to be assured of, was in abundance. He stated:

62

IMF adjustment under the National Resistance Movement

I do not expect your ideological commitment to either free market solutions or a planned approach to blind you to the actual realities of this country . . . I suggest that in devising solutions to our problems, you should be guided by our social, political and economic realities rather than experiments based on known theories which might prove totally inapplicable in our context.[2]

In the meantime, the NRM, while continuing to pay its debts to the IMF, kept the latter at bay for most of 1986. It would appear that the first NRM Minister of Finance, apart from his political connections and professional competence, was primarily given the job on account of his critical views of IMF-supported programmes in Uganda between 1981 and 1985.

The NRM's cautious, even suspicious, attitude towards the IMF would appear to have been based on two fundamental grounds: the perceived failure of IMF-supported adjustment programmes in Uganda between 1981 and 1985; and considerable evidence of repeated failures of similar programmes elsewhere in Africa.

Structural adjustment in Uganda, 1981–4

Available evidence suggests that the Obote 2 administration afforded the IMF laboratory conditions for its programme. The administration accepted the entire set of IMF conditionality terms and literally handed over the economy to be subjected to them. The story goes that the IMF team was engaged in a dialogue with a team of Uganda 'negotiators' from the Ministries of Finance, Planning, Education and the Bank of Uganda. When the Uganda team questioned some of the IMF assumptions and conditionalities, the IMF team stormed out of the meeting and drove directly to President Obote, who promptly signed the agreement. The Ugandan 'negotiating' team only learnt of the signing from the news media.

In 1981, the exchange rate regime was liberalized by a massive devaluation from UShs8.4 to UShs78 to the US dollar. Another devaluation followed in July 1982 under which the rate of exchange on 'window' 2 (W2) was auction-determined. It was hoped that the W2 depreciated rate would reduce the volume of transactions conducted on the parallel market and in any case, produce revenue for the government. As a liberalization measure price controls were abandoned; a selective squeeze on recruitment for government employment was imposed; and quantitative ceilings on total domestic credit and net credit to government were put in place with a view to promoting economic growth while dampening inflationary pressures.[3]

Both the government and the IMF appear to have regarded the foregoing as a success story, complete with 'incontrovertible' evidence. Between 1981 and 1983 real GDP recovered at an average growth rate

63

of 5.4 per cent; per capita income registered an average growth rate of 2.6 per cent and monetary GDP was said to have recovered steadily. Further, macroeconomic indicators suggested that inflation rate was reduced from 100 per cent to an average rate of 30 per cent. Moreover, the budget deficit was presumed to be under control, having been reduced from 75 per cent of total expenditures in 1980/81 to 41 per cent in 1981/82 and 29 per cent in 1982/83.

The government cheerfully reported that excess liquidity in the economy had been absorbed and balance of payments (BOP) deficits had been brought under control.[4] Judged by the IMF's macro-economic criteria, the programme was pronounced a success. In the words of the IMF: 'After a decade of continuous deterioration, Uganda's economic and financial situation improved during the two fiscal years 1981/82 to 1982/83. Reflecting increases in both agricultural and industrial production, real gross domestic product (GDP) grew at an average annual rate of 7 per cent.'[5]

Behind these macro figures, however, were other ramifications. The introduction of W2 had diverted most IMF dollars intended for Uganda to Kenya's parallel market. The bidding system meant that the Uganda shilling was freely convertible into dollars at the prevailing market rate. Meanwhile, the Kenya shilling was also easily, even eagerly, convertible into Uganda shilling. In practice, therefore, IMF W2 dollars found their way into the private foreign bank accounts of Kenyan businessmen. A conservative estimate of US$4 billion is thought to be illegally held in foreign bank accounts by Kenya residents, and Uganda is a principal source of these funds. Uganda's two-tier system also strengthened the Kenyan shilling; for many years the black-market premium for the Kenya shilling remained under 20 per cent because of the supply to Biashara Street, Nairobi, of IMF dollars through W2. The total impact of this phenomenon upon Uganda's economy has been a matter of intense debate.

The industrial sector, which depended on imported inputs, was starved of credit and foreign exchange as a result of tight conditionalities already abstracted. By 1985, the total production of the manufacturing sector had shrunk by 22 per cent. Particularly affected were textile and garment industries. Only beer (in spite of apparent shortages) and tobacco industries showed a slight rise in production.[6] Evidently the IMF programme did not provide for sustaining real import levels for the productive use of foreign exchange. It is not suprising, therefore, that industrial capacity utilization averaged 20 per cent betweeen 1983 and 1986.[7]

At the same time, Uganda experienced unprecedented total neglect of its infrastructure: the number of schools went up but the quality of education went down exponentially; medical services came to a complete standstill; and, in particular, the transport sector was neglected to the point where all roads, including the one leading to the President's State House, disintegrated into the proverbial potholes amongst which only drunken drivers were able to drive in straight lines.

The Obote 2 administration tended to develop an overdependence on IMF and World Bank funds – both contributed more than 50 per cent of external financing. Predictably, when this institutional funding began to dry up, the economy took a further nosedive in 1984. The period from 1981 to 1985 also saw a dramatic increase in external borrowing that was soon translated into a heavy debt burden. The debt-service ratio jumped from 18.9 per cent of total government export earnings in 1981 to 55 per cent in 1985. As arrears accumulated, the ratio of annual debt obligation to export earnings has since risen to around 73 per cent. To date, Uganda's foreign debt stands at US$1.65 billion and is rising. A further sobering fact is that, as a result of heavy borrowing in the early 1980s, the IMF transfers more dollars from Uganda than it lends the country; i.e. there is a net outflow of resources to the Fund.

The foregoing analysis fully vindicates NRM's initial reluctance to deal with the IMF. There was ample evidence that the Fund-supported adjustment programmes were difficult to sustain; a few positive effects were easily overwhelmed by a host of external and internal shocks. In time, the NRM has had to discover the bitter truth that once a poor country is hooked on IMF stabilization programmes the tendency is to go back for more loans again and again.

Lessons to be learnt from Uganda's 'stabilization' experience during 1981–5 were aptly summarized by the IDRC report:

> Economic programmes cannot work in an insecure, indisciplined and corrupt environment; the IMF programme did not provide for sustained real import levels for the productive use of foreign exchange; IMF financing was high cost, early repayment money; the shift in income distribution away from the urban sector was too rapid; the budget ballooned to compensate for this on account of huge defence expenditure; there was no expenditure control and no ability to raise productive expenditure; and local industries were starved of credit and foreign exchange.[8]

The failure of IMF-supported adjustment programmes in Africa

The second major justification for the NRM's cool attitude towards the IMF was the failure rate of Fund-supported programmes elsewhere in Africa. While the continent has become increasingly beholden to the Fund, recent history is littered with failed programmes. African countries with strong Fund-supported structural adjustments achieved an overall negative average annual growth rate of 1.53 per cent compared with a positive average annual growth rate of 1.22 per cent among countries with weak adjustments during the period 1980–7.[9]

Furthermore, the World Bank data files indicate that the sub-Saharan African countries implementing orthodox structural adjustment programmes (SAPs) experienced, after adoption of SAPs, GDP growth decline from 2.7 per cent to 1.8 per cent; a decline in the investment/GDP ratio from 20.6 per cent to 17.1 per cent; a rise in the budget deficit from 6.5 per cent to 7.5 per cent of GDP; and a rise in the debt service/export ratio from 17.5 per cent to 23.4 per cent.[10]

Even in cases of longer-term extended facilities, 16 of 30 programmes have failed because of the inability of recipients to meet targets. In any event, the IMF is now a net recipient rather than a net lender of funds in developing countries. Currently, the Fund takes US$500 million more out of Africa per year – repayment of earlier loans – than it lends in new money.[11]

The lessons to be learnt from the failure of IMF-supported programmes in Africa are sobering in many ways: under the somewhat flamboyant nomenclature of structural adjustment/policy reform, African nations have been compelled to perform major surgery – on themselves; the continent's marginal and vulnerable role at the edge of the global division of labour has been reinforced further; the continent's residual political independence has been eroded even further; the Fund's obsession with balanced budgets and financial equilibrium, it has been argued, has thrived at the expense of equity and economic transformation; in particular, severe cuts in social spending – an integral part of adjustment – have exacted intolerable burdens on vulnerable social groups unable to defend themselves. To date, African per capita expenditure on education and health is by far the lowest in the world and is still declining. As the AA-SAP study points out, 'Africa may begin the next millennium with a greater proportion of its population being illiterate and unskilled than it did at the beginning of the post-independence era in 1960.'[12]

To attribute Africa's lack of economic transformation and recovery to the IMF alone would, however, be naive. It would be a repetition of the cruder versions of dependency theory of the 1960s. It has to be said that the constraints imposed on Africa by the contemporary international economic system are supplemented by home-grown socio-political and administrative disabling factors: incompetence, technological backwardness, crude selfish interests of the ruling elites and lack of democratic processes – all of which have facilitated the imposition of inappropriate reform packages. The external and internal dimensions have played themselves out to their logical conclusion: the African economies, which are increasingly producing what they cannot consume and consuming what they cannot produce, have acquired built-in tendencies to generate crises within and assimilate others from the international economic system.

66

IMF adjustment under the National Resistance Movement

As letters of intent to borrow from the IMF replace the five-year development plans, and as economic decisions of the gravest consequences are acceded to by a few bureaucrats, one cannot help but observe Africa's accelerating marginalization in the international economic and monetary system. Even more depressing is the brutal reality that Africa's mention in world affairs primarily arises out of its external indebtedness. To reiterate the central thrust of this chapter, NRM's initial hesitation to deal with the IMF had valid and legitimate philosophical, economic and political justification. Later in the chapter we shall examine how the NRM abandoned its initial stance and has since sought closer cooperation with the Fund.

IMF conditionality versus economic tranformation

In order for a country to qualify for IMF loans it must agree to a set of policy reforms and criteria of performance. The two constitute the core of the Fund's 'conditionality'. The usual conditionality package involves devaluation, credit restrictions, liberalization, and restrictive monetary and fiscal policies. The idea is to restrict domestic aggregate demand; create incentives to shift resources from non-tradable to tradable goods, and therefore enhance exports and improve the balance of payments position; remove distortion by way of freeing markets; and slow down inflation. The problem is not that the Fund imposes conditionality *per se*, the real charge is that conditionality is either unfair in its application and imposition of cost, or faulty in its advice, or both;[13] and that the IMF lending conditions are not adapted to the structural capacities of the poorest countries.[14]

Acrimonious arguments against conditionality have a long historical record. Faced with balance of payments pressures of a structural character in the 1940s, European countries, especially Britain, France, and the Netherlands, insisted on the need for access to a large volume of unconditional resources from the Fund. As Sidney Dell observes, those countries only need to look back at their own files and position papers of the early postwar period to understand the current predicament of African countries. The arguments then and now are startlingly similar. The problem, however, is that what was sauce for the goose in the early 1940s and 1950s does not seem to be sauce for the gander in the 1980s and 1990s.[15]

For African countries conditionality issues became crucial in the mid-1970s. Before then low conditionality loans, mainly composed of the Compensatory Financing Facility (CFF), Oil Facility Subsidy Account, and Trust Fund, accounted for 80 per cent of Africa's loans. By 1980 the situation had been reversed: high conditionality funds accounted for 70 per cent of the continent's loans from the Fund. Since then the basic tenets of the reform programmes have been subjected to relentless criticism.

Structural adjustment on trial

The merits of devaluation have been put under the microscope: it may increase receipts of exports but at the same time drive up import costs; with declining terms of trade rampant in Africa, income loss from imports may far exceed gains from exports, leading to overall decline of purchasing power and contraction.[16] Devaluation also has implications for distribution: it tends to redistribute wages to profits; middle-class bureaucrats defend their income levels by massive allowances; and its real efforts may therefore be nullified by inflation.[17]

The intention of liberalization is to free markets from restrictions and distortions, restore competition and efficiency, and thereby clear the economy for rapid economic growth. But liberalization quite often leads to reckless use of scarce foreign exchange and helps strangle local industries. Besides, liberalization is not necessarily the most viable route towards transformation: the newly industrializing countries (NICs), particularly the Asian Gang of Four – Hong Kong, Singapore, South Korea, Taiwan – were highly interventionist, protectionist, *dirigiste* states that protected their local industries with subsidies. And they developed much faster than many economies during the last 25 years.[18] In any case, it can be argued that the crucial question in Africa is not the freeing of markets but their creation.

Monetary and fiscal restraints have caused brutal cuts in income and economic expansion without demonstrating that the sacrifice leads to full utilization of capacity, satisfactory growth rates and low inflation.[19]

Export-led development does not seem to be viable: export markets are crowded; issues of fallacy of composition are still enduring; between 1973 and 1981 Africa lost 23 per cent of the purchasing power of its exports to buy manufactures. In any event, expansion of production and export of traditional commodities, particularly agricultural products, appears to be a strategy that has consigned African states indefinitely to relative poverty, as the world's hewers of wood and drawers of water.[20]

Thus, contrary to conventional wisdom, structural adjustment in Africa may be a long-term pain for a short-term gain; it may mean adjustment to poverty; a matter of running harder in order, at best, to stay in place; a misplaced emphasis on financial balances and price structures rather than economic transformation. In the words of one expert:

> Far from encouraging a fully integrated, self-reliant, self-sustaining and evenly balanced development, policy reforms instead function to reinforce patterns of dependence, external dominance, disarticulation and regional disintegration.[21]

The foregoing brief critique of the IMF model used in policy-lending programmes is a third pillar on which NRM's caution towards the Fund was, or should have been, based.

68

AFRICAN ALTERNATIVE TO
STRUCTURAL ADJUSTMENT PROGRAMMES

Before we deal with IMF/NRM relations, it is imperative to refer to the most current, and probably the most articulate, alternative to the orthodox adjustment programmes. The UNECA's position paper, 'African Alternative to Structural Adjustment Programmes (AA-SAP): A Framework for Transformation and Recovery', locates the roots of the African crisis at the levels of production, consumption, technology, exchange, employment, and socio-economic political organization. It identifies disabling factors (domestic, external, historical, and contemporary) that have prevented structural transformation. Instead, those factors have led to narrow, disarticulated, ill-adapted economies with weak inter-sectoral linkages, backward productive bases, and excessive dependencies on external factors.[22] It advocates democracy as a prelude to mobilization; a need to move from trade dependence to trade viability; and transformation at the level of production, particularly regarding issues of what to produce and how to produce, i.e. choice of technology. It lays particular emphasis on employment generation, equity and satisfaction of the essential needs of the African populace. It proposes a framework for 'adjustment with transformation' based on three macro entities: operative forces, available resources and their allocation, and basic needs to be satisfied. It reaffirms the goals outlined in the Monrovia Strategy, Rabat Resolutions, and Lagos Plan of Action: self-reliance, self-sustaining development, sub-regional economic cooperation and integration, and food self-sufficiency.[23] AA-SAP strongly objects to the logic of balanced budgets at the expense of growth, production, and equality.

The critique mounted by AA-SAP is refreshing and activist. Its presumptions, however, remind one of the old basic human needs (BHN) approach. Indeed, there are many old ideas in the new alternative framework. AA-SAP nevertheless provides a coherent broad framework within which discussion of attempts at recovery in Uganda can be analysed.

NRM-IMF RELATIONS

The first half of 1986 ushered in a palpable sense of recovery in Uganda: freedom of speech, security and civil liberties were restored in large measure; a significant percentage of about 950,000 displaced Ugandans were slowly returning to their farms; and the nascent NRM administration was learning fast on the job.

In economic terms, however, 1986 was a difficult year: the war in the north and northeast escalated government expenditure; inflation rose by 237 per cent; the public sector investment programme remained in suspended animation; the balance of payments deteriorated sharply and the accumulation of external payments rose by US$21 million; imports grew by 30 per cent and the current account swung into deficit by US$82 million, which represented one per cent of GDP; the volume of coffee exports decreased by 12 per cent while, at the same time, coffee prices on the world market fell; and the budget was expenditure-driven, rather than income-driven, and getting out of control. It took some time for the administration to appreciate the dynamic linkages between the war, deficit spending and inflation. The government responded by increasing the money supply, which only made matters worse. By the fourth quarter of 1986 the economic situation was almost untenable. The administration realized that economic chaos was beginning to erode the political capital the NRM had built up. There was growing anxiety to prevent the germination of new seeds of popular discontent. In November, NRM made sweeping changes in the Ministries of Finance and Planning and the Bank of Uganda by installing a new team in each of the institutions. More importantly, the NRM finally decided to begin serious negotiations with the IMF.

A profile of negotiations between the IMF and the NRM
NRM's philosophical position towards the IMF, perhaps circumstantially, assumed a new direction by the last quarter of 1986. The new attitude was that as long as the NRM dealt and negotiated with the Fund carefully and thoroughly, the former would take advantage of the loans and sustain its programmes.

The first negotiation encounter between NRM and IMF, however, was difficult, bordering on farce. The Ugandan negotiating team (the authority) was entirely new, having no previous experience in such negotiations; there was no clear-cut demarcation as to who was to do what amongst the authorities, neither was there an agreed framework to present to the IMF. In fact, it would appear that those groups representing the authority – drawn largely from the Ministries of Finance and Planning, and the Bank of Uganda – had each a working model, and they were models that did not necessarily agree. The IMF quickly dismissed as untenable the position(s) put forward by the authority and presented an alternative model upon which the authority made little comment.

The following example illustrates the unpreparedness of the Ugandan team. During the negotiations it appeared that the Ugandan negotiators were unaware of some assumptions and formula used to calculate revenue from petroleum products, a crucial aspect of the negotiation. As it turned out, however, one of the oil companies in the country had previously worked out the formula and it had been operational for some time. The IMF knew this, and the Ugandan negotiating authorities did not.

The internal conflicts among the authorities and the resultant negotiating weaknesses must have been abundantly clear to the IMF side. Indeed, as it turned out, the package that was announced was largely an IMF affair.

On 15 May 1987, the government announced a comprehensive IMF-supported package that had all the ingredients of shock treatment: tough budgetary measures; massive devaluation – from UShs14 to UShs60 to the US dollar, increased interest rates, introduction of Open General Licence (OGL), and currency conversion.

Before the IMF began releasing funds to support the programme, the Ugandan government announced budget measures that were substantially inconsistent with the agreed package, measures that astonished the Fund. Within a week the Ugandan negotiating team was in Washington, and within days of their arrival, the NRM was 'persuaded' to abandon its budget and make a new one (or else the agreed programme and funding would be called off). The result was what is popularly known as the Telex Budget, referring to the intense consultations between Kampala and Washington as the new budget took shape.

Soon after, the IMF released about US$40 million as part of SAF and a further US$33 million as a compensatory facility, and signalled that Uganda would now be able to attend the Paris Club for debt rescheduling. Once the IMF was satisfied, the World Bank invited Uganda to attend the consultative meeting; it also disbursed US$55 million as the first tranche of the economic recovery credit. Shortly thereafter, the EEC and the UK signalled their willingness to release US$15 million and £10 million respectively. Thus IMF's leverage is not simply related to the money it loans out; it acts as a gatekeeper for almost all other funds, both multilateral and bilateral – i.e. cross-conditionality.

Economic performance, 1987–8

Despite the adjustment lending programme, the economy was not improving: general prices went up; inflation was galloping at 240 per cent; the balance of payments position worsened, partly because coffee prices declined. There was, however, modest economic growth, largely because of growth in the private sector. Many stated stabilization objectives were not achieved. There were several reasons for this: the IMF was insensitive to the lack of capacity in the economy; policy changes required by the programme were impossible to implement given the war in the north as well as expansionary programmes the government was putting in place; the government did not have its heart in the programme, partly because there was a feeling that the programme was not designed by the government but by the Fund. Indeed, this was dramatized by the government decision to reduce interest rates by 50 per cent, obviously paying no attention to the IMF package. Whatever the government's attitude to the programme, there were also administrative, managerial and technical bottlenecks. The essential message NRM was sending to the Fund was that Government wanted Fund resources without stringent conditionality.

In order to qualifty for the second tranche, the Ugandan government had to show that it was following the package and earning good marks on performance criteria. As noted earlier, the performance on the latter was fairly poor. In March 1988, the IMF and World Bank insisted on nothing less than draconian policy measures if any funds were to be released. In spite of strong objections the only concession Uganda won from the Fund was that the shock policy measures would wait until budget day before they were announced.

The 1988/89 budget, which was preceded by massive speculation, announced the most draconian measures yet: interest rates were raised to between 30 and 40 per cent; currency was devalued from UShs60 to UShs150 to the US dollar; and extremely tight monetary measures and ruthless income-driven budget controls were put in place. A monitoring committee was set in motion to oversee and enforce the policy changes; for once the government appeared committed to the programme.

The IMF expected the shock to achieve a balance between demand and supply. To some degree this was achieved: after initial instability, prices began falling by September–October 1988, and remained stable for a while; shortages were less visible; and the budget appeared to be under control.

These shock measures had further profound ramifications. There was a major slump in industrial activity, with the index falling by 25 per cent; by October 1988 total production had been cut to March 1987 levels;[23] the government radically reduced spending on development projects as well as other social services; and almost all payments approved by June 1988 were cancelled.

Enhanced Structural Adjustment Facility (ESAF)

Meanwhile, both the IMF and World Bank were so impressed by the performance of the economy that in September 1988 a conference was organized at which US$550 million was pledged by the international community.

The Enhanced Structural Adjustment Facility (ESAF), a new facility that came into existence in 1988, is even more stringent in its conditionality than the usual SAFs. In the Ugandan case, the IMF team insisted on continuous adjustment of the exchange rate, stringent ceilings that demanded that the government not only pays the Bank of Uganda but also deposits large sums with the Central Bank, huge increases in interest rates up to 50%, expansion of OGL to encompass more sectors, export liberalization in which the Coffee Marketing Board (CMB) would

72

compete with private firms for coffee exports, and an export retention scheme.

The NRM government initially disagreed with several aspects of conditionality, particularly the credit ceilings, which looked untenable and unreasonable. Again the negotiators were unable to change the IMF formula, except the timing of the measures' announcement. Finally, the ESAF deal was struck in April and the first disbursement was made, but not before Uganda became current with the Fund. Once again, when it came to the budget the NRM government announced measures that were different from those agreed with the Fund. The IMF's wrath was somewhat subdued by the Special Import Programme II (SIP II), started in June 1989, which was not only *de facto* partial devaluation, but also made it possible for the government to have a bigger budget.

Crop finance

Probably the most contentious issue between the NRM and the IMF, and central to monetary control, is crop finance. Sometime toward the end of 1988, NRM realized that coffee farmers had not been paid for several seasons in succession. The intermediaries, principally cooperative unions, had siphoned off money intended for farmers. This issue was both political and economic: political because the government wanted to be seen to be responding to farmers' needs; economic because farmers were gradually losing interest in coffee growing and were switching to other crops.

The CMB had neither the money nor the capacity to collect and market coffee efficiently, and commercial banks were operating under a considerable squeeze as part of the Fund package. The NRM government therefore decided to escalate its efforts to pay farmers by using the Bank of Uganda as an agent of finance to the CMB. In effect, the CMB was given an unlimited overdraft with the Central Bank. As the exercise gathered momentum domestic credit ceilings came under pressue, creating inflationary spirals; by mid-1989 private sector credit (UShs41.5 billion) exceeded bank *deposits*; crop finance jumped from UShs6.8 billion in December 1988 to a staggering UShs20.1 billion in May 1989. This escalation was not matched by coffee shipments or foreign exchange earnings. Currently, considerable energy is being spent to reverse the impact of this policy. Needless to say, the IMF is unimpressed by this kind of performance and must be using all its leverage to push NRM policies back on track before more disbursements are made.

THE ADJUSTMENT PROCESS AND POLITICS

Although the financial imbalances are glaring and other indicators show economic difficulties ahead, the NRM's broad thrust on economic recovery and transformation is conceived in broader political terms. There is a serious exercise under way to strengthen the political infrastructure and democracy through resistance councils (RCs), the idea being to sensitize citizens and invite them to participate in the political process at the grassroots level. This is an essential prerequisite to further attempts at economic transformation, as AA-SAP clearly points out.

There is a determined effort to improve the physical infrastructure, particularly roads and transportation, another crucial prerequisite for economic recovery. A drive is under way to bypass speculators and deliver agricultural inputs directly to the farmer to enhance production and encourage non-traditional exports. There is a welcome trend toward involving women, who form the backbone of agriculture, in decision making in all political and economic structures. There is an unprecedented number of women in the National Resistance Council (NRC) – the equivalent of parliament – and several in the cabinet; appropriately, the Minister of Agriculture is a woman. Investing in women's involvement and mobilization has enormous political and economic capital that NRM is deliberately cultivating.

Transformation and recovery cannot occur in an enviroment of instability and turmoil. This fact has not been lost on the NRM government, which is seeking to generate consensus by broad-based representation in government that deliberately promotes the politics of inclusion. Relentless efforts have also been made to hammer out a political solution with insurgents in the north and to redirect scarce resources to development projects. Indeed, if peace initiatives are to be sustained in the north and northeast, they must be accompanied by a sustained drive towards economic reconstruction.

The NRM has also invested time and money in reducing the level of moral turpitude, particularly in public life. Through political education and improved management some sectors have improved without recourse to the traditional adjustment programmes. One outstanding example is revenue collection by the Customs Department. By simply appointing new management, while retaining the old structure, customs contributions to government revenues have risen from an inconsequential and negligible figure to 43 per cent.

CONCLUSION

The NRM's initial reluctance to deal with the IMF was justified in terms of the less than successful earlier adjustment programmes in Uganda and elsewhere in Africa as well as doubtful assumptions made in the IMF model. In time, the NRM has lived with the reality that the IMF is a reflection of the global distribution of power in a contemporary economic system in which Uganda happens to be pretty much on the margin. It has also had to recognize that the IMF, through cross-conditionality, is

74

even more powerful than first meets the eye. And while IMF conditionalities have become increasingly harsh and unpalatable, external and internal pressures have made adherence to IMF performance criteria nearly impossible. Thus, though the NRM has made remarkable strides in socio-political arenas, teasing problems regarding the possibility of economic transformation still abide.

Notwithstanding the intractable nature of some of the inherited problems and the NRM's inability to influence the IMF in negotiations, the government is shrewdly investing in building political and physical infrastructures that are unavoidable prerequisites for economic transformation.

Within the tight parameters noted earlier, and in spite of initial false starts, the NRM government, unlike its predecessors, has evolved a position that it presents to the IMF during negotiations. The government has also learnt that adjustment, in the light of internal and external factors, is totally unavoidable. The question is not if, but when and how. Beyond this point, however, analyses and prescriptions part company. Analysts on the right wonder why Uganda, and sub-Saharan Africa as a whole, should be 'paid' to undertake policy reforms that are in their best interests; those on the left object to such imposed conditions, which they regard as part of the recolonization of Africa.

The Ugandan experience offers some sobering lessons: the Fund reflects the contemporary global distribution of financial and political power; its primary agenda of stabilizing the world financial system is such that it hardly yields any ground when negotiating with developing countries; additionally, there appear to be information/data gaps on the part of both the Fund and country authorities such that negotiations between the two, as Helleiner aptly put it, are conducted by badly prepared antagonists of modest ability employing data of dubious quality.

African countries have home-grown problems that are somewhat independent of the pressures exerted by the contemporary international economic system. In addition, Uganda, like many other African countries, has urgent problems other than those of economic growth and financial balances. These are legitimate priorities to which the IMF has not shown sufficient sensitivity.

Lastly, there are questions that Africa cannot avoid addressing: do IMF packages thrive best in authoritarian regimes, or do they, additionally, induce repression, or both? Is the Fund's role neocolonialist tutelage? Should IMF dealings with African governments remain secretive or should they be subjected to rigorous scrutiny in order to hammer out a more durable social contract? By accepting IMF conditionality is Africa essentially adjusting to poverty? What should be the role of the state in attempts towards recovery and transformation? If the state made a major retreat in economic management and intervention, who would perform this function? Is the state part of the problem or a potential part of a future solution? Can economic transformation occur without similar transformation at the political level? Is Africa unnecessarily blaming self-inflicted economic mismanagement and misfortunes on external factors? Does Africa have an alternative to the orthodox structural adjustment programmes, as AA-SAP seem to posit? Can single countries travel the road of economic transformation alone? Can the Balkanized, unviable states in Africa survive the next millennium in their present form? Are African states preparing their positions in the light of events in Eastern Europe and in Western Europe in 1992? Should continental and regional unity be imposed on Africa even if it means doing so by force? And who will do that? As the NRM prepares Uganda for the 1990s and the next millennium these abiding questions will have to be confronted. Other African countries have no choice but to confront them squarely as well.

Notes

---

1. The views expressed in this chapter do not reflect those of the Uganda government or the Bank of Uganda.
2. IDRC, 1988, p. 1.
3. Ministry of Planning and Economic Development, 'Uganda: Stabilisation and Structural Adjustment Programmes in the 1980s', unpublished paper, 1988, pp. 1–3.
4. *ibid*, pp. 7–8.
5. IMF, 'Uganda – Staff Report for the 1984 Article IV Consultation', Washington, January 1985.
6. Ministry of Planning and Economic Development, 'Index of Industrial Production to December 1988: Statistical Bulletin No. Ip/1', Kampala, 1989, p. 2.
7. Ministry of Planning and Economic Development, 'Background to the Budget, 1989–90', Kampala, July 1989, p. 62.
8. IDRC, 1988, p. vii.
9. UNECA, 'African Alternative to Structural Adjustment Programmes (AA-SAP): A Framework for Transformation and Recovery', Addis Ababa, April 1989, pp. 3–11.
10. *ibid*.
11. Lancaster, 1989, p. 2. See also, Commonwealth Secretariat, 1987, p. 12.
12. See, UNECA, 'African Alternative to Structural Adjustment Programmes', pp. 3–13.
13. See Helleiner, 1983, p. 11.
14. *ibid*, p. 20.
15. Dell, 1981, pp. 14–15.
16. Taylor, 1987, p. 40.
17. Mamdani, 1989, pp. 2–3.
18. See Harris, 1986.
19. John Williamson, 1987, p. 2.
20. Lancaster, 1985, p. 149.
21. Quoted in Copeland, nd, p. 8.
22. UNECA, AA-SAP, p. 1.
23. *ibid*, pp. 1–2.
24. Ministry of Planning & Economic Development, 'Index of Industrial Production', p. 3.

Map 2   *Administrative Divisions of Uganda after 1976*

77

FIVE
The agrarian context of the Ugandan crisis

Vali Jamal

The crisis afflicting Uganda during the last two decades has important lessons for the more general 'African crisis' and its suggested remedies.[1] Although the Ugandan crisis – unlike that in the rest of Africa – originated in the modern sector, with Amin's 'War of Economic Independence' against the resident Asian community, it soon joined the mainstream African crisis whose origins lie in the export sector – agricultural, mineral, and in some cases foreign remittances.[2] In Uganda import capacity was reduced to only one-third of its level in the early 1970s and the country went into a free fall, with huge declines in per capita income and wages. Starting in 1981 the government – Obote 2 – began to apply a strict Structural Adjustment Programme (SAP) under the aegis of the International Monetary Fund and the World Bank. The shilling was devalued heavily and producer prices were raised more or less in parallel with the devaluations.

What we get in Uganda is thus everything in the 'fast forward' ('fast backward'?) mode: the collapse of the modern sector and urban wages, the decline in exports and the devaluations all proceeded much faster than elsewhere. In some ways Uganda is thus an exception. But it is one that has much to teach us since it shows within a condensed time-frame what happens to an economy that undergoes a massive decline and an equally massive SAP. In short, it offers a unique laboratory case of structural collapse and structural adjustment.

The roots of the African crisis have often been sought in 'surplus extraction': governments, it is alleged, have squeezed the agricultural sector to death through discriminatory pricing policies.[3] This squeeze, it is held, pampered the modern sector industries and urban wage earners, the mechanisms for transfer on the urban side being tariff protection and minimum wage legislation, and on the rural side export taxes and exchange rate manipulations. I will concentrate in this chapter on rural–urban relations in Uganda from a broad historical perspective. I will show how these have changed dramatically in just the last decade and a half and bring out the implications for pricing policy and adjustment.

78

The agrarian context of the Ugandan crisis

THE CATASTROPHE

According to the World Bank's latest report on Africa (World Bank, 1989, figure 1.2), Uganda had the worst growth performance of all sub-Saharan countries between 1961 and 1989. Per capita GDP fell at 2.1 per cent per annum, or altogether by over 40 per cent. Even Chad and Niger, which are perennial under-achievers in Africa, did better than Uganda, as did Ghana (– 1.4 per cent per annum), despite the many parallels that have often been drawn between the two countries. The decline was all the more serious as it was concentrated between 1972 and 1980, implying a contraction in per capita incomes of something like 5.5 per cent per annum. To give even a more dramatic picture of the 'free fall', three-quarters of the decline in the 1970s came in just two years, 1978–80. Table 5.1 shows these statistics.

The debacle in the 1970s was in sharp contrast to the performance in the 1960s and to some extent in the early 1980s.[4] In the immediate post-independence period, with high savings and investment rates (13 per cent of GDP), a trend growth rate of 4.1 per cent per annum was achieved in GDP, with the monetary economy leading with 4.2 per cent. Inflation was kept to a minimum, government revenue exceeded expenditure, and a positive current account balance was registered in most years. Industry posted the highest growth rate (6.5 per cent per annum) and accounted for 14 per cent of monetary GDP by 1971. Uganda had already passed the phase of import substitution and was beginning to make a successful entry into export production, especially to the East African Common Market partners, Kenya and Tanzania. All these growth rates turned negative in the 1970s and the economy went into a 'subsistence mode', with the destruction of the industrial base in the urban areas and the collapse of the export sector in the rural.

As already noted, a large part of the economic collapse happened between 1978 and 1980, *after* the overthrow of Amin. Are we to conclude from this that Uganda's misfortunes arose more from the destruction of the Liberation War than the ravages of the Amin years, a viewpoint that is sometimes expressed in Uganda? The answer is no, or at the most that is was only partly so. The war was certainly a catastrophe for Uganda, but Amin cannot escape so easily, for by the time of his downfall the economy was well on its way to ruin; exports were down to 37 per cent of their 1970 volumes and all other sectors were operating at 20–30 per cent of capacity.

The divergent trends actually tell us something instructive about the relative role of external and internal factors in Uganda's growth. The full impact of Amin's mismanagement was masked by the great boom in commodity prices that occurred in 1977 when the unit value of Uganda's exports practically doubled (1.9-fold increase) while import

Table 5.1 GDP growth rates and composition in Uganda, 1963–87

	1963–72	1972–8	1978–80	1980–1	1981–2	1982–3	1983–4	1984–5	1985–6	1986–7
Growth rates (% per annum)										
Total GDP	4.1	−0.8	−7.7	3.9	8.2	4.3	−5.4	1.0	1.1	2.9
Monetary GDP	4.2	−3.0	−6.1	0.0	9.1	2.6	1.2	2.6	−0.6	3.3
Subsistence GDP	3.8	3.3	−11.3	10.3	6.9	7.0	−11.6	−7.0	−2.1	2.2
Total GDP per capita	1.8	−3.0	−9.8	1.0	5.3	1.5	−7.9	3.7	−3.8	0.1
Monetary GDP per capita	1.9	−5.1	−8.2	−2.7	6.1	−0.2	3.8	−0.2	−3.2	0.5
Composition (%)[a]										
Total GDP	68.3	68.9	60.3	62.5	60.2	60.7	59.6	62.3	64.6	65.2
Monetary agriculture	1.04	1.12	1.57	1.40	1.61	1.52	1.46	1.50	1.27	1.34

Note: (a) Based on constant (1966) price series. Figures relate to first year – i.e., in 1963 68.3% of the GDP was monetized, etc.

Source: World Bank, 1983 and 1988.

prices remained constant (1.1-fold increase). The improved terms of trade maintained the purchasing power of Uganda's exports at 89 per cent of its 1970 value, despite a reduced volume of exports. After the liberation this trend was reversed and amplified the purely internal impact of mismanagement and insecurity that became Uganda's lot in the three years following Amin's defeat. (Three administrations struggled unsuccessfully to run the country between 1979 and 1981.)

In concluding this section we present in Table 5.2 some statistics of output performance in 1980 compared with a peak-year performance, which was generally around 1970. These figures corroborate the picture of widespread decline of the Ugandan economy. Export and imports fell to two-fifths of their peak values, industrial production fell by a staggering 80 per cent, vehicle fleet and electricity consumption fell by two-fifths, while revenue fell even as a proportion of a low GDP. 'Economic collapse' would certainly be an apt term for the catastrophe that hit Uganda in the 1970s.

INCOMES AND INCOMES DISTRIBUTION BEFORE 1972

The massive decline of the economy was accompanied by equally massive shifts in structures and income distribution. These shifts signify a complete turnaround in the economic relationships that existed in Uganda before 1972.

The historical evolution of the Uganda economy after the introduction of British rule and cotton cultivation resulted in huge inequalities along racial, occupational and geographical lines.[5] Throughout the colonial period – and right into the early 1970s – the basic division of labour comprised Asians and Europeans as entrepreneurs and Africans as farmers and wage earners.[6] After independence this structure began to crack a little, with the emergence of an African trading class, but by and large by the time of the Asian expulsion Africans were still conspicuously absent in large-scale activities in the modern sector. The predominant racial and occupational differentiation was most apparent in southern Uganda, causing a clear north–south divide. Apart from growing 60 per cent of the cotton, the north had practically no other monetized economic activities; the south, by contrast, grew the rest of the cotton and 90 per cent of the coffee, and had a majority of all the wage employees and most of the other modern activities. As a rough order of magnitude it may be estimated that around 1970 the south, with 35–40 per cent of the population, had 75–80 per cent of the national income, implying income differentials of the order of 6 : 1. Table 5.3 shows estimates of income distribution and tax incidence along occupational lines around the mid-1960s.

The major features of Table 5.3 may be underlined. Non-Africans, comprising just 1 per cent of the population, received 28 per cent of the

Table 5.2 Output performance in Uganda in 1980 compared to a peak
year, c. 1970

	Peak year (= 100)	1980
Exports	1970	37.7
Imports	1971	43.2
Coffee exports	1969	36.1
Cotton exports	1970	15.4
Industry		
Fabrics	1970	15.1
Beer	1974	26.3
Soap	1966	2.7
Average	1970	
	– 74	10.0
Vehicles	1971	57.4
Electricity		
consumption	1970	57.6
Government	1972	1982
revenue: GDP	= 14.0	= 4.3

Source: Based on World Bank, 1982 and 1983 (two reports): text tables 4.1
and 5.1 and appendix tables 3.7, 9.2 and 10.1 in the 1982 report, and
text table 1.8 in the 1983 report.

monetary GDP, or 20 per cent of the total GDP. Sixty per cent of their
income came in the form of operating surplus from their enterprises, and
rent. Of their wage income (UShs396 million), UShs123 million represented wages from their own enterprises. Thus the importance of enterprise income for the Asians is clear. However, it is worth noting that they
took 28 per cent of the total wage bill, which should help dispel any
simple notion that the Asian dominance was mostly in entrepreneurial
income; it was quite significant even in the wage sector.

For the Africans, wages provided 30 per cent of monetary income
compared with 54 per cent from farm incomes. Taking account of subsistence income, wages came to 18.4 per cent of total African income.
Wage earners formed less than 10 per cent of the total African labour
force at this time, so that we can see the disparity between them and the
farmers. Another feature of African incomes worth emphasizing is the
place of trade income. Although a small part of total African income,
trade was nevertheless an important and growing feature of the African
economy by the late 1960s and a vast improvement over the 1940s when
Africans were practically absent from the trading sector.

With respect to tax incidence we should note that farmers paid at a
high rate – 10.4 per cent (21 per cent of cash income) – compared with
13.6 per cent for the 'rest' group and 5.1 per cent for African wage

Table 5.3 Income distribution in Uganda, c. mid-1960s

	Total income, 1967 (million of shillings)	Households ('000)	Average income (shillings p.a.)	Tax incidence, 1964 (%)	After-tax differentials (farmers = 1.0)
African	3796				
Farmers	2706	1600	1691	10.4	1.0
Wage earners	701	180	3894	5.1	2.4
Traders	389	80	4862	12.4	2.8
Rest	1166				
Parastatal	170				
Non-African	996	18	55330	13.6	31.6
Wages	396				
Operating surplus	600				
Total	4962				
(Monetary GDP)	3525)				

Source: Total income and tax incidence based respectively on Jamal, 1976a and 1978. Tax incidence for 1964 is assumed to apply to 1967. Household members based on demographic characteristics: i) farmers 85 per cent of total population and five members per family; ii) 1.33 wage earners per wage-earning family; iii) African trading families around 45 per cent of wage-earning families; iv) non-Africans around 90,000 and five members per family. Blank spaces imply figures cannot be derived or are not relevant.

earners. Moreover, in the above calculations only direct taxes – income tax, export tax and trading licences – were included; indirect taxes, such as customs and excise, could not be accounted for because of lack of data. Being generally regressive taxes, these would reinforce the conclusion about the regressive nature of taxation in Uganda.

At this period – the late 1960s – one spoke of wage earners as the 'labour aristocracy' in Uganda – in relation, that is, to African farmers, not to non-African entrepreneurs.[7] The minimum wage had been raised fivefold since 1957, whereas coffee prices even in *current* terms had declined by a half and those for cotton by 27 per cent. In real terms this amounted to a fourfold increase in wages compared with declines of 40–60 per cent for export crops. Such huge wage increases completely changed the nature of wage employment and the structure of incomes in Uganda. In 1957 the minimum wage would have bought only three-fifths of the food requirements of an average size family in towns, whereas by 1967 one-half of the minimum wage would have sufficed.[8] Simultaneouly, the structure of African incomes changed in favour of the wage earners.

The turnaround resulted from deliberate government policy. These were the early years after independence and the government wanted to demonstrate the fruits of freedom to the electorate, which in pragmatic terms meant urban residents. More fundamentally, the government was now embarked on a policy of 'stabilization' of the labour force, a policy derived from Kenya as enunciated in the 1955 *Report of the Committee on African Wages*. This report dominated wage policy in both Kenya and Uganda into the 1960s. The 'target worker' was at the centre of this policy; it was considered that he was harmful to both urban and rural sectors, as he would have no foothold in either sector to improve his productivity.[9] The transitory and migratory pattern of wage employment this engendered could only be curbed by enabling the worker to earn a wage in the city sufficient to support his family. The report recommended an immediate change in the basis of the statutory minimum wage – 'from one which takes account only of the needs of a single man to one based on the needs of a family unit.'[10] The family-based wage remained the norm in wage-fixing from the late 1950s through the first decade of independence. Under its influence the minimum wage was increased sixfold in 13 years between 1957 and 1970, representing an almost fourfold increase in real terms. The 'labour aristocracy' was well-ensconced by the mid-1960s.

INCOMES AND INCOME DISTRIBUTION AFTER 1972

Both the Asian and the labour 'aristocracies' were destroyed in the 1970s, the Asian one by a stroke of Amin's pen in 1972 and the labour one somewhat gradually in the few years following. Gradual though the change was, it was nonetheless decisive for the structure of incomes in Uganda.

In expelling the Asians, Amin was not motivated by notions of equity, but simply by a dislike of what he considered to be foreign domination of the economy. The rounds of redistribution of Asian assets benefited mostly Amin's henchmen. The bigger industries were handed over to parastatals. Gradually the assets lost their productivity because of the lack of spare parts, foreign exchange, maintenance and, perhaps more importantly, lack of funds and managerial experience. Under-utilization of capacity became the norm.

This was the time when the *magendo* economy ruled. *Magendo* refers to activities carried on in the parallel market, as opposed to the controlled market in which official boards were supposed to import and export goods, and price controls were enforced. After the mid-1970s the parallel market became dominant in Uganda; goods could be imported unrestrictedly if a person had foreign exchange abroad, produce was smuggled out by individual farmers and middlemen, price controls were widely ignored. One could say the market was operating freely – and what is wrong with that? In fact, the competition was loaded in favour of the power brokers who ultimately controlled *magendo* operations. Those who had access to factory or farm supplies made fortunes, and these were of course those who had the protection of the government. Access to imports became a similar source of windfall gains. These imports came in at what after the mid-1970s was certainly an overvalued exchange rate. At the retail level the imports were priced at the 'shadow exchange rate', which was then 8–10 times the official rate. Thus *magendo* was a preferential freeing of the markets. Its distinguishing feature was not free markets but illegality, breakdown of law and order, and corruption. In a situation in which money could most easily be made illegally and honest work did not pay, the erosion of morals this engendered can only be guessed at. Many observers fear that this newly induced attitude to work is now a major hindrance to establishing normal work patterns in Uganda.

Putting together the selective allocation of Asian properties and the operation of the *magendo* economy it would be difficult to say that urban income distribution improved during the Amin years. Per capita incomes were falling, so that here was a case of 'stagnation with redistribution', a twist on the 'growth with redistribution' theme. The greatest irony was that in the last few years of Obote's regime some Asian businessmen (around 200) had returned to reclaim their assets, but mostly to set up in trade, where turnover was quick and profit margins enormous. Under the laissez-faire system prevalent in Uganda after 1982 – a part of the economic reforms agreed with the IMF – this handful of businessmen gained control over practically the whole import sector.

How people cope

One would shudder to estimate the distribution of income in urban Uganda in 1990.

While the Asian aristocracy of 1972 went through these metamorphoses (first the '*magendo* aristocracy' and then the partial Asian aristocracy of the 1980s), the labour aristocracy was not as fortunate. With the decline in modern sector productivity a wage structure that supported an independent class could no longer be sustained. Either the labour force had to shrink or wages had to fall. The labour force actually *increased*, from 329,800 in 1972 to 367,600 in 1977 (the last year for which wage data are available), so that adjustment had to come through a fall in real wages and the mechanism for this was inflation. Table 5.4 shows the rise and fall of the wage-earning class. The figures are so fantastic – the minimum wage down to 10–15 per cent of its 1972 level – that one is bound to wonder whether there is not an error here somewhere – perhaps all those zeros in the inflation?[11] Well, inflation was a hard fact of life in Uganda after the mid-1970s and the arithmetic of deflation does indeed yield the figures in column 3 of Table 5.4. To clinch the issue, in column 4 we have shown the purchasing power of the minimum wage in terms of the basic staple, *matoke*. In 1972 the minimum monthly wage would have brought 1.67 times an average family's food requirement (reciprocal of column 4); by July 1988, even with a wage hike, only 19 per cent could have been bought – just five days' supply.[12]

With the wage down to 10 per cent of its 1972 value, people also effectively worked that much less at their wage employment. Some of the free time was devoted to growing food in the *shamba* (garden) and some to 'business', the buying and selling of small items of consumer goods, the opportunities for which increased because of the gap left by the Asians. Compared to the situation before 1972, one cannot but be struck by the visible increase in street-trading in Kampala. Of course something like that has happened in most African cities but in Uganda the reasons were different; the fact is that unlike other African countries rural–urban migration actually slowed down or even reversed[13] and yet the informal sector grew. What happened was that a great part of the trade previously in the hands of the Asians was shared by an increasing number of petty traders.

It may be seen from the above that the whole structure of the urban economy has changed. Before 1972 there was an Asian entrepreneurial-cum-wage-earner class, an African wage-earner class, and a class of African petty traders. After the expulsion, the Asian group of course disappeared, and the African wage group lost its viability. The petty-trader group expanded, in numbers as well as income, sharing some of the Asian wealth. This group absorbed most of the wage earners, growing into a conglomerate trader-cum-wage-earner-cum-*shamba* group. These kinds of 'fusions' helped to keep most wage earners above food

86

Table 5.4 **Minimum wages in Uganda in nominal and real terms, 1957–88,
selected years**

	Minimum wage (shillings per month)	Price index (1972 = 100)	Real wage (1972 = 100)	% of minimum wage required to purchase 9,000 calories
1957	33	61.4	29	164
1959	75	62.4	65	
1962	138	67.0	111	
1964	150	70.9	114	
1967	150	75.2	108	49
1970	185	90.2	111	
1972	185	100	100	60
1976	240	368	35	
1980	400	3348	6	
1981	950	6068	8	
1984	6000	22000	15	
1988 (July)	165000	1350000	7	600

Source: Minimum wages up to 1972 from reports of minimum wages advisory
boards and Knight, 1967; after 1972 from information provided by
the Ministry of Labour. Price index up to 1984 from Uganda: *Statistical Abstract* and idem: *Background to the Budget*, various years, thereafter
World Bank, 1988, table 8.8 for implicit figures up to 1987 (see Table
5.6 below), linked to old series at 1984, and 1988 from IMF 1989, table
on Uganda. Figures in the last column derived from *matoke* price data.
For further details see Jamal, 1985.

poverty – as opposed to the starvation implied by the wage figures – but
to the urban living standards still fell by at least two-fifths.

In the rural areas too fundamental changes occured in the structure
of incomes after the mid-1970s, which can again be attributed to inflation. The prices of food crops, which were increasingly traded on
the free market, rose sharply whereas export-crop prices fell. Simultaneously, export volumes declined. Export income, which in the 1960s
had easily dominated farm incomes, was therefore relegated to a minority role. These changes are all the more remarkable when it is realized
that they effectively happened in just five years after 1975.

The differential trends of cotton and coffee as opposed to food crops
caused a worsening rural income distribution. Cash incomes in the south
fell less than in the north, where cotton, the most important cash activity,
was practically wiped out. The picture changed again after 1980 when
the shilling was floated and huge price increases for export crops were

granted. By 1984 the original income structure (export crops dominating food income) was probably restored in the south, but with cotton production continuing to stagnate, this was not so in the north. Thus income distribution continued to disfavour the north.

PRICING POLICY

Given the massive structural shifts in the economy, pricing policy for agricultural export crops and the way it has been articulated since 1981 are at the heart of macro-economic management in Uganda. This section examines various aspects of pricing policy, paying particular attention to the parity between export crops and food crops, the balance between rural and urban areas, and the implications for overall income distribution.

I alluded earlier to the reversal in rural incomes in the 1970s as a result of divergent price trends between food crops and export crops. Table 5.5 helps to pinpoint these trends. By 1980 the structure of prices was in complete disarray. Food-crop prices had increased by 20 to 25 times, whereas export crop prices had increased less than sixfold. In real terms, food-crop prices were up 64 per cent (*matoke*) to 150 per cent (maize) of their 1972 values whereas export prices were 20 per cent. There is no doubt that such trends contributed to the decline in exports. However two factors must be recorded.

First, we must not jump to the conclusion that export crops declined at the expense of food crops. For this to hold we would expect to see an increase in food crops of a similar magnitude to the fall in export crops. There was no such increase. Here we must remember, given that most farmers operate within a subsistence context, that price ratios have an impact only on food crop *marketing*. There is no reason to believe that marketed surplus increased during this period. There was no dramatic increase in urbanization – if anything there was a slowdown or even a decline – and urban incomes fell. The decline in exports thus signifies an enforced withdrawal into leisure.

Secondly, price was not the only cause of the decline in exports. Cotton, being an annual crop, provides the best test of the importance of prices. Cotton output had begun to fall soon after 1973 when prices were still fairly high and when food-crop prices had yet to start their steep ascent. Thus by 1975 cotton output had already fallen by 57 per cent compared with 1973, at a time when prices had declined by (only) 28 per cent. An elasticity of two would not be claimed by even the most ardent proponent of prices. Clearly other factors were at work, the most important of which was the breakdown of the infrastructure – transport, marketing, and processing facilities. Since cotton is a weight-losing commodity, these are critical inputs in its marketing. Ginning is especially crucial; the breakdown of ginning capacity set in as early as 1973.

Table 5.5 Crop prices in Uganda in nominal and real terms, 1972 and 1980

	1972	1980	1980:1972	1980 in 1972 terms	1980:1972 real terms
	Shillings per kilogram				
Prices					
Coffee	1.19	7.00	5.9	0.21	0.18
Cotton	1.25	6.00	4.8	0.18	0.14
Matoke	0.17	3.00	21.4	0.09	0.53
Maize	0.60	20.00	33.3	0.60	1.00
Returns ratios					
Matoke: coffee	0.9	3.8			
Maize: cotton	0.6	5.7			

Source: Uganda, *Background to the Budget*, various years, for coffee and cotton prices; matoke and maize prices based on Ministry of Agriculture data.

If we look at the situation in 1980 compared with 1972 the inescapable conclusion is that we have to 'get the prices right'. When we look at sub-period trends and their underlying reasons we find that other factors were also at work. Thus 'getting prices right' may be a necessary condition for increasing exports but not a sufficient one. We shall see that government policy relied almost exclusively on prices to increase production, with serious implications for macro-economic management. But before that we have to elaborate on certain implications of the price structure from a historical perspective.

Figure 5.1 shows the returns to Uganda and Ugandan farmers for growing cotton. The Uganda figures are based on the f.o.b. (free on board) price of lint and c.i.f. (cost, insurance, freight) price of cloth, while the farm figures are based on the producer price for lint equivalent[14] and the retail price of cloth. In a special sense the two graphs show the 'terms of trade' of Uganda and Ugandan farmers for cotton. Uganda's terms fluctuated considerably although data intervals may be partly responsible. The trend decline after 1973 comes through clearly, as well as the relative profitability of growing cotton in the earlier years. Actually one discerns a trend decline for the whole period 1914–87. Concretely put, around 1914 the country could import 197 yards of cotton textiles for 100lbs of lint, whereas by the mid-1980s the equivalent terms had fallen to around 65 yards of cloth. The same applies to the farmers, with cotton growing being much more profitable at the inception of the industry than in the 1980s. In fact, a trend decline in producer prices set in around the late 1950s.

The most important thing that Figure 5.1 enables us to establish is the persistent nature of farm taxation in Uganda, given approximately by the gap between the two terms of trade. A more precise calculation

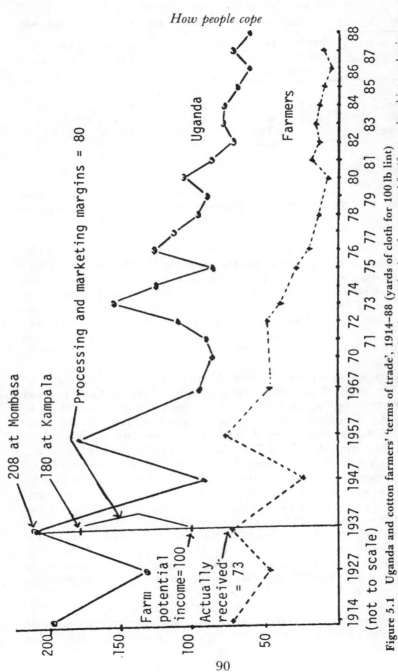

Figure 5.1 Uganda and cotton farmers' 'terms of trade', 1914–88 (yards of cloth for 100 lb lint)
Source: Jamal, 1976b, table v.4 up to 1957; then for 'Uganda' real external price of cotton and for 'farmers' real internal price of cotton, both from Table 5.6, linked at 1957.

would require that the country's terms be modified to reflect prices of exports and imports at producer point and not in Mombasa or New York as in the figure, and that in the case of farmers allowance be made for processing and marketing costs for both cotton lint and cotton cloth. Calculations for 1937 are shown in the figure. Compared with the 208 yards of cloth for 100lbs of lint at Mombasa, the value in Kampala would be 180 yards. However, not all of this could be distributed to the farmers since ginners had to be paid for processing the seed cotton and traders for distributing the cloth. These essential charges would absorb some 45 per cent of the export proceeds, leaving 100 yards of cloth available for potential distribution to the farmers. Farm prices actually granted could purchase only 73 yards, the difference going as export tax, import duty on cloth and income taxes. By 1972 the import duty had been effectively commuted into a 'tax' to support the local textile industry. By the late 1980s the divergence between what the country received and what the farmer received for export crops had reached ridiculous proportions because of the operation of the 'overvalued exchange rate'.

Table 5.6 shows information complementary to that in Figure 5.1 in terms of cotton and coffee producer prices since 1927. Cotton and coffee real prices in the USA since 1950 are also shown.[15] In the recent period the government has at least tried to maintain the real price of export crops and there is a vast improvement compared to the nadir of 1980. Yet prices are at a fraction of their 1972 level. As may be seen, the trend in the internal terms of trade was much more sharply downward than in the external terms, signifying increased 'taxation'. Rough figures for 1989 show that robusta coffee producers received (new) UShs5,400 million, whereas export tax itself amounted to UShs4,700 million. Newly enforced import and sales taxes took a sizeable proportion while the rest of the 'taxation' was in the form of increased marketing costs under conditions of infrastructure breakdown, and increased profit margins under conditions of scarcity and oligopoly.

While producer prices have fallen they have certainly not fallen as much as urban wages, and farm *incomes* have fallen even less than producer prices and by now are certainly much higher than most urban incomes. Both of these facts depend on giving a proper valuation to subsistence consumption. When this is done, farm incomes in total fell by less than 30 per cent or so[16] compared to the 30–50 per cent fall in urban incomes, not to mention the 90 per cent fall in wages. As for absolute incomes, in 1984 we would have to give the farmers UShs456,000 as the imputed value of their subsistence consumption.[17] On top of that, coffee farmers made around UShs60,000 from coffee and UShs17,000 from food-crop sales. Thus their total income would come to UShs553,000 – *nearly one-half* of *average* urban incomes – for all intents and purposes average *trading* incomes. Because of stagnant output cotton

Table 5.6 Cotton and coffee producer prices in Uganda in current and real terms, 1927–87, and US real price, 1950–87, selected years

	Cotton (safi) price (shillings per kilogram)	Cotton real (1972) price (shillings per kilogram)	Coffee (robusta) price (shillings per kilogram)	Coffee real (1972) price (shillings per kilogram)	Uganda price index (1972 = 100)	US cotton real (1972) price (US cents per kilogram)	New York coffee real (1972) price (US cents per kilogram)
1927	0.39	1.94	–	–	19.8		
1937	0.22	2.26	0.13	1.31	9.9		
1947	0.47	1.05	0.37	0.83	44.6		
1950							130
1957	1.21	1.97	1.65	2.69	61.4	124	
1960	1.06		1.10			111	90
1967	0.88	1.17	0.88	1.17	75.2	60	87
1972	1.25	1.25	1.19	1.19	100	76	99
1973	1.30	1.04	1.19	0.96	124	106	94
1974						86	87
1975	1.90	0.76	2.50	1.00	251	60	81
1976	1.90	0.52	2.50	0.68	368	87	167
1977						76	277
1978	3.00	0.32	3.50	0.37	946	67	171
1979	6.00		7.00			63	168
1980	6.00	0.18	7.00	0.21	3348	73	132
1981	30	0.49	35	0.58	6068	59	84

1982	40	0.32	50	0.40	12510	49	90
1983	60	0.38	80	0.50	15852	55	100
1984	70	0.32	131	0.59	22000	54	98
1985	125	0.21	262	0.44	59200	47	97
1986	200	0.13	723	0.48	179500	42	117
1987	1000	0.21	1820	0.38	475700	49	80
						42 (88)	

Source: Uganda 1927–67 prices from Jamal, 1976, various tables; 1972 onwards from Uganda *Statistical Abstract* and *Background to the Budget*, various years and World Bank 1988, table 8.7. Consumer price index as in Table 5.4. *Safi* refers to Grade A cotton, usually 80 per cent of the total crop; robusta is the predominant (80 per cent) coffee in Uganda. US cotton and coffee prices from IMF, 1989 table p. 180 for current prices ('US 10 markets' for cotton and 'Uganda coffee (New York)') deflated by US export unit value index from IMF, 1989, table p. 722. Earlier years from corresponding tables in IMF, 1985.

93

farmers did not fare as well but even their 'income' would easily come to 40 per cent of urban incomes in real terms. These figures are obviously not offered as the last word on the subject but merely to show that in a subsistence context price trends of export crops do not tell the whole story about levels of living, or income distribution.

Thus we have two perspectives on farm prices: in relation to agricultural taxation and in relation to wage increases. Given the generally declining external prices further price increases can only occur if the level of taxation is reduced or if wages are reduced. There is no scope for the latter since wages have already fallen as far as they can. Greater scope exists for reducing taxation, both overt in the form of export taxation and covert in the form of inefficiencies and excessive profit margins. Granting the difficulty of lowering export taxes because of their importance in total revenue, the choice finally boils down to reducing the costs associated with processing and marketing. In fact without measures in this direction higher prices are doomed to be negated by self-generated inflation. At least four lacunae need to be filled. First, there is a total lack of transport and processing facilities. This in particular explains the poor response in the case of cotton. Secondly, the most basic farming implement, the *jembe* (hand-hoe), is not available on the farms. Farmers have to make do with hoes that should have been discarded years ago. Thirdly, consumer goods are scarce in rural areas, another reflection of the breakdown of the infrastructure. Finally, farmers are not paid on time for their produce. The last two factors ensure that the price increases do not translate into anything tangible. Lack of consumer goods has kept the farmers in the 'subsistence mode', while late payment has broken their confidence in the marketing authorities. Farmers would rather take their *debe* (tin) of maize to the roadside and sell it to passers-by for instant cash than grow cotton, to be paid in chits.

Thus it is not surprising that high farm prices have failed to elicit a significant supply response. In the meantime inflation has become an integral part of the economy, an outcome of the exchange-rate regime in operation, for the fact is that with the economy now more than ever dependent on imports, the higher foreign-exchange price is translated directly into higher prices for consumer goods. Thus the country is caught in a spiral of devaluation–inflation–high prices–devaluation.[18] While the original devaluation was justified to pay higher prices to farmers, later devaluations have become simply a part of a vicious circle in which the real sufferers are the fixed-income earners. The prospects of them again becoming full-time wage earners, university professors or government officials are continually receding and this cannot but be at the expense of productivity in the economy.

CONCLUSION

The Ugandan economy underwent massive structural shifts in the last two decades. In the rural areas exports declined catastrophically, to the extent that for a while food crops came to rival export crops as a source of cash income. In the modern sector wages were continually eroded and wage earners ceased to be a viable and independent economic class. Real incomes fell in all sectors, but more so in the urban than in the rural sector, where the preponderance of subsistence production cushioned the fall.

Given the dominance of export crops in the economy, its revival now requires an increase in their production and this puts agricultural pricing policy at the core of macro-economic management. In the 1970s the basic parities between food crops and export crops were completely disrupted as inflation increased and, even with the market for food crops limited (mostly to urban areas), food crops came to rival export crops as a source of cash income for the farmers. Other factors, such as insecurity and the breakdown of the infrastructure, contributed to the fall in exports. However, with the price structure in disarray there can be no doubt that government had to intervene in the price field and that, with local inflation having gone way out of line with imported inflation, the basic remedy was a devaluation – and a massive one. This came in 1981 and prices were raised in real terms. After this the currency was kept on a float and underwent almost continuous devaluation. Farm prices were adjusted periodically to keep pace with the inflation. These subsequent actions are open to question. They place preponderant weight on higher prices as the cure for export expansion, whereas the poor output response has vindicated the importance of non-price factors. The virtual floating of the shilling has by itself become a source of inflation in Uganda because of the country's new reliance on imported consumer goods. The continuing erosion of urban fixed incomes that this implies is detrimental to the revival of a diversified modern sector.

Thus one cannot but be dismayed by the immensity of the task that remains to be accomplished. Nothing less than the reintroduction of export crops is involved, not unlike the situation at the start of the colonial period, with its concomitant investments in marketing, processing and transport facilities. And it involves recreating the whole modern sector. No doubt, even without this the Ugandan farmer will continue to grow his own food and the towns may become even more self-sufficient, but the economy will have taken two steps backwards.

Notes

1. The author is Senior Research Economist, ILO, Geneva. Views are expressed in the author's personal capacity. To avoid unnecessary complication all figures are given in terms of old Uganda shillings (= 100 times new shillings).
2. For the typical African country agricultural exports provide up to three-quarters of total exports in the 1980s. However there are also some prominent mineral-based economies – Nigeria, Gabon, Zambia, etc., while remittances (from South Africa) are important in the Southern African countries and (from the Gulf) in Somalia and Sudan.
3. See, among others, Lipton, 1977; World Bank, 1981; Bates, 1981. Other notable contributions to the debate include Commins *et al.*, 1986; Lofchie, 1986; Jamal and Weeks, 1988.
4. A vivid account of the state of the economy on the fall of President Amin may be found in Commonwealth Secretariat, 1979. The report was written under the leadership of the late Professor Dudley Seers soon after the liberation of Kampala. See also the many excellent articles in Hansen and Twaddle (eds), 1988.
5. For the early economic history of Uganda see Wrigley, 1959; Ehrlich, 1965; Jamal, 1976b.
6. A history of the East African Asians may be found in Mangat, 1969. For their socio-economic profile in the 1960s see Ghai, 1965 and for issues centering on the expulsion of the Ugandan Asians, Twaddle (ed.), 1975.
7. Knight, 1967 contains an analysis of wages policy in Uganda in relation to farm incomes.
8. These figures are specifically shown in column 4 of Table 5.4.
9. For the development of wage labour in Uganda, see Powesland, 1959; Elkan, 1960.
10. Kenya, 1955, pp. 11, 142, quoted in Weeks, 1971.
11. A note is in order here about the impact of inflation on our tables. In many tables I have dropped the decimal point after the 1970s. This is not only because it would be spurious to retain it in most cases, but for a more down-to-earth reason: where figures are in shillings the decimal implies shillings and cents. With inflation, the cent can buy nothing and has completely gone out of circulation. Even shilling coins have stopped circulating.
12. See Chapter 6 below for vivid accounts of how urban families have survived in the face of collapsed wages.
13. The growth rates (percentage per annum) of the four largest towns between 1969 and 1980 were as follows: Kampala 3.2; Jinja −0.7; Mbale 1.7; Tororo 0.5. Compared to this, the overall growth rate was 2.8 per cent. Now up to 1972 the towns were growing at 5–6 per cent per annum. Thus betwen 1973 and 1980, all towns (including Kampala) registered lower growth rates than natural population increase, implying reverse migration. Source: Uganda, 1982, table 1.26, p. 50.
14. It is worth emphasising that comparisons between producer prices and f.o.b. prices must be done at an equivalent stage of processing. Producer prices in the case of cotton are for *seed cotton* whereas export prices are for *lint*. The conversion factor is 100 kg seed cotton = 33 kg lint.
15. These prices show New York prices for Uganda coffee and for cotton (unspecified)

deflated by the US manufacturing price index; thus they approximate Uganda's real prices – or terms of trade.

16. A notional figure based on the fact that cash incomes formed around 30 per cent of total farm income (including subsistence production/consumption) in the 1960s. Even if we assume that all of the cash income disappeared, the drop in total income would be only 30 per cent.

17. Based on the cost of a 2,200 calorie per capita diet in urban areas, scaled up for an average size rural family. This estimation of farm subsistence incomes has to be used as GDP accounts do not give current-value figures of subsistence production (as of other components). In any case we might have resorted to this approximation, the underlying argument being that equal baskets of food should carry equal price tags. The operative assumption thus is that farmers produce and consume at least a minimum food basket.

18. For a further discussion of this issue see Loxley, 1989. It may be pointed out that Loxley was a member of the Uganda Study Team that advised the government in 1986 on issues of macro-economic management. See IRDC, 1986.

SIX

Women, children and a 'living wage'

Christine Obbo

The decline of Main Street, the proliferation of petty trading in all side streets and on uncontested space in towns and on major and rural roadsides, and the commoditization of nearly every activity and of domestic and wild products are outstanding features of the present Ugandan economy. These result from changes in the economy in the last 20 years that have threatened the 'living wages' of the majority of Ugandans. Most families from all socio-economic strata need at least two, or even three, income-generating activities to survive. Survival means being able to pay the inflationary rates of school fees, rents, taxes, food bills etc. The result of all this has been a blurring of the distinctions between formal and informal economic activities, commercial and domestic spaces, public and private concerns and business, and moral and amoral parameters.

This chapter shows the resilience of Ugandans as they struggle to recover from Amin's 'economic war' that never was, and the subsequent Structural Adjustment Programmes (SAP) of the International Monetary Fund (IMF) and the World Bank, which have pressured the government to live within its means by balancing its budget, controlling wasteful expenditures and presumably generating enough foreign exchange to repay its 'development' loan debts. One of the SAP provisions, currency devaluation, has caused progressively high inflation, thus increasing the number of people unable to live within their means. It must be pointed out, however, that the real causes of poverty existed before SAP and that SAP only aggravated the situation of the vulnerable – the aged, women and children.

This chapter unapologetically does not deal with activities within the formal structures of fanned or air-conditioned offices. Rather, it deals with the *njua kali* (hot sun: informal sector) activities in building and city street alleys and corridors, city pavements, suburban kerbs and garages, some village schools and village paths. These are the areas where the struggles for the living wage are fought out each day.

The chapter also focuses on women and children because they

98

predominantly operate in the *njua kali* sector, and they are often over-looked in discussions of SAP, which tend to over-report activities in the formal sector. Often the linkages between the formal sector and the *njua kali* sectors are not made. Yet it is important to know what happens to individuals and families as they balance production for subsistence and market and at the same time attempt to maintain social, physical and economic wellbeing.

In the 1950s and 1960s self-employment was a survival strategy for people who had no education or skills to secure jobs in the government or private sector. The informal sector was a last-resort employment solution for rural–urban migrants and school drop-outs. Its activities lay outside official job definitions, renumerations and taxation, but operators did not escape from harassment by officials. As some of the activities generated lucrative incomes, those in formal employment sometimes joined in as a means of getting rich while maintaining respectable pensionable jobs.

By the mid-1970s in Uganda, as in other African countries, the rapid migration of peasants to cities had begun to overload the health, educational, housing and employment services. The informal sector became the predominant mode through which services were provided through a mixture of entrepreneurial and self-help endeavours. At this time, too, the supposedly illicit, illegal or city-blighting activities came to be known as the informal sector, and governments and planners began to regard this sector as the solution to the unemployment problems. By the late 1970s, the formal economy had for all intents and purposes collapsed. There were still employees in all public government jobs but 'things were done' in the private sphere. This became known as the *magendo* economy which combines blackmarketeering in foreign exchange and overcharging to make up for the losses incurred during the process of doing business in Uganda.

The proliferation of *magendo* activities has at the same time been caused by and has exacerbated the erosion of confidence in public service and institutions. The result has been that most civil servants spend more time on their private activities, which they feel generate the income that their families live on, than on government jobs that still have prestige because they indicate a person's high educational status, but which pay starvation wages. The government has failed to adjust the wage structure to the high inflation.

The *magendo* economy has created a sharing of wealth mechanism that has become the accepted way of conducting business in Uganda. The 'right to survive by eating' has been recognized as a basic right by most Ugandans. Incomes earned by exacting extra fees for services that the public is ostensibly entitled to for free or at officially fixed prices partly supplement the wages of most civil servants. Those who are inclined to complain about the injustices of this are easily silenced by a simple, 'my friend what shall I eat?'

In all districts, the RCs work as public-spirited public servants operating at the grassroots. The RCs enjoy a lot of power that they can easily use to their advantage. In West Nile an RC1 chairman imposed a stiff fine of UShs5000 on four youths who had been found hawking second-hand clothes and brooms in the village. When asked why he was fining the youth beyond their means, he did not dwell on the illegality of the activities and the necessity of stopping them, he was concerned with 'what shall I eat?', i.e. the source of income. Local people claimed that this was a lucrative source of income for the RCs. One RC1 chairman in Rakai asserted that the ordinary people in Uganda will never improve their lot because those in responsible positions insist on lining their pockets from public coffers and the sweat of peasants. This comment was prompted by an incident at a massive search for arms house to house and at road blocks, which resulted in losses for traders as their produce was confiscated. This is not unique; in Tororo district some RCs had got into the habit of confiscating peoples' produce on the way to the market. This affected peoples' ability to pay their taxes and their children's school fees. The people complained to a broadcaster in one of the local languages, he aired their complaints and the practice stopped. The basic point was that in most cases the peasants were suffering from double loss; they were not eating their food crops because they were treating them as sources of cash, yet they were stopped by RCs from realizing the cash as well.

Corruption is a collective disease in Uganda that most citizens have problems passing judgement on. But when all the rationalization for it has been done – such as maintaining standards of living, maintaining children in school, surviving – one finds that there are some Ugandans who somehow manage without resorting to corrupt practices. Those who find themselves giving bribes in order to get things done in reasonable time (or done at all) do not like it, but they maintain the attitude of 'Do not judge another person until . . .'

In the urban areas the sharing mechanism operates through a new category of jobs in the interstices of the formally recognized job structure. In all ministries it is impossible to deal directly with officials in charge. One has to go through different people to accomplish tasks like renewing a passport or licence, or acquiring and transferring land titles. The interstitial jobs now provide employment for a large number of people. These are predominantly young men who know the price of every service and their way around known places of business such as airport customs, traffic control offices, foreign exchange black markets, land offices etc. Some operators are so established that people seek them out in the strategic places they frequent; others (particularly the women) are sought in their places of work, and still others periodically check in at offices where they have contacts to see if there are any jobs or errands that require action. The interstitial operatives live by their wits and their delivery of services saves their clients possible embarrassment, loss of face and unnecessary delays. Behind their backs they are referred to as *bayaye*, hustlers.[1]

In many ways the best jobs in Uganda are perceived to be those that give access to and control over public resources and assets that can either be transferred to private use or used to generate incomes. The Salaries Review Commission concluded that the failure to ensure living wages for civil servants has created 'a retainer fee syndrome', i.e. the tendency to regard salaries as a means of retaining positions in government. 'The Civil Servant had either to survive by [losing] his standard of ethics, performance and dutifulness or remain upright and perish . . . [there is] suggestive evidence [that] the average Ugandan is still morally sound and not only capable, but also proud of good work if only there was an improvement in his real income'.[2]

The High Level Manpower (HLM) Survey in 1967 classified wage employment into the following groups: top managers, junior managers, professionals, technicians, clerical workers and office executives, and others, including schoolteachers. The HLM estimated that professionals comprised 20 per cent of the total wage employment, and the unskilled and semi-skilled represented 80 per cent. It is doubtful that the percentages have changed. However, the distinctions between modes of earning a living cannot be clear-cut as many wage earners also employ people to hawk or sell merchandise on back city streets *(kikubo)* and suburban roads. Still others divide the work day into a few hours for official business and the rest of the day for other businesses. Workers in various ministries devote a lot of time to moonlighting. They either use the official facilities and resources to earn the second income or seek other employment such as trading or driving taxis.

With the deterioration of standards of living, it is recognized that working conditions need to be improved in many cases thus raising morale. Many companies and agencies try to boost morale in the workplace by giving reasonably decent wages and providing comforts like food, tea and transport. Many civil servants say that they stay in their jobs because of the housing and transportation provided. Messenger boys continue to make tea and clean offices because if they are creative they can shave off enough provisions for their own daily lunch and dinner. One told me that the tips he got for errands eventually add up. The 'tip' is expected if one wants to have a job done and to avoid delays or misappropriation of resources or damage to merchandise.

It is a class issue, the underlings feel that under most circumstances they are not accorded due recognition for all they do for the elite, so the least they deserve is some financial reward. Some employees recognize that 'underlings' need 'to eat' and automatically tip them for services performed, but others are forced to comply by threat of what might happen if they do not. The class antagonism is recognized by the elite, who employ the 'underlings' to deal in situations in which they would be delayed, made to lose face or compromised. The 'underlings' resent any elite they deem as 'trying to be clever', i.e. using them. All in all, however, the elite and others enjoy give-and-take relationships because they are dependent upon each other. The domestic 'underlings' are much more easily contained than those in the public places of work and services. Nevertheless, there is a saying in Uganda that one cannot be both poor and stubborn. Unskilled labourers are expendable because there are many others who will gladly replace them, and this puts a limit on their assertiveness.

However, judging from the number of young people selling an assortment of food and other items on the streets, some 'underlings' are paying for the consequences of their assertiveness. As one put it 'you either endure *njua kali* or you suffer servitude for pathetic wages'.

PETTY TRADING: THE TONINYIRA MUKANGE SYNDROME

M is an expectant school drop-out who lives with a distant relative working for a private organization in Kampala. M has to get up at 6 am to sweep the house, wash the laundry and dishes (if she did not do so the day before) and get breakfast ready. Some days she has to be at the wholesale food market by 6am so as to get first pick and good prices.

At 8am M and her patroness B leave the apartment and do not return until six in the evening. M and B's days differ remarkably. B's organization provides tea breaks in the morning and afternoon, has contracted two women to provide cooked food at lunch, and encourages workers to meet regularly to discuss any problems they encounter. The employer says that he pays decent wages to his employees (including the office messenger/cleaner) and feeds them in order to ensure that staplers, toilet paper, cups and chairs do not end up in the possession of someone else. B, however, needs more money to send her daughter to a good boarding school. She saves on rent and transportation because she is a squatter in one of the abandoned Asian houses in Kampala, and she walks to work. B is better off than most of the female household heads. She says that she hardly ever visits her village now that her parents are dead. Her three siblings also live in Kampala. However, there is no shortage of relatives like M – to be accommodated while attending school.

B rents half a market stall from an old acquaintance and it is here that M sells the produce. Unlike other sellers M only deals with things in season – such as pineapples, passion fruits, mangoes and limes. She does not compete with the established sellers of staples like bananas but does sell cassava and sweet potatoes. M knows that she is lucky to have a job that does not involve sitting in the sun or being covered with dust on the pavements or sidewalks.

On those days that she does not sell much at the market she walks for two miles to sell at another market that operates in the evenings between 6pm and 10pm. This market is known as *Toninyira mukange* ('do not step on mine') because it is so congested with sellers that there is hardly moving room.[3] This market is situated on the edge of the Kibuli–Namuwongo–Wabigalo–Kisugu group of low-income areas. Sellers of such goods as meat, fish, fresh and cooked food, industrial plastic items and second-hand clothes congregate there. Bachelors enjoy reasonably priced square meals while sitting on rail tracks. Suburban housewives pick their way in high heels to buy spinach or cassava, bananas or fish. Housegirls, while socializing with each other or boyfriends, buy food or sandals or plastic water containers and basins. Toninyira is an overflow from the evening markets that existed in the surrounding low-income areas during the 1970s. Things have not changed at this market; business is brisk, things are cheap and it attracts people from all socio-economic classes. It is also the only market where the rich are not overcharged, after all the idea is to sell off either 'hot' items, food before it spoils, or to make desperately needed money for an immediate target – need.

The most exciting aspect of the Toninyira syndrome is its spread to strategic places on suburban routes, or near suburban homes. The sellers are housegirls, houseboys and other unemployed relatives of suburban residents. The sellers either generate capital to deal in seasonal items like fruits or snacks for schoolchildren, or are employed by homemakers, who need money to cover the daily expenses of maintaining their homes. These suburban sellers operate all day (but in some cases and in specific locations they open in the evenings because the sellers have regular nine-to-five jobs in town). These markets show great sensitivity to the market. For example, during school time roast peanuts, sliced pineapples, sweets, bananas and cough drops are sold to schoolchildren. In the evening milk, sugar, tea and bread are briskly sold to those returning from work or to housegirls in a hurry. The market serves unanticipated needs like candles for sudden power blackouts or butter, salt, soap and toilet paper for emergencies. The sellers make on average a 20 per cent profit. There is openness about the profit as buyers pay for the convenience and the sellers inform them during the bargaining process that they only make so much on such and such items. Some of the homemakers complain that on most days these sellers go early to the supermarket so that by the time the workers go there the shelves are empty of salt, sugar, soap, etc. In other words, the only way working people can get things is by buying them at Toninyira market or Toninyira suburban kiosks.

How people cope

WOMEN'S DIFFERING EXPERIENCES

The overcrowding of petty trading in one physical place or the overcrowding of the same line of business previously referred to as the *Toninyira mukange* syndrome is also the predominant pattern in all the busy business parts of the city. *Kikubo* ('corridor') businesses are also characterized as *katimba* ('hang to show') because the mechandise is put up in the morning and packed up in the evening. Clothes, cloth, cosmetics, shoes, bags, etc., are some of the items brought in cars or carts in the morning and wheeled away in the evening. The operatives are predominantly employed by middle-class people who have salaried jobs but who feel that it is expensive to rent rooms in the city building premises and that is in 'this dust and filth where money is to be found'. This is the place for ordinary people and people who consider themselves middle class and as such are ashamed to be seen here.

In one incident, Joy, an employee of a prestigious institution who owned a stall in *katimba*, spotted her employer waddling through the area, she crawled behind the fabrics and when she thought it was safe she emerged only to find Mary, a churchmate, standing there, with an amused expression. 'I have been looking for you! What are you doing here?'. The mutter about visiting a friend there did not really convince either of them. This incident is interesting because it reveals a lot about the common practices and sensibilities with regard to realities of supplementing wages, and shopping for bargains; and the location not being quite appropriate for educated people. The employer and churchmate were there to hunt for bargains and Joy was sitting in that morning for her employee, who had taken a baby to hospital.

Although in conversations educated people claim that the *kikubo* area is too congested, unsafe and a shopping place for the ordinary people who use the taxi park facilities, in fact the educated do at strategic times frequent the area to shop, to collect the money from their stalls, and to drop off employees. Some wives of prestigious men such as civil servants or university professors own stalls and sell in them. This is not a threat to the family name because these wives are usually less well known than their husbands and are never taken to public functions. Some of these 'anonymous' wives even sell vegetables or secondhand clothes at the markets. In addition to having salaried jobs, the owners of the stalls may own small hairdressing salons or sell lunchtime snacks. The reality is that not all wives of educated people can own large hairdressing salons and shops in the desirable parts of town, nor can they own butcheries, piggeries, dairy farms or bakeries. But public sentiments still relegate petty trading and informal sector activities to the poor and unskilled segments of the society who cannot get good employment.

The myth about the sources of incomes of the different segments of

104

the population is maintained because the elite can manage to buy the commodities that are traded and then employ a poor dependent to sell them in city stalls or suburban street corners. Informal sector workers cannot be automatically assumed to be self-employed, but usually the volumes and the regularity of the goods give some indication of the source of employment. Obviously a young man or woman selling two kilos of groundnuts, dry roast maize and a dozen sweets is self-employed, whereas one selling five kilos of roast groundnuts, or a dozen packets of milk and loaves of bread is working for someone else.

The pavement traders are predominantly young men, young children and young women with babies. They sit in the sun and seem to sell little, as indicated by the volume of their commodities. The sellers face competition from mobile young men who sometimes hawk the same items, such as cooked groundnuts and maize. The solution has been for pavement sellers to specialize in quick snack items that are suited to different tastes. Small banana leaf bundles containing 100 cooked and dried coffee beans are traditional in the rural areas but have become popular with poor urbanites. Roast groundnuts, maize and sim-sim are now a standard fare on the pavements. Sweets, cough drops, biscuits and cigarettes are popular items. Some sellers have a regular lunchtime clientele that passes by to buy single cigarettes that are lit for them on the spot. The sellers make a 100 per cent profit and sometimes even offer cigarettes on credit.

The goods and commodities on sale in the streets and markets are usually available in the wholesale shops and the amounts one buys are determined by one's capital. Goods that are imported come in by both legal and illegal means. Being an importer requires having interstitial contacts among customs officers at the ports of entry, with licensing officers and of course at road block security points. In general doing business in Uganda is expensive as importers must pay informal fees to many service people along the way before the goods reach the shops. However, this is cheap compared with operating through the right channels where it is felt that the taxes are very high.

The most famous of the importers are the 'Dubai traders', who buy duty-free goods from Dubai and import them on the weekly flight. These traders are reputed to bring large volumes of electronic equipment and expensive-looking clothing compared with the less flashy goods of traders who import from India, Kenya or the United Kingdom. Although the Dubai trade is dominated by men, the women, roughly a quarter of the category, are the ones who excite the public imagination. These women are visible because they dress in a flashy manner, are stereotyped as plump (although some are young and slim), and know their way around the system. These women do business in the most expensive way, but still manage to make commodities available at prices that are comparable to

105

local and non-Dubai goods. While some have trading licences, others rent the right to use the trade licence from male traders. Airport officials seem to harass them more and so do security officials on road blocks. The Dubai women are regarded ambivalently because they are associated with the *magendo* trade that has been in existence for the last 20 years.

In all fairness it must be observed that the traders who engage in import trade work hard to acquire foreign exchange outside the banks in order to save time, there is no evidence that they are among the many players in currency black-market activities that were characteristic of *magendo*. The issue of causes and participants in the parallel money market will be discussed after the following glimpse at the changing fortunes of a former 'Dubai' woman.

Julia's husband was a long-distance trucker who transported petroleum products from the Kenyan port of Mombasa to Rwanda and Zaire. On the return journey he brought coffee for export through Mombasa. His travels made it possible for him to supply Julia with cotton prints from Zaire and expensive clothing which she sold to the wives of *mafuta mingi* (i.e. soldiers and businessmen with money), a group which was famed for its consumerism. Eight years ago her husband, who had converted to Islam, went to work in the Gulf states. He used to return once every three months via Dubai where he bought consumer goods for Julia to sell. Julia was the envy of all her associates struggling to gain access to businesses. In 1987 Julia's husband deserted her for another woman. Her source of trade vanished. She tried selling second-hand clothes but even this venture soon failed. She currently calls herself 'unemployed but looking for opportunities'. She rents two square yards of space from a *katimba* trader. She says the monthly UShs30,000 for rent and the daily UShs 100 for storage are going to drive her out of the cloth trade. The real reason is that there are too many traders, she does not sell enough cloth because she is new to the business area, does not have an established clientele, and does not have a wide selection of cloth.

The struggle for a living wage affects Ugandans in both the rural and urban areas. However, men and women experience it differently. The differential gender experiences are aptly illustrated in the following example.

A man who had been attending board meetings all morning in an air-conditioned office was surprised when his wife appeared to be flustered about her experiences one Friday. The dialogue was recorded verbatim as follows:

Husband: 'How was your day?'
Wife: 'My car licence is expiring today, and I spent the whole morning with X trying to get it renewed, but his contact at

	the police station was not there. We are going back in the afternoon'..
Husband:	'Why did you wait until the last moment?'
Wife:	'It has been a hectic week and I totally forgot about the licence. On Monday, the landlord tripled the rent and if I cannot raise it I will have to close the shop. On Tuesday the soldiers again came bothering my shop girls by demanding tips. I do not make enough money and I certainly do not have money to subsidize their salaries.
Husband:	'But why do you pay them. It is illegal. Report them.'
Wife:	'Where can I report them? On Wednesday, one of my three shop girls quit and left me in a lurch. She left with some money. The other girls are demanding more money for lunch because they want to eat matooke. I am going to get rid of them. I cannot buy them matooke when I cannot afford it for my family. The business does not bring in enough money either.'
Husband:	'They probably eat one meal a day and want it to be good. At work we have stopped matooke and serve posho (maize meal) for the free lunch. There were a lot of complaints at first until we suggested that we would contract a matooke seller to come and sell to them like other institutions do.'
Wife:	'Anyhow, I spent all yesterday recruiting new girls. I may even have to close the shop.'

This was not the only couple that had had different experiences of making a living wage by virtue of operating in offices or dealing with street reality. In a recent seminar elite men criticized the attention paid to women petty traders operating on the pavements in the sun because they maintained that the women who matter – those who run shops, hardware stores, flower shops and private schools – were not dealt with. 'Dwelling on black-market activities and street traders does not make us look respectable,' one declared.

This elitist attitude, which demands the over-reporting of the activities of the minority, is unacceptable. It is the activities of the majority of ordinary Ugandans that make the economy of Uganda dynamic. Women bear the brunt of trying to make ends meet because ultimately they have to ensure that their dependants and families are fed, clothed and receive medical care and education. Women with babies are ubiquitous in low-income jobs, as street traders, road sweepers, and public garden maintainers. Women continue to predominate in providing cooked food to office workers. In fact young girls who do not have enough capital are increasingly banding together in groups of five to eight to share the expenses, the work and income from cooked food. Some cooked-food sellers have become so sophisticated that they bring charcoal stoves to keep the food warm and to make after lunch tea for those who want it. The profit margin of food sellers appears to be low when one compares the price of raw food with what they charge for large portions of food.

Men and women along busy roads have a ready market for farm produce. Urban dwellers appreciate the freshness of the products and the reasonable prices. Some shrewd sellers greet customers on bent knees and call them 'auntie', particularly if they drive Mercedes-Benz cars. The commoditization of food is affecting the health status of children. Women sell eggs, fruits and vegetables to generate incomes and then spend some of the money on medical treatment for malnutrition problems. In some places older children work with their parents or for others to sell food and to thrash and winnow beans and groundnuts. Still other young people collect wild fruits and catch river fish to sell to passers-by.

In many rural areas that are poorly served by road networks, the food rots in the villages or women walk long distances (with heavy baskets) to reach market places. (Children also have to walk long distances to and from schools.) The only freely mobile people are middlemen who possess bicycles.

Labour and services are also expensive in rural areas. Farmers complain that they cannot afford to hire labourers. They claim that hiring tractors is cheaper. This situation has led to the revival of communal labour teams throughout Uganda. In Buganda, fellow villagers are now an integral part of wedding preparations; helping to build the 'tent', bring food, supply beer, etc. In West Nile young men work in return for an agreed reward such as beer or meat. Cultivating a 100 yards by 50 yards field yields a return of a goat valued at UShs4,000. But ten women in the same location ploughed a field of the same size in three days in return for one kilogram of coarse salt each.

THE PARALLEL MARKET AND A 'LIVING WAGE'

In a recent government seminar on Uganda's economy since 1986[4] sponsored by the Chartered Institute of Bankers, participants spent a lot of time on the issues of the parallel market and a 'living wage'. Government participants asserted that the government did not have enough revenues to increase wages. Apparently before the 'living wage' became an issue the government spent over half its budget on wages compared to the 10 per cent currently spent.

Private individuals are just as preoccupied as the Central Bank with how to gain access to foreign exchange. Those in jobs requiring travel abroad to conduct government business guard this privilege jealously. Those who gain access to jobs requiring sanctioning or signing contracts for foreign companies, foreign aid, or foreign businesses usually get a 10 or 15 per cent cut in foreign currency. This practice is so common that

recently a foreign official who had been sent to negotiate an 'aid' contract
to Uganda privately fumed to another foreigner who went to visit her at
her hotel room about a permanent secretary: 'He is a pain in the neck,
he will not accept anything. I have wasted one week working on him.'
This Ugandan should be applauded and those who assert that foreign aid
corrupts should not be dismissed out of hand as troublemakers.

Construction is the fastest growing business in Uganda because it
is an investment that soon pays for itself. Owners of modern houses can
rent them to expatriates and other foreigners. Many people are envious
because landlords are sometimes paid in US dollars. Anyone who can
acquire foreign exchange outside Bank of Uganda channels is regarded
as engaging in black-market activities. The black market enjoys such
a high profile that it can rightly be regarded as the fifth column. A
local paper, *Weekly Topic*, routinely publishes the black-market (*kibanda*)
rates on the same page as the official rates. In a recent meeting it was
asserted that the major participants in black-market activities are people
in powerful political and bureaucratic positions. Apparently it is their
wives and relatives who are the most active players.

Ugandans use all loopholes in the economy to maintain living
standards. One of the commonest is multiple employment. Workers in
various ministries devote a lot of time to moonlighting. They divide the
work day into a few hours for the official business and the rest of the day
to other businesses. It is recognized that this is stealing government time.
At the same time it is argued that if people received a living wage then
they would not divert time from work. This, however, is not perceived
generally to be as bad as stealing government money through hidden
expenditures or allowances. The commonly cited examples are the uses
and reimbursements made on government departments' vehicles, vehicle maintenance and transportation of workers. The result is that most
government expenses go to servicing the workers. However, the allowances are not distributed evenly because some people have access
to vehicles, others get to go more often on field trips, and still others
have more access than others to the permanent secretaries who authorize disimbursements. As described previously, those with no access to
government resources to exploit, or to claims, resort to interstitial operators, and this leads to loss of government revenue. For example, if a
government fee or tax is high, the operative is paid a fee and he lowers
the rate to be paid.

Techniques for extracting a living wage can leave both private
individuals and public organizations as victims. Telephone subscribers
often complain of bills for calls they did not make. It is well known that
one can 'rent' time on other people's phones. While I was waiting in a
government office a phone rang and a young man rushed in to answer
it. From his conversation, which lasted 30 minutes, I learnt that he was

109

from another ministry, that he was calling the US, and that he was talking to four friends whom he asked to send him pairs of jeans for sale as there was great local demand for them. After the call he counted out 3,000 shillings and handed them to someone in the corridor before leaving the building. That indeed had been a cheap call to make!

It is a common complaint that international calls often go dead in the middle of conversations because someone has been allowed to 'rent' the line. This irritation is one of many; others include getting no response at the telephone exchange while in background operators engage in the conversations about sales of mattresses, beds, shoes, etc.

The adjustment of the actual wages earned to bring them up to a living wage is not confined to civil servants. Apparently the appropriation of agricultural field officers' and teachers' salaries to finance trips by ministers is a rampant problem. Money is diverted in the capital city while the civil servants in the rural areas have to wait three to four months to be paid.

The result is that, for example, teachers in some rural schools spend little of their time on teaching, and concentrate on growing food for cash. Some just stay at home to cultivate; others mobilize the labour of schoolchildren for at least 12 hours a week. This sometimes causes tensions between headmasters and parents. However, this is usually rationalized on the ground that few graduates from the rural schools will ever escape being farmers so it is in their interest that they be taught agriculture. While some schools have an agricultural curriculum, in most schools agriculture is another name for cheap school childrens' labour. So in some ways the parents object rightly that they do not sent their children to school to be peasants. Female teachers, who usually do not enjoy access to resources like lorries, often find it convenient to give up teaching and engage in multiple activities like horticulture, tailoring and crafts. One woman, whose husband is a headmaster, gave up teaching to grow tomatoes. These fetched a good income which she spent on family clothing and school fees. She was, however, forced to stop that business because her husband had started appropriating the money after each sale and never spent it on household needs. A friend trained her to be a tailor. She borrowed money to buy a second-hand sewing machine and she is now the village tailor. Her husband, she says, has no way of ever laying hands on her money because she invests the payments in new fabrics and threads.

What about teachers in urban areas? K is a 49-year-old teacher and her husband is a middle-level civil servant. Their combined incomes do not constitute a living wage. Furthermore, they have five children in institutions of higher learning on whom they have to spend a substantial amount of money for travel, as well as accommodation and classroom supplies.

110

Women, children and a 'living wage'

K engages in multiple money-generating activities. She raises chickens in her backyard. She says that the eggs and chicken sales help put food on their table. She has converted her garage into a general store selling second-hand clothing, beer, soft drinks, cigarettes, matches, tea and sweets. On different days she makes 20 or 30 per cent profit on these items. K also employs a school drop-out and distant niece to sell bananas, pineapples, bread, cigarettes, tea, milk, sweets and cough drops on a busy suburban street. K and her family have managed to maintain a decent standard of living through her hard work, which she says is 'necessary but exhausting'. 'I am always tired because I have to prepare lessons, I have to feed the chicken, I have to cook while minding the shop, and I have to take care of the house and laundry. I do not go to bed before midnight and I wake up at five. We manage but we have many unfulfilled obligations and projects back home.'

K and her husband are considered lucky because their homeland is far from where they live and so they are not bothered by a constant stream of relatives. Visiting ruralites have always bothered urban dwellers in low-income brackets. However, nowadays middle-class people also complain of 'uninvited rural guests who expect to be provided with money for the return journey'. But poor relatives are not always an inconvenience for urbanites; they are quite useful as unpaid help around the home and additional income generators.

CONCLUSION

The majority of young women and men are either hawking food and other low profit margin commodities on the streets or they are employed for low wages by someone. Young women are employed as messengers, traders, hairdressers, housegirls, etc.

Middle class professional women have either given up their jobs or are supplementing them with garage shops, hairdressing salons and pavement trade. Some middle-class women with the right connections still control sizeable business concerns and they are established business people in their own right. People experience the struggle for a living wage differently, depending on their gender, their socio-economic positions, their access to public resources and the availability of road services.

Notes

1. The word *bayaye* originally referred to the unruly, marijuana (*njaye*)-smoking young men from Kyagwe county who were very active during the reign of Kabaka Mwanga. In the 1970s Amin glorified the unruly urban, uneducated, unemployed hustlers who harrassed people in the rural and urban areas. They even became a role model for rebellious youths who rebelled against their parents and teachers, and sought a short-cut means of earning a living. Currently informants referred to *bayaye* as anyone who successfully hustles and outwits one in a given situation. However, the hardcore *bayaye* are stereotypically seen as 'unemployed', shabbily dressed, foul-mouthed young men operating in city markets places and taxi and bus parks.
2. Uganda Government, 1982b, p. 109, section 163.
3. The phrase *Toninyira mukange* has a three fold meaning – it refers to a specific market place; it applies to the ubiquitous marketing of numerous vendors within a few inches or yards of each other on the pavements of nearly every street corner; and it is descriptive of the tendency of traders to deal in the same items or business. It is a question of too many traders chasing a limited number of clients.

   Three illustrative examples will suffice. If one trader manages to sell off pineapples or bananas or wax candles in one day, then all the other traders jump on the bandwagon, often sustaining losses. If a shopkeeper succeeds at the right time (i.e. before Christmas and before Easter) to sell off a consignment of Italian ladies shoes, then other shopkeepers also stock it only to watch slow sales. Or the promise of great profits has made hairdressing salons the most ubiquitous business in Kampala and many hairdressers complain of the slowness of business.
4. The Seminar, held from 11–17 December 1989 at the International Conference Centre, was sponsored by the Chartered Institute of Bankers, and was attended by leading academics, government officials, civil servants, bankers and members of the National Resistance Council.

PART THREE
THE HEALTH OF UGANDANS:
THE SOCIAL SECTOR UNDER PRESSURE

SEVEN
Living on the edge:
changing social structures in the context of AIDS

George C. Bond & Joan Vincent

Uganda, it has been suggested, has come to symbolize Third World disaster in its direst form. "Famine; tyranny; widespread infringements of human rights, amounting at times to genocide; AIDS; malaria; cholera, typhoid, and a massive breakdown of government medical services; corruption, black-marketeering, economic collapse; tribalism, civil war, state collapse" (Hansen and Twaddle, 1988, p. 1) have characterized that period of Uganda's history between the overthrow of Milton Obote in 1971 and the present. This chapter suggests something of the interdependence of these social pathologies through a preliminary account of conditions in rural southwest Uganda in 1988. Also, and more importantly, it emphasizes their historicity.

In the 1960s regionalism and ethnicism were frequently singled out to account for differences between districts or Ugandan peoples. Today, several trends have been observed that are common to all of them. We would argue that it is critically important not to assume the existence in Uganda of enduring infrastructural frailties (Banugire, 1989) but, instead, to recognize that the events of the past 17 years have force in their own right to fashion the social fabric and the lives of survivors.

The familiar continuities of infrastructure may be features of a longer-term analysis: for example, uneven regional development accompanying capitalist expansion, the construction of ethnicity in the service of colonial administration, and the public institutionalization of gender inequalities. But they are of less significance than the emergent social phenomena reported in recent surveys for the analysis of the immediate national and local present and its restructuring after more than half a generation of unchecked violence and war. Survival appears to have ironed out cultural and ethnic variation, for the present at least. This may relate to the lessening of competition at the state centre, the collapse of the export economy, the remodelling of the armed forces, or the greater awareness among Ugandans at all levels of society (as among academics) of global forces, their strengths and their fragilities.

This leads us to the second object of this chapter, which is to suggest the need to analyse the current social structure of Uganda's districts in the light not simply of local and national interests but of geopolitics.

113

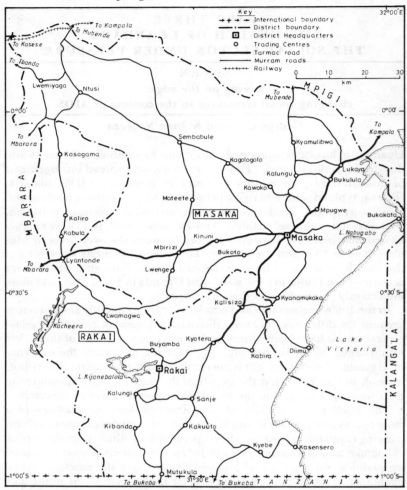

Map 3 *Masaka and Rakai Districts in Western Uganda*

The internationalization both of the Ugandan citizen's personal experience of the modern cosmopolitical system and of public relief measures for the amelioration of Uganda's ills have implications for centre-periphery relations within the nation, and for Uganda's sovereignty.

UGANDA: A SOCIAL PROFILE OF THE 1980s

Between September 1983 and July 1984 a comprehensive social survey was carried out in four districts in Uganda: Kigezi, Masaka, Busoga and

Living on the edge: changing social structures in the context of AIDS

Teso (Jaenson, Harmsworth, Kabwegyere and Muzaale, 1984). Inquiries were conducted in three locations in each of the districts. One of the locations thought to be in Masaka was actually in Rakai (then a comparatively newly created district) and we will refer to Masaka/Rakai.

Table 7.1 shows the composition of rural households in Masaka/Rakai in 1983–4. These trends are characteristic, with small local variations, of all four districts. Eight trends are singled out here because of their relevance for AIDS dispersion and intervention, their reflection of changes in the Uganda economy and their reflection of the effects of violence throughout the countryside.

(1) A significant trend towards one-person households of widows or widowers. The survey noted that these individuals' adult children had migrated in search of wage employment or better land.

(2) An increasing proportion of single-parent, especially female-headed households. This is exceptionally high (39 per cent) in the Masaka and Rakai localities, in part because one housed many of the girlfriends of *mafuta mingi* (literally 'those with much fat') who enriched themselves during Idi Amin's regime. Many of these women had been abandoned by their menfolk during the war (Jaenson, Harmsworth, Kabwegyere and Muzaale, 1984, p. 39).

(3) An increase in the number of grandchildren living with household heads. The survey explains the high figure for Masaka as due to 'the strong custom of all Ugandans of loving to live with grandchildren' and the 'more permissive attitude toward illegitimate children of their daughters and sons' (Jaenson, & c 1984, p. 53).

(4) A clear indication that polygamy accompanies wealth and that, in rural areas, the educated are more likely to be polygamous than the unschooled. They are also likely to travel more. The rate of polygamy was considerably lower in Masaka district than in the other three districts. This was attributed to 'accepted practice in Buganda for a household head to bring home to his housewife the children he had produced outside the home with . . . mistresses' (Jaenson, & c 1984, p. 50).

(5) Continuing heavy investment in education both in terms of cash for school fees and labour forgone. Rural households expected education to provide them with an escape from poverty.

(6) A marked decrease in the size of landholding per household since the Agricultural Census of 1982. Over half the respondents in the survey had fewer than five acres and over half that number probably had less than two acres.

(7) A substantial minority in all rural areas now depend on non-agricultural activities for their main source of income.

(8) Social welfare services have decreased everywhere. The survey attributes this to a lack of government expenditure and to the large

115

Table 7.1 Rural Household Composition in Masaka/Rakai, 1983–4

Ego-centred households	% of the total population
Lone householder	39
Lone householder with grandchildren	35
Lone householder with old parents	6
Total	80
Affinally-centred households	% of the households
Male householder, wife and children	66
Male householder, wives, and children	6
Plus adult sons	17
Plus adult sons and their wives	7
Total	96

number of qualified people who have left the country. From 1935 until the mid-1970s the Ministry of Health alone received between 7.5 and 10 per cent of the country's budget. In the early 1980s it received less than 3.5 per cent (Dodge, 1987, p. 102).

These findings reflect changes in the social structure of Uganda since the magisterial Agricultural Survey of 1962. Then, academics accounted for differences between districts in terms of regional development patterns and ethnic particularities. In the first half of the 1980s, similarities may be accounted for in terms of the black-market economy, state violence and civil war, and the entry of the new republic into a new, global arena.

THE *MAGENDO* ECONOMY

Underlying the development of this complex of social structural features was the emergent *magendo* economy which (as we can now see) provided the economic and communications infrastructure of AIDS in Uganda. Amin's economic policy froze agricultural prices, drawing a large proportion of crops into a black market, including the market garden products of southwest Uganda on which Kampala relied (Green, 1981; Sathyamurthy, 1986; Banugire, 1987, 1989). The *mafuta mingi* were then able to spread *magendo* into the primary food-producing sector of the economy (with the active encouragement of the state) by gaining a monopoly over road transportation (Sathyamurthy, 1986, p. 677ff.). Crops were purchased where they were grown and then transported to *magendo* compounds where they were sold at a huge black-market profit. This, along with the smuggling of coffee and gold out of the country, created a *magendo* economy heavily dependent on world capitalism. The profits from this external trade were invested in housing, commercial buildings, and land.

Aidan Southall has described how, in southwest Uganda, paraffin

116

Living on the edge: changing social structures in the context of AIDS
and sugar were smuggled to Tanzania in lorries mounted with sub-machine guns (1980, p. 647). Lake Victoria ports in Rakai changed almost overnight from remote fishing villages to thriving smuggling entrepôts with heavily armed, high-powered launches running coffee to the Kenya shores. A brief passage from Southall's 1980 account (pp. 646–7) sets the stage for the appearance and dispersion of AIDS in Uganda:

> The basic supply-route from the port of Mombasa, through Nairobi to Uganda, ran like a great artery of corruption from western Kenya to Kampala, on north to the Sudan, on west and south to Rwanda, Burundi and Zaire. Long stretches have been beaten to pieces as hundreds of huge trailer-trucks pound continuously up and down the roads. The tough drivers and crews, who are paid overtime and danger money, change their Kenya shillings at the border. They are often delayed for days, drinking in the bars, eating in the hotels – one plate of chicken for lunch costs 65/-, which is one quarter of the unskilled monthly wage – and sleeping in the brothels which line the route. From this main artery corrupting tentacles of the black market with its illicit deals and violent transactions penetrate into the Uganda countryside, pulling into its stream the desperate, the opportunistic, and the down-and-out.

AIDS IN UGANDA

AIDS is a disease that is numerically insignificant. In May 1988, 91,905 cases had been reported to the World Health Organization. Of these cases, 10,992 were from Africa, 68,338 from the USA, 241 from Asia, 11,445 from Europe, and 889 from Oceania (Mann, Chin, Piot and Quinn, 1988). The numerical insignificance of the disease is highlighted by the fact that the 11,000 cases reported from Africa represent 0.00002 per cent of its estimated population of 500 million. Concern over AIDS appears at first sight to be out of proportion to the present number of cases (Bond and Vincent, 1988).

The appropriateness of the concern lies in the fact that AIDS is incurable and has a devastating potential for human beings. The number of persons carrying the human immunodeficiency viruses (HIV-1 and 2) is unknown. It is estimated, however, that 'over 250,000 cases of AIDS have already occurred, that between 5 and 10 million people worldwide are infected with the AIDS virus and that within the next five years about one million new AIDS cases can be expected' (Mann, Chin, Piot and Quinn, 1988, p. 82). International agencies and the Uganda government deploy social scientists, to varying degrees, to establish areas of intervention for the purpose of prevention. The immediate solution appears to rest with behaviour change and not medical cures.

AIDS is also distinguished by characteristics that bring it directly into the domain of the social and cultural. There are no non-human vectors;

117

it is we who are the carriers and the active agents of its transmission and distribution. As an incurable disease transmitted primarily through sexual activity, it may affect our notions of ourselves and others as sexual, social, moral, and religious beings. It has practical economic and demographic consequences at the macro-dimensions of political economy and the micro-conditions of personal relationships. Global and national macro-economic and political factors affect the flow and movement of individuals, placing them in situations conducive to acquiring HIV. Some of these factors are related to ecology; modes of production; market forces; the movement of labour, goods and services; commerce and trade; violent upheavals; and the consequences of droughts and famine. Our perspective here is one that includes both the macro-dimensions of political economy and the micro-conditions of specific contexts. Notions of time, place and location are viewed as aspects of process. We found it necessary to recognize multiple spatial patterns in the distribution of AIDS, each one related to specific histories of movement. Uganda today reveals a layering of overlapping distributions. Finally, as a social disease, AIDS has a moral and a political dimension.

Uganda has been one of the few African countries to declare AIDS a national problem and open its doors to international agencies. This policy of openness and willingness to cooperate with international health agencies has produced a range of information on Uganda's health situation. In Uganda, AIDS is primarily a heterosexually transmitted disease that has a markedly higher distribution rate in certain localities, among certain occupations, and within specific age-ranges. At the moment these can be narrowly specified, but AIDS is a disease on the move, its progress unimpeded by all forms of boundaries.

The highest rates of AIDS in Uganda are in the south, where apparent stability and visible prosperity reflect vibrant industry among a population geared towards rehabilitation and development after years of civil strife. Yet, it needs to be stressed, AIDS is neither a regional nor, for that matter, a Ugandan problem. It is intimately tied into the international movement of labour, goods and services, commerce and trade, soldiers and pilgrims.

In Uganda, the head of the National AIDS Control Programme (NACP) vividly traced the movement of AIDS as it progressed from fishing village to small commercial centre to the capital. The first cases of AIDS appeared in 1982 in Goma, a small lakeshore village in Rakai. The following year AIDS appeared in Kyotera, and then in Masaka. As it progressed across southwestern Uganda, the number of cases increased month by month and year by year. When it reached Kampala, something of an explosion occurred; it was transmitted rapidly and the number of cases increased. Today, mortality from AIDS in the southwestern region is explained by the local people in terms both of its movement

118

along trade routes and of local sons, engaged in migrant and more permanent labour in the cities, 'coming home to die'.

In a speech to the US House of Representatives Select Committee on Hunger, Ambassador Kibedi (1988) observed that 'indications are that cases are doubling every six months. The increase has risen from 17 cases in 1983 and 29 in 1984 to 2,700 by December 1987'.[1] The disease has thus moved along the commercial and trading routes into main population centres, increasing in scale as it progresses. By 1988, its impact was also being felt among the young urban middle-class, and government policy was gearing up to a fresh assault on AIDS, assisted by new proposals for intervention, mainly in the form of education, from the international agencies.

The extension and proliferation of AIDS in Uganda is an unintended consequence of the macro-order of international political and economic relations. Yet, it has an immediate effect on the everyday activities of specific regions and localities, affecting how individuals conduct their daily lives. It is to this that we now turn.

THE FIELD LOCALE: RAKAI, 1988

The report that follows focuses on the east of Rakai district, south of Kalisizi trading centre, and the west of the district, between Kyotera and Rakai town.[2] At the southern edge of Uganda on the Tanzanian border, this small district is now at the heart of international attention.

The metalled road from Masaka to Kyotera has few stopping places along it. The road from Kyotera to Mutukula (on the Tanzanian border) is a dirt road that is now being rehabilitated by China Sitco, a Republic of China construction company under contract to the government. Modern hotels have recently been built at the junction of the highway with the Rakai Town road. These have among their clientele Western journalists and international AIDS agency officials. A small settlement, Kibale, has developed at the junction of the highway with the dirt road from the Lake Victoria fishing village of Goma – known to the media as Kasensero, a name also used by AIDS Control Programme (ACP) personnel.

The first 'Slim' disease/AIDS cases to be recognized came from Goma, a village of some 30 wooden shacks quite unlike the stone or mud and wattle housing of most of Rakai's population. Of the first 15 traders tested for evidence of HTLV-III antibodies, ten were positive. These admitted to heterosexual and homosexual casual contacts (Serwadda, Sewankambo, Carswell, *et al.*, 1985, p. 852). By May 1988, 181 cases (3.8 per cent of the total for Uganda) had been reported from Rakai. Goma itself is a port to which traders and smugglers come from Tanzania and Kisumu in Kenya, as well as from other Ugandan lakeshore

119

villages. This is the locality where, it is said, 'it all began' (Personal communications; Hooper, 1987; Caputo, 1988).

The road from Goma to Kibale junction passes through a string of villages that are strikingly similar in their appearance and physical plan. They consist of a series of structures strung out along the dirt road: small, well-stocked stores, and two or more 'hotels', which served food and beverages and provided a resting place for travellers and the steady stream of traders between Goma and Kyotera and Masaka. Always, too, in each village and alongside the road that linked them were dwellings with closed shutters and derelict forecourts – all too visible an indicator of the 'plague' that had struck the area. From inquiries about their owners and what had happened to their families, we were able to reconstruct the process by which AIDS was devastating Rakai.

Trade along the Goma–Kibale–Kyotera–Masaka–Kampala route is conducted by bicycle traders and heavy trucks. The last eight miles of the 15 mile feeder road from the highway junction to Goma has been torn up by the huge trucks owned by traders from Masaka, who are among the wealthiest in Uganda. Local truckers are more likely to employ bicycle traders (many of them young men and boys from Kyotera) to traverse the now poor road surface, transferring their goods at Kyotera onto Kampala-bound trucks. Although traders have asked the government to repair the road, locals believe the requests are being ignored in order to put an end to smuggling.

People in Rakai speak of Slim/AIDS being found on one side of the highway (the east) but not on the other (the west). They also speak of the disease having been introduced by the Tanzanian army. The disease's concentration along the main communications arteries has certainly been reported. Yet, because of the openness of the border and the easy passage of family members, migrants and bicycle traders from one side to the other, as well as the widespread distribution of small markets in roadside settlements away from the main trucking routes, it is now likely that the disease is much more widely found than clinical studies show. The presently understood distribution of AIDS in Rakai District may well be a function of the sampling and survey methods used.

The Rakai region has a long history of labour movement from Tanzania, Rwanda, Burundi, and other parts of Uganda. In 1950 Audrey Richards carefully documented the routes used by some 62,000 immigrants and 52,300 emigrants entering and leaving Buganda (Richards, 1954). Sixty-six per cent of the immigrants were from Rwanda and Tanganyika. The main destinations for these labour migrants and sojourners were Mutukula and Kyotera in Rakai, and Masaka and Kampala. At that time the system of public and private transport was poorly developed and large numbers made the journey on foot. Many of them are now among the grandparental generation in today's Rakai, and their family networks and social ties continue to foster movement throughout the region. It is somewhat ironic that Richards is already quoting the 1927 annual report of the Uganda Protectorate's medical department to report 'the devastating and increasing diseases which threaten every caravan and trade route' (Richards 1954, p. 58). More recently, Louise Pirouet (1988) began to document the chaotic movement of refugees, and particularly Rwandans, in the Masaka and Rakai regions during the past 17 years. About 80 per cent of the people of Buwunga sub-county were born in the area, made up of people of Baganda, Banyarwanda, and Banyankore/Bakiga extraction.

Quite clearly, Tanzania, Rwanda, Kenya, and even Zaire and Zambia should be included in any assessment of AIDS in Rakai, Masaka, Kampala and other parts of Uganda. Their inclusion is largely related to patterns of population movements reflecting economic activities that distribute and bring individuals together. Traders from Zambia purchase goods in Rwanda and refresh themselves at 'hotels' and bottle stores on the long journey home; Zairean prostitutes and Rwandan migrant labourers seek employment in the cities and on sugar and tea plantations in Uganda, desperately seeking a living wage that will permit them to make remittances to families at home; fishermen and traders ply the waters of Lake Victoria, crossing to and from lakeshore villages in Kenya, Tanzania and southern Uganda. Pastoralists move freely across the northern part of Tanzania and southwestern Uganda. Bukoba, the trading and commercial centre in western Tanzania, is known to have high rates of AIDS, and its traders move regularly across the border into Rakai. Truckers, traders, and travellers stop at 'hotels' in the small and large towns situated along the main thoroughfare from south to north. Add to this political tensions and expulsions within Uganda itself, many of them focusing on parochial and chauvinistic ethnic discrimination against such truckers, traders, and immigrant workers, and the transnational dimensions of AIDS becomes even more significant.

In the press and in popular opinion AIDS is particularly associated with Rakai although, as we found, more cases have actually been reported from neighbouring Masaka and from Kampala. Two journal articles with worldwide distribution (Hooper, 1987; Caputo, 1988) have served to focus attention particularly on Rakai. In an article published in *African Affairs*, Hooper reported that 76 per cent of the prostitutes tested in Rakai in 1987 proved to be carriers of the antibody to the HIV virus, as were 33 per cent of the truck drivers passing through the district. Photojournalist Robert Caputo's article in the *National Geographic* focused on Kyotera. Fear now exists in several areas where international AIDS agencies have been working in Rakai and we found in certain locations (and specifically in Goma) extreme alienation and opposition to clinical research into the disease. Notoriety is itself becoming a factor in the restructuring of the situation.

THE EFFECT OF WAR ON RAKAI DISTRICT

Military conflict, population dispersals, refugees, and the resurgence of diseases such as malaria and sexually transmitted diseases, AIDS and malnutrition figure prominently in the discourse of Rakai. The desire of Ugandans from all walks of life to discuss their personal and collective experiences of war lay very close to the surface in 1988. They talked of relatives, friends and neighbours who had fled into the bush only to confront armies on the move. The number of deaths from military and civil strife is hard to assess but the experience of wars and disease are uppermost in their minds. There is a clear sense of past devastation.[3]

Rakai is, indeed, a social landscape devastated by the shellings and bombardments of modern warfare. Whole towns and villages were razed to the ground and populations fled into the bush for months, even years, on end. Masaka and the district headquarters were extensively bombarded in the war of 1979. One of the fastest-growing towns in Uganda in the 1960s, its population was 640,596 in 1969. In 1980 it was 905,714. Amin's army invaded Tanzania to reclaim for Uganda the border area (the Kagera salient) in 1978. It was rebuffed and the Tanzanian army pursued his troops across the international boundary between the two countries, utterly destroying the border town of Mutukula en route. Many of the civilian population were killed and bulldozers flattened what remained. Rakai became a battleground for the two warring armies. After the successful overthrow of Amin in April 1979, Obote again formed a government. This was opposed in the southwest by the National Resistance Movement (NRM). Rakai rose to support the NRM and again became a battleground from 1981–5.

One may conjecture that the heaviest toll was among young men of military age throughout these 17 years. They were recruited into the armies and were thus the ones most likely to be killed in combat or in arbitrary attacks on civilian populations. These conditions might well have been conducive to 'sexual promiscuity' or temporary unions. Women might have had to rely more on older men and children for support than hitherto and themselves have engaged more in cash-earning activities. Since that time, rapid and marked inflation has characterized the re-establishment of a settled economy. Not until Yoweri Museveni took office in January 1986 did the people of Rakai consider life to have returned to normal.

The population of Rakai suffered considerably under Amin's regime (1971–9) although they believed that, by and large, atrocities were not committed among the rural population. They claim to have suffered more under Obote's second regime (1979–85) although there were no such massacres of the peasantry as in the Luwero triangle. Years of shelling, seeking refuge in the bush and supporting troops living off the land took their toll. The towns of Mutukula, Kyotera, Kalisizi and Masaka were flattened; most of the houses to be seen there date from 1980. Whereas Amin's troops kept to the highway, those of Obote and the Tanzanian army spread through the countryside. Schools, convents, and the homes of wealthy families were first occupied and then looted by the troops. Women were raped, and men, women and children killed. Graffiti and graves are today's reminders of past war.

It is important to recognize, however, that even during these extended periods of military strife and upheaval the basic source of food, the banana groves, were not destroyed. The resilience of the south is attributable to this fact: no scorched earth policy was put into effect. Through the entire period of military activity the banana groves remained intact. This feature of the natural order is in stark contrast to the social and personal dramas that marked everyday life. AIDS in southwest Uganda is one more disruption in an enduring landscape. The picture is likely to be very different in the north and northeast of Uganda, where AIDS exists in a context of civil strife, disorder and famine that is today utterly destroying all means of livelihood for a population made up almost entirely of pastoralists and millet farmers.

For many in Rakai, AIDS was simply yet another disaster that had befallen the region. The number of known deaths attributed to the disease was negligible compared with the mortality of men, women, and children during the fighting between 1978 and 1986. The impression we gained from our field trip to Rakai was in line with the findings of Sarah Forster and Kemlin Furley, whose mimeographed report (1988) we read on our return. They found that in Kigezi district and Kampala AIDS was mentioned as a problem by only 4 per cent of the rural villagers interviewed; by 2 per cent of those living in Kabale Town; and by 5 per cent of those in Kampala. Poverty, other diseases (malaria, measles, typhoid and tuberculosis) and high school fees caused more concern than AIDS. 'The majority,' they reported, 'regarded AIDS as just another disease which would take its toll like all the others before a cure was found. Such fatalism,' they concluded, 'is not unjustified; in many ways it reflects reality in a country where many people are dying from other diseases and in civil war. But what the survey does show is that where people do see there is a choice between an early death and a way of avoiding it, most are interested in opting for the latter' (Forster and Furley, 1988, p. 7).

AIDS AS PROCESS

AIDS mortality has had an impact on societal patterns in spite of its comparatively short period of recognition. This situation is particularly apparent in customs and rituals related to death and burial. Bodies are

123

usually buried within a day or two of death, which allows little time for kin to come from a distance to funeral and mourning ceremonies. They are attended more by immediate neighbours and friends. They mostly take place in the early evening and several might be attended in one evening at neighbouring homesteads. It is the cumulative effect of AIDS mortalities (i.e. several occurring in one village, or several occurring in one week) that brings home the enormity of AIDS to the people.

In response to direct inquiry, we were told that families took in and cared for AIDS sufferers and, after their deaths, their children. Widows and their children continued to live in the houses of the deceased, using the *matoke* that surrounded them. Some might continue to use the subsistence staple while choosing to live elsewhere (presumably with their own consanguine kin). An increase in the number of female-headed households was certainly reflected in the survey referred to earlier.

Indirectly, however, we learnt of cases where widows with very young children (i.e., those not well established as affines in their husband's kin group, or those with no grown children whose labour was valued) might be forced to leave. It would be unlikely that such a woman could remarry. Some might sell sexual favours, having no other means of livelihood and child support. Sometimes children were left abandoned by the roadside or at the doors of schools and hospitals. This was clearly related not solely to AIDS and orphans but to children 'unwanted' because there was no means of supporting them. The problem of the care of children and their mothers was considered by Rakai's district administrator to be a major issue.[4] It is spoken of as Child Survival.

Since AIDS was first recognized in Rakai in 1982 it has come to be appreciated that only male children aged 5–15 and female children aged 5–12 formed a 'safe' cohort within the population. These children have now reached the age of sexual maturity. Many of those whose parents have died are now being cared for by old people. This, too, would appear to be reflected in the survey. Many of the guardians lack access to funds, having recourse only to the subsistence economy and the compassion of neighbours. Given the practice of a girl receiving 'presents' from a sexual partner, it seems likely that this category of orphan will also engage in 'promiscuous sexual activity' or 'prostitution'. The process of AIDS transmission has thus entered for the first time upon its reproductive phase.

The domestic industrial revival we observed in Rakai in 1988 was related not simply to economic inflation but to the cash needs of these two sectors of the population – the very old and the very young. Woven mats, baskets, pots, and wooden bedframes and tables were offered by the roadside along the entire 110 miles from Kampala to Rakai. AIDS mortality among the 15–45 male and female cohort has robbed old people of the children they had thought would support them in their declining years. They incur the expenses of funerals; they may incur the expenses of raising their grandchildren and those of friends and neighbours. They are likely to lack both a labour force made up of kin to maintain banana and coffee plantations, and cash to employ one. Where child labour is employed (as in Rakai, where truckloads of children were transported to work) children are being deprived of the schooling that would enable them to get better jobs. They are also being deprived of the AIDS-related health education programmes being given in primary schools, which appear to be the most hopeful form of AIDS intervention in Uganda so far.

The social implications of AIDS are apparent even in patterns of marriage. We observed the celebration of a mass wedding ceremony to mark the end of the Marian year. This was held for 86 couples at Kitaredde parish church, just north of Kyotera. A few young people exchanged vows, but most were partners in common-law unions who were choosing to sanctify their relationships. All were testimony to the persuasive campaign of the Church in Uganda encouraging Catholics to 'love faithfully' which stood in contradistinction to the admonition of the Aids Control Programme to 'love carefully'.

But the mass ceremony revealed more than this. We were struck by the number of elderly or old men marrying young brides. It may be assumed that some were men of moderate wealth or standing who chose girls they thought to be free of AIDS. Some might be polygamous second or third marriages, the older or senior wife welcoming both the solidarity of gender and the additional labour under circumstances in which AIDS was likely to have struck down the cohort of the population that formerly provided domestic agricultural workers, male and female. There may also be an increasing shortage of suitable young partners, given the apparent tendency for AIDS mortalities to nucleate. In all societies, geographical contiguity plays a large part in the selection of mates. In Rakai, a young virgin may come from a locality in which most eligible partners have died (i.e., where there is heavy labour migration or an infected 'prostitute'). Such young women might welcome marriage (as might their parents) to wealthy, elderly men. Yet ethnographic evidence suggests that when old men are unable to satisfy the sexual needs of young wives, the girls will turn to young lovers. In Rakai and Kampala, we were given to understand, a world of sexual 'corners' and 'tricks' opened up before every adolescent, male and female, and tempted every man and woman, married and unmarried. Premarital sexual experience was valued and extramarital sexual adventures expected. Should such winter–spring marriages become the norm, a new at-risk population would be in the making.

THE RESPONSE OF THE CATHOLIC CHURCH IN RAKAI
Various religious organizations in Uganda have long tried to curb the behaviour that spreads the AIDS virus. Today, sermons preach with renewed force the dangers of sexual promiscuity, urging members of the congregation to mend their ways. The AIDS Bible is used ecumenically. The population of southern Rakai is predominantly Roman Catholic. The recent rise in popular religious activity and enthusiasm there is not expressed in a proliferation of independent African churches, prophets and ritual practitioners, as is common elsewhere in the continent, but appears to be contained within the religious framework of the Catholic Church. The Church is carefully and self-consciously monitoring, evaluating, and regulating local religious manifestations, such as 'seers', visionaries, and spiritual herbalists (or 'witch doctors' and 'finders'). It has contained the contending cross-currents of beliefs and explanations, allowing notions of pragmatic science and religious mysticism to coexist within the single moral and spiritual order of the Church.

The Catholic Church has recognized the physical, social and moral disruption of war and disease and is attempting to provide medical treatment alongside spiritual and moral leadership and guidance. Through its hospitals and dispensaries it has provided Western medical facilities and treatment and through the activities of Brother Anatoli of the Bannakaroli Brothers in Kitaredde and his staff it has encouraged the use of herbal treatments, hygiene, and instruction about the body and the spread of diseases.

Brother Anatoli does not only explore the medical properties of local plants. He also demonstrates that the efficacy of herbs in treating diseases and their symptoms is unrelated to indigenous religious beliefs. He holds that the efficacy of herbal medicines stems neither from the powers of the ritual practitioner nor indigenous deities, but from the intrinsic medical properties of the herbs, and the knowledge and skills of the herbalist. The zeal with which he pursues his herbalist vocation has led to intense skirmishes with indigenous local practitioners. These concern not only mundane properties of herbal medicines and treatments but also controversies over the nature of explanations, epistemology, and morality or the moral life. It was surely no accident that Brother Anatoli was invited to conduct the mass wedding ceremony, which brought together priests, nuns, and parishioners from churches throughout the parish. Brother Anatoli has extended his activities to Kampala where he dispenses herbal medicines to a large number of patients. He is a public figure with ties into Uganda's southern intellectual elite.

The type of medical, social and moral issues raised by Brother Anatoli and his practice are also expressed in the rise of the Catholic parish of Mbuye as an international centre of spiritual healing and religious

Living on the edge: changing social structures in the context of AIDS
pilgrimage.[5] In 1987 a young Catholic woman living in Rwanda called Spacioza apparently claimed a vision from the Virgin Mary, instructing her to leave her home and go to a small Catholic parish in Uganda. Spacioza selected the parish of Mbuye and settled there in November 1987. She was the first of several women seers to claim visions and messages from the Virgin Mary. They proclaim that the Blessed Virgin is concerned about AIDS and through them delivers messages preaching sexual chastity and morality, and warning that sexual promiscuity will lead to death through AIDS.[6]

Mbuye has a number of contradictory features. It is the centre of a religious and moral revival, and yet it attracts large numbers of pilgrims, many of whom avail themselves of the more worldly activities of the booths and markets set up directly across the road from the parish church, shrines, and sacred enclosure. Prostitutes were available in the market areas; religious festivals may therefore not only be a source of morality, but also provide for the dissemination of AIDS.

These two examples – the activities of Brother Anatoli and those surrounding the Mbuye seers – point to the parochialism and yet international sophistication of Rakai. They illustrate the ability of the Roman Catholic Church (itself an international organization) to absorb and contain local, popular religious movements. They also suggest the strength of ties among local and regional elites and the relationship of these elites to those of Kampala. The regional ties take on a political meaning when one realizes that many of the officers of the resistance councils (RCs) are also important Church laymen. Thus AIDS has facilitated a resurgence, if not a renewal, of Catholic ties after their attenuation during the Amin and Obote regimes. It has empowered the elite with a cluster of moral and religious issues that transcend ethnic parochialism and establishes its concern with the plight of all humanity. Through Brother Anatoli's herbalist activities and the Church's hospitals and dispensaries, the elite is on the side of science, technology, rehabilitation, and development. Through its sponsorship of the Mbuye seers, it has become the arbiter and controller of popular religious movements.

CONCLUSION

This chapter inquires into the social conditions in Rakai that need to be understood to supplement clinical inquiries into AIDS among the population, and to provide for informed preventative intervention. Since our visit, legal measures have been introduced in Uganda to extend greater protection to minors, and in France and the USA hopes have been raised for medical advances.

Some of our findings have implications for other regions of Uganda, and particularly for the northeast, where military conflict, malnutrition, starvation, and an absence of medical facilities remain the order of the

The health of Ugandans: the social sector under pressure

day. We found in Uganda in 1988 an international spatial orientation
that minimizes the north and northeast even while it extends the purview
of the south to the Middle East, Europe and the USA. The urbane parochialism of the south is contained not only in AIDS but also in commerce
and education. AIDS, especially, is a further renewal of international
ties and, at the same time, the circumscription of local particularistic
relations. Too heavy a burden for the existing support system to maintain, AIDS has brought southern Uganda back into the international
community.

The two central theoretical and methodological issues raised by
our field inquiry remain to be addressed more widely. First, the need to
recognize as an historical and social condition the effects of war and its
aftermath on a population and region, even if this means setting aside,
for the short term, the concepts and constructs of an earlier academic era.
And, secondly, the need to build into any analysis of structural adjustment and revolutionary change in Uganda a full accounting of their
geopolitical dimensions.

Notes

---

1. This quote is derived from a public address made by Ambassador Wanume Kibedi to
the United Nations. The figures provided in this paper are from public documents and
thus fully available to those concerned with the study of AIDS.
2. A brief trip was made to Rakai in August–September 1988 as team members of the
International Advisory Group, HIV Center for Clinical and Behavioral Studies, New
York State Psychiatric Institute and Columbia Presbyterian Medical Center. The group
is conducting anthropological research in the USA (Dr Ida S. Susser), the Dominican
Republic (Dr John Kreniske) and Uganda (Dr George C. Bond and Dr Joan Vincent).
3. A methodological point needs to be made here to support historians Michael Twaddle
(1986) and Shula Marks (1986) in their calls for a more dialectical form of inquiry, looking at alternative viewpoints, exploring the dialectical relationship between the researcher and the world in which we live and act. Anthropologists also recognize the need
constantly to bring together 'structure and meaning, process and consciousness, to
engage in a constant dialogue with empirical data and theory, and to use the former to
refine and modify the latter' (Marks 1986, p. 175). Nevertheless, one should, perhaps,
beware of too whole-hearted a commitment to the Histoire Immediate that emerged out
of the Congo crisis. Anthropologists, as they set out to historicize Masaka/Rakai's
experience, might also be more concerned to take up a comparative perspective, viewing
Uganda alongside Northern Ireland or Lebanon, in studying the effects of prolonged
violence and war.
4. The District Administrator of Rakai listed as her development priorities in the district,
boreholes; improving health; orphans; education; and income generating activities for

women. She called for practical assistance, not research, and for technological assistance and programs, not personnel.

5. It was the signatures in the visitors book at Mbuye that first alerted us to a new parochialism among our hosts and respondents. The furthest point north they ever mentioned was Hoima. Yet, they often referred to places in the USA, Europe and the Middle East as well as places nearer home in Tanzania, Kenya, Rwanda and Zaire.

6. Many of the Bannakarole Brothers, the guardians of the Mbuye seers, attribute the cause of AIDS to man's failure to adhere to biblical commandments related to adultery and sexual promiscuity. They view AIDS as a punishment, similar to the great biblical flood, sent by God to punish man for his failure to pursue a moral life. They did, however, stipulate their understanding of its spread into southwestern Uganda, namely, through the sexual practices and movements of traders and soldiers.

EIGHT
Medicines and self-help:
the privatization of health care in eastern Uganda

Susan Reynolds Whyte

The breakdown of government health services in Uganda has been documented by Dodge & Wiebe (1985), but little has been written about the explosive growth of private biomedical care in the troubled years since 1971. The Report of the Health Policy Review Commission of 1987 (pp. xv–xvi) underlines its significance:

> When Government Health Units were functioning well in the 1960s Private Practice was on small scale, but as the services deteriorated and the economic conditions became severe . . . private clinics, Medical laboratories, and Pharmacies mushroomed all over the country, involving even the health personnel employed in Government. The general breakdown of law and order in the country made it impossible to enforce statutory controls laid down in the various Acts governing health. Although good private practice is a very important service to the population, the existence of many illegal private clinics and the indiscriminate peddling of drugs by unqualified persons pose a threat to the lives of the people of Uganda.

This chapter describes the privatization of biomedicine in a part of Tororo district in eastern Uganda,[1] emphasizing the significance of Western pharmaceuticals in the transformation of the social relations of healing. Although there are many examples of misuse of medicines, the issues involved in privatization are not simply negative ones of state breakdown and lack of control. The processes I describe are examples of local initiative and self help and they have implications that go beyond health care.

BACKGROUND

In the 1960s Uganda had one of the best health care delivery systems in Africa (Dodge, 1987, p. 105). Drugs were available without charge at government health facilities, which were heavily attended. During the Amin years, hospitals were critically affected by the expulsion and emigration of trained personnel; from 1968 to 1974 the number of doctors dropped from 978 to 574, and pharmacists from 116 to 15 (Scheyer & Dunlop, 1985, p. 34). For rural health centres and dispensaries, which never had resident doctors or pharmacists, lack of medicines seems to have been the most severe problem. A recent WHO report (1988)

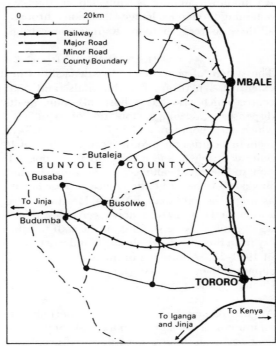

Map 4
Bunyole County

estimates that attendance at government health units dropped by half from 1976/77 to 1988, and attributes this to 'gross shortages of drugs'.

An Essential Drugs Programme was initiated by UNICEF in 1981; in 1985 DANIDA provided funds through the Danish Red Cross for an Essential Drugs Management Programme (EDMP). Drug kits are now being distributed to 809 rural health facilities (including non-governmental ones) and kits are also being supplied to the out-patient departments of 49 government hospitals and 31 run by non-governmental organizations. Although many health units complain that supplies are still insufficient, the senior pharmacist advisor in the EDMP asserts that enough drugs are now being provided to the rural health units and that there would be no shortage of essential drugs at rural facilities were medicines properly managed.

In addition to the Essential Drugs kits, there are other sources. Central Medical Stores in Entebbe provides medicine for hospitals and some for lower-level facilities. Joint Medical Stores supplies mission facilities, and many of them also receive donations of medicines from abroad. A para-statal, Uganda Pharmaceuticals Ltd, sells medicines to licensed drug outlets, and several private firms import medicine for sale to retailers.

An unknown amount is smuggled in, thus avoiding the difficulties of obtaining foreign exchange allocations through official channels. Given all these sources, there are a great many drugs available in Uganda.

GOVERNMENT MEDICINE IN 1989

The system of government health facilities in Tororo district is fairly extensive. There are four hospitals (and a trypanosomiasis research centre which also has a hospital), nine health centres, and 22 sub-dispensaries, serving a population of about 700,000. In Bunyole county, which has a population of 75,000, there has been a substantial improvement in facilities since Amin's coup in 1971. A 100-bed hospital has been built at Busolwe, and a sub-dispensary opened at Nabiganda, in addition to the old health centre at Butaleja and the sub-dispensary at Bugalo (Busaba). But attendance at these facilities is not nearly as heavy as might be expected. Butaleja Health Centre used to have 300–500 patients a day in 1970; it now receives less than 100. On the day I visited it, 12 patients were waiting for the staff to come on duty at 10am, a far cry from the crowds we always found when we brought sick people there in 1969–71.[2] Admission of inpatients is far under capacity. Butaleja is supposed to have 30 beds (including maternity); 15 are in working order (though without mattresses), but only four to eight were being used. Most of the beds at Busolwe Hospital were empty when I was there in August. Although there has been a decline in measles admissions since an immunization campaign a couple of years ago, morbidity in general does not seem to have gone down. If people are not making heavy use of government facilities, it is not because they are healthier.

Complaints about service at the government units are legion. Patients have to wait for hours. Staff members do not report for duty on time and do not give adequate attention to patients. They demand money for services that are supposed to be free. One man claimed that a hernia operation at Tororo Government Hospital cost UShs5,000 by the time one reckoned 'tea' for porters, payments to nurses, something for the surgeon, etc. The price at St Anthony's, a private mission hospital in the same town, was only half that, although it was officially a fee-for-service hospital, while the government one was ostensibly free.

Medicines were a major point of discontent. Often patients were told that medicines were out of stock; they were advised either to return another day or to purchase medicines privately. Some people believed that medicines given at government facilities were diluted; a health centre staff member asserted that her colleagues diluted the PPF for injections.

The Uganda Essential Drugs Management Programme recently completed an analysis of material on use of five drugs selected for monitoring at 99 government health units. When the amount of drugs

132

delivered was compared with the patient registers and the drugs remaining in stock for given periods, it was found that one third of drugs were unaccounted for (*Findings 1986–9*). As the report suggests, there are several possible explanations. One is 'misappropriation'. I think there can be little doubt that large amounts of government drugs find their way out of health facilities through 'informal' channels. It is difficult to estimate this flow. The EDMP analysis was based on the patient registers kept by health staff. But several people indicated to me that these are sometimes padded; names and prescriptions can be entered although the patient is told that the drugs are out of stock.

The criticisms and condemnations of the government health system are voiced by staff as well as patients. Many health workers still hold to an ideal of how the service should function and sigh over the lack of discipline and private appropriation of government resources. But they shrug and ask: 'What to do? We have to live.'

When I left eastern Uganda at the end of August 1989, the Ministry of Health staff had not yet been paid for April, June or July, let alone August. When salaries do come, they are impossibly low. Group employees (porters, dressers and nursing aides) get UShs1,500 a month, enough to buy three kilos of sugar in Busolwe. Enrolled midwives and nurses receive between UShs2,000 and UShs3,000, the price of a bunch of *matoke* (cooking bananas) in Tororo market. Yet, remarkably, people still come to work and many patients still receive free medicine at government health units. I heard several stories of workers who did *not* demand 'tea' or steal medicines. The person in charge of one health unit remarked pointedly that it was curious that extra medicines were never used at night when the *mulokole* ('saved') nurse was on duty.

How do health personnel manage? Some obtain land and cultivate; I heard complaints about a medical assistant who was always in the swamp working on his rice. At one large facility, the staff had worked out a rota for brewing millet beer to sell. A nurse sold *enguli* (homemade rum) from her staff quarters. Government cars and bicycles could be used to earn money. But of course the most obvious way for a health worker to survive is to use his position; that is, to draw upon his experience, his contacts and his access to medicines.

PRIVATIZATION

A simple way to do this is to ask for payment for services rendered in the government facility. This can be done on an institutional basis, when workers agree among themselves to charge and share the money. I heard of one health centre, for example, that was approached by the local resistance council (RC) with the demand that treatment should be given free as it used to be; the staff refused. Busolwe Hospital has an outpatient arrangement for 'Grade A patients'; those who are prepared to pay

UShs100 for faster service. More commonly, however, individual workers get money as they can from individual patients. These transactions are variable and difficult to quantify, but are mentioned in several reports (Kinuka *et al.*, 1985; Kironde, 1985; Odurkene, 1988).

Proposals are under discussion to initiate registration fees for outpatients at all government health facilities: UShs200 at hospitals and UShs100 at health centres. This would be an effort at 'cost recovery'; the idea is that it would help to finance the services. But it must be set against the fact that many patients are already paying at government health facilities and may have to continue to do so.

Another common form of privatization is that health workers give treatment in their own homes; some do this after retirement, but others engage in home private practice while still in government service.

The most conspicuous indications of privatization, however, are the private clinics and drug shops that have mushroomed in the rural areas. Nearly every trading centre now has at least one clinic being run by a government health worker who has rented premises where people come for examination and treatment. Many have drug shops as well. In 1971 there were no private facilities in Bunyole county; today there are at least 11 private clinics and four drug shops, despite the fact that government facilities have also increased substantially.

This is typical of other parts of Tororo district I was able to visit, and of the country as a whole. A survey carried out by the Uganda Red Cross in 1985 showed that 41 per cent of those who sought treatment in rural areas went to private clinics or drug stores, while 47 per cent went to government centres and 10 per cent to mission facilities (Kinuka *et al.*, 1985, p. 9).

Before 1971, private clinics, many of them run by Asian doctors, were only found in towns like Tororo and Mbale. In eastern Uganda the boom in rural private clinics and drug stores seems to have occurred in the mid-1980s. The first clinic in Busolwe opened in 1984, in Nagongera in 1985. The Health Policy Review Commission also reports that the trend towards part-time private practice by government health workers 'worsened in the 1980s when even unqualified personnel started operating clinics and laboratory services which have mushroomed in the whole country' (Report . . . 1987, p. 82).

Why did privatization receive such an impetus at this time? The Commission mentions two factors: health workers' need to survive economic hardships, and the failure of government health services 'because of deteriorating physical facilities and shortage of funds to purchase adequate drugs and medical supplies' (*ibid.*). There is no doubt about the first factor. But as to shortage of medicines, it is striking that the supply of drugs to the government system was actually improving at the time when so many clinics and drug shops began to appear. The Essential

Drugs Programme started in 1981. In the report of the evaluation of 1984, Mburu (1985, p. 90) gives information about the availability of drugs in health centres.

> Antibiotic capsules and injectables disappear from stocks at a much faster rate than do others. However, in visits to local pharmacies near each health centre, I found the drugs in short supply at the health centres well stocked. It is thought that shortage of these items in the public sector may be related to supply in the private sector. But there was no easy way of identifying during the field visit whether or not the drugs came from the health centre.

The point I would stress is that whether or not drugs pass directly from a health centre to the shop next door, the total supply of drugs to Uganda increased in the 1980s, so that more drugs became available, through one channel or another, for sale in clinics and shops. Stock (1985, p. 129ff) has come to similar conclusions about Nigeria.

A clinic is supposed to be licensed by the Uganda Medical Council. Only a doctor may obtain a licence and this permits examination, prescription and dispensing of medicine, but not retailing of drugs. The DMO makes recommendations on licensing and is responsible for inspecting clinics. While a clinic is supposed to be run by a doctor, a dispensary may be operated by a medical assistant, and a maternity home by an enrolled midwife; but both of these must be supervised by a doctor whose name is registered as Visiting Physician. Pharmacies are licensed by the Uganda Pharmaceutical Board, on the recommendation of the DMO. They may not examine, prescribe or treat. No special training is required to sell class C drugs (proprietary drugs like Aspro, Malaraquin, etc.), but only a pharmacist should be allowed to sell class A and B drugs.

These rules bear some relationship to reality, which is surprising since there are almost no mechanisms for enforcing them. The licensed clinics and drug shops are registered in the names of doctors. (There are only 45 pharmacists in the entire country [Report 1987:50], so the requirement that a pharmacy be operated by a pharmacist is unrealistic.) In a number of cases individual doctors had several licences, but I did not find any case in which a doctor actually supervised the daily operation of his facilities. With one exception, the doctors who held licences did not live in Tororo district; one was working in Nairobi, several were in Kampala, or in neighbouring districts. The visiting doctor for one maternity home had gone to the UK for further studies.

In some instances the doctor actually owned the business, paying a salary to the people operating it. In others it seems that the owners paid the doctor a fee for being allowed to register under his name. Workers in these places tended to have experience, if not formal training, in

135

government health facilities. Many were simultaneously employed in hospitals and health centres. Other drug shops and clinics were not licensed; these tended to be owned by medical assistants, but they might employ people with less medical training to actually run the business. I visited clinics that were being operated by nurses' aides, dressers, and porters, yet many others had medical assistants and nurses in place. At one extreme was a clinic in a very small trading centre, owned by the medical assistant at a health centre in the same county. It was being operated by two young girls who had no experience in health work and were being 'trained on the job'. At the other extreme was a clinic on a main road owned by a doctor working in the MOH in another province. He had employed a retired senior medical assistant/anaesthetic assistant who was even able to do hernia repairs and other simple operations under local anaesthetic at the private clinic.

Health workers who combine private practice and government employment arrange suitable schedules. Several who worked at a hospital had 'special duty'; they worked nights only, and since there was usually little to do at night they could sleep, and be rested for work in their drug shop or private clinic during the day. Others had arrangements with colleagues who covered their private practice on the days when they worked in the hospital or health centre.

Wages for private sector health workers seem to be about twice the government wage for a given job category. Although these salaries still do not go far (one clinic worker pointed out that he had 12 children in school), at least they are paid on time.

The economics of these private clinics varied, but my impression is that a profit of UShs5,000–10,000 a month could be made. These are modest profits (UShs10,000 was worth US$50 at the official rate and US$17 at the parallel market rate in August 1989). In terms of buying power, the owner of a private clinic was worse off in 1989 than he had been when living on his government salary alone in 1971 (see M.A. Whyte, 1988 on the changed situation of the rural salariat). At one maternity home, the owner paid UShs5,000 in salaries to her two employees, and UShs3,000 in rent. In May and June 1989, the clinic had an income of UShs38,000 and UShs40,000 respectively. She estimates that 75 per cent of these proceeds went to buy drugs and other supplies. At a clinic owned and operated by a medical assistant, the average daily income was UShs800–1,000. His rent was only UShs1,000 (he had one room in a trading centre), so about UShs25,000 a month was left over, from which he had to buy medicines. The profitability of these ventures clearly depends on drugs expenditures.

Some medicines are obtained free from the government system. For example, a health worker might substitute empty vials for full ones when on night duty and record having given injections to fictitious patients. In

136

this way he is able to supply injectables to his own clinic. However, private practitioners seem to buy most of their medicines rather than stealing them personally, although the medicines they buy may well have been misappropriated by other health workers. I was told that prices were good in Entebbe, where drugs from Central Medical Stores were sold cheaply. Although drug vendors in the Mbale market display only proprietary drugs, inquiry revealed that they also sold antibiotics whole-sale. I was offered a tin of 1,000 ampicillin capsules for UShs18,000. Some of these drugs have undoubtedly been diverted from their intended uses. Karamojong are said to bring drugs to Mbale market that donors have sent to relief projects in Karamoja.

The parastatal, Uganda Pharmaceuticals Ltd, only sells to licensed drug shops. But these sometimes make purchases for unlicensed shops on commission. UPL has a branch in Mbale, but none of the clinics and drug shops visited in Tororo district relied exclusively on this source. Better prices are often to be had elsewhere, for example from private drug shops in Iganga, Tororo or Busia. Rice traders who go regularly to Jinja and Kampala bring back medicines. In general, private practitioners buy drugs where they have good contacts. One man told me that he bought in Mbale because he had friends there with whom he had trained as a medical assistant.

So far I have described private practice in which government health workers are directly involved. But there are other sources of drugs that must be mentioned before a discussion of how the public actually uses medicines. Some drug shops are owned and operated by people who have no training in medicine. More common still, many general shops sell a variety of pharmaceuticals including antibiotics. A shop may display only proprietary drugs, but if a customer asks for capsules, these are brought out from under the counter. In one case, a shopkeeper showed me a plastic sack full of many different kinds of capsules, from which the interested customer might choose. In other shops, especially in smaller trading centres, many different types of 'strong' drugs are displayed together with soap, batteries, bicycle spares and salt. In one such shop I saw tetracycline, Septrin, Flagyl, ampicillin, sulphadimidine, ephe-drine, mebendazole and Largactil, in addition to Andrew's Liver Salts, Ulax and Aspro. The vendors who sell drugs in markets may have some knowledge about what they are selling, but it is often gathered in a very haphazard manner and adjusted to notions of what the client might like and how much he can afford. 'Bush doctors', usually self-taught, give injections and sell medicines in the village. Most of these untrained people have connections to the formal medical system. Health workers sell them medicines; I saw containers with the EDMP mark, not in the health workers' own clinics and drug shops, but in the shops of untrained people. And some 'bush doctors' seek advice from trained people.

The health of Ugandans: the social sector under pressure

SERVICE IN THE PRIVATE SECTOR

Both patients and practitioners (also those concurrently holding jobs in the public sector) emphasized the convenience and superior quality of service in private clinics and drug shops as compared to government facilities. There is no long waiting time, practitioners are concerned and courteous, and patients are more certain of getting drugs. Many people feel that more competent treatment is given in private clinics.

> On one Monday morning in August, for example, I found 12 patients waiting in a private clinic in Busolwe; but the dresser who operated the clinic was hard at work and patients were moving through. A woman with a sick child came from the outpatient department at the hospital; she had given up waiting there, and besides, the severe abcess on her child's buttocks was the consequence of an injection received earlier from the hospital. Over at the outpatient department, I found 50–60 patients waiting. No one had received any medicine yet, although it was 10:30 in the morning.

Both private clinics and drug shops received patients who had gone first to government facilities and been told the necessary drugs were out of stock or who were dissatisfied with the treatment they have received. Not uncommonly, these patients brought their treatment slips ('Medical Form Five') to the private facility, either to ask for the medicine prescribed or to get another opinion as to the treatment.

Two patterns of service were offered both by private practitioners and vendors of medicine. They prescribed medicines for customers who did not know what treatment was needed, and they sold medicines to those who already knew what they wanted. That is to say, private clinics also retailed medicines, and drug vendors also prescribed treatments. In this section I will discuss prescription practices and in the next I turn to folk patterns of self-medication.

The skills brought to bear in private clinics are similar to those in government facilities, insofar as the same health workers are involved. Several reports have shown that prescription skills of medical and paramedical staff in the government system need to be improved. There are tendencies to give too many and inappropriate medications, and too many injections and unwarranted antibiotics (EDMP Findings 1986–9; Minde & Kalyesubula 1985). A systematic study of private clinics would probably reveal the same patterns. But other characteristics of private practice should be noted.

At private clinics, and even more commonly at drug shops, medicines may be given without seeing the patient. This is a great convenience for customers, and it is a carry-over of the pattern obtaining in the 'traditional' sector where diagnosis and prescription are frequently made without a physical examination of the sick person. But thoughtful practitioners realize the problems.

A man came into a private clinic in Busolwe saying his wife had abdominal pain and diarrhoea. The medical assistant gave him Panadol and Flagyl (an anti-bacterial and anti-protozoal, indicated for amoebic dysentery and certain abdominal and gynaecological infections). Afterwards he commented to me that abdominal pain is a very broad symptom – he did not really know what he was treating. But he had to give something. He says that at least 50 per cent of his customers are people coming on behalf of someone else. Often men come to get medicine for their wives. Men have the money and they want to show their wives that they care for them, '. . . but they don't really show that, because they don't bring them for proper examination . . . Now this man may go and buy drugs at a drug shop, and give his wife different medicines without ever getting to the root of the problem.'

At drug shops, inquiry is almost always made about the age of a patient, to avoid giving adult doses to children. But most sales are made rather quickly on the basis of the customer's spontaneous naming of the absent patient's symptoms, with no attempt to probe into the details of the sickness.

A man came into a drug shop saying, 'I have a patient at home who is bleeding too much.' The dresser who operated the shop asks, 'Why didn't you bring the patient? Do you have a syringe?' The customer affirms that he does and is sold a vial of injectable ergometrine and 15 Flagyl tablets. Afterwards the dresser says he assumes the woman has aborted. Ergometrine is given to stop uterine bleeding, and Flagyl is given for her abdominal pain.

A customer comes to the same shop saying, 'I have a child of 1½ years, who coughs too much.' Without further questioning, the dresser gives him chloramphenicol syrup and instructs him to give a teaspoonful three times a day for seven days.

The next point about private practice is that a wider variety of drugs is available here than in government outpatient facilities. The Essential Drug Kits contain 26 different medicines. All of these are available in the private sector, but this also carries many more. Government workers sometimes tell patients to go and buy drugs that are not included in the kit. In one case, for example, a man came with a 'Medical Form Five' for his one-year-old child, who was suffering from diarrhoea. At the hospital he had been given oral rehydration salts, which is the internationally accepted treatment. But the health worker had also written that he should buy Flagyl, which is definitely not recommended by the EDMP for routine treatment of childhood diarrhoea.

Drugs regularly prescribed in the private sector for common symptoms that are not included in the kits include phenylbutazone

(Butazolidin) given for backache (indicated for certain types of arthritis); Dapsone, which is crushed and put on wounds (indicated for leprosy); and chloramphenicol for diarrhoea (a strong antibiotic indicated for typhoid fever and certain kinds of meningitis).

A further characteristic of private practice is that prescriptions are adjusted to the customer's ability to pay.

> A man comes into a private clinic asking for Aspro and aspirin. The medical assistant asks how much money he has and the man lays a banknote on the table. When the practitioner explains that Aspro and aspirin are the same thing, the man asks for Nivaquine instead and is given four chloroquine to take at once. After he leaves, the medical assistant remarks that this is not a sufficient dose to treat malaria; but the man did not have enough money for the full course of chloroquine. Anyway, he added, he did not know whether his customer really had malaria; he just assumed so because the man had asked for Nivaquine.

In drug shops, people were seldom given a full course of antimalarials or antibiotics. If a customer did not want to spend more than a certain amount, he would lay his cash on the counter while describing the symptoms for which he needed medicine. This adjustment of treatment to pocketbook is of course even more marked in self-medication; people ask for the amount they can afford. They might ask 'Do you have tablets to stop diarrhoea? I want 60 shillings worth.' or 'I want white capsules. I have 80 shillings.'

In private practice, you must please the customer. While some trained health workers tried to maintain a certain professionalism, explaining to customers what they thought the proper treatment should be, they all had to try to attract and retain clients. Sometimes they seemed to put to the back of their minds what they had learnt during their training, as in the case above of the medical assistant, who knew that a patient should be examined in person, although he sold medicine to her husband anyway.

> A health visitor told of calling upon a friend, a nurse, who runs a drug shop in Tororo. A customer came in, wanting four tetracycline capsules. After he left, the health visitor asked why she had sold him only four. 'You're a nurse, you know that's an underdose.' The nurse replied, 'I can look at a customer and know whether he can afford a complete dose. Besides, if I don't sell to him, he'll go elsewhere. This is a business.'

Sometimes trained workers actually seemed to accept that folk practices, such as emptying the contents of capsules directly onto sores, were effective, even though this contradicted their earlier training. In many cases the omnipresence of this kind of 'knowledge' gradually affects other knowledge acquired long ago, and never refreshed with any follow-up courses.

Several times I encountered the popular conception that a mixture of different capsules and tablets was particularly efficacious. The attitudes of private practitioners to this notion are instructive. An untrained medicine vendor, who worked the weekly market in a small trading centre, usually prescribed a blend of drugs, because he thought this attracted customers.

> An old man came up to the vendor's stall, saying he had diarrhoea and chest pain. The vendor asks how much money he has, and the man gives him 200 shillings. The vendor sells him 2 penicillin V tablets, 2 Panadol, 2 Butazolidin, 2 ampicillin capsules, and 2 chloramphenicol capsules, with instructions to take them two by two, always pairing different types.

For other customers, he gave other combinations, advising that the tablets be pounded and mixed with the contents of the capsules, the mixture to be taken in spoonfuls over several days.

In contrast a trained nurse recounted her reaction to this folk practice of combining medicines.

> A man came into my drug shop, saying he had 'visited somewhere', and was now feeling headache and stomach ache. (He was probably afraid he had contracted gonorrhoea.) He asked for 2 ampicillin, 2 Septrin, 2 tetracycline, 2 chloroquine, 2 chloramphenicol and 2 aspirin. He started to crush the tablets and empty the capsules, and asked for a glass of water so he could take the mixture all at once. I told him to go home and take the medicine. Let him die from home, not from my shop!

She sold him the drugs, however.

PHARMACEUTICAL SELF-HELP

The ultimate in privatization is not the obvious mushrooming of private clinics but the tendency of people to avoid clinical relationships altogether by acquiring medicines and treating themselves. To a certain extent this reflects a 'family care' pattern in many African cultures; in Bunyole, experts did not have the authority and monopoly on knowledge that characterizes, for example, the European relation between doctor and patient. The family, not the specialist, had the primary responsibility to decide on a diagnosis and treatment (Whyte, in press). In Bunyole, everyone knows a few herbal medicines at least, so they can treat members of their own families. Within a neighbourhood, certain people have more specialized knowledge of herbs for specific symptoms, and they sell these for a small fee (Whyte, 1982). But herbal medicines have never been commodities to the extent that Western pharmaceuticals are. Even now, when a trend is developing to prepare, package and market 'African medicine' (*obulesi bw'ehimali*), there is no comparison between the booming business of a drug shop on market day and the leisured pace of the market stall selling herbal medicine.

The desirability of 'European medicine' is a mark of the earlier success of the government health system. And the wide availability of pharmaceuticals as ordinary commodities makes it possible for people to help themselves, now that the public system has deteriorated. By and large the people I spoke with in Tororo district were not at all concerned about the misuse made possible by easy popular access to drugs. Rather they emphasized how health workers were helping people by opening drug shops and clinics. I heard of cases where health workers had been invited to open shops or clinics in communities that lacked them. Even a sub-county health assistant, when asked what he thought of the untrained market vendor who sold blends of drugs, said he was helping people by bringing these medicines on his bicycle from Busoga. In the face of continuing high morbidity, people are taking health care in their own hands and are pleased to find the tools they think they need available in shops and markets.

At least half the transactions in drug shops, and maybe a quarter of those in clinics, involve customers who come to buy a specific drug they have decided to use rather than to seek advice. Even when being served by a trained health worker, they are, so to speak, prescribing for themselves. A few examples will illustrate what I mean by self-help.

Customer: 'Could you give me the drugs I usually buy?'
Shopkeeper: 'Capsules?'
Customer: 'Yes.' (Places money on the counter and is given tetracycline capsules.)

A customer says he has a patient suffering from a cough. The shopkeeper, a dresser, recommends Septrin tablets, but the customer refuses, saying he wants vitamin pills. The shopkeeper does not have vitamins and explains that, anyway, vitamins do not treat cough. But the customer refuses to buy anything else and leaves.

A customer comes in asking for Septrin syrup. The nurse asks whether the sick person is a child or an adult. When she learns it is an adult, she recommends Septrin tablets instead, as syrup is used mostly for children. The customer buys the tablets, and the syrup too, saying he will use both at once.

A soldier asks for gentamicin for gonorrhoea. The nurse says she does not have it, but recommends injectable 'Dawadur' (a form of penicillin) which she says is the very best treatment for gonorrhoea. The soldier refuses it, saying he only wants gentamicin.

Medicines and self-help

A customer wanting medicine for worms is given mebendazole. He is told the dosage and pays 240 shillings for 12 tablets and leaves. A few minutes later, he comes back saying he has just seen Atotaper, a drug he found effective some time back, in the next shop. He asks for a refund, which he is given, and thanks the shopkeeper. After he leaves, the shopkeeper explains that such instances are not uncommon; he always handles them carefully so as not to discourage the customer from coming another time.

There is considerable variation in people's familiarity with drugs. Some know the names, and ask for Valium or ampicillin. Others ask for capsules by colour: red and yellow (tetracycline), or red and black (ampicillin), or white (chloramphenicol). Still others ask in ways that are commonly understood: tablets for blood (ferrous sulphate), tablets to put on sores (penicillin V), or the yellow tablets for diarrhoea (Flagyl).

I bought a variety of pharmaceuticals available in a local drug shop and asked people to show me the ones they knew and tell me how they used them. Everyone recognized many more drugs than I would have in a similar test in Denmark. Some people described usages that seemed idiosyncratic, but there were a number of common patterns that constituted a local tradition of self-medication, strongly divergent from 'government' treatment. There was clearly a cultural reinterpretation of medicines as they passed into the local popular sector (see Bledsoe & Goubaud, 1988). Emptying capsules directly into wounds is general practice, as has been described not only from another study in Uganda (Odurkene, 1988), but also from elsewhere in Africa (Pradervand, 1985). The contents of tetracycline and chloramphenicol capsules are also emptied into infected eyes, or mixed in milk to counteract vomiting. One or two ampicillin or chloramphenicol capsules are taken for stomach pain. Chloroquine and aspirin together are used to treat headache and also any fever, but the treatment is only continued until the symptoms lessen; there is no notion of taking a course of chloroquine.

The popularity of injections in many Third World countries is well known. They were in great demand in Bunyole in 1970, as they still are today. In those days there were injectors (*ab'epsihyo*) who provided injections for those who did not want to go to the health facilities (for example those suffering from venereal disease). Nowadays so many people know how to give injections, that it is hardly necessary to seek out the local injector. One injector explained that his business had fallen off very sharply because nowadays people buy ampoules at the drug shop and inject themselves.

The widespread use of disposable needles has no doubt facilitated this development; there are many more needles around than there were in 1970. Although I did not see them for sale in drug shops, I was told that health workers took them from hospitals and health centres for their friends or to sell. (One alcoholic nurse was reputed to sell them for 70 shillings, the price of a Kimbo tin of millet beer, when he was really thirsty). Trained health workers taught their friends and family how to give injections, and even lay people showed each other how to do it. A young man I knew wanted a shot of chloroquine; his mother had a large vial she had bought from the drug store, but he did not want to inject himself. So he explained the procedure to one of his friends and got him to give the injection, though the friend had never tried it before.

People inject at home partly for convenience. Even families who live near the hospital in Busolwe do not want the trouble of having to go and wait for treatment. In particular, families with many children – there always seems to be at least one child sick – preferred not to be dependent on the government health system.

For some, there is also a safety aspect; they are afraid of dirty needles at the hospital. Since the public education campaign on AIDS, many people are aware that needles should be sterilized. People want to avoid abcesses as well as AIDS.

A 3-year-old boy was given a course of 30 PPF injections at the hospital. He developed a severe abcess, which finally had to be excised leaving a deep scar. When his little sister fell ill (various diagnoses were suggested – measles, kidney problems and chronic malaria), a medical assistant recommended 24 Ex-pen injections to be given 4 per day. The child's older brother administered the injections, because it was inconvenient to take the patient to the health worker four times a day, but also to avoid another infection.

Home injections, like self-treatment in general, are economical. It is cheaper to buy medicines and administer them oneself than to go to the private clinic of a health worker. One ampoule of chloroquine costs 150 shillings in the shop, but a chloroquine injection at a clinic is likely to cost 200–300 shillings.

Medicines are a kind of therapy that may easily be separated from healers; anyone can use them. Europeans are used to thinking of certain kinds of drugs as properly belonging within the control of experts. But this association between biomedical experts and pharmaceuticals has proven fragile everywhere in developing countries. People want medicines, but they do not necessarily want medicine in the institutional sense (Alland, 1970). In Uganda, the process of separating drugs from the health institutions that were meant to control them has been facilitated by the private activities of the health workers themselves. But widespread popular access to drugs means that even clinical relations with private practitioners can be avoided. Self-medication is so widespread that the most realistic course now may be to accept that people *are* treating themselves, and to try to educate them about how to do it more safely and effectively. I am not suggesting that training and retraining of health workers should be neglected; they clearly continue to play an important role in the popularization of biomedicine. However, it is not enough to improve the skills of experts, when lay people have already so eagerly taken curative medicines into their own hands.

CONCLUSION

The processes of privatizing biomedicine certainly involve potential threats to health, to the extent that privatization facilitates misuse of medicines. Misuse may pose an immediate individual danger of complications or even death; in the long term, improper use has negative effects for everyone in that certain disease-causing organisms may become resistant to commonly used drugs. Yet it is important to remember that inappropriate use of drugs also occurs in the public system and that privatization does not necessarily mean poorer health care. On the contrary many people think it is an improvement.

There are two aspects of privatization that require our consideration: the relation between the public and the private sectors; and the relation of privatization to local forces and initiatives.

It is evident, first of all, that the privatization of health care and medicines is intimately connected to developments in the public system, as has been demonstrated for other African countries (van der Geest, 1988; Stock, 1985). A weak public system motivates development of private activities, which in turn help keep the public system weak. Underpaid health workers, who have developed private practices, are little motivated to strengthen the state system. Yet public health care does not collapse totally, because it is supported by private practice both in the sense that health workers can afford to keep their underpaid state jobs and in the sense that for patients the private sector supplements the public one. When the health centre runs out of drugs, they are available in the drug shop. In Uganda, donor organizations are playing an important role in helping to prop up the national health system. But the intertwining of the public and the private sector means that infusing resources into the public system, especially strengthening the supply of drugs, stimulates growth in the private sector.

This connectedness of government and private health care should be taken into account in a positive way by seriously considering what health tasks must be carried out by government and what can be done by private enterprise. Given shortage of resources, it may be that government should concentrate more on training of health workers and on preventative work, accepting the fact that a good deal of curative work will be carried out in the private sector.

It is significant that most discussions of the importance of community participation in health care do not relate this to the private sector. The

145

assumption is that community health workers (CHWs) are to be trained and supervised by national programmes or by NGOs with international support, even though they may be selected by members of their community. In an excellent overview article on the dilemma of essential drugs in primary health care, Bennett (1989) outlines the questions of what kinds of medicines CHWs should be allowed to administer and how people should pay them for drugs. The lesson from Uganda is that these issues are already being worked out by people completely outside a planned framework of community-based health care. In spite of its questionable practices, the privatization of biomedicine really is a grassroots movement that local societies have welcomed in the absence of planned programmes initiated from the outside. The need for cost recovery is clearly recognized. Instead of sending selected villagers for training, communities are relying on people who have already received training. And there is very little sense that lay people are incapable of managing their own health problems. Although one may legitimately be concerned about some of the practices involved, it is necessary to recognize that local initiatives exist and to try to work with them rather than forbidding them.

How could this be done? Radical rethinking will be required and I put forward these suggestions not as answers but as ideas for discussion. Those who operate private clinics and drug shops should be offered training courses in appropriate use of drugs. After this training they should be allowed to buy essential drugs at cost price. This would be a positive motivation that would build on the existing situation rather than ignoring it. The training programme could be an opportunity to improve prescription habits.

The present system of government registration and control does not work effectively to prevent unqualified people from selling drugs and practising biomedicine. Perhaps local resistance councils should have a greater role in deciding who can sell medicine. They are the ones who know who actually runs shops (as opposed to licence holders). This would mean that discussions should be held with them and information provided so that they have a proper basis for making a decision.

I have already mentioned the need for public education campaigns and I would like to stress that in the present situation of widespread lay medication this is the single most important step to be taken. Education about drug use needs to be specific about indications and proper dosages and even about how to give injections safely. Dangerous practices should be discouraged, but it is unrealistic to advise people to take only medicine prescribed by health workers. Given that the relevant health worker may be in private business, it is vital that the customer have sound guidelines for buying. And given that people have a keen interest in drugs and are already learning on their own how to use them, an education effort is entirely appropriate.

The processes of privatization described here may be seen as specific examples of more widespread state dynamics, not only in Uganda but in many African nations. In summing up contributions to a recent volume on society and the state in Africa, Chazan (1988) emphasizes the importance of a broad approach to the problem of state deterioration in Africa. It is not simply a question of the breakdown of state structures, but of the broader field of power and politics – what she calls the relations between society and the state. As the state becomes weaker, people devise new means of coping 'furnishing a vivid demonstration not only of the breakdown of state mechanisms but also of the resilience and flexibility of indigenous constructions of social and material life' (Chazan, 1988, p. 333). The result is the burgeoning of a 'second system', an informal or non-formal sector, which has important and complex connections to the state system, not least in that it is dominated by people who have had access to state resources. Chazan (1988, p. 338) concludes that the primary challenges facing us today have to do with grasping 'the connections between the macro and the micro, between state and society, between autonomy and dependence.' A discussion of structural adjustment and the rehabilitation of government agencies must be based on an appreciation of the complex intertwining of these connections.

In analysing the privatization of health care, I have tried to place the state system, consisting of trained personnel and technology in the form of drugs, in the broader context of private enterprise and self-help. I have described the 'second system' (which is the primary system for many people) in some detail, so that its problems will be clear to us all. Yet I do not see a return to the golden age of free state medicine as feasible; we somehow have to deal with the problems of what exists, rather than dream that the clock can be turned back to the 1960s. Confidence in the ability of a paternalistic state to provide health care has been lost. What is needed now is a new conception of the state's role and recognition and guidance of people's efforts to care for themselves. Only in that way may confidence in the state be restored.

Notes

1. The research upon which this paper is based was made possible by a grant from the Danish Council for Development Research, for which I am very grateful. I would like to thank Knud Christensen, Jørn Korn and Sjaak van der Gees for kindly reading the draft and sending me helpful suggestions. To Birumi and to old friends and new in Bunyole, let me say *mwebale luhulu lweene*.
2. My husband, Michael A. Whyte, and I carried out research in Bunyole county of what was then Bukedi district from February 1969 until April 1971. My interest then was focused on more 'traditional' modes of treating sickness and misfortune. They are still important today, but I do not deal with them here since I have published on them elsewhere.

NINE

The quest for therapy in Moyo district

Tim Allen

Inya niya? Inya niya?
Te buni ya? Te buni ya?

Do I produce to die off? Do I produce to die off?
To be buried? To be buried?
(*Madi lullaby*)

This chapter draws on fieldwork carried out in West Moyo county of
Moyo district from March 1987 until October 1988. A return visit was
made between July and September 1989.[1] During this period I resided
in Laropi, a parish with a small trading centre and a population of 3,500.
About 10 miles from the Sudan border, it is the site of the Nile ferry. In
1980 most people from Moyo district had fled north of the border
because of atrocities perpetrated by Uganda National Liberation Army
(UNLA) soldiers and the ensuing guerrilla war. In Sudan, the majority
were settled in refugee camps. Several of these camps on the East Bank
of Sudan's Equatoria Province were attacked by the Sudan Peoples'
Liberation Army (SPLA) in 1986, prompting the Ugandans to start
returning home. Many of those settled in the West Bank remained in
Sudan until the following year or until 1988, but almost the entire
population of Laropi returned in mid-1986. It was for this reason, and
because the food situation beside the river was then very bad, that Laropi
was chosen for a base. It was my intention to try to understand how communities are reforged in adverse circumstances (see map on p. 163).

The people of Laropi (and of most of Moyo district) speak Madi, a
Sudanic language closely related to that of the neighbouring Lugbara of
Arua district. Madi-speakers are invariably referred to as belonging to
the Madi tribe, and refer to themselves in this way. However it is worth
bearing in mind that the idea of a Madi 'tribe' only gained currency during the colonial era, and has never implied any sort of cohesive political
entity. The Madi society of the past, in so far as it is possible to talk of
such a thing, was essentially clan-based, the patrilineages being loosely
linked into small chiefdoms that sometimes included other patrilineages

149

speaking other languages. Thus the multilingualism so widespread today has long roots. During the second half of the nineteenth century the power of some *opi* (chiefs) in the area was greatly increased as a consequence of alliances made with ivory traders, or the Turco–Egyptian invaders, who rewarded allies with guns.

I refer briefly to the past at the outset to emphasize that there is little that is traditional or static in Madi society. The incursions of the ivory traders caused widespread devastation, wiping out large herds of cattle. Catholic missionaries have been active for three quarters of a century, and by the late colonial period the Madi were a heavily commoditized peasantry producing cotton as a cash crop to pay taxes and school fees. Many also migrated to southern Uganda to work as labourers, or joined one or other of the government services. Even though the area has been politically and economically marginal, acutely so today, commitment to education is remarkable, even by Ugandan standards. English is widely spoken, and the BBC World Service listened to avidly every evening by those with radios, and by their neighbours.

When people talk about 'traditional' ways in Moyo district, they in fact often refer to the late colonial period or the 1960s, when taxes were paid and state services provided; when it was possible to take fish to Kampala on the bus and come back on the same day; when salaries or the returns from growing cotton were enough to buy bottled beer, clothes, a radio, bicycles and to pay school fees. As elsewhere in Uganda, the era when the state worked is talked of in glowing terms, and is continuously compared with the present situation, when salaries, if paid, are almost meaningless. It is extraordinary to an outsider how the ideal of what things should be like and a sense of duty seem to be enough to keep teachers and civil servants turning up for work relatively regularly. People want to grow cash crops for government buyers, and feel that they ought to. Many would have grown cotton in 1988 and 1989 if the seeds sent had not failed to germinate, and if the rehabilitated ginnery in Adjumani had not broken down. Even so, and in spite of what are in effect very low farm gate prices, some have planted it. The variety of cassava sold in markets for turning into *waragee*, the local liquor, is jokingly referred to as 'cotton cassava' since selling it, or making *waragee*, is the only source of income for several families.

Unlike in Arua district to the west or, increasingly, Gulu district to the east, the population of Moyo has not been able to opt into the dynamic parallel economy, which has become such an integral part of life in other parts of Uganda. The land is not fertile enough to produce large quantities of food crops for sale in the capital, and in any case transport is extremely difficult. Many shops in Moyo town and Adjumani are almost empty, and prices are prohibitively high because of transport costs from Kampala. River transport is unavailable, and roads are in

150

poor repair and occasionally insecure because of bandits operating from Zaire and the remnants of the Holy Spirit movement.

People continue to look to the state for services that cannot be provided, and in lieu of the state look to the international non-governmental organizations (NGOs). The NGOs, in effect, operate as parastatals but, understandably, lack the will and resources to take on responsibility for long-term service provision, and avoid any form of direct administration. Thus people have had no option but to fall back upon themselves, to draw upon the archive of their culture, on their experience as refugees, on what is recalled of the past, and on what has been learned at school or from the radio, to find ways of rubbing along with neighbours they may never have lived with before running to Sudan, and of winning a living in difficult circumstances.

Here I shall discuss some aspects of the part healing plays in this process, both in the sense of curing sickness, and in the sense of explaining, and coping with, what would otherwise be inexplicable misfortune. Therefore I will be concerned partly with the allopathic curing of disease, but also with the way in which sickness forms part of the texture of moral discourse, part of the way in which a degree of social accountability is established, often painfully, at a time when old ways of organizing village life are unworkable and the local state structures that replaced them are chronically weak.

From the point of view of 'scientific' allopathic medicine there are major problems in Moyo district. During 1986 and 1987 the UN/ Ministry of Rehabilitation relief programme was unable to distribute adequate relief food to the returnees. According to United Nations High Commission for Refugees (UNHCR) figures from East Moyo county, through which over 30,000 returnees passed in 1986, including those destined for West Moyo, only 10 per cent of expected cereals, 14 per cent of beans, 12.5 per cent of cooking oil and 20 per cent of salt arrived and were distributed in the first five months of the repatriation exercise. Things did not improve in 1987; the consequence was that much of the population relied on gathered 'famine' foods like water lilies from the Nile, wild roots, and the leaves of various plants. Feeding centres have remained full at both Moyo and Adjumani hospitals and, particularly in the hungry season between March and June, there have been fears of widespread malnutrition. In September 1989 large quantities of relief food from the Food and Agriculture Organization (FAO) were expected in the area, though in the event these were subsequently redirected because of improvements in the situation. Rather surprisingly, surveys carried out by MSF (France) and by the Red Cross have not revealed a serious nutritional problem. All the surveys undertaken have indicated a relatively low figure for children under five years in the less than 80 per cent 'weight for height' category (between 2 per cent and 6 per cent).

151

However, these figures for malnutrition have unfortunately not been linked to mortality rates, which people assert are very high. This might be expected since Moyo district has one of the lowest levels of immunization coverage in the country (less than 20 per cent). But diarrhoeal diseases and malaria are also very common (often being found in combination with anaemia) and probably account for the majority of deaths. Children who look healthy suddenly waste away and die in a matter of days, and would therefore not usually appear in occasional nutritional surveys based on anthropometric surveys.

Malaria is also a major cause of adult morbidity, as are schistosomiasis, intestinal worms, eye infections, infected wounds, tropical ulcers, meningitis, tuberculosis and trypanosomiasis (sleeping sickness). Venereal disease is also fairly common, and the level of HIV infection is rising, although it has not reached the levels recorded in southern Uganda. So far deaths from clinically defined AIDS have been few, but have been much discussed, because some of those affected have been well-known individuals.

It is perhaps the sleeping sickness situation that is most disturbing. In 1960, because of intensive treatment and vector control, the disease was almost eradicated. Since that time control measures have become haphazard and many Ugandans were infected with the disease in Sudan. In 1989 the prevalence was estimated at 5 per cent in some parishes of West Moyo and Obongi counties, and it is thought to be rising. The present control and treatment programme is clearly incapable of dealing with the scale of the problem, in spite of improved methods of screening and treatment. Like tuberculosis, sleeping sickness requires a prolonged course of treatment, which continues for long after the patient feels better, making it extremely difficult to administer. Coming to terms with the disease will require far more resources than are currently being made available, a more effective propaganda campaign and probably also some form of legislation to enforce screening and attendance for treatment. There is little immediate prospect of these things happening, and in spite of the best efforts of the district medical staff and medical NGOs, the situation can be expected to become worse.

Government health care services in the district are overstretched, as they are elsewhere in Uganda. Drugs are often unavailable in the static dispensaries and patients have to purchase them from the parallel market. Some medical staff are extraordinarily selfless, and work extremely hard, but resources are severely limited, and it is impossible to turn up for work every day unless some alternative income is available. One conscientious midwife I know makes ends meet by brewing beer on Sundays.

MSF (France), an NGO, has been assisting in allopathic health care provision in the area since 1984. The organization has been involved in

152

renovating Moyo Hospital and several static dispensaries, and supplies additional medicines and equipment. There are usually about ten expatriates based in Moyo town, working on all wards of the hospital except the surgical, supervising the renovation of buildings, and providing some in-service training of medical staff. They are also involved in the child vaccination and sleeping-sickness control programmes.

The attitude of the population to allopathic healing is complex. It is not uncommon to meet people living as peasant farmers who have a remarkably detailed knowledge of biology, largely derived from O-level and A-level textbooks. One day, when I was helping to harvest a field of groundnuts, the man working next to me commented on the various birds busily flying about in the field. He observed that the reason that they are always so active must be related to the fact that their blood temperature is 114°F while that of human beings is only 97°F.

Not surprisingly, attitudes to particular diseases are partly determined by education level. But whether or not there is a word for the disease in the Madi language is also important, something which is often linked to eradication and control programmes during the colonial period. Thus there are words for sleeping sickness (*mongoto*), yaws (*loboto*), venereal diseases (*njuku*), and the word 'malaria' has been incorporated into the vernacular to refer to any kind of headache. For such diseases, conceptions of empirical sickness causality promoted by the Catholic Church, medical staff and others are generally accepted, and it is recognized that there are allopathic, manufactured medicines that can cure them. The difficulty is perceived essentially as one of access. This is similarly the case with lesions and bacterial infections. People will usually use district health services in these cases if they are available, or try to purchase drugs for home treatment. For one reason or another, the treatment a patient ends up obtaining is often in an inadequate dose, or involves taking the wrong drug, a problem that is particularly acute with respect to home treatment with antibiotics.

The paucity in allopathic medical resources, combined with high demand for them and several half-hearted attempts to professionalize what are thought of as indigenous healers, has led to the emergence of many local healing specialists who do not use manufactured allopathic drugs. They call themselves 'daktaris', 'herbalists', or *erowa dipi* (owner of medicine). Such specialists have operated in the district for quite a long time, but there now appear to be many more practising than formerly. Much of what they do involves direct mimesis with what is understood of 'Western' health care. *Erowa dipi* often deal exclusively with sicknesses that are perceived as having an impersonal aetiology; for these they give their own herbal remedies, or use other techniques, which they claim have been revealed to them by God (*Rubanga*) in dreams. They give these remedies with the specific intention of curing the symptoms of the

153

ailment, and they often vehemently deny any connection with *ojo*, the professional spirit mediums about which I shall have something to say in a moment. They assert that they provide similar services to the district medical staff. Unlike district medical staff, however, they openly charge for their services. The charge is made in instalments, the first being for the identification of the disease, and the giving of the treatment, which may cost UShs300–400 plus a cock, and the second being after the treatment has been successful. Charges vary, but one healer I interviewed demanded UShs5,000 for successful treatment of a man, and UShs6,000 for a woman. Several of them work close by one of the rural dispensaries and have cases referred to them by staff working there, particularly when drugs are unavailable or the disease cannot be treated by manufactured allopathic medicine (such as in cases of hepatitis). It is also widely believed that some diseases can only be treated by these specialists, notably *burule* ulcers and 'false teeth'.

Burule is a particularly virulent form of tropical ulcer caused by bacteria that live on a grass growing in riverine areas. Often it does not respond well to antibiotics and sometimes surgery is necessary. *Burule* are therefore normally taken to an *erowa dipi* for treatment. This involves deep cuts being made to drain off pus, in combination with the use of herbal lotions. It is widely believed that the infection is caused by eggs, which in serious cases may be cut out. These 'eggs' are in fact the patient's swollen nodes, and I know of cases where people have died as a consequence of this treatment. 'False teeth' are the lower canine milk teeth of small children. At the time of teething many children have diarrhoea and fever, and it is believed that these are caused by worms in the gums. The treatment is to cut out the lower milk teeth of these children with a razor blade or nail. This also sometimes causes death.

Other treatments administered by *erowa dipi* tend to be harmless, and some are probably effective. They usually have medicines to soothe pain, and have purges that are much used in particular cases of 'poisoning' when it is thought that a toxic substance has been swallowed. These specialists can be male or female, but the majority of those working purely with treatments of this kind are men. The women are often birth attendants who combine massage and herbal treatments with attempts to make the mother experiencing a difficult delivery reveal what secrets she is hiding, since this is widely thought to be the real cause of the problem. Other female *erowa dipi* may combine their work with spirit mediumship and, as a rule, with female healers there is a less clear line between impersonal/empirical sickness aetiology and interpersonal/moral interpretations. It is to this latter area that I now turn.

I have said that there are words used by people in Moyo district for particular diseases; there is not, however, a specific word for sickness. The word used is *laza*, but this can also mean affliction or misfortune in

154

general. The notion that all affliction has an interpersonal cause was paramount before the promotion of empirical causality as a complete explanation of disease aetiology during the colonial period, and it still competes with or overlaps empirical explanation. Things do not happen by coincidence: *awo otu kwe ku*, 'crying does not climb a tree'. Sometimes it can be accepted that a patient has sleeping sickness, or died from drowning, but an additional explanation is also sought. Why did that particular person and not another experience misfortune? The explanation is almost invariably linked to the intervention of spirits of deceased people, or the actions of living individuals.

In the past, the manner of dealing with affliction in what is now Moyo district seems to have been similar to that described by John Middleton (1963) for the neighbouring Lugbara, based upon fieldwork done around 1950. In many cases, particularly serious ones, a moral explanation would be sought. It would be assumed that the problem was caused by (normally patrilineal) ancestors who were irritated by the behaviour of the living. Healing was attempted by elders making promises to 'feed' the ancestors, at the lineage shrine. On such occasions grievances were discussed, and pressure might be brought to bear upon those whose behaviour was interpreted as being the root of the problem. Alternatively, the cause of the problem might be interpreted as *inyinya* (sorcery).

The effects of colonial administration, state formation, commoditization and the migration of young men out of the area in search of work had greatly weakened the capacity of elders to act as effective moral arbitrators even before the upheavals of the 1980s. In exile, the people of Laropi had often lived among non-kin in refugee settlements. In 1986, they had little option but to return to live in their ancestral lands, something that a number of them had not been doing before they left, since they had been resident in other parts of Uganda. Old people, not necessarily those who are elders in terms of inherited lineage authority, try to use this enforced recongregation to assert themselves in the fraught process of establishing a degree of community cohesion. They do this by drawing upon old beliefs, of which younger people profess ignorance. They argue that harvests are poor because ceremonies should be performed to placate the ancestors, and to clean the land of the blood spilt upon it. In most instances these assertions are tactfully ignored. In Dufile, the neighbouring parish to Laropi, the ceremony to purify the land, and call upon the ancestors to help ensure good rains and fruitful harvests was only performed in 1989, three years after returning. In Laropi it has never been done. Even the house in which the rain stones should be kept has not been rebuilt.

With respect to personal affliction, however, elders may be more successful in promoting their interpretation. Particularly when the afflicted

155

person is an ex-soldier, affliction may be linked to past antisocial behaviour, now being punished by outraged patrilineal ghosts. Stories are told of individual men dying, or becoming deranged with remorse in the vicinity of shrines. In these cases elders are less involved with therapy as such than in explaining misfortune with reference to a morality they seek to promote. The affliction shows justice being done. I never encountered an instance where a promise to perform a sacrifice at a shrine was the only therapy adopted, but it is often combined with an allopathic cure. Thus, in the case of a boy with sleeping sickness, his aged step-grandmother insisted on a commitment to 'feed' the ancestors before she would agree to his father taking him for treatment at Moyo Hospital. More often, elders are called upon to play a role only when a healer specialized in the divination of interpersonal causality reveals that ancestral ghosts are involved.

These specialists are known as *ojo*, or sometimes by the Acholi word *ajwaka*, or by the English term 'witch doctor'. In the past *ojo* were usually women who were possessed by God as adolescents and acted both as diviners and herbalists. Nowadays people tend to go to *erowa dipi* for herbal remedies, and almost all *ojo* are women possessed by named spirits not by God. The particular manner in which Madi mediums now divine has been borrowed from Acholi, and it is common for them to speak in the Acholi language when entranced. One *ojo* in Laropi is possessed by five named spirits, including an Acholi and a murdered bishop, and like most other *ojo* she understands her possession as something that brings her close to God. The room in which she divines is decorated with pictures of the Virgin Mary, she has to pray several times each day, and singing hymns is the way in which she calms her spirits when they become too excited.

This connection with Catholicism is accepted by clients, many of whom are those most active in church activities. The connection is reinforced by the persistent association that has been made by missionaries between spirits and the Devil. The spirits of an *ojo* are often referred to as *Satani*. In this context the Madi word *onzi* is important. It is a word that is normally translated into English as 'bad' or 'evil', but is actually far more ambiguous. It also has connotations of power, especially metaphysical power, of something that cannot be fully comprehended. God may even be referred to as *onzi* in this sense, and women often are. The very word for women incorporates the term with a slight change in pronounciation (*izonzi*). Thus to refer to the Devil and the spirits as *onzi* is to underline the importance of trying to find ways of communicating with these things and perhaps controlling them.

Ojo cannot cure affliction caused by ancestors, but they can find out if this is the problem and will refer the patient to his or her lineage elders. But *ajwaka* can be directly efficacious in the treatment of some kinds of *inyinya*, and can treat others possessed less benignly than themselves by spirits. Both of these sicknesses are so common that many think of them as daily hazards.

The meaning of *inyinya* is sorcery, although it is invariably translated as poison, and indeed the English word poison is nowadays often used instead in conversations in the Madi language. There are various types of *inyinya*, some involving a mere touching of the victim, others involving leaving something on a path, or putting something into food. The translation of the term as poison is probably connected to the introduction of allopathic medicine, and the promotion of notions of empirical causality in the colonial period. It was not possible to make an open accusation of withcraft or sorcery in a court, but an accusation of poisoning was acceptable. A file in the Uganda Archives in Entebbe dating from 1922 reveals that colonial administrators working in the area took pains to find out if native 'poisons' really were toxic, with inconclusive results.[2]

Similar cases are still regularly brought to court, but are eventually dismissed since conviction requires a postmortem examination of the victim, and a witness to state that the accused has actually made and administered the concoction. Obviously this is untenable in instances where the accused is supposed to have left the *inyinya* on a path, or to have poisoned by touch alone. Even where poison is supposed to have been swallowed, a postmortem is impossible, since it requires disinterring the body and sending internal organs to Entebbe for examination. Nevertheless, all court officials I spoke to accepted that many of those released were actually guilty and, in effect, the accused may serve prolonged periods in prison, since they are sent there on remand, partly for their own protection, and may remain there for months until the case is heard.

Since the people of Laropi did not live together in exile, even closely related neighbours may be strangers to each other. However, in part because of the re-assertion of the moral values associated with patrilineal relations, those not of the patrilineage are more suspect than others. The motive for *inyinya* is *ole*, envy, or *aya*, jealousy between co-wives. It is thought of as being practised most commonly by women, or by marginal men, such as those living with affines (who are therefore 'like women') and *mwalimu*, the religious teachers among the Muslim traders in the district. As a rule it is women who are accused directly. Usually they are women for whom little or no bridewealth has been paid, and who have no children with a man within the patrilineage. They are individuals who are 'of the outside', whose loyalties are not completely clear since they have been married in from another patrilineage. They are *onzi*, unpredictable; potentially dangerous, possibly evil. Middleton tells us that in the 1920s and 1930s it was quite common for an accused woman to be killed by cutting off her limbs, burning or spearing, and Barbara

157

The health of Ugandans: the social sector under pressure

Harrell-Bond has recounted some awful situations that occured in the refugee camps in Sudan.[3] In numerous instances (I heard of 10 that occurred in the Laropi area during the course of my fieldwork), the accused still end up being severely tortured and killed.

Belief in the capabilities of poisoners remains almost universal. A recently ordained Catholic priest from the district assured me that he had actually seen a poisoner affecting his victim by just touching, and the August 1989 edition of the Catholic newsletter of neighbouring Arua Diocese reported with approval the expulsion of three familes from Vurra Division that had been found guilty of poisoning, even going so far as to print the names of the accused.[4] It is worth quoting at length from this piece since it is very revealing about the role played by the new resistance councils (RCs). I have removed the names of those involved.

> RCs and Chiefs of Vurra Division in Arua District have uprooted and expelled 3 families of people whom they found guilty of killing a total of 7 people, by poisoning using native drugs, and for practising witchcraft. According to the RC2 (Parish level) Secretary for Information, the 3 were tried in June at the county Headquarters where they all admitted guilt and were accordingly rejected by their own people and handed over to higher authorities to save lives and to clean up their division . . . The first accused, a woman who fled to neighbouring Arivu Division was arrested with the help of RCs of that Division. On interrogation by RCs and Chiefs, she reportedly admitted that she had killed 4 people by poisoning including her own mother, her own daughter, her husband, and the daughter of her close relative. She said she possessed 5 types of witchcraftly poison . . . She also named 2 of her accomplices in the deadly profession, who were also arrested and interrogated . . . (One of these) reportedly admitted that he had 8 types of poisons and had killed 3 children using them. His (poison) involves rubbing the substance on his own hand and face and transmitting it by handshake or a hard fixed look at a person he wants to kill . . . Among those at the trial of the three were the political mobilizer for Vurra County, the Chairman RC3 Vurra Division, the Sub-County Chief, and the Vice Chairman RC4.

I know of recent cases where RCs have been involved in judging accused women in a similar way, and two where they participated in burying them alive when found guilty. On another occasion, a young man from outside the area ('like a woman') was accused, and eventually handed over to the local NRA detachment. The soldiers tortured him by dripping burning plastic on him until he admitted his guilt. He allegedly then ate his own poison, but several people stated that he had really been beaten to death. Since the courts are incapable of effectively punishing those accused, and in some cases even convict individuals who end up taking the law in their own hands, villagers have had recourse to other

158

institutions. RC officials, who are supposed to be directly accountable to those who elected them, are inevitably placed under considerable pressure. The RCs in East Moyo county have lobbied their RC5 (county level) representatives to ask the President to give them power to try cases officially, and execute the convicted.

Ray Abrahams (1985) has described a somewhat similar situation, where local level officials became involved in a 'witch-hunt' among the Lango in 1967. In this case the movement petered out following exposure in a Ugandan English-language newspaper, and it can only be hoped that the same thing will happen in this case. On 30 November 1989, *New Vision* published the following report under the headline 'Witches flogged to death':

> Three people believed to have engaged in witchcraft . . . were clubbed to death by villagers of Ezuku parish in Vurra county, Arua district . . . The incidents occurred between November 25 and 27, 1989 . . . Following a meeting of the RCs and the villagers in the parish last Saturday to flush out bad elements the people hung a burning jerrycan in a tree and forced (the accused) to sit under it while the hot liquid dropped on his bare body. The RC II Secretary for Security in the parish . . . told *The New Vision* that the old man admitted having sold (poison) to six other persons. He said he had disclosed the names of at least 30 people he and his colleagues killed in the country using charms.

The report goes on to explain how the man, his son and a friend were clubbed to death, and how a large quantity of charms were recovered from their houses. Villagers stated that the poison could be transmitted by either the shaking of hands or 'by the witch fixing his eyes at the person he wishes to kill'.

Neither of these reports mention *ojo* or 'witch doctors'. Nevertheless, it is highly likely that they were involved, at least initially, for when someone suspects he or she has been poisoned in Madi and Lugbara, an *ojo* is commonly employed to find out who did it and why. As a rule the *ojo* will refuse to reveal the name of the poisoner, but will make vague hints, and offer advice about what to do. Sometimes she administers herbal remedies herself, or refers the patient to an *erowa dipi*. She can also find poison put on a path, or buried in a field, which may afflict an entire neighbourhood, and receives considerable rewards for doing so.

Ojo are similarly paid well for successfully dealing with cases of spirit possession, again a phenomenon closely associated with women. Wild spirits seize a victim, almost always a woman, and cause her to do peculiar things, like sleeping in a tree, or dancing wildly in the bush. Her male relatives will take her to see an *ojo*, who will arrange a ceremony at which she will go into a trance-like state, dancing wildly together with the patient and other women. Young men play drums, and strong

159

alcoholic drinks are consumed. It can be very exciting. The spirits of the *ajwaka* will speak through her, calling upon the spirits possessing the patient to reveal themselves, and explain what they want. When they do so, in strange, high pitched voices, sometimes a grievance concerning the home is revealed. In one case a woman turned out to be possessed by her dead father; through her he castigated her brothers as drunkards. The ceremony is relatively expensive, and often further ones have to be organized, particularly if the spirits 'love' their medium, and decide to stay permanently. If this is so, she may be initiated as an *ojo* herself.

In part this widespread phenomenon of spirit possession can be thought of as a way of coming to terms with the recent past. The relationship between the peoples now referred to as Acholi and Madi is extremely complex. On the one hand there is a tradition of antagonism. For the Madi, the term 'the Acholis' has become synonymous with the marauding UNLA and, more recently, with the UPDA and the Holy Spirit Movement. On the other hand, although their tongues are grammatically very different, the two groups are culturally close and certain key words are the same in both languages (including *kaka*, the term for close relative). Many strong associations are made between the spirits now possessing women and that which is of 'the bush' – which cannot be fully understood or tamed. The mediums have been seized by forces outside 'normal', moral intercourse, and *ojo* are powerful precisely because they have ready access to these forces. Thus the use of the Acholi language when entranced becomes highly meaningful, as does the use of the Acholi kind of spirit mediumship itself. But it is also tempting to see many cases of spirit possession as a form of female expression, or even resistance, rather than as sickness. Speaking through its medium, a spirit will regularly make economic demands on male relatives, and castigate them for their personal failings. In this way spirit possession highlights the weakened control men have over women as a consequence of the refugee experience, and the chronic instability of marriage. It also confirms to men the irrational and dangerous nature of women. Several times I heard men complain that possession has become an epidemic simply because women enjoy the seances.

Summarizing, the following points may be made. First, allopathic curing in Moyo district is limited and insufficient to satisfy need. Second, and partly as a consequence of this, there is widespread recourse to home treatment with allopathic manufactured medicines, and to healers who are seen, and see themselves, as in some sense linked to 'Western' health care. Third, there is a complementary and overlapping conception of sickness not as disease but as a form of affliction that makes manifest interpersonal and moral issues. Sickness in these cases may be due to intervention in the lives of the living by deceased ancestors, to the activities of poisoners, or to possession by wild spirits. In part these latter kind of sicknesses make sense of appalling social trauma. Most terrifying of them is sickness caused by poisoners, who are widely believed to be responsible for the death of hundreds of people. It is surely significant in this respect that RCs have become involved in dealing with those accused. While this is obviously not in itself always a positive development, and the killing of presumably innocent people cannot be condoned, it does underline the degree to which these new mechanisms for village organization have taken on an indigenous meaning, and are playing a part in making reforged communities more socially meaningful.

Notes

---

1. Research in Uganda was financed by the University of Manchester, England, and the European Economic Community. Logistical support was provided by the Makerere Institute of Social Research and the Lutheran World Federation. None of these institutions are responsible for the views expressed.
2. U.P. File No. 73 Native Affairs: Poisons.
3. Middleton, 1963, pp. 266, 274; Harrell-Bond, 1986, pp. 309–12.
4. *Nile Panorama*, August 1989, p. 5.

PART FOUR

PROPHETIC RESISTANCE, EXTERNAL CHALLENGES AND HUMAN RIGHTS ISSUES

TEN
Is Alice Lakwena a witch? The Holy Spirit Movement and its fight against evil in the north

Heike Behrend

In a paper delivered at Makerere University in September 1987 at a conference on 'Internal conflicts in Uganda', a leading official of the NRM, called Alice Lakwena 'a lunatic prostitute of Gulu Town turned witch'. In various newspapers that reported on the Holy Spirit Movement she was either called a prophetess or a witch. In this chapter I will show that the accusation that she is a witch is by no means accidental.

Anthropological productions are stories about stories which were told by people we, the anthropologists, are studying (Bruner 1986: 10). The number of stories that can be told is endless. But in particular historical eras there are dominant narratives that are most frequently told and that function as paradigms or guiding metaphors. There are, of course, always conflicting and competing stories, but they are generally discounted and are not given equal weight in the discourse of a period. Because anthropology is embedded in a political process, dominant stories are units of power as well as of meaning (Bruner, 1986, pp. 18–19).

There are different stories told about the Holy Spirit Movement (HSM):

■ A story about a revolutionary movement of mainly ex-soldiers, who having been defeated and banned to the periphery are trying to conquer the centre again. (The HSM is not a peasant movement. Although there were and still are peasants involved, the main part of the movement is formed by ex-soldiers of the UNLA and UPDA.)

■ A story about a movement based on ethnicity.

■ A story about internal conflict in Acholi; an attempt to solve tensions and contradictions between the established authorities and young men, mainly soldiers, returned to Acholi after having been defeated.

■ A story of a movement in which some numbers of women participated, many in order to seek refuge from tensions, discrimination and oppression within their families (those of their fathers and/or their husbands) and to gain status by fighting and being granted military rank.

■ A story about an attempt to purge and eradicate witchcraft and sorcery.

Although this can only be a preliminary discussion, I will talk about the HSM as a story of a movement to eradicate witchcraft and sorcery. First, I will describe the historic events that led to its emergence. Second,

162

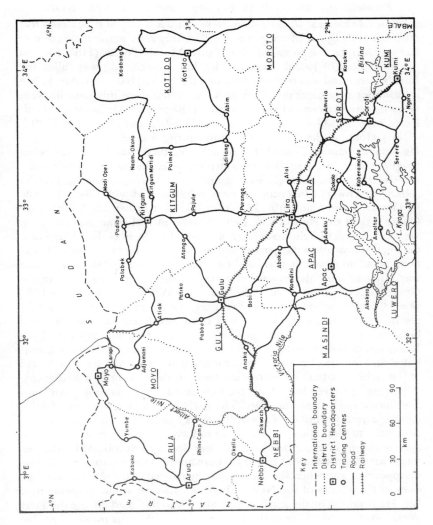

Map 5 *Northern Uganda*

I will give an insight into the HSM's ideology and organization. Third, I will reconstruct the history of the Acholi concepts of chiefship, priesthood, and witchcraft – that is what we call politics and religion – to demonstrate how during colonial and postcolonial times, chiefs, priests and later prophets tried to fight evil, that is, witchcraft and sorcery.

The HSM already has a history of its own and has undergone some

163

substantial changes. In fact, there were at least three, at times even five different Holy Spirit Movements. I will mainly refer to the movement of Alice Lakwena, the so-called Holy Spirit Mobile Forces (HSMF), and the movement of Joseph Kony, which in the beginning was called the Lord's Army and was recently renamed the United Salvation Army. My information originates mainly from a report that some missionaries were given by three Lakwena fighters in June 1987 and from information I collected myself in Gulu and Kampala in October and November 1989.[1]

'His Holiness the Lakwena, a holy spirit, was sent to the north of Uganda on January 2nd 1985.'[2] At this time there was a civil war being fought. Many Acholi soldiers who formed the main part of Obote's army were killed in the guerrilla war against the National Resistance Army (NRA) of Yoweri Museveni. Museveni had stayed with Obote in exile in Tanzania and together in 1979 they had overthrown Idi Amin. After Obote rigged the elections in 1980, Museveni had gone into the bush with 27 soldiers to fight his former ally. An elder from Gulu told me that during this time not a day passed without some families in the neighbourhood being informed that one of their sons had been killed in the guerrilla war. In addition, there were rivalries in the army between Langi – Obote's ethnic group – and Acholi soldiers. When on 2 December 1983 Oyite Ojok, a high-ranking Langi officer, died in an accident many people in Acholi suspected that he had been murdered on Obote's order because he had become too powerful. When Ojok was replaced by a Langi junior officer and not by a senior Acholi, many Acholi felt humiliated and the idea became even stronger that Obote had tried to get rid of the Acholi soldiers by sacrificing them in the war against Museveni.

Having appeared in Acholi, the holy spirit Lakwena took possession of different spirit-mediums. On 25 May 1985, he took possession of Alice Auma, a young woman of about 27 years from Gulu who had recently converted to Catholicism. He is said to have taken possession of her in such a violent manner that he made her deaf and dumb. Although her father asked more than 11 healers to cure her they were unsuccessful. She disappeared, and when she came back she related that she had stayed 40 days in the waters of the Nile.[3] There the Lakwena took possession of her. He is said to be the spirit of an Italian who had died during the First World War, aged 95, near the sources of the Nile. His mission was 'to help as a doctor. He cured a number of people suffering of different diseases at that time, because of the prevailing situation in Uganda: of bloodshed, of national disunity, and immorality.'

When in July 1985 Obote was overthrown by Bazilio and Tito Okello, Alice, the Lakwena's spirit-medium, continued to heal in Acholi. Many Acholi soldiers now used their chance to take revenge. They passed through the homelands of their former enemies in Lango, doing much looting, killing, and raping. When the Okellos were

164

Is Alice Lakwena a witch?

overthrown by Museveni on 25 January 1986, a great number of Acholi soldiers retreated to the north. They returned to their villages, buried their weapons and tried to take up the lives of peasants again. But only a few succeeded. While in the army they had learnt to despise the peasant's way of life and had made an easy living out of looting. Conflicts in the villages increased when some of them began looting and raping their neighbours. Moreover, because they had been defeated by the NRA, they were ridiculed by other villagers. In addition, they were viewed as killers and impure because they had not been cleansed of the blood spilt. Their immoral behaviour offended the ancestors, and the elders feared the latter's punishment.

On top of that, at the beginning of 1986 the first cases of AIDS were reported in Gulu.[4] This sickness was seen as being caused by *kiroga*, a sort of sorcery. The elders related the misfortune that hit Acholi to the immoral behaviour of the soldiers and to the general increase of sorcery and witchcraft. In a situation of internal crisis where the regime of the spiritual had got out of hand, there now appeared an external threat: On 8 March 1986, Gulu was conquered in three hours by the NRA. They met little resistance. Soon afterwards the 35th Battalion of the NRA was sent to Kitgum. This battalion included remnants of the UNLA who had surrendered, and ex-Fedemo troops who, being mainly Baganda, had been formed to resist Obote (see Chapter 13 below). They took the opportunity to loot, rape and murder. To escape this some of the Acholi ex-soldiers took up their weapons again and went into the bush to join the newly founded UPDA. Others followed when the NRA started searching for ex-UNLA soldiers in order to disarm and confine them to camps for rehabilitation and politicization.[5]

This was the moment that His Holiness the Lakwena changed his orders. On 6 August 1986, he became the commander of the Holy Spirit Mobile Forces and told Alice, his spirit-medium, to fight.

> The Lakwena appeared in Acholi because of the plan drawn by Y. Museveni and his government to kill all the male youths in Acholi as a revenge for what happened many years back. So the Lakwena was sent to save the male youth from that malicious plan.
>
> The good Lord who had sent the Lakwena decided to change his work from that of a doctor to that of a military commander for one simple reason: it is useless to cure a man today only that he be killed the next day. So it became an obligation on his part to stop the blood-shed before continuing his work as a doctor.

In early November, Alice, following the orders of the Lakwena, approached the UPDA near Kitgum and was given weapons and soldiers to build up the HSMF.[6] A few weeks later the HSMF fought a major battle gainst the government troops at Corner Kilak and won. After this victory many more soldiers of the UPDA joined the HSMF because

165

'Alice had power'. From Corner Kilak the HSMF marched to Lira and in October they reached Tororo and Busoga. At the end of October they lost the decisive battle near Jinja. It is said that the NRA won this battle because Museveni had asked a powerful witch doctor from Ghana (or Tanzania) to give medicine to his soldiers. According to another version, Alice lost her power because she had ceased following the instructions of the Holy Spirit. Although he had forbidden her to talk to strangers she had given an interview to some BBC reporters. To punish her the Lakwena made her lose the battle. In this battle she was wounded but escaped from the NRA. In December she crossed into Kenya and was imprisoned because she had no identity card. She was released in April 1987 and granted political asylum. She stayed in a United Nations refugee camp in Thika. In spring 1989 a riot broke out and she escaped. According to another version, she stayed, and still stays, in a convent near Nairobi.

The fighting in northern Uganda continued. Alice's father Severino Lukoya, who was possessed by the spirit of God the Father, continued to offer resistance. He surrendered in August 1989 because his soldiers had left him. In November he was still under arrest in the barracks at Gulu. In April 1987 a young man called Joseph Kony, a school drop-out from Gulu, approached the UPDA and was given the so-called 'black battalion'.[7] Up to now he and his soldiers are in the bush fighting the NRA. In June 1988 UPDA soldiers surrendered following the government's offer of amnesty. Soldiers of the HSMF who had been forced to join the movement also took the chance and left the bush. Many of them were integrated into the NRA or militias, so-called Local Defence Forces (LDF), to fight against their former allies.

A progressive dehumanization took place on both sides. Lack of discipline, looting, raping, and killing by NRA soldiers caused many Acholi, women and men, to go into the bush and join the HSM. The atrocities by some NRA soldiers were met by more atrocities on the side of the HSM who had now been given the name *otontong* ('people who cut'). The desperate cycle of violence accelerated again under Joseph Kony. Caught in this cycle, the purest aims inevitably became soiled.

> Lakwena means 'messenger' in Acholi[8] and is a holy spirit[9] . . . Now being a spirit he is not visible. Nobody has seen the Lakwena and we should not expect to see him anyway. Being a spirit he has no relatives on earth. He speaks 74 languages including Latin.

Thus, the Lakwena transcended particularistic interests and limitations based on language and ethnicity and claimed a universalist position.

Why did God send the Lakwena to Acholi?

A number of people of Uganda is asking why the Lakwena appeared in this part of the country. His appearance in the Northern part of Uganda, specifically in Acholiland, is by no means accidental. It was

166

a planned event by God. According to the Lakwena two tribes had the most bad records in the history of Uganda, namely the Acholi and the Baganda. But top on the list is the Acholi. They have been notorious for murder, looting, raping, etc, etc. It was therefore planned by God to help the Acholi to be converted by [i.e. from] the evil ways of life to Godfearing and loving people before continuing to do the same in other parts of Uganda.

The Acholi's claim to leadership was founded on negative attributes: because they were the most sinful of all ethnic groups in Uganda, God sent the Lakwena to them. Thus, their sinfulness guaranteed their salvation.[10] Their claim to be, like Israel, the chosen people was based on their experience of exile in Tanzania and the Sudan under Idi Amin. And, like the people of Israel, their sinfulness and guilt was transformed into a claim for leadership.

Alice preached that the Day of Judgement was near. The people had stopped praying to God. They prayed to material items. They had not followed the commandments of God. They only believed in the power of the gun. God had sent the Lakwena to give a sign that it was not too late to change for the better. After the overthrow of Museveni a flood, a thunderstorm, and an earthquake would come. Snakes would punish those who did not repent of their sins. The fighting of the HSMF was a holy war that would purify Uganda from evil, sinners and non-believers. After the victory, 200 years of peace would follow.

One of the aims of the HSMF was the cleansing of Uganda from evil; that is, from impurity, witchcraft and sorcery. Alice used the power given her by the Holy Spirit to expose and eradicate witchcraft and sorcery. The soldiers of Alice's HSMF had to undergo an initiation ceremony in which they were cleansed. They had to take off their clothes and their magic charms, all of which were then burned. They had to swear, the Bible in the right hand, that they would stop practising witchcraft and sorcery. They were anointed with shea-butter oil and made holy.

The Lord's Army of Joseph Kony also cleansed initiates from witchcraft and sorcery. The initiates lined up in the formation of a cross in the 'defence', the soldiers' camp, in front of the 'yard', the ritual centre of the defence. Their magic charms were burned and they were sprinkled with a mixture of shea-butteroil and water. The ceremony was called 'loading *malaika*' (*malaika* are angels in Kiswahili) because the initiates were 'loaded' with an angel who would protect them in the battlefield. After this the initiates had to remain for three days without eating with or speaking to non-initiates. After the three days they were allowed to mix again with other people.

The HSM, like Maji Maji (Iliffe, 1967, p. 508), was a 'millennial assault on witchcraft and sorcery'. Initiation into the forces was an

167

initiation into a cult group that purged witchcraft and sorcery and inaugurated what Roy Willis has called the 'instant millennium'.

The fight against witchcraft and sorcery made the HSM not only fight the NRA, the enemy from outside, but also healers and diviners, in Acholi *ajwaka*, who were viewed as internal enemies. These *ajwakas* were mainly women who used the power of different spirits (in Acholi *jogi*) for sorcery, but also to fight witchcraft and sorcery. The HSM fought not only witches and sorcerers but also witchhunters and the hunters of sorcerers.

In addition, initiation into the HSMF created a new morally generated life, conducted by new rules:

> As a result of the chief-commander, his Holiness the Lakwena
> issued the holy spirit safety precautions which are 20 in number:
> 1. Thou shalt not have any kind of charms or remains of small sticks
>   in your pocket, including also the small piece used as a tooth
>   brush (Lev. 19,4,31; Is. 3,18–20; Ez. 13, 17–23).
> 2. Thou shalt not smoke cigarettes (1 Cor. 3, 16–20).
> 3. Thou shalt not drink alcohol (Prov. 21, 1; 23, 20–21; Is. 5, 11–12
>   20–22; Num. 6, 1–4).
> 4. Thou shalt not commit adultery or fornication (Deut. 5, 18;
>   Gal. 5, 19).
> 5. Thou shalt not quarrel or fight with anybody (Prov. 17, 12–13).
> 6. Thou shalt not steal (Lev. 19, 11; Deut. 5, 19; Rm. 13, 9).
> 7. Thou shalt not have envy or jealousy (Lev. 19, 17; Prov. 27, 3–4).
> 8. Thou shalt not kill (Lev. 19, 16; Deut. 5, 17; Rm. 13, 9).
> 9. You will execute the orders and only the orders of the Lakwena
>   (Deut. 5,7).
> 10. Thou shalt not carry any walking stick in the battle field.
> 11. Thou shalt not take cover on the ground, in the grass, behind
>   trees, ant-hills or any other obstacle there found. (Deut. 7, 21–24;
>   9, 1–3; Ex. 23, 27–28).
> 12. Thou shalt not pick from the battlefield any article not recom-
>   mended by the Lakwena (Deut. 5,21; 6, 25–26; Jos. 7,10–11,
>   19–21).
> 13. Thou shalt not kill prisoners of war (Lev. 19, 18, 33–34; Mt. 6,
>   14–15).
> 14. Thou shalt follow the right words of command, and never argue
>   with the commander (Lev. 19, 2–4; Deut. 5, 20; 1 Cor. 4,1).
> 15. You shalt love one another as you love yourselves (Lev. 19, 18;
>   Mt. 22, 37–39; Rom. 13, 8–10; Gal. 5, 14–15).
> 16. Thou shalt not kill snakes of any kind (Ex. 7, 8–13; 8, 1–4;
>   Os. 2, 18).
> 17. Thou shalt not eat food with anybody who has not been sworn in
>   by the holy spirit.
> 18. Thou shalt not branch to any home or shake hands with anybody
>   while on route to battlefield.

19. Thou shalt not eat pork or mutton and oil of the same (Ex. 12, 14–18; Lev. 1, 10–11; 7, 11; 19, 26; Lk. 8, 32–33).
20. Thou shalt have two testicles neither more or less.

Injuries and deaths in the battle were seen as a punishment for sinful behaviour, that is for breaking any of the Holy Spirit Safety Precautions. But even if some of the soldiers died in the battlefield, Alice promised that as soon as the HSMF conquered Kampala and overthrew the NRA government they would be resurrected and receive cars and houses.

The HSM had its own mobile hospital to care for wounded soldiers. Alice and the HSMF did not use Western medicine. A book was found on the battlefield near Kitgum containing prescriptions given to the chief pharmacist, a lady with a degree in political science from Makerere University, by the Holy Spirit. Ingredients of pounded snakes, frogs, scorpions, and chameleons were mixed with water and injected. For each wound made by different weapons another kind of mixture was prepared.[11] In contrast to Alice, Joseph Kony used Western medicine. Besides this he also used a mixture of sim-sim oil (sesame oil) and water from a hill named Odek (where Joseph's home is situated), called Holy Spirit Drug, and another concoction called 'combine' which was made of pounded snakes, scorpions, frogs and chameleons boiled with parts of NRA soldiers' bodies. The fluid was distilled like local liquor (*waragi*) and injected. The logic behind this was the idea of immunization, that is, making the soldiers immune by injecting the inimical. The Lakwena had also promised Joseph and his soldiers that he would send a drug to heal AIDS.

In addition to the Holy Spirit Safety Precautions four commands were given to the population in the liberated areas:

1. Yaa oil (shea-butter oil) must not be eaten at all because it is for anointing the soldiers and for treatment.
2. Honey must not be eaten because the bees are fighting to preserve the infrastructure of the country.
3. The snakes must not be killed because they belong to the wild life and they are fighting against the NRA and are removing bad leadership from family level to top level.
4. Prayers and Sunday service have to be taken seriously by everybody otherwise they will meet snakes in the field.

This is the time of judgement. We have to fear so that all Ugandans may become Godfearing people. Let all Ugandans have faith, hope, and love. Final message: Blessed are those who believe.

The second and the third commands can be understood when they are considered in relation to the peculiarity of the HSM's war. Three forces combined to win the war:

Prophetic resistance, external challenges and human rights issues

1. spiritual forces which number 140,000;
2. human forces whose number we cannot reveal;
3. wild life forces, snakes and bees, all of them are under the command of his Holiness the Lakwena.

The war of the HSM was a cosmic uprising in which human forces, the forces of the wilderness, and spiritual forces took part to create a new society.

Besides the Lakwena, the Italian spirit, Alice was possessed by some other spirits such as Miriam, Medina, Sheban, Invisible Chairman, and Wrong Element (Allen, 1989, p. 15). But the commander-in-chief was His Holiness the Lakwena: 'The operation plan for any battle is drawn by the commander himself, that is the Lakwena. We don't have intelligence staff. The Holy Spirit is doing it.' Before a military action took place the Lakwena took possession of his spirit-medium Alice. She and her soldiers prayed in the 'yard' where a charcoal stove was used as a shrine. She dressed in a white *kanzu* and wore a rosary around her neck. Then the spirit spoke through her. The chief clerk of the *laor* (the Acholi word for medium) had the duty to write down the words of the spirit. 'If the spirit says do not move, we do not move.'

Joseph Kony, too, was possessed by different spirits who had their own names, origins, functions and spheres of influence. Like Alice his supreme spirit was the Lakwena. He oversaw and controlled the work of the other spirits. Following him was Silly Silindi, a female spirit from the Sudan, who was the chief operation commander. Silly Silindi directed the war and ordered the soldiers to go to such-and-such a place to fight NRA soldiers. She was also in charge of the women fighters.[12] Silly Silindi's second-in-command was a Chinese spirit named Ing Chu. His special duty was to command spirit jeeps so that the NRA would see jeeps coming towards them. Another Chinese spirit was El Wel Best, who planned operations. Major Bianca, a female spirit from the USA, observed the movement of the NRA and was head of intelligence. She reported to Silver Coni, a spirit from Zaire, who was commander of the 'yard', in order to plan the necessary operations. King Bruce, another American spirit, worked as commander of the stone bombs which turned into grenades when they reached the NRA. The third American spirit was Jim Brickey or 'Who are you?', who fought on both sides. When the Holy Spirit soldiers did not follow the Holy Spirit Safety Precautions then Jim Brickey helped the NRA to fight the HSM as a punishment. Chairman of the spirits was Juma Oris, the spirit of a government minister under Idi Amin, who is still alive and lives in the southern Sudan.[13]

The number of named spirits fighting for the HSM was constant and their identities were unchanging. They only possessed Joseph and Alice respectively and did not fall on other people. Although being spirits

170

from faraway countries they were regarded as guardians of the new moral order issued by the Lakwena.

To receive the orders of the spirits Joseph dressed like Alice in a white *kanzu* and wore a rosary around his neck. He sat down on a chair of metal. A glass of water was put in front of him. He dipped one of his fingers into the water and made the sign of a cross. He rose up slowly, his face changed now, his eyes red. One of the spirits had taken possession of him and started to speak through him. A secretary was sitting next to Joseph writing down the words of the spirits. The spirits who introduced themselves by giving their names, would say: 'You move off from this side because the NRA will come and you will show them that following people is not good.' Or: 'You go to such and such a place and there you will find guns and amunition.' Or a spirit would order some punishment: 'The son of man [Joseph] does not listen to me anymore, he should be given 50 strokes.' And then Joseph would be punished and given 50 strokes by Major Ojuku, second lieutenant.

Joseph Kony himself did not fight. He prayed and worked the whole day with his assistants, ten young boys, in the 'yard'. Five or six charcoal stoves stood there. Their fires were not allowed to die. He laid out some models of guns, tanks and helicopters made out of wire on the stoves and sprinkled water over them. These actions caused the NRA weapons to malfunction and enable him to predict the intensity of the coming battles. On the ground of the 'yard' a map of the Nile and all its tributaries was drawn. Joseph poured water into the 'rivers' so that the NRA could not cross and would be confused.

Once a year Joseph and all his soldiers gathered at a place near Kitgum on the Aswa River, where they prayed and sacrificed a black ram by burning the animal in a big fire. They prayed and sang hymns until the animal was consumed by the fire and then went back to the defence. The HSM had four basic aims:

1. Removal of bad leadership
2. Reconciliation in the spirit of no revenge
3. National unity
4. Returning to democracy (to elect the government will be the people and not the HSMF)
   The army is not fighting for any particular individual and it has no link or association with any of the past leaders of this country. It is not fighting for any particular group of this country, not even for any particular tribe or religion.

After the liberation of Uganda, the liberation of the Sudan and South Africa was planned. The political programme of the HSM was pan-African. The HSMF were organized into a Central Office, which worked out national politics and its political programme, and a Frontline Coordination Team (FCT) whose duties were:

171

1. To link the soldiers to the civilians in whose area troops are staying to get food and other requirements.
2. To preach to the people Lakwena's Gospel.
3. To provide moral and political education to the soldiers and to the public.
4. To act as a spokesman of the HSMF.

A Mobile Institute of Moral Political Rehabilitation also existed 'to educate the soldiers and all Ugandans of good will.' In training camps 'Guerrilla Tactics' and 'Holy Spirit Tactics' were taught. Not only men but also a substantial number of women were fighting in the HSM. When attacking the enemy the soldiers sang a hymn praising the Lord and shouting 'James Bond'.

The liberated areas were strictly controlled. Road blocks were built. The inhabitants were not allowed to enter regions that were controlled by the NRA. People who were found carrying tax tickets, identity cards or the new currency were accused of collaborating with the NRA and were punished. Today the new currency or poll tax tickets are no longer identified with collaboration with the government. But if the soldiers of Joseph Kony find somebody who is a member of a Resistance Council or who carries a letter from one of the RCs he will be cut into pieces.

In a situation of internal crisis and external threat the Lakwena came and asked Alice to work as a healer. When he told her to organize the HSMF and to fight she invented a new role. From being a healer in a local, peripheral cult of affliction she became the prophetess of a millenarian movement whose aim was to take over the centre. The 'undercurrents' of messianism in a peripheral cult gave rise to a prophetess with innovatory abilities (Lewis, 1986). As a healer Alice had to deal with the powers of life. When she became a prophetess she began to use violence. She started to kill, using the powers of death like a witch, the notorious opponent of a healer.

In the course of their history the Acholi have made use of their cultural archive in different ways to redefine the world and to fight evil. In response to penetration from outside, and to inside tensions and contradictions, they invented and reinvented different cults and changing modes of discourse. Central to an understanding of the different cults and discourses and their transformation is the Acholi concept of *jok*, power.

As Okot p'Bitek has shown, for the Nilotes in general and for the Acholi in particular, there were different categories of *jok*, each *jok* being independent from other *jogi*. There were the chiefdom *jogi*, the ancestor *jogi*, the free *jogi*, a *jok* in the bundle which was brought from afar and bore the name of the country from which it came, and there was the harmful power of witches that was also called '*jok*'. The *jogi* were ambivalent powers that were used to interpret misfortune. They were responsible for misfortune and at the same time were a power against it.

172

Is Alice Lakwena a witch?

In rituals different *jogi* were approached and appeased. They could be exorcised and killed or endorcised,[14] which means they were domesticated and became the centre of a cult of affliction.

The different *jogi* cannot be understood as belonging either to the political or the religious sphere. They belong to both and have to be perceived along other lines. In Acholi thought the powers of different *jogi* were opposingly used in either the public or the private sphere and were regarded as being either productive, life-giving, or destructive, death-bringing. The power of a *jok* used for personal gain in private and for destruction constituted witchcraft, while the same power used in public for legitimate ends belonged to the chief and the priest (MacGaffey, 1986 p. 168).

In precolonial times four kinds of people had to deal with *jogi*: first the chief, in Acholi *rwot*; second, the priest of the chiefdom *jok*, in Acholi *won ngom*, both of whom worked in public for the well being of the people and the land; third, the priestess of free *jogi*, in Acholi *ajwaka*, who worked in private but for the wellbeing of the client; and last the witch, in Acholi *la jok*, who worked in private for destruction.

In precolonial times there were more than thirty chiefdoms in Acholi-land[15] which were constantly splitting up and reintegrating. Each chiefdom was made up of a number of villages under the political and ritual control of a chief. Before the penetration of the slave and ivory trade to Acholi, the position of the chief seems to have been rather weak. He had no means of coercion and although all the adult male inhabitants of a chiefdom were required to render a tribute to the chief, which consisted of certain animals' skins and meat, there were always villages that refused to pay tribute and then moved away to set up independent chiefdoms of their own (Girling 1960, p. 94). Most of the chiefdoms had a ritual centre, the shrine of the chiefdom *jok*. The duty of the priest, who was called *won ngom*, father of the soil, was to serve this shrine. The chief and the priest were both responsible for making rain and for the fertility and wellbeing of the people, the cattle, and the land. The chiefdom *jogi* had no part in sorcery or witchcraft. They were guardians of the moral order. Most of the chiefdom shrines belonged to clans of commoners who provided the line of priests, while the chiefs belonged to the so-called aristocratic clans. It was the priest of the chiefdom *jok* who invested the chief with chiefship. He initiated the chief into the cult of the chiefdom *jok*. In precolonial Acholi society chiefship can be interpreted as a cult of a chiefdom *jok* and chiefs as persons initiated into this cult.[16] Once a year, a feast took place at the shrine of the chiefdom *jok*. All the people of the chiefdom gathered at the chief's court and then followed the priest to the shrine of the chiefdom *jok*. It was essential that those who went to the shrine be women and men of clean hearts, which meant that they had to be free of witchcraft and sorcery. It was one of the duties of the chief

173

and the priest to cleanse the country once a year from witchcraft and sorcery.

There were different kinds of witchcraft and sorcery among the Acholi. A witch was a person 'who had *jok* in his head'. This *jok* made him or her become unwillingly a 'night-dancer', a 'kite' or have 'the evil eye'. A witch, when caught, might be killed and buried without funeral rites taking place. Whoever killed a witch was not considered a murderer and was not punished.

There were different *jogi* from afar, called *jogi aoma*, who could be bought and used by sorcerers to harm and kill people. The most dangerous kind of sorcery was *awola*, poisoning. Poisons, extracted from snakes, were put in the food or drink of the victim. This caused him to die on the spot or to fall sick with a permanent disease.

The *ajwaka* or priest-diviner of free *jogi* was the one to fight witchcraft and sorcery. But, in contrast to the priest of the chiefdom *jok*, the *ajwaka* used her power in private to heal individual, rather than collective, afflictions. People who wanted to harm somebody could use the service of an *ajwaka*. Because she used the same power as a witch or a sorcerer she had to prove that she worked for the wellbeing of the patient and did not intend to kill him as a witch would do. The *ajwaka*, when she failed, could be accused of being a witch.

The catastrophic experiences of the Acholi in the last century – slavery, various epidemics and the loss of nearly all their cattle – manifested themselves in the coming of new *jogi* like Jok Ala, the *jok* of 'Arabness'; Jok Marin, the *jok* of 'armyness'; Jok Rumba, the *jok* of 'Europeanness'; Jok Rubanga, the *jok* responsible for tuberculosis of the spine; and Jok Omarari, who became the centre of a new cult when bubonic plague swept Acholi (Okot p'Bitek, 1978, p. 11). These *jogi* – some of whom came from Bunyoro and were an extension of the *mbandwa* spirits – became the centre of different cults of affliction, in which an *ajwaka* divined and cured individual afflictions. The new *jogi* were more diverse, violent, and unregulated than the chiefdom *jogi*. They could be bought and used for witchcraft and sorcery.

It seems that the chiefdom *jogi* who had the duty to punish the breaking of the moral order were not powerful enough to cope with the situation. While the public efficacy of the priest of the chiefdom *jok* lost some of its importance during the colonial era, the chiefs – or at least some of them – succeeded in gaining political power. Because of their involvement in the slave and ivory trade, they acquired firearms and built up their own means of coercion. In this way, they assumed the power to kill. When the Acholi population was disarmed in 1913, after the Lamoghi rebellion, the chiefs retained the monopoly on arms and used it to enrich themselves and to take revenge. They did not employ their power to serve the public wellbeing but to further their private interests.

Is Alice Lakwena a witch?

The Acholi translated the oppression and exploitation they had to endure into the idiom of witchcraft and sorcery. During the Second World War, for example, a new form of witchcraft, called *abiba*, spread through Acholi. Witches sent their *jok* power *abiba* into a kite which then flew over the head of the victim or alighted on the roof of his house and sucked up his intestines. The image of kites with balls of fire in their anuses, sowing dysentery in the countryside, was probably derived – as Okot p'Bitek has suggested – from the sight of enemy bombers raining fiery balls and spraying machine gun bullets (Okot p'Bitek, 1978, p. 128).

Because of the failure of the colonial and postcolonial government to deal with witchcraft and sorcery a collective response to witchcraft and sorcery was no longer possible, though the internal tensions and contradictions between rich and poor, elders and young men, and women and men did not decline but rather increased.

With the coming of Protestant and Catholic missionaries to Acholi a highly complex process of reorganizing and reformulating of meanings and relationships between the Acholi concept of *jok* and different Christian concepts started. In this process the ambivalence inherent in the concept of *jok* was split into a moral dualism. The Christian God, given the name of Jok Rubanga, the *jok* responsible for the tuberculosis of the spine, became the absolute goodness while the other *jogi*, as lesser spirits, equated with Satan were now called *jogi setani* and were thought of as being evil in themselves. Jok Rubanga became the centre of the new Christian cult, which developed from a peripheral to a central cult or religion.

Moreover, new sorts of spirits made their appearance. These were the Christian *jogi*, such as Jok Jesus, the *jok* of the Holy Mary and the *jok* of the Holy Spirit whose power could not be used for evil and private ends because they were good in themselves. There developed the tendency to call these spirits *tipu*, the Acholi word for the ghost of a dead relative. *Tipu* was used by the Catholic missionaries to translate the concept of the Holy Spirit, *tipu maleng*. With time and the spread of Catholicism in Acholi (the Verona Fathers have been in Gulu since 1911) the word *tipu* became increasingly associated with Christian *jogi* while the old 'pagan' *jogi* were seen as coming from Satan and being evil.

At the beginning of the 1970s, a married woman in Atiak developed some mental problems and her husband wanted to leave her. 'Then the thing got her', a new spirit took possession of her. She went into the waters of the Nile and stayed there for four days. When she came out of the water she held a fish in her hand and started preaching. The new spirit who had taken possession of her was Jok Jesus. This *jok* gave her the power to heal and to prophesy. When Jok Jesus spoke through her she dressed in a white *kanzu* and wore a rosary around her neck. In

175

contrast to the *akwaka* she worked in public under a mango tree, using for healing only prayer, holy water, and oil, and not the 'pagan' objects the *ajwaka* were working with. To mark the opposition to the *ajwaka*, this woman and her followers were given the name *nebi*, from the Hebrew word *nabi* for prophet in the Old Testament.

More and more *nebis* started to work in Acholi. Many people followed them because they worked in public and were possessed by morally unequivocal good spirits (*tipu*), who could not be used for sorcery and witchcraft. They became rivals of the *ajwakas*.

Alice Lakwena began working as a *nebi*. The Holy Spirit Lakwena, a *tipu*, took possession of her and asked her to heal the sick and wounded. Working as a *nebi* she fulfilled in an evolved form the basic functions of the precolonial chief and priest of the chiefdom *jok*. Like the latter she worked in public and was possessed by spirits who were the guardians of the moral order and had no part in sorcery and witchcraft. Moreover, like the priest of the chiefdom *jok*, Alice and Joseph once a year made a special sacrifice to appease the spirits and to cleanse the world of witchcraft and sorcery.

In a situation of existential crisis, the Lakwena ordered Alice to heal society and to cleanse the whole of Uganda from witchcraft and sorcery. But to heal society she had to use violence, the power to kill. In doing so she, like the *ajwaka*, used the means she pretended to fight. Although she was fighting witchcraft and sorcery she used the means of a witch, because she used her power to kill. And this explains why she was accused of being a witch.

Notes

---

1. This is only a preliminary essay as I hope to continue research. I wish to thank Tim Allen, Alja Epp-Naliwaik, Ronald Kassimir, Patrick Olango and Catherine Watson for their help.
2. Quotations given without a reference are taken from the report that some missionaries were given by three Lakwena fighters in June 1987.
3. The sojourn in the water is a motif known also from other movements like Maji Maji of Jakan as a sign of the vocation of a future prophet.
4. There may have been earlier cases, but they were not classified as AIDS.
5. In fact, the conditions of these camps were so bad that Acholi died there. At home it was said that they died of poisoning.
6. Personal communication from Catherine Watson.
7. *ibid.*

8. Lakwena is the name of the spirit himself. In Acholi the name means 'messenger'.
9. It might be possible to see the Lakwena as a manifestation or refraction of the Holy Spirit who is conceived in terms of *jok*, the Acholi concept of power.
10. This claim for leadership makes the HSMF violate their own political programmes which postulates the equality of all ethnic groups in Uganda.
11. Personal communication from Catherine Watson.
12. *ibid.*
13. *ibid.*
14. I am following here the terminology used by I.M. Lewis given in a paper on gender and religious pluralism in Mainz in 1989. He calls *endorcism* what Luc de Heusch calls *adorcism*.
15. The ethnonym 'Acholi' did not of course exist in precolonial times.
16. Here I am following MacGaffey's interpretation of Bakongo chiefship.

ELEVEN
Uganda and southern Sudan 1986–9:
new regimes and peripheral politics

Peter Woodward

Since writing on peripheral politics and neighbour relations in the earlier collection of essays published as *Uganda Now: between decay and development* (1988), nothing has caused me to change my mind significantly about the basis of relations between Uganda and southern Sudan, and their importance for each other's domestic politics.[1] Apart from their being neighbours they have, on the face of it, relatively little in common, and there are few historical ties between them.

True, they share the White Nile, but to fertile Uganda the river is not that important, while to arid Sudan it is very significant (if less so than the Blue Nile flowing from Ethiopia). In human terms there is an artificial border between the two that divides indigenous communities such as the Acholi and the Kakwa, but such borders are not inevitably socially divisive, and may on occasions be exploited by local inhabitants, who are able to avoid the demands of authority by cross-border migration.

The essence of the relationship, then, lies not so much in shared physical or human resources as in similar internal problems – specifically the positions of the peoples of northern Uganda and southern Sudan within their own countries, and the implications of these for the neighbouring state. In considering this in my earlier chapter I suggested that the greater the political alienation of either area nationally, the greater the spillover in terms of refugees and other consequences of violence into the neigbouring state and, as a corollary, the greater the political incorporation of either area the less significant impingement there is on the neighbour. And impinging was what could happen: refugees, increased flow of arms, and cross-border use of remote territory for military and political purposes – all had an impact on the neigbouring state, which could prove destabilizing.

Since Uganda's independence there have been three broad phases in the relations between the two countries. First, from 1962 to 1971, the civil war in southern Sudan had an important Ugandan dimension, as well as some impact on northern Uganda. Southern Sudanese refugees were concentrated more in Uganda than any other neighbouring

178

country, and it was there that the main external southern party, the Sudan African National Union (SANU), was established. Ugandans came to show sympathy for their fellow 'Africans' in the struggle against the 'Arabs', and Uganda became the main supply route for Israeli weapons for the Anya Nya guerrillas in southern Sudan (ironically helping the latter to unite, an important prerequisite for the Addis Ababa agreement of 1972 which ended the war). In the second phase, from 1971 to 1979, it seemed to many that the southern Sudan was increasingly entering into Ugandan affairs. Idi Amin's infamous regime has been depicted·in a number of ways, but there was clearly a southern Sudanese dimension. His own synthetic Nubi community had an historical connection with the region, while with peace in the south ex-Anya Nya guerrillas were among those who joined the sinister forces that sustained Amin's rule. But with Amin and the north in power in Uganda, and southern Sudan at peace with the north, relations between the two countries were for a while (important to President Numeiri's regime) relatively quiet. Problems arose once more, however, in the third phase from 1979 to 1986 for now both countries developed new problems in their border areas. The downfall of Amin was followed by a wave of refugees into southern Sudan, and though the north, in the form of Milton Obote, eventually took power once more there were still various troubles in Amin's home area of West Nile and the refugee population mounted. Meanwhile in southern Sudan the Addis Ababa agreement was rapidly falling apart, eventually leaving the country with an even worse civil war from 1983 than the earlier one and with an increasing spillover from the conflict into northern Uganda.

In time the shortcomings of the governments in both countries brought about the downfall of both, and by coincidence at almost the same moment. President Yoweri Museveni finally fought his way to power early in 1986 and in Sudan, following Numeiri's overthrow by the *intifada* (popular uprising) in April 1985, elections were held a year later that installed Sadiq al-Mahdi as prime minister for the second time, only to fall to a further coup in June 1989. Museveni came from western Uganda, but in broad terms his rise to power appeared to be that of the southern part of the country, which had for so many years been under the sway of men from the north; while Numeiri's successors were northern Sudanese inheriting a civil war in the south. The question arose of how the new regimes in both countries would tackle the problems of their peripheries in north and south respectively; and what would be the implication of their respective actions for the neighbouring country?

INTENSIFIED CONFLICT

Typically the initial aim of the new governments was military consolidation, a move in which Museveni obviously had better prospects from the

179

outset. Museveni's National Resistance Army (NRA) had its tail up following the capture of Kampala, and Basilio Okello's men were forced to retreat northwards towards Gulu. But in retreating north the 5,000-strong force that remained under Okello's command was returning to areas that were largely its home territory, especially the lands of the Acholi peoples, and it looked as if a much stronger test awaited the NRA than the capture of Kampala had posed.

In fact Gulu was captured more easily than initially appeared likely. The nearby town of Lira put up stronger resistance, but when that fell and the attack on Gulu began, Okello and a substantial force moved north towards his own home town of Kitgum; and Gulu was taken after only a three-hour battle. But it soon became clear that Okello and his men had determined not to stand and fight in the northern towns but retreat to the countryside and to southern Sudan where it would conduct a classic guerrilla war exploiting the border. In this they had two important advantages – their own cross-border ties and the attitude of the Sudanese authorities.

The Acholis and other peoples of northern Uganda, have, as mentioned, close ties with kin across the border, and the 5,000 or so who retreated north were following in the footsteps of the remnants of the earlier regime of Idi Amin. As many as 15,000 ex-Amin men were believed to be in the south, and the anti-Museveni forces soon linked up with these, creating in mid-1986 a common front, the Uganda Peoples Democratic Army (UPDA).

As for Sudan, the feeling there was that Museveni and the leader of the Sudan Peoples Liberation Army (SPLA), John Garang, were in cahoots. The two men had studied together in the then hotbed of African radicalism, the University of Dar es Salaam, and remained friends. Museveni had had a remarkable army that had come from the bush to overthrow the existing regime in the capital by a popular guerrilla campaign, a rare success in Africa for all its internal wars. Garang appeared to have the same aim, since he sought not the secession of the southern Sudan, but the eventual uprising of all the deprived peoples of Sudan against the corrupt Khartoum-based elite that in one guise or another had dominated Sudan since independence. It was thus understandable that the Sudanese authorities in Khartoum, and in the main southern city of Juba, should regard Museveni's rise as a threat since it would encourage, if not support, Garang. Sudan thus took a tolerant view of meetings between Okello's man and ex-Amin groups, not only in the south but even in Khartoum, where Basilio Okello for a while stationed himself.

The UPDA then proceeded to launch a series of attacks in northern Uganda, including an attack by about 3,000 men on Gulu itself in August 1986 (which Museveni claimed included 1,200 who had been permitted to cross the Sudan border) but which was fought off by the NRA.[2] By the end of the year Museveni was claiming peace in most of the country but admitted that there was still resistance from various groups in Gulu, Kitgum to the north and Karamoja to the east. (Meanwhile the UPDA itself suffered from the factionalism common to guerrilla armies and the Uganda Peoples Front and Uganda National Unity Movement appeared.) Furthermore, following the August attack on Gulu he was openly blaming the Sudanese for encouraging the attacks, claiming that Sudanese soldiers based at Nimule on the border had helped the UPDA. In response the Uganda border with Sudan was closed, which ironically made it harder for the Sudan government to move supplies from East Africa to the increasingly beleaguered town of Juba, and other centres in eastern Equatoria.

While there was a cross-border dimension to the problem, it was clear that much of the trouble was indigenous, with the Acholi in particular taking sides for or against the NRA, while many civilians suffered the attention of both NRA and guerrillas. The latter necessarily lived off the land and included those for whom banditry as much as political resistance had become a way of life, but the NRA's clean reputation was also somewhat smeared. Amnesty International was later to report that this was because of the replacement of the original NRA units by those made up of other anti-Obote factions – the Uganda Freedom Army (UFA) and the Federal Democratic Movement (FEDEMU) – which were less disciplined.[3] And although attempts were made to add a political dimension to the pacification of the north by establishing political cadres right down to the village level, during the second half of 1986 they were increasingly attacked by the guerrillas as government collaborators, so that by the end of the year, while the NRA held the towns, the guerrillas, then estimated at 4,500, could range freely across the countryside.

1987 opened very much as a continuation of 1986. Opposition in northern Uganda became more fragmented, but no easier to control for all that. At its most bizarre it produced Alice Lakwena, herself an Acholi from Gulu, and her 'Holy Spirit Battalion', which suffered so heavily in battle with the NRA at Corner Kilak. But more in the tradition of at least the senior figures of the UPDA were those who still continued to operate from southern Sudan. And while such fragmentation posed a decreasing military threat to the NRA on the battlefield, it made security if anything worse, since instead of rival armies it threatened a situation of anarchy. In a bid to put pressure on the UPDA, which was already rumoured to be considering talks with the NRA following a series of defeats, Museveni felt that the time was right to try and mend fences with Khartoum.

As for the Sudan government it became clear during successive rainy seasons, when their own forces were largely confined to urban centres, that the SPLA was making overall headway from its strongholds in Upper Nile down into eastern Equatoria. Hitherto Equatorians had shown resistance to what was after all depicted as the Dinka-dominated SPLA (against whose influence the whole Equatoria-backed re-division movement in the Southern Region had grown up at the start of the decade) and some, such as the Mandari, had been armed by the Sudan army to operate as tribal militias, effectively contributing to an anarchic drift in southern Sudan as well. But with growing incursions of the SPLA, and the army largely confined by the rains, reports grew that peoples of Eastern Equatoria such as Mundari, Toposa and Kakwa were going over to the SPLA. If the SPLA established itself firmly in Eastern Equatoria, and if Khartoum continued to support the UPDA, then there was a real prospect of counter-backing from Museveni to the SPLA.

IMPROVED RELATIONS

Thus Sudan was willing to try and improve relations and Museveni duly visited Khartoum in June 1987 for talks with Sadiq al-Mahdi. It was agreed that both governments would take measures to improve border security, including moving refugees away from borders. This referred to Ugandan refugees in Equatoria, still estimated at 100,000, amongst whom UPDA sought recruits. Extradition arrangements between the two countries were also to be improved, while barter trade would be expanded. But Museveni made it clear that he was not changing his sympathies entirely, for he would not 'wage a war against Garang in the name of Sudan and expected the Sudanese armed forces not to side with Ugandan rebels'.[4] Instead he offered to mediate between the Sudan government and the SPLA, a position he was to pursue publicly in the following months.

The spirit of conciliation he was seeking to promote among the warring Sudanese also became increasingly apparent in his approach to the UPDA. While continuing to use the stick against the UPDA, still reported to be operating across the Sudan border in spite of the talks in Khartoum, Museveni appears to have turned as well to carrots, offering amnesties to UPDA members who surrendered. This was something of a concession on his part, for with the ending in August 1986 of the original amnesty offered when he came to power he had branded his opponents as criminals and sworn to destroy them once and for all. In March 1986 his initiative showed some success when Moses Ali, a former henchman of Idi Amin, surrendered and some refugees returned from Equatoria to Uganda. Basilio Okello and his followers had remained in the field but in the summer of 1988 they opened talks with the NRA in Gulu. As a result an estimated 80 per cent of the leadership and 3,000 men (the majority of the UPDA) agreed to end their resistance, and many were in fact incorporated into the NRA.

With so many of the UPDA turning from poachers to gamekeepers the number left to carry on fighting was much reduced. A year after the amnesty it was put at less than 1,000. They were, moreover, fragmented, exhibiting ethnic rivalries and tensions that gave rise to suggestion of embryonic local warlordism. The largest single group was a new version of the Holy Spirit Army, now led by one Joseph Kony, mainly operating around Gulu but not showing the growth experienced by Alice Lakwena's earlier movement. Having offered the carrot and absorbed many UPDA into the NRA, the military commanders decided the time was ripe for a violent push against the remaining opposition. The targets were not just rebels but also villagers, with one commander saying that he was 'denying the enemy food and shelter'.[5] Soon 130,000 had sought refuge in Gulu from a scorched-earth policy that seemed in principle not dissimilar from the one used by Obote's army in the Luwero triangle against the NRA. It remains to be seen whether absorption of UPDA, losses of the remaining rebels in battle and weariness of persecuted villagers will finally bring some form of pacification to northern Uganda.

UGANDA'S POLICY TOWARDS SOUTHERN SUDAN

Between 1986 and 1989, it appears that Museveni was constantly aware that peace in the north would depend on developments in southern Sudan as well as on government policy within Uganda. As mentioned, his sympathies are drawn towards the SPLA, but he recognizes the danger of alienating Khartoum in a situation in which anything he does, though significant, will not be decisive in the outcome of the conflict; as a result he professes neutrality in Sudan's war. In consequence since his 'mending of fences' with Khartoum in 1987 he has sought to promote dialogue whenever an opportunity recurred. At the end of that year he was one of the East African leaders (the others were Mengistu and Moi) who hosted a series of talks between the SPLA and leaders of the southern parties in Khartoum, touring under the title of the Sudan African Parties (SAP). Progress was made but, as so often in Sudanese politics, when the SAP returned to Khartoum it turned out to be a broken reed. A year later Museveni arranged for Sadiq al-Mahdi and Hasan al-Turabi, leader of the Muslim Brother-backed National Islamic Front, to fly to Kampala to meet with John Garang; but the latter feared he was being set up for a propaganda coup for the Islamists and declined to attend.[6] In December 1988 Museveni was in Tripoli where it was announced that he was discussing a peace plan that would encompass not just Sudan, but northeast Africa as a whole, though little more was heard of it. At the time of writing in 1989, with a peace process under way, but struggling to maintain its momentum, and with the further complication of a new military government in Khartoum, Museveni remains one of Sudan's several neighbours trying diplomatically to maintain progress.

Meanwhile the war itself was expanding as the SPLA pressed further into Equatoria from its natural heartlands of Upper Nile and Bahr al-Ghazal. This brought both good and bad news. The SPLA were anti-UPDA, both because of Garang's sympathy for Museveni and because the SPLA believed that the Sudan army had sought to use the UPDA against it; moves such as the capture of the border town of Nimule from the Sudan army checked the UPDA's movements and supplies, for they had bought ammunition there on the open market. At the same time, the spread of warfare in Equatoria spilled over into Uganda, causing other problems of security there. There were reportedly violent incursions by SPLA groups into northern Uganda (though some said they were UPDA masquerading as SPLA) while many Equatorians fled, not only from the war, but out of dislike for the SPLA, especially in western Equatoria. In March 1989 it was reported that 500 refugees were crossing into Uganda each day and already totalled 40,000, with UNHCR preparing to receive a further 30,000. As well as receiving refugees, Uganda was also a centre for organizing the relief supplies of Operation Lifeline Sudan, which was designed to prevent a repeat of the estimated 250,000 deaths from famine and related suffering in 1988.

CONCLUSION

In such a brief time, and in such fluid circumstances, it is much harder to discern any kind of pattern than it was in writing earlier on the period between 1956 and 1985. The problems of northern Uganda and southern Sudan remain essentially those of centre–periphery relations and, as such, solutions are internal to those two countries. At present the military situation reflects not parallel, but very different circumstances. While the NRA appears to have used both carrot and stick to quell the UPDA in large measure, across the border the SPLA has been sweeping towards victory, at least in southern Sudan: and in consequence in the short term the perspectives of four years ago have changed, for the political impetus is moving away from rather than towards the border between Sudan and Uganda. No longer is there much talk of an Equatorian state from Equatorians and their cousins from northern Uganda;[7] instead the NRA wants to rebuild the Uganda state, while the SPLA appears firmly committed to a united 'New Sudan'.[8] Yet both remain a long way from their respective goals. Northern Uganda may be largely quelled, but the methods used have so far done little to suggest significant political (let alone economic and social) integration, and it remains to be seen if the NRA and the kind of state Museveni is establishing is capable of achieving this much more difficult and elusive task. Similarly with the SPLA: the dream of ethno-regional solidarity rising in northern Sudan to overthrow the old Khartoum-based elite still seems far off, as the recent SPLA moves to negotiate with that elite implicitly acknowledge. In the event of the failure of that process it is likely that the military situation in the south will mean de facto division of the country. But it remains to be seen whether in 'liberated areas' the SPLA will be capable of following its destructive successes with constructive achievements. Great problems could lie ahead, including renewed hostility amongst at least some Equatorians to the SPLA leadership.

Thus while the cross-border dimension of politics in both countries appears somewhat reduced at present, the potential for future trouble is still there. 'Between decay and development' is still unresolved in Uganda, for any optimism must be cautious, while Sudan's future is anybody's guess. But whether united or divided, the problems of Equatoria, as of northern Uganda, still appear unresolved in political (as opposed to military) terms and as such the neighbour dimension remains, with the possibility of refugees, new guerrilla movements and cross-border fuelled conflicts.

Hitherto it has mainly been managed at best by attempts at military-oriented agreement. When there has been mutual recognition, for whatever reasons, of the dangers of the situation, Kampala and Khartoum have talked to each other about a solution, as in 1987. Probably such talks and agreement do have some effect, but given the tenuous control of both states on these peripheral areas any agreements is likely to be only partly implemented. A new lasting peace for both countries is likely to be established only when a degree of constructive cooperation is also possible. Since development in either could suffer from the effect of decay in the other, there is an incentive to encourage cooperative activities. There are already signs that this is at least implicitly recognized. Uganda has allowed the transportation of humanitarian relief to southern Sudan and the 1987 talks included the topic of improved trade. Again it may be asked how far states can effect policies, especially in an area (together with northern Zaire) where the informal economy has been so significant. But that too indicates that if more regulated and integrated economies are to develop in that part of Africa, then that too will require more effective inter-state cooperation, if the relatively open borders are not to continue to be exploited for smuggling with its potentially damaging effect on economic improvement. Development, in all its forms can never be a wholly national affair, and Uganda's relations with its neighbours will continue to be a significant element of its efforts to recover.

Notes

1. This account is largely drawn from media sources, especially *Africa Confidential*, and some personal interviews and information gathered in Khartoum in April 1989.
2. *Africa Contemporary Record* **19**, 1986–7, p. B480.
3. Amnesty International, 1989.
4. *Africa Contemporary Record* **19**, 1986–7, p. B480.ı
5. *Africa Confidential* **30**, (3) 3 February 1989. This violence against civilians was supported by interviews with refugees from the area, who reached Khartoum in 1988.
6. John Garang, personal interview.
7. Woodward, 1988, pp. 236–7.
8. A phrase much favoured by SPLA leader John Garang, by which he means political, economic and social restructuring of Sudan.

TWELVE

Kenya's relations with Museveni's Uganda

David Throup

At 9.45 am on 7 March 1989, according to the Kenyans, an unidentified aircraft crossed the Uganda–Kenya border in the remote northwest of Turkana in the direction of Lokichoggio, where it dropped eight bombs, killing three people. The Kenya government despatched a strong protest to Kampala, reinforced its marine bases on Lake Victoria and sent two extra platoons to the border post at Busia, which had been the scene of a confrontation with Ugandan forces in December 1987. Only five days before the Lokichoggio raid, Kenyan troops had killed 72 heavily armed Ugandan cattle rustlers in West Pokot.[1]

Three years earlier, in June 1986, relations between the two states seemed to be excellent. Museveni had apparently overcome the Moi government's doubts about Kenya's new 'revolutionary' neighbour and to have been forgiven for abrogating the 1985 peace treaty. Within 18 months, however, the two countries were on the verge of war. The Kenyans claimed that Ugandan troops had crossed the border near Busia in Western Province, firing on Kenyan border guards. The crises of December 1987 and March 1989 emphasized the deep suspicions that had developed between the two regimes. What had caused them and why did relations between the two states deteriorate so dramatically? This chapter will attempt to answer such questions using material in the Kenyan and Ugandan press. Through media analysis of events we shall identify shifts in the Kenya government's attitude towards the NRM and assess the crises of December 1987 and March–April 1989.

KENYA'S ATTITUDE TO THE NRM'S VICTORY

When the Museveni government came to power in January 1986 most Kenyans were willing to trust it and expected that it would assert control over remaining centres of resistance in Acholi without too much bloodshed and reconcile diverse political and ethnic factions.

When Museveni made a one-day state visit to Kenya on 16 June, six months after seizing power, even *The Weekly Review*, which had emerged as one of the NRM's strongest critics, heralded 'the spirit of regional cooperation'. The two countries then agreed to appoint a commission to

187

examine financial, energy, transport and border security issues.
Museveni praised the Kenyans' mediation in the futile peace negotiations, assuaging certain grievances. This visit marked the high point of
inter-government relations. For the first time in nine years, a Kenyan
cargo train, carrying 800 tons of sugar, crossed the border and Kenya
Railways announced that two cargo trains a day would operate from
Nairobi to Tororo, reducing freight costs for Uganda's imports and
exports.[2]

THE ROAD TO BUSIA
In the second half of 1986, however, relations dramatically deteriorated.
By September 1986, the Kenyan press was beginning to be more critical
of the NRM. Museveni's clamp-down on political parties, his refusal to
co-opt Baganda monarchists, the continuing military turmoil in the
north, rumours of attempted coups, and the arrest of dissident Baganda
clan heads intensified doubts about Uganda's political stability. Within
Kenya, the deteriorating political situation with the discovery of the
dissident Mwakenya organization, and KANU's confrontation with the
churches following the abolition of the secret ballot in the party's primary
elections, intensified concern about its radical neighbour. This increased
after the Libyan leader, Muammar Gaddafi, visited Kampala in September, when he castigated the Christian churches as agents of neocolonialism. Many Ugandans were equally irritated by the three-day visit,
especially by the arrogance of Gaddafi's guards, who virtually took over
control of central Kampala, pushing the Ugandan authorities aside.[3]

Antagonized by the visit, Kenyan businessmen and politicians vented
their displeasure at being excluded from the lucrative Ugandan black
market. Many senior officials, moreover, were still irritated by the
NRM's abrogation of the peace treaty with the Okello regime only three
weeks after it had been signed. Others were concerned about the high
level of Ugandan military expenditure, which the 1987–88 estimates
revealed would absorb 34.6 per cent of the budget, compared with 14.2
per cent on education and 7.3 per cent on agriculture, which was supposed to receive priority under the development plan. Such military
expenditure, however essential to defeat the NRM's opponents in the
north and east, exacerbated the Kenyan government's fears.[4]

Relations deteriorated further when Uganda expelled Kenyan residents, and matters were made worse when some of the buses carrying
them to the border were ambushed by guerrillas, compelling the refugees
to make their way to the border at Busia on foot. By February 1987, the
two governments were accusing each other of harbouring dissidents,
while many Ugandans came to consider the decline in trade as a
deliberate policy of destabilization by Kenya.

The Kenyan press provides a good indicator of the fluctuating relations between the two governments. Throughout 1987, press coverage inflamed the conflict. In May, for example, *Weekly Review* editor Ng'weno warned that 'the Kenya government needs to take stock of what is going on in Uganda very seriously.' Statements such as 'Kenya faces a formidable foe that must be dealt with before things get completely out of hand' did little to reduce tensions. This barrage of criticism led the Ugandan government to take the unprecedented decision in May 1987 to stop all shipment of coffee through Kenya, even though this meant ferrying 2,800 tons across Lake Victoria to the railhead at Mwanza in Tanzania.

Although negotiations were held in June 1987 between Justus ole Tipis, the Kenyan Minister of State in the Office of the President and his Ugandan counterpart, Balaki Kirya, the situation deteriorated. In late August, the Ugandan government moved its troops to the frontier, ostensibly to prevent guerrilla bands operating in the area, but with the implication that Kenya was assisting them. The situation there was tense and it was perhaps only a matter of time before Kenyan border guards and police became involved in a shooting incident with the NRA, who were attempting to turn back refugees fleeing from the fighting with the Holy Spirit Movement in eastern Uganda.

In contrast to the press, the Kenyan government's initial response to the deployment of Ugandan troops was restrained. It declared that Kenya was 'firmly committed to the principle of good neigbourliness and non-interference in the internal affairs of other countries'. Some Kenyan officials suspected that the NRM had provoked the crisis to divert attention from Uganda's domestic problems. After 18 months in office, Museveni's authority seemed to have weakened. Rebel forces had regrouped and were mounting renewed challenges to the NRA in the north and east, diverting attention from national reconstruction. Inflation had reached a new high and peasant producers appeared to be retreating once more from the market, evading the demands of the state.

Speculation in Kenya grew that Museveni would not survive much longer as anti-NRA forces in the north consolidated their position and advanced from Acholi and Lango deep into Eastern Province to within six miles of the Owen Falls hydroelectric station at Jinja, which supplies western Kenya as well as Kampala. Lakwena's advance compelled the Ugandan government to suspend steamer services on Lake Victoria to Kisumu as the Holy Spirit Army briefly controlled the Buvuma and Rosebery channels from Jinja. When Museveni delayed his return from the 1987 Commonwealth Prime Ministers' Conference at Vancouver for three weeks to visit the United Nations, Washington and Accra, Kenyan papers claimed that he had fled and would not return to Kampala.

On Monday 14 December, approximately a hundred NRA soldiers attempted to cross the border near the Kenyan town of Busia, firing on

Kenyan security guards when challenged. Sporadic fighting continued throughout the day. Following the clashes at Busia, the Ugandan government held an emergency cabinet meeting, which decided to reinforce the garrison at Tororo, ten miles from the border. Trucks and buses were used to ferry troops from Kampala to the frontier-and it seemed as though the two countries were on the verge of war.[5]

The *Weekly Review* took an extreme anti-NRM line, warning Kenyans to be alert for further Ugandan incursions and on the look-out for spies attempting to establish contact with Mwakenya dissidents. The magazine warned that 'in President Museveni, Kenya is dealing with an ideologically committed leader who happens to have some very grand ideas of what he can achieve beyond the borders of his country. He has a ruthless, though at the moment inefficient political and military machinery sufficient to contain his domestic opponents. By implication, he has plenty of flexibility in spreading mischief beyond the borders of Uganda.' Many Kenyans shared the view that Uganda's hostility to Kenya was ideologically motivated rather than a result of the NRA's battle to establish control after nearly two decades of civil strife spilling over the border. In any case, the Ugandan government had been clearly warned that Kenya would tolerate no further provocation.[6]

KENYA-UGANDA RELATIONS IN 1988 AND EARLY 1989

The immediate crisis was defused by a meeting between the two presidents on 28 December 1987, at the Kenya border town of Malaba. Moi had requested the meeting and Museveni seemed defensive, claiming that he had no alternative but to deploy the NRA along the border because the Ugandan police force had disintegrated. Uganda agreed to withdraw its anti-aircraft guns and missiles and to provide better security to Kenyan truck drivers waiting to transport 10,000 tons of goods to Kampala. It was also agreed that Kenya Railways would carry 5 million bags of coffee to Mombasa. The Kenyan press acknowledged that Museveni appeared eager to end the crisis and re-open the border. In return, the Kenyan government agreed to prosecute Alice Lakwena and her followers in the Holy Spirit Movement, who had sought refuge in Kenya, and reportedly sentenced Lakwena and seven of her associates to four months' imprisonment at Thika. Shortly afterwards, ole Tipis announced that more than 100 of Lakwena's followers had been gaoled and warned that the government would deal firmly with all illegal immigrants.[7]

Full resumption of normal diplomatic and business relations was still hampered by Nairobi's hostility to Libyan influence in Uganda. Kenyan politicians feared that Colonel Gaddafi was also manipulating Islamic fundamentalist groups in Kenya, especially in Coast Province, in order to destabilize Moi's pro-Western regime. The Muslim-dominated Coast

190

Province had long been an important element in the political coalition that sustained Moi. Although its importance had declined during the 1980s as he successfully restructured the Kenyan state, directing patronage to the Rift Valley and Western provinces to cement the support of more important elements in his coalition, the growth of Islamic fundamentalism threatened his old allies at the Coast and weakened his own authority. Gaddafi's support for Mwakenya provided an even more direct challenge. It was also rumoured that Iraq, another radical Arab state, had financed a dissident group associated with the veteran Luo politician Oginga Odinga.

Even more startling allegations were soon made when at the trial of former Assistant Minister Kimani wa Nyoike he was alleged to have contacts with Mwakenya. Along with former cabinet ministers Charles Rubia and Masinde Muliro, wa Nyoike had been an outspoken critic of Moi's purge of the KANU apparatus after the downfall of Njonjo. Alone in the National Assembly they had resisted the government's plans to concentrate power in the party and to reduce the autonomy of such institutions as the churches and the legal profession, which had dared to criticize changes in the constitution and the abolition of the secret ballot. At wa Nyoike's trial the prosecution claimed that Museveni and former President Nyerere of Tanzania had had contacts with Kenyan exile leaders such as Koigi wa Wamwere and Andrew Ngumba. It was alleged that Wamwere had informed wa Nyoike that 'Museveni was assisting him in many ways, including the training of guerrillas and the provision of arms and funds.' It was also revealed that Raila Odinga's Kenya Revolutionary Movement had despatched recruits for training in Libya through Uganda.[8]

Such revelations and continuing minor border incidents prevented the normalization of relations, between the two regimes, exacerbating their ideological differences. Kenya protested about the build-up of Ugandan troops along the frontier and was alarmed by reports of the NRM government's support of Mwakenya, while Uganda was concerned that Kenya would close its border, hindering the free movement of essential supplies and exports, and believed that Nairobi was actively attempting to destabilize Museveni's administration. Neither country, fortunately, could afford a full-scale war, even if both feared that adventurist factions in the other regime might push them into open conflict in order to consolidate their power.

With relations deteriorating once more, Kenya introduced stricter control over Ugandan residents and dismissed many exiles from their jobs in an attempt to court popular support. In November 1988, beset by acute economic difficulties and mounting unemployment, the Kenyan government announced that the employment of foreign nationals would be reduced 'to a bare minimum'. As a result, more than

191

Prophetic resistance, external challenges and human rights issues

2,000 Ugandan secondary school teachers were declared unemployed. Many refused to return home and sought help from the United Nations High Commission for Refugees. Before the two countries became locked in confrontation, arap Moi and Museveni met in Arusha early in December 1988. They discussed the security situation and agreed not only to withdraw support from dissidents but also to expedite the flow of Ugandan goods through Kenya and to an increase in the charges for electricity supplied to western Kenya from the Owen Falls dam.[9]

THE POKOT AND LOKICHOGGIO INCIDENTS

Three months later, in March 1989, Kenyans had cause to fear renewed conflict with Uganda and the threat of deeper Libyan involvement. As the *Weekly Review* observed, 'is Uganda once again spoiling for war with Kenya?' The speculation was provoked by two incidents: the incursion of 400 heavily armed raiders in military uniform into West Pokot and the bombing of Lokichoggio, a remote Turkana town.

The bombing of Lokichoggio aroused particular concern. The Kenyan government announced that it regarded the attack and the deployment of Ugandan troops along the frontier as a 'flagrant and unwarranted violation of its airspace and territorial integrity by Ugandan armed forces'. Uganda, it declared, should not 'construe Kenya's policy of peaceful co-existence and good neighbourliness as a weakness' and warned that 'the Kenya Government cannot sit idly by and let these unprovoked attacks continue unabated, because it has a responsibility to protect its citizens and their property'. This denunciation was perhaps premature since later more careful analysis cast doubt on Kenya's claim that the aircraft had come from Uganda. It seems likely, rather, that a Sudanese aircraft attacking SPLA bases had strayed over Kenya. The Kenyan government, however, adopted a militant stance, clearly believing that Uganda was responsible.[10]

The two incidents, the most serious clashes since the Busia conflagration in December 1987, seriously injured relations between the two countries. The Kenyan press as usual adopted a very hostile attitude towards Uganda. The *Weekly Review* urged the government to pursue invaders back across the border and denounced 'the track record of the Museveni government', which it compared unfavourably with Idi Amin's. Despite Uganda's denials, the Kenyan authorities remained convinced, at least publicly, that the attack on Lokichoggio had been launched from Uganda. They insisted that the aircraft, believed to be a MiG 21 fighter, had crossed into Kenya from Uganda with two other aircraft as escorts and had turned back in the same direction after the raid. On 12 March, in a 35-minute address at the airport, on his return from a tour of western Europe, Moi lamented the assistance that Kenya had given various Ugandan governments, noted how he himself had attempted to

192

mediate between Tito Okello and the NRM, and asserted that 'whoever abuses or challenges Kenya's sovereignty will get what he deserves'.[11]

The Ugandan government dismissed the findings, observing that the report of 'the Kenya Government-appointed investigating committee is at best a matter of sheer speculation and at worst a perfect lie contrived to provoke and to mar Uganda's reputation at home and abroad.' The Foreign Ministry in Kampala argued that 'no one should be expected to believe the findings of the committee . . , [with] conflicting roles, namely, that of an accuser, of a prosecutor and of a judge, and called upon Kenya to appoint 'an objective machinery of inquiry.'[12]

THE LIBYAN CONNECTION AND KENYA'S PARANOIA

Even when the fracas over Lokichoggio receded, Nairobi continued to view events in Uganda with grave concern. Every sign that Museveni was strengthening Uganda's ties with Islamic states, especially Libya, created a mixture of fury and fear, even though Museveni assured the Kenyan government that he was merely attempting to secure more aid from the Islamic Development Bank for water development projects and road reconstruction. The NRM preserved its close relationship with the Libyan government, which had been one of the few willing to support its guerrilla struggle against Obote, securing $12 million of cheap oil (as well as aid and military expertise) through agreements to barter coffee, maize and soya beans. Early in February 1989, for example, Uganda Radio had announced that the government had signed three agreements with Libya. These secured a US$130 million loan at 4 per cent interest with a repayment period of 12 years financed by barter exports; the rescheduling until 31 December 1999 (including accrued interest) of an US$11 million loan that had been secured by Idi Amin in 1974; and a general investment protocol 'to promote and strengthen economic cooperation between the two countries.' By comparison it ought to be noted that Uganda had received US$170 million of aid from Britain since the NRM had come to power in January 1986. Despite Uganda's dependence upon Kenya the NRM could not afford to abandon its old ally merely to improve relations with Nairobi. As *The Guide*, a Kampala newspaper, observed, several Muslim non-governmental organizations were assisting Uganda's rehabilitation 'because of President Museveni's positive policy towards the Muslim community in the country.' Although the NRM could ill afford the economic costs of a confrontation with Kenya, it was essential to secure additional technical and military aid from Libya and other Arab states. The Kenyan government became even more alarmed in May 1989, when Kampala announced that Museveni had signed a barter agreement with Cuba, whereby Ugandan coffee, beans, processed leather and soya beans would be exchanged for sugar, salt, paper, chemicals and medicines.[13]

Prophetic resistance, external challenges and human rights issues

By contrast, only 1–2 per cent of Kenya's exports went to Arab states and it had recently decided to re-establish diplomatic relations with Israel. Indeed, following the bombing of Lokichoggio, a Kenyan military delegation and the head of Kenya's intelligence service had visited Jerusalem. While Uganda was seeking economic assistance from the Arab world and was joining Sudan in an attempt to eradicate dissidents on their common border, Kenya had adopted a pro-Israel stance in order to improve its alliance with the USA, which had been strained by reports of human rights' violations by the Moi regime.

Although President Museveni and the NRM attempted to improve their reputation in Western countries and to dispel Nairobi's fears that Uganda, the Sudan and Libya were plotting to destabilize Kenya, the Kenyan government reacted with great alarm at any sign of troop movements along its borders, still considering Uganda to be a close ally of the Libyan Arab Jamahiriya. Few businessmen or Kenyan government officials believed that Museveni and his colleagues in the NRM had abandoned their Marxist opinions. Articles and editorials in the Kenyan press continued to denounce the Ugandan leader. Anti-Ugandan sentiment was widespread among many sections of Kenyan society and the government's resolute stance attracted mass support. Since independence Kenyan politicians had courted popularity by attacking the Asian community; now they were able to demonstrate their patriotism without endangering the stability of the economy or discouraging foreign investment by attacking Ugandan refugees. The government capitalized upon these sentiments, announcing that expatriate employment would be phased out over the next five years. Ugandan exiles, employed as teachers and clerks or as skilled workers in direct competition with Kenyans, were likely to be the first affected by the plan.[14]

CONCLUSION

We need to consider whether there were any immediate causes for Kenya's suspicions about Lokichoggio or for the intensification of the crisis in March 1989. *Africa Confidential* provided a succinct analysis, suggesting that 'a number of issues lay behind the Lokichoggio dispute. It is clear that Uganda's vocal autonomy threatened Kenya's claims to regional pre-eminence, with economic dominance very much at the forefront. Kampala's relations with Libya, a source of weapons, petroleum and funding for its political schools, have consolidated Kenyan mistrust of President Yoweri Museveni.' Nairobi's insistence on blaming Uganda for the attack seems to have been designed not only to incite anti-Ugandan sentiments among the masses but also to avoid a confrontation with the Sudan, which might have revealed Kenya's role as a major supply route for the SPLA. The Kenyan government believed that the SPLA would eventually force concessions from Khartoum and emerge as an interlocutor in the politics of the whole region, fundamentally shifting the balance of power in the area. By contrast, despite Museveni's long association with John Garang, dating back to their time at the University of Dar es Salam, the Ugandan government seemed to be increasingly aligned with the regime in Khartoum and had provided refuge for more than 40,000 Sudanese government troops in Moyo district, who had fled before the SPLA's advance.[15]

President Museveni insisted that the people of Uganda and Kenya had no conflict. The difficulties were simply being created by the elite. He explained to *'Al-Dustur*, an Arabic magazine published in London, that 'there is no conflict between Kenya as a country and Uganda as a country. If some tensions and disagreements surface, they are attributable to the people in charge. There is no conflict of interests between Kenya and Uganda, because their interests are interconnected . . . The people in charge and the manner in which they control their countries' affairs may create false and fabricated tensions . . . All this is manufactured by the rulers in these countries.'

Museveni considered that the troubles had three causes. In September 1986, certain Kenyan leaders had begun to use the press to lecture Uganda on its internal affairs. Secondly, some prominent people in Kenya wanted to create political instability in Uganda and to get rid of the NRM. Museveni observed, 'we didn't say much about this in the past but the time has now come to expose this matter, because we possess a great deal of proof of the involvement of a number of Kenyan officials in plots to threaten our country's stability and security.' Thirdly, he asserted, most Kenyan leaders were ignorant of the real situation in Uganda and the changes the NRM had made. For example, as the NRA asserted control over the remoter parts of the country, stopping cattle-rustling, the rustlers had been forced to move over the border into Kenya, taking with them the sophisticated weapons they had acquired from two decades of turmoil and civil strife. There were similar problems along the border with Sudan, but whereas the Ugandan and Sudanese government were collaborating to restore order, he complained, 'the Kenyans insist on considering this activity a Ugandan military invasion'. Museveni also suggested that the conflict between the two countries – there had been another exchange of gunfire at the Busia border post in July 1989 – was hindering economic development. Uganda's recovery was being stifled, while Kenya was losing revenue by obstructing the flow of Uganda's exports and imports through its own territory to and from Mombasa.

The Kenyan government remained deeply suspicious of what it considered the neo-Marxist programme of the NRM and its alliance with powers like Libya. Museveni's government, on the other hand, appeared convinced throughout the period we have reviewed that big business

195

interests close to important ministers and civil servants in Nairobi, who had earlier been trading partners with the Amin, Obote and Okellos regimes, were determined to subvert it and profit not only from smuggling but also, perhaps, their actual downfall. Vested interests, mutual suspicions, and mutual distortions precluded either government from making the first move to restore normal diplomatic and economic relations. Further complicating the situation were the continuing civil war in the southern Sudan, the Kenyan government's fear of Islamic fundamentalism undermining its authority in its own Coast Province, and Somali irredentism having a similar effect in the northeastern sections of its territory. The dispute between Uganda and Kenya thus threatened to become part of a wider regional conflagration in the late 1980s as the two governments attempted to strengthen their domestic positions by denouncing their neighbour. Sadly, at the time of completing this chapter, this situation appears to be continuing in the immediate aftermath of the Rwandan imbroglio of October 1990.

Notes

1. FBIS-AFR-89 March, 1989, p. 1; FBIS-AFR-89-044, 8 March, 1989, p. 2.
2. *Weekly Review*, 20 June 1986, pp. 14–15; 27 June 1986, p. 9; and 11 July 1986, p. 17.
3. *Weekly Review*, 11 July 1986, p. 14; 29 August 1986, pp. 11–12; 5 September 1986, pp. 15–16.
4. *Weekly Review*, 18 September 1987, p. 58.
5. *Weekly Review*, 25 December 1987, p. 1.
6. *Weekly Review*, 18 December 1987, p. 1; 8 January 1988, p. 1.
7. *Weekly Review*, 8 January 1988, pp. 34–5.
8. *Weekly Review*, 28 October 1988, pp. 8–10.
9. *Weekly Review*, 25 November 1989, pp. 20–1; 24 February 1989, p. 16.
10. *Weekly Review*, 10 March 1989, p. 35; FBIS-AFR-89-044, 8 March, 1989, p. 2.
11. FBIS-AFR-89-047, 13 March 1989, p. 6; *Kenya Times*, 13 march 1989, p. 10.
12. FBIS-AFR-89-076, 21 April 1989, p. 3.
13. *The Guide*, 30 November 1988, p. 4; FBIS-AFR-89-001, 3 January 1989, p. 6; *New Vision*, 4 May 1989, p. 12; FBIS-AFR-023, 6 February, 1989, p. 2.
14. FBIS-AFR-89-024, 7 February 1989, p. 12; FBIS-AFR-89-056, 24 March 1989, p. 6.
15. *Africa Confidential*, 28 April 1989, pp. 3–4; *The Guide*, 18 May 1989, pp. 1, 8; FBIS-AFR-89-134, 14 July, 1989, p. 3.

THIRTEEN
Human rights issues in Museveni's Uganda

M. Louise Pirouet

In the Preamble to the OAU's African Charter on Human and People's Rights the signatories state that they are

> Convinced that it is henceforth essential to pay a particular attention to the right to development and that civil and political rights cannot be dissociated from economic, social and cultural rights in their conception as well as universality and that the satisfaction of economic, social and cultural rights is a guarantee for the enjoyment of civil and political rights.

While we will probably agree that there are links between development and human rights, we may find it more difficult to agree with the last part of this declaration, that the 'satisfaction of economic, social and cultural rights is a guarantee for the enjoyment of civil and political rights'. It is possible to argue, as black South Africans do, that economic, social and cultural rights *result from* respect for human rights. It would certainly be dangerous to suggest that respect for human rights might have to wait upon development (nor does the text of the Charter suggest that this should be the case). This reference to the linkage between human rights on the one hand and development and economic, social and cultural rights on the other, serves as a reminder that a consideration of human rights in Uganda is not marginal to the concerns of this volume, but central to it.

The National Resistance Movement (NRM) led by Yoweri Museveni came to power promising to restore security to the people of Uganda after 14 years of tyranny and massive violations of human rights. Speaking about the *10-Point Programme* before the National Resistance Army (NRA) victory, Museveni stated:

> As soon as NRM takes government, not only will the state-inspired violence disappear, but so will even criminal violence. Given democracy at the local level, a politicized army and police and absence of corruption at the top, as well as interaction with the people, even criminal violence can disappear. Thereby security of persons will be restored and so will security of legitimately earned property.[1]

197

Prophetic resistance, external challenges and human rights issues

At his swearing-in ceremony as President, Museveni returned to this theme:

> The second point on our programme is security of person and property. Every person in Uganda must [have absolute] security to live wherever he wants. Any individual, any group who threatens the security of our people must be smashed without mercy. The people of Uganda should die only from natural causes which are beyond our control, but not from fellow human beings who continue to walk the length and breadth of our land.[2]

Museveni went on to explain that during the Nairobi talks leading to the abortive peace agreement he had been urged to be diplomatic with 'the criminals across the table', but had retorted: 'But diplomacy, does it also apply to criminals?' The security of persons was to be underpinned by new structures through which democracy would work from the bottom up. Resistance councils (RCs) would be established at all levels, and emphasis was laid on the importance of giving people a voice at the lowest level of hierarchy, a level at which even the humblest could feel that he or she had a voice that counted.

Four years later it is apparent that the restoration of security has been only partly achieved, though a network of RCs has been set up, and is working well in many parts of the country. Elections to these have been held without the violence and allegations of ballot rigging that characterized the 1980 elections. Some areas of Uganda are experiencing a measure of security that they have not known for years; other areas that had been relatively peaceful are now suffering very great insecurity. Amnesty International's 1989 report, *Uganda, the Human Rights Record 1986–1989* documents a lamentable catalogue of human rights abuses, mainly in the context of this regional insecurity, though Amnesty International (AI) is careful to qualify its stance. It notes the massive legacy of human rights abuse that Uganda has suffered, and 'the return of security to many parts of the country, the improved behaviour of the army, increased respect for the law' (p. 2). The conclusion to the report (p. 48) notes:

> Any assessment of the NRM government's human rights performance is, perhaps inevitably, less favourable after four years in power that it was in the early months. However, it is not true to say, as have some critics and outside observers, that there has been a continuous slide back towards gross human rights abuse, that in some sense Uganda is fated to suffer at the hands of bad government.

The Minority Rights Group's report No. 66, *Uganda* (July 1989) reaches a similar conclusion. Warning that 'there is no such thing as a quick military solution' to the problems of continuing insurgency in the north, it concludes: 'We believe that it is not yet too late for Uganda to incorporate the Acholi and Teso, and we urge both the Ugandan government and the dissident leadership to think again while there is still time' (pp. 26–7).

Why do human rights violations still occur and why did discipline in the army break down from time to time, resulting in human rights violations in the combat zones? Is the Uganda government serious about protecting its citizens and restoring security of persons and property to them? Have the problems of insecurity simply been transferred from one area of the country to another, as some people aver? How can a society overcome such an appalling legacy of gross human rights abuse as that inherited by the present government? Are AI and the Minority Rights Goup (MRG) being unrealistic when judging Uganda by the standards of the UN Universal Declaration of Human Rights? A British diplomat is alleged to have remarked: 'This is Africa; things are different. Amnesty International has its work to do, but you can't apply those standards here'.[3] (This piece of diplomatic cynicism can be dismissed out of hand as racism. If Britain had chosen to act on human rights abuse in Uganda no doubt it could have done something to alleviate Uganda's suffering, but it chose to put commercial considerations first.[4]

First, then, why have human rights violations continued to occur, almost all in the context of military operations in the north and east? A variety of factors help to explain why the NRA, which came to power with a reputation for respecting civilians and their rights, has not succeeded in maintaining that reputation unimpaired. In the first place, it is not the same army, as the AI report notes (p. 14). After the fall of Kampala in January 1986, the Okello faction and elements of the UNLA that had kept Obote in power fled north. They were expected to make a stand en route, but to everyone's surprise they melted away over the Sudan border, and the north was peacefully occupied. The behaviour of the NRA was in complete contrast to that of the UNLA which, even when fleeing, had murdered and looted.[5] However, by August 1986 sections of the forces that had fled had regrouped and returned across the border to harass the population and attack Gulu. The NRA had to be quickly reinforced and the 35th Battalion was sent to Gulu. This included the remnants of the UNLA that had surrendered and ex-FEDEMO troops (FEDEMO was one of *the* smaller groups, mainly Ganda, that had been formed to resist Obote). These men had received only the briefest training, and had not absorbed fully the need to respect civilians that had been induced in the NRA through long training and harsh punishments when the codes of conduct were broken. 'When Museveni's men first came they acted very well – we welcomed them,' said one villager, 'but then they started to arrest people and kill them'.[6] Former NRA troops became infected with this indiscipline: reports insist that they, too, were involved in the trouble that followed.

199

Prophetic resistance, external challenges and human rights issues

In incorporating ex-UNLA and FEDEMO soldiers, and many more have been incorporated into the NRA since, as well as members of insurgent groups who have surrendered, Museveni has begun to abandon his earlier position of having no truck with 'criminals'. Attempts at reconciliation are desirable, and the NRA stood in urgent need of the extra troops who came over to it, but the policy has nevertheless backlashed to some extent so far as the army has been concerned.

There are further reasons for the breakdown of discipline. The NRA had originally been trained as a guerrilla army, and now found itself having to act as a standing army in counter-insurgency, a notoriously difficult position. Civilians found themselves caught between two forces, the insurgents, who called themselves the Uganda People's Democratic Movement/Army (UPDM/A) and extorted support and food, and the NRA, who punished civilians suspected of aiding the insurgents. Mission hospitals were closed because they treated everyone in need, no matter which side they were on, crops and grain stores were burnt, and civilians were rounded up and subjected to interrogation. Reports multiplied of *kandooya*, 'three piece tying', in which the arms were tied tightly behind the back at wrists and elbows. *Kandooya* strains the chest and impedes breathing, and sometimes so severely damages the nerves of the arms that amputation becomes necessary. Young men suspected of supporting the insurgents were marched off to 're-education camps' in the south, or were held in barracks, though the latter was technically illegal. The detainees were reported to have been treated reasonably well: apart from *kandooya*, systematic torture such as characterized Obote II was not reported, but prison conditions were very harsh.[7]

No doubt the unfamiliar territory in which the NRA now had to operate, their ignorance of local languages, and their fear of being isolated in an unfriendly countryside all contributed to the breakdown of discipline. By the time the 35th Battalion was replaced in October 1986 much damage had been done. Orders that *kandooya* was to cease eventually had an effect, but the population had been antagonized, and the results of this are still apparent. The army is still using counter-insurgency tactics and these are bound to antagonize people who might have supported them or been uncommitted. It is clear that the NRA perceives the insurgents and their supporters, willing or otherwise, as 'groups who threaten the security of our people [who] must be smashed without mercy'.[8] The problem was, and still is, to find a way of smashing the enemy without smashing the civilian population and turning them into enemies too.

The insurgent groups in the north are also guilty of human rights abuses against the civilian population, which found itself caught between the NRA and several groups of rebels: the UPDA, Alice Lakwena's Holy Spirit movement and its successors, and groups that can best be

Human rights issues in Museveni's Uganda

described as bandits. In mid-1988 it was reported that in the previous three weeks more than 35 innocent people had been killed, dead bodies were left to rot unburied, and more than 30,000 people in Kitgum town were homeless after their homes had been burnt by cattle raiders, rebels, or the army, which was pursuing the rebels. These people were described as being without food, clothes or medical services. For the third year in succession the schools were closed. It is clear from this report among others that human rights abuses were by no means confined to the NRA, as some insurgent leaders have suggested.[9] The rebels also reportedly used *kandooya*.[10] Not all of Lakwena's followers were willing adherents of her movement.[11] Hundreds of ordinary villagers had fled to the comparative safety of the NRA-held towns.[12] The insurgent groups had fought among themselves:

> The UPDA hates the Holy Spirit [movement] because it constantly harassed the UPDA in the bush, stealing guns and men. The UPDA is also embarrassed for it was former UNLA/UPDA commander Lt. Col. Ojuku who gave Alice Lakwena her first guns and men.[13]

The same report went on to claim that the rebels abused the civilians more than the NRA did. No wonder that one observer described the people as fleeing to the forests and mountains to hide from both the rebels and the government troops.

The so-called Holy Spirit movements led by Alice Lakwena and, after her defeat, by her father Severino Lukoya, and by Joseph Kony, (see Chapter 10), have all been poorly armed and have trusted to a mixture of spells, magic potions and traditional and Christian prayers to protect them from bullets. These movements have something in common with some other resistance movements, of which Maji Maji in Tanganyika in the early 20th century and the Xhosa movement led by the prophetess Nongqawuse in the 19th century are the best known. In the case of the Ugandan and Xhosa movements they seem to have been born out of despair, relying on supernatural means of deliverance when all else has failed. The very existence of the Holy Spirit movements is, then, a testimony to the depression and powerlessness felt by the people. The NRA has taken very few prisoners after battles with these rebels, though hundreds have been killed. There have been disturbing reports that on at least one occasion in August 1987 soldiers deliberately shot the wounded.[14]

The Teso have suffered more insecurity because of Karamojong raids than anything else. Cattle raiding got completely out of hand when the Teso militia, which had provided some protection under Obote II, was disarmed and disbanded by the NRA, which saw them as a possible threat. The NRA was unable, and possibly also unwilling, to protect the Teso in early 1986, and the Teso suffered terribly as a result. Insurgency

201

in the area has been fomented by Peter Otai, who claims to be fighting for the restoration of democracy and human rights. In view of his past record as Minister of State with responsibility for the army during Obote II, there is reason to be sceptical of his aims.[15] Economically both Teso and Acholi have been set back decades by the insecurity from which they are suffering. The government launched a famine relief appeal for Acholi in June 1988, estimating that 372,000 people who had fled to the towns needed food aid and 540,000 needed non-food items. A Western aid agency called in to help considered this an underestimate, if anything, and noted that people were even worse affected in the rural areas. This appalling situation was entirely due to war, the people having been deprived of their right to food and shelter by both the rebels and the army.

While most of the abuses of human rights by the NRA have taken place in combat areas, there have been reports from elsewhere. Details of extra-judicial executions (some of a horrifying nature), torture and detention without trial are given by AI in its 1989 report, *Uganda: The Human Rights Record 1986–1989*, and there is no point in repeating that information here. Although the incidents described had been reported to the Uganda government, AI claimed that in most cases no action had been taken. AI's delegates were prevented from entering the Gulu area in January 1989 although they had permission from Kampala to do so. We must, therefore, turn to the second question raised at the beginning of this: Is the Uganda government serious about protecting its citizens and restoring security of persons and property to them?

In spite of all that has been said above, the answer to this question is yes. They have not yet been successful, and they find it difficult to control the army, but there are, nevertheless, a number of pointers to their seriousness about the restoration of human rights.

First we should notice the setting up in August 1986 of the Commission of Enquiry into Violations of Human Rights that had occurred between 9 October 1962 when Uganda gained its independence and 25 January 1986 when the NRM took power. This Commission is an important plank in the government's programme. It is, however, dealing with past abuse, not with current abuse. The government has told both Amnesty International and International Alert that a successor organization to deal with ongoing complaints is to be established, though the form it will take is yet to be decided.[16] The Commission does have some relevance to the present in that one of its functions is educational. It moves around the country to hold its hearings, and people are described as learning for the first time that they have rights. This is potentially very important, and some indication of the government's intentions, as a repressive government usually prefers to keep its subjects as much in the dark as possible about their rights. Then, too, an Inspector-General of

Government has been appointed who has wide-ranging powers and is directly responsible to the President. He can issue search warrants and subpoena witnesses, and is having some success in dealing with corruption, which currently occupies much of his attention. But his remit also covers allegations of human rights abuse (including arbitrary killing, arrest and detention, unfair trials, torture, and illegal acquisition of property), the extent to which law enforcement agencies themselves respect the law, and maladministration and abuse of office, this last being the normal sphere of an ombudsman. There is clearly considerable potential here.

The government's intentions are also demonstrated by its signing and ratification of the UN Convention against Torture and Other Cruel, Inhuman or Degrading Treatment or Punishment, and the OAU's African Charter on Human and People's Rights. This latter came into force on 21 October 1986, having been signed by 30 out of the 50 OAU member states. The signing of such documents may not mean much: by no means all the states that had signed the OAU Charter by October 1986 had unsullied human rights records. But, as AI points out in its 1989 Report on Uganda (p. 2), 'By its adherence to international treaties . . . the [Ugandan] government has shown that it wishes to be judged by absolute standards'.

The NRM government has been willing to receive delegations from AI on several occasions, and has allowed its representatives to visit prisons and interview prisoners. The government was reported to be very angry when AI's 1989 report appeared, but a further mission to Uganda followed soon after the report was published, and President Museveni himself received AI's Secretary-General, Ian Martin. The government has also received missions from International Alert, but this organization was considered less of a potential threat. The 1987 Seminar arranged by International Alert, which produced very useful work,[17] was something of a public relations success for the Uganda government. Another international organization that has been able to visit Uganda is the International Committee of the Red Cross (ICRC), which was expelled by Obote, and was never permitted by his government to visit barracks where detainees were held and where torture was frequent and horrific. The NRM has permitted the ICRC to visit civil prisons (in which a number of detainees are held), and a number of barracks and major police stations. In accordance with ICRC practice reports are made only in confidence to the government concerned; they are not published. However, the willingness of the Uganda government to admit to the existence of these detainees and to allow ICRC visits to barracks is encouraging and helps greatly to provide protection for those held in them.[18] It is believed that the number of detainees held in the main military barracks is small, a few hundred rather than thousands.

203

However, some 3,000 detainees were held in civil prisons in April 1989.

It is particularly important to examine the government's attitude and actions on army discipline. During the war that brought the NRM to power the army was strictly disciplined by two codes of conduct, and soldiers who abused the civilian population were severely punished. These codes of conduct became law when the NRM took power. AI describes their operation thus:

> The Code of Conduct for the National Resistance Army prescribes a mandatory death sentence for murder, treason, rape and disobedience of a lawful order resulting in loss of life. Soldiers are tried by a unit disciplinary committee chaired by the unit's second-in-command. They have no right to legal representation and no right of appeal. All death sentences must be confirmed by the Chairman of the High Command, President Museveni. The NRA's operational Code of Conduct defines a series of offences related to the army's operations in the field, including desertion, disobeying lawful orders, misuse of arms and failure to perform one's duties. All the offences listed in this code carry a maximum penalty of death. Defendants may be tried by a unit tribunal, a field court martial or a general court martial, all of which can impose death sentences. There is no automatic right to have a lawyer and no right of appeal. Death sentences passed by a unit tribunal or general court martial must be confirmed by the High Command. The Chairman of the High Command has the prerogative of mercy; the High Command advises him on how to exercise this.
>
> Many of the executions of soldiers have been carried out in public, often soon after the offence was committed . . . The government's rationale is that speedy and public justice reassures the people that the army is under control.[19]

Although AI considers it remarkable how many soldiers are convicted on criminal charges by the criminal courts, indiscipline in combat zones has been much less easy to control. The government is extremely sensitive to criticism of the army; enquiries have taken place that have sometimes, but not always, resulted in soldiers being brought to justice. We have noted that the 35th Battalion, whose behaviour so sullied the NRA's reputation in the north, was replaced and that *kandooya* largely ceased. In December 1988 AI specifically raised some horrific instances around Gulu where it was alleged that villagers had been forced to remain in their huts when these, and their crops, were burnt in order to deprive the rebels of assistance. It was reported that the divisional commander in the area was removed, and an inquiry set up, and a senior general sent to Gulu. Fifty NRA soldiers were reportedly being held for indiscipline, at least five of them for murder.[20] The final outcome of this is not yet known though AI was told during its April visit to Uganda that the enquiry was due to report soon, and that any soldiers found guilty would be brought to justice.[21] A further appalling incident occurred on

204

Human rights issues in Museveni's Uganda

11 July 1989 in eastern Uganda. On this occasion 279 people were rounded up in a sweep organized to apprehend rebels. Forty-one of these were taken to the district headquarters as suspected rebels. The others were cleared, but instead of being released, they were locked into a railway wagon where 47 died of suffocation. On this occasion the army was quick to acknowledge responsibility. Major General Salim Saleh, the Commander-in-Chief, broadcast an apology, and 14 soldiers were placed under arrest, including two majors and a captain. Major-General Saleh was reported to have told the press, 'It's the worst thing I have seen in the NRA. It's a clear case of gross criminal negligence. We don't know whether it was intentional or accidental, but someone will have to die for it'.[22]

People detained by the army are known in Uganda as 'lodgers'. Batches of these have been released from time to time: in June 1988, 1,671; in October 1988, 950 as well as several hundred ex-UNLA soldiers; and in July 1989, 1,086. But the total prison population does not seem to have fallen, because there have been further arrests.

There are, then, some restraints on the army. The unrestrained criminality of Amin's army and the UNLA is not being repeated, and there is some evidence that the Uganda government is sincere in its commitment to restore security of persons, though it is not always able to fulfil its intentions, and the evidence from the combat zones is that too often soldiers who offend are not punished as they should be, even when their guilt is known. Dealing with insurgency is extremely difficult in any circumstances, and the NRA has been too prone to practise precisely the kind of counter-insurgency tactics that are likely to lead to abuses of the type it complained of in the past. An ominous development that must qualify our answer still further is that since late 1988 the President has been empowered to declare any part of the country to be 'in a state of insurgency'. In such areas magistrates' courts may try offences usually referred to the High Court, including cases punishable by death, and cases that may occur outside their local jurisdiction; the President may appoint magistrates as he wishes and they need not have any legal training; when capital cases are heard the magistrates will sit with two assessors, one of whom will be an NRA soldier; no bail will be allowed; the rules of evidence will be suspended so as to admit hearsay evidence, and the burden of proof will be shifted from the accuser to the accused; and soldiers will be given the same powers of arrest as police officers.[24] The Law Society of Uganda has rightly objected to this legislation and to the setting up of special courts to deal with banditry.[25]

Many Acholi would argue that they are now suffering what the people of the Luwero Triangle suffered previously, and that insecurity has merely been shifted from one area to another. A doctor who visited the north and east in mid-1988 noted that apart from signs of fighting such

205

as burnt-out houses and buildings riddled with bullet holes, and stories everywhere of rape, looting and killing, many of the people met were surviving on the bare minimum of food. There were cases of severe malnutrition, including adult kwashiorkor, an unusual occurrence. It was noted that in most areas there was a complete lack of functioning health and immunization facilities, and that, though no casualty figures were available, the death toll had been very high. But, unlike the people of the Luwero Triangle, these people did not hold the army responsible for all their sufferings. Much of it had been caused by Karamojong raids – and these had taken place as far west as Nebbi in West Nile – Alice Lakwena's people, and other rebels, though the army had played its part, and had been unable to protect the people. Although they can cause plenty of trouble still, the rebel groups cannot offer any alternative to the present government, nor can they provide protection or offer any programme for the future. Most of the UPDA has surrendered to the NRA, and Tito Okello has returned to Uganda under an amnesty. The fighting is said to be dying down, and the people returning to their villages. Whether the problems of insecurity have simply been transferred from one area of Uganda to another is a question that cannot be given a straight yes or no. Yes, insecurity now occurs in different places, but no, the problems are not exactly the same as they were, nor is the general situation in which they arise. Today's insecurity can be more easily marginalized than could insurgency under Obote II, and Museveni is therefore likely to be more securely in power. If, however, the NRA were unable to protect the north and east from rebels, bandits and cattle-raiders, there is the possibility that a more coherent resistance might appear that would constitute a more serious threat to the government than does the present low level. What the present insurgency does succeed in doing is wasting the country's resources and impeding development.

In considering whether or not the present Uganda government is serious about restoring security of persons and property to its citizens we looked at two new structures which have been set up, the Commission of Enquiry into Violations of Human Rights, and the office of the Inspector-General of Government. Both were established to meet urgently expressed needs, and both are now operating effectively, though both were hampered to begin with by a lack of resources. The Commission of Enquiry has shown the need for a permanent commission to monitor human rights, and this is under consideration. The greatest need for structural adjustment in the human rights field is the army. The guerrilla NRA was the best-disciplined army Uganda has ever had. Since coming to power it has undergone major change, as has been noted: it has increased hugely in size in order to counter insurgency and carry out duties that would normally be the responsibility of the police. Its recruits, many of them drawn from previous armies, lack the commitment to discipline and respect for civilians that characterized the NRA before 1986. Its command structures and ranking system are no longer the more egalitarian ones of the bush army; the ranking system of the old regular army seems to have been restored. In 'areas of insurgency' soldiers are given powers in magistrates' courts that are wholly inappropriate for the military to carry out. The difficulties that have been experienced in bringing culprits to justice for human rights abuses in areas of armed conflict illustrate the difficulty the authorities are facing in controlling the army and making it politically responsible. The army seems to be edging its way towards trying to recover some of the immunities and power it possessed under Amin and Obote II. It will be a disaster for Uganda if it succeeds.

After the army mutinies of 1964 Tanzania disbanded its army and replaced it with a People's Defence Force whose first recruits came from the ranks of the politically dependable Youth League of TANU. The People's Defence Force did not only have a military function: it was also to contribute to development, and was trained to be socially responsible. Museveni had something of the same vision for the NRA, which was originally more akin to the TPDF than it is now. The army was to be politicized, he promised, and before 1986 it did possess a measure of social responsibility, though the harsh punishments that had to be meted out from time to time bear witness to the difficulty of inculcating these virtues in an army, particularly after such an appalling recent history as Uganda has suffered. Nyerere was able to impose such a radical solution as the disbanding of the army and re-establishment of the TPDF because he could act from a position of strength.[26] Already Museveni's power is limited *vis-à-vis* the army by the fact that he depends on it, so that it is doubtful if the army could be restructured along the lines it followed during the bush war. All armies demand to be given sufficient power and freedom to do what they consider to be their task, and problems of control are acute when an army has to be involved in countering insurgency. It is Museveni's and Uganda's misfortune that the NRA had to revert to the same type of structure as previous armies, though once the need for speedy reinforcement had arisen, perhaps this was inevitable.

Finally we asked whether the appalling legacy of violence and human rights abuse that the present government inherited could be overcome; were AI and the MRG simply being impractical and idealistic in judging Uganda by absolute standards? The cattle raiding, banditary and rebellion in the north and east are a depressing inheritance indeed. That such legacies can be overcome there is no doubt: Europe in the 14th century was strikingly similar to Uganda today; the British diplomat who thought that in Africa one could not expect civilized standards was forgetting that less than two hundred years ago the slave trade was in full swing, with

Prophetic resistance, external challenges and human rights issues
Britain at the centre of it; and transportation to Australia continued well after the slave trade had been made illegal. It took vigorous and long campaigning to end the slave trade and transportation. If Uganda's legacy of human rights abuse is to be overcome, it will surely be because Ugandans themselves demand it of their government. For the first time in years the Law Society is able to voice its objections to the introduction of insurgency laws, and the Commission of Enquiry is beginning to teach people that they have rights which they must defend. The group known as the Human Rights Activists is able to function in Kampala, and there is considerable freedom of the press. These are hopeful signs. But they need to be supported by development, as the OAU African Charter on Human and People's Rights suggests. Human rights cannot be fully restored until insurgency ends, but much greater respect for human rights by the army could help to create a climate in which insurgency would be more likely to wither. The past *can* be overcome; whether it will or not is still not entirely clear.

Notes

---

1. Museveni, 1985, p. 52.
2. *BBC Summary of World Broadcasts*, ME/8171/B/8, 31 January 1986.
3. *The Independent* (London), 22 February 1986.
4. Hooper and Pirouet, 1989, pp. 19, 27; Furley, 1989.
5. *The Times* (London), 11, 13 February 1986; Amnesty International, 1989, p. 24.
6. *New African*, December 1987; see also *The Independent*, 24 July, 6 August, 11 September 1987.
7. Hooper and Pirouet, 1989, p. 24.
8. Museveni, 1985, p. 52.
9. See also *Amnesty International*, 1989, p. 26.
10. *New African*, December 1987.
11. *The Observer* (London), 8 November 1987; *The Guardian* (London), 10 November 1987.
12. *Africa Confidential*, 23 September 1988.
13. *Africa Analysis*, 20 January 1989.
14. *The Independent*, 11 September 1987; Amnesty International, 1989, pp. 26–7. For the large numbers of dead, see, for example, *Sunday Times* (London), 23 August 1987; *South*, October 1987; *The Times*, 6 October 1987; *The Observer*, 8 November 1987; *The Guardian*, 23 March 1988. This last claims that 7,000 of her followers may have died.
15. *Africa Events*, October 1987.
16. Hooper and Pirouet, 1989, p. 23.
17. Rupesinghe (ed.), 1989.
18. Amnesty International, 1989, p. 35.

19. *ibid.*, p. 15. Amnesty International is concerned at the summary nature of this justice and is campaigning against the death sentence.
20. *Africa Analysis*, 20 January 1989.
21. *Amnesty*, no. 40, August/September 1989.
22. *The Independent*, 24 July 1989.
23. *ibid.*, 21 July 1989.
24. Amnesty International, 1989, p. 20.
25. Hooper and Pirouet, 1989, p. 23.
26. Omara-Otunnu, 1989, p. 56.

PART FIVE

THE CONSTITUTIONAL BASES OF REVOLUTIONARY CHANGE

FOURTEEN
Legal adjustment to revolutionary change

Sam K. Njuba

Many revolutions in Africa have failed because of the attempt to embrace foreign ideology. This inevitably leaves out some people and in many cases it is the majority that are left behind. The National Resistance Army/National Resistance Movement revolution in Uganda was aimed at carrying along all the people or at least a greater majority through purposive and positive mobilization programmes. Thus, in the NRM one finds ultra-right and ultra-left members, monarchists, socialists, Marxist-Leninists, republicans etc., happily working together. The main thrust of the ideology is aimed at doing good for Uganda – true nationalism. This is not an easy thing to attempt. It has been said that it is one of the weaknesses of this revolution. But we believe it is its strongest attribute to pull together all the people for the best of the entire country. From the experiences already referred to, the NRM leadership is convinced that this approach is the best under the Ugandan circumstances.

In the NRM there is an apparent dichotomy between the legal order and the revolutionary moves of the NRM. I deliberately use the word 'apparent' because to some people the revolutionary spirit appears to have been retarded by the NRM sense of a need to carry everybody along. They have a mission to accomplish. The extremists in the NRM are therefore not too happy because their mission is retarded by the need to carry everyone along and also revive the legal order. The latter they perceive as unnecessary, affecting the speed of the revolution and hence delaying its consolidation.

It remains important at one stage in the revolutionary process to establish a legal framework within which the principles and norms of the revolution can operate. Having replaced the oppressive and dictatorial regimes through armed struggle the next task of the NRA/NRM was to establish a legal order by streamlining the administrative structures of the state. The amendment to the Local Administrations Act that legalized the resistance councils (RCs) and the recent establishment of a Constitutional Commission (both discussed in more detail later in the chapter) are part of efforts to establish a legal order.

Legal adjustment to revolutionary change

An attempt will be made in the rest of this chapter to reflect upon these and other legal adjustments that are taking place in Uganda. It is important to note that in making these changes the NRM is making every effort to carry everybody along and achieve maximum unity and economic progress. In effect the major task is to revitalize the legal order rather than introduce an entirely new one.

CONSTITUTIONAL ADJUSTMENTS

Legal Notice No. 1 of 1986 amended the 1967 Constitution in some parts, e.g., the legislature and provisions relating to the head of state. These amendments left largely untouched the judicial system and presidential powers. A legislature was introduced to enact laws. The same notice provided for the expansion of the NRC political organ to include other fighting and political groups. This change was intended to involve all parties and partisan groups in the management of government. This provision was very much welcomed by the country and many references were made to it through the subsequent years. In February 1989, finally, the proposed expansion was effected. The expansion of the NRC was one of the undertakings of the movement and was categorically set out in Legal Notice No. 1 of 1986, at the takeover. This expansion was significant in two respects. First, the method of effecting the expansion and, second, the quality and functions of the new enlarged body. It was also a fulfilment of the NRM philosophy of accommodation, otherwise referred to as the politics of inclusion.

METHOD OF ELECTIONS

The NRC (political organ) was until February 1987 the supreme policy-making body of the NRM as well as the legislative authority. It was faced with the task of deciding the best method of enlarging itself. It could have nominated political personalities from various corners of the country to the NRC. To a certain extent this was employed when the President appointed ministers who were not original members of the political organ. These then sat and enacted laws in the NRC when it sat as a legislative body.

Another alternative would have been for the NRC to direct the district councils (RC5) to nominate people from their respective districts to the NRC. But the organ decided to employ elections throughout the country. The general elections hitherto held in 1961, 1962 and most recently, 1980, were all carried out under secret ballot. They were all discredited, especially the 1980 one, which was massively rigged. Most Ugandans suspected that even the then-proposed elections (1989) would suffer the same fate. Our detractors argued that it was a ploy by the NRM to impose hand-picked members of the NRC on the people to the exclusion of others. In fact the political organ had no such intention. The success and mass acceptability of the 1989 elections dealt a heavy political blow to detractors who had hoped they would flop and once again throw the country into political chaos from which they stood ready to take advantage.

Incidentally, it was that rigging that was the immediate cause of taking to the bush to fight in 1981 by the various forces. An unconventional method of election was therefore devised. The candidate stood at the voting place and those who wished to vote for him lined up behind him. To people in the West it was a rude shock, for it violated the familiar electoral norms of a secret ballot element with its separation of choice and expression. None of us in Uganda can pretend that it was a perfect method, yet it was necessary to inject some sanity into the system in order to revive life in the body politic. The body politic was so corrupt that it was needed to avoid rigging these elections. It was a balancing act – the need for secrecy on the one hand; and the need for getting rid of corruption on the other. The sum total was a peaceful election with indeed few petitions alleging violation of the rules of the elections. But the greatest achievement of the exercise has been the fact that the NRM was exonerated from the charge that it was manipulating or manoeuvring to bring its own people into the NRC to the exclusion of others of contrary political views.

Another achievement of this exercise has been the qualitative change in the NRC. Its membership of almost 300 is dominated by relatively young men and women in their early 40s whose allegiances to the old politics of parties and other sectarian interests are not as deep-rooted as other politicians. The law provided specifically for district and municipal women representative to be elected, so that over forty NRC members are now women. (There are 34 districts and municipalities). This did not merely bring to the national legislature a feminine touch, but rather a real female force, as evidenced by the lively debates that have since taken place. The law also provided room for representation of the armed forces in the national legislature. The 1967 Constitution as amended in 1986 introduced provisions for members of the armed forces to be part of the national legislature. The NRM has, however, gone further in that while previously the armed forces representatives were nominated by the President, the present members are elected by the army itself through its council. All in all the introduction of two new special constituencies, namely the army and woman in addition to the ordinary member, has been a fundamental and qualitative change. But more significant still is the experiment of a partnership between the armed forces and the civilian in the running of the state.

Another significant innovation has been the creation of an executive of the NRC. This is known as the NEC. This is entrusted with the task of vetting ministerial and other senior political appointments and acts as a check on the otherwise extensive presidential powers over appointments.

PARTICIPATORY DEMOCRACY AND THE ADMINISTRATION OF JUSTICE

As already indicated, it is not possible in a revolutionary situation to sustain or maintain the previous order. Soon after the takeover, for example, members of the armed forces began to consider that the judiciary was not acting fast enough for the revolution. Soldiers who were politically conscious did not fully appreciate how the legal system functioned and hence grew impatient with the ordinary courts of law. For instance the army found it extremely hard to believe that a man whom they had arrested the previous day could be released on police bond or court bail. Army personnel could not appreciate how a man in possession of a gun could have used it to kill another while drunk and yet plead diminished responsibility. Above all, with the entire society having been corrupt: it was considered that the judiciary, especially the lower bench, was no exception to this rule.

The NRM therefore drew upon its experience in the bush where the ordinary people looked after their own affairs, including the administration of justice. Thus the institution of resistance councils (RCs) and committees was introduced throughout the country. This institutional framework is designed to play an increasingly important role in the future. The changes were basically contained in two pieces of legislation that amend the Local Government Act to institutionalize and legalize RCs and another that vested limited judicial powers in them.

The amendments substantially modified the structure of local government in order to reflect the functions and powers of RCs. The district commissioner, previously a civil servant who was the executive head of a district, was replaced by a political cadre appointed by the President. His role, besides administration, is to mobilize the population to appreciate the NRM political programme as contained in the *10-Point Programme*. He has a council (RCs) and an executive of nine people known as a district committee that handles the affairs of the district. The council is composed of two representatives of each sub-county in the district. The sub-county RC is composed of nine executive members of each parish. Each parish has a council composed of 9 executive members of each village in that parish. The lowest council is the people in the village over the age of 18 who elect their executive committee, which is known as a resistance committee 1 (RC 1).

This set-up, designed originally to assist in the struggle in defence of the population, and for mobilization and communication within an area, was adopted and introduced throughout Uganda. It has given the people real authority over their local affairs. They are free to deliberate and

213

make proposals on anything in their area. Developmental plans, instead of being from the top, start at the lowest level of administration and are thus appreciated by the ordinary people who, after all, are supposed to implement them. These resistance councils and committees have taken root and have become a permanent feature of Ugandan local government. In effect the way these RCs have been embraced by the people has turned out to be a major change in the power structure of the country. Their popularity is a result of people's participation in decision making at all levels, which is participatory democracy. For the first time in years the ordinary citizen is feeling that he is part of the government and that he has authority and can continuously exercise it, which was not the case in the past. Previously people used to exercise their right to choose leaders once in ten years, that is if elections were held at all. Even then, these elections were so often rigged that they are not worthy of being accorded the status of democratic process.

Another major readjustment has been in the trials of certain offences by resistance committee courts. The judicial powers granted them provide jurisdiction in certain categories of criminal and civil matters. In effect a two-tier judicial system has been set up. The RC courts operate parallel to the ordinary courts. The advantage and indeed the main difference is that while the ordinary courts strictly adhere to legal procedure, the RC courts are more flexible and pragmatic. They are guided by good sense and have so far been able to promote reconciliation among people in their jurisdictions.

CONSTITUTION-MAKING

Following the assumption of power by the NRM government in January 1986, a Minister of State for Constitutional Affairs was appointed for the first time in Uganda. This was part of the NRM's commitment to create a permanent and lasting peace, jealously guarded by the supreme law of the land, the Constitution. Government views the Constitution as a document that should have its roots in the social, political and economic conditions of the people. It must be a document based on the firm understanding that government exists to serve the needs of the people and not the other way round. The Constitution must recognize that people have individual rights – human rights – that should not be unlawfully infringed. Further, the Constitution must have a national character and must create a national consciousness, so that when it is attacked, the attack is seen to be on the Ugandan consciousness and the Ugandan character.

The NRM is seriously committed to the restoration of democracy. Long before it took over power it worked out proposals for a political programme that has come to be popularly known as the *10-Point Programme*. To an encouraging extent this programme has been

Legal adjustment to revolutionary change

implemented, as evidenced by the expanded NRC and a fully functional RC system. The NRM is aware that the political problem remains the root cause of other problems including the economy. The NRM believes that an acceptable constitution is a step towards creating political stability. To be acceptable, the people of Uganda must be involved in constitution-making powers. It is against this background that in December 1988 the NRC enacted The Uganda Constitutional Commission Statute, which set up The Constitutional Commission.

This statute clearly spells out the Commission's duties. These are:

(1) the duty of collecting ideas from people throughout the country;
(2) the responsibility of studying and reviewing the present Constitution with a view to making proposals for enactment of a national Constitution which will among other things,
   (a) guarantee the national independence, territorial integrity and sovereignty of Uganda;
   (b) establish a free and democratic system of government that will guarantee the fundamental rights and freedom of the people of Uganda;
   (c) create viable political institutions that will ensure maximum consensus and orderly succession to Government;
   (d) recognise and demarcate division of responsibility among state organs of the Executive, the Legislative and the Judiciary, and create viable checks and balances between them;
   (e) endeavour to develop a system of Government that ensures people's participation in the governance of their country;
   (f) endeavour to develop a democratic, free and fair electoral system that will ensure true people's
   (g) establish and uphold the principle of public accountability by the holders of public offices and political posts, and guarantee the independence of the judiciary.

In carrying out their mandate the Statute requires the commissioners to seek the views of the general public and to stimulate public discussion and awareness.

AFTER THE COMMISSION

By law the duration of the Commission should be two years although the minister can extend this should he deem it expedient, especially if it is for purposes of enabling the Commission to complete its work. At the completion of its work the Commission will submit its report to the minister. It is expected that the minister would then table the draft constitution before a national constituent assembly. Ugandans who live abroad are free to submit written memoranda to the Constitutional Commission and some already have.

215

The constitutional bases of revolutionary change

CONCLUSION

In many respects the NRA/NRM revolution has been a unique one. It has represented a major departure from the more common practice in Uganda and other parts of Africa where comparable changes in government have been characterized by victimization of sections of the population and minority groups that have opposed change. Rather than victimize, harass and oppress opposition, the NRM has opted to educate such groups so that they can re-adjust their attitudes and appreciate the need for unity. Already this strategy is bearing fruits because the level of opposition has been drastically dropping as the NRM has step-by-step implemented the *10-Point Programme*.

It has not been easy for the NRM to harmonize the spirit of the revolution with the legal order that earlier prevailed in the country. This is not surprising because, as pointed out earlier, legal order and revolution are not necessarily congruent but seemingly present an inherent contradiction. Slowly but surely, however, the two are now being harmonized. There is little doubt that when finally the Constitution in which all people have participated is put in place, then chances of total harmony will be tremendously increased.

For those who may entertain any doubts on the NRA/NRM revolution, they should take heed of Museveni's words at the time of the takeover. The new regime was, he said, not a mere change of guards but a fundamental change.

FIFTEEN
The rule of law and human rights in Uganda: the missing link

E. Khiddu-Makubuya

UGANDA'S CONSTITUTIONAL LEGACY

One of the most persistent features of Uganda, at least since 1966, has been breaches of the rule of law and violations of human rights. These have persisted whether the regime in power was civilian or military. It is important to figure out their genesis if preventive and remedial measures are to be effectively taken. I note that the National Resistance Movement (NRM) has set up a Commission of Enquiry into Violations of Human Rights covering the period 1962 to 1986. The Commission is required to inquire, inter alia, into "the causes and circumstances" surrounding the whole range of human rights violations and breaches of the rule of law.

The Commission's final report should provide sound insights into the causes of human rights violations and breaches of the rule of law. Meanwhile, it is my view that any serious attempt to figure out their causes and antecedents will have to reckon with the interaction of the following factors:

(1) Colonial rule, during which disparate nationalities were brought together in a loose and artificial association. The colonial state was certainly not rooted amongst the people of Uganda. It was a structure superimposed upon them. It thus became necessary for the colonial authorities to resort to draconic and authoritarian legalisms to compel compliance. The post-independence state is hardly more rooted among the people than the colonial one. The state has continued to be an external structure artificially and forcefully superimposed upon the people. It should not come as a surprise that the said post-independence state inherited and embraced the colonial framework lock, stock and barrel and found it imperative to use it to subjugate the people.

(2) Ethnicity and ethnic identity has been a major factor and a basis of sectarian and factional orientation in public life. To this perennial threat of disintegration a weak, incompetent, and unimaginative leadership has reacted simplistically with oppressive strategies and tactics.

217

The constitutional bases of revolutionary change

(3) Religion has also led to division along clearly marked lines. This must certainly be seen as adding to the insecurity of the leadership. The infusion of ethnic and religious identity into the public life of Uganda has often led to the politics of ascription, which are themselves unstable.

(4) Differences in levels of development, economic activities, modernization and receptivity to change and innovation. Those different levels of development are explicable historically. For example, while the British encouraged other Ugandan nationalities to adopt modern ways of life, they deliberately preserved the Karamojong in a pristine and raw state. Those differences coexist with differences in visions and world views. These two have often bamboozled the political leaders, whose usual reply has been hostility and repression.

(5) The massive poverty in which the majority of Ugandans live readily supports a system of cheap patronage, opportunism and political exploitation. The repressive structures have not lacked philosophers, supporters, henchmen and operatives, whose lowest denominator is socio-economic opportunism and illicit gain.

(6) Over the period under review Uganda has not been blessed with competent or capable political leaders. Some of them have lacked even basic education. On the whole, most past Ugandan rulers have clearly not measured up to the task. There have been problems of lack of vision, inferiority complex, and susceptibility to flattery and sycophancy. Some leaders have viewed and conducted themselves as tribal chieftains. They have craved for the company of inferior and mediocre minds. This has led to political myopia, narrow-mindedness, and lack of imagination and creativity. The leadership has failed, on the whole, to live up to the challenge of statesmanship.

(7) Foreign interests have also not left Uganda alone. The neocolonial economic structure left in place in 1962 has been a major springboard for the entrenchment of other foreign interests. Some foreign interests have been instrumental in servicing and generally propping up authoritarian regimes.

(8) Uganda was, throughout the period under review, politically underdeveloped. The level of political consciousness has generally been very low. This lack of politicization generates credulity and naivety among the populace to unprecedented degrees. It promotes political inertia and the Messiah syndrome. People tend to mistake political forms and technicalities for substance. Political ignorance conduces people to cooperate with their oppressors until it is too late to withdraw or meaningless to try to do so. A major component of this political underdevelopment is a large margin of ignorance regarding the rule of law and basic human rights and the relative unwillingness to enforce them or to fight for them. It is this political underdevelopment

218

that accounts for the lack of nationalist political organizations to roll back repression and to translate the lessons of history into practical politics. Most of the so called political parties that have existed in Uganda have espoused primordial, sectarian and, indeed, foreign interests while others have shaped up as defence mechanisms to such backward, primordial, sectarian and foreign-oriented initiatives.

(9) The practice of politics by other means. This term refers to forms and practices intended to achieve political objectives other than by peaceful, honest or straightforward means. These may take the forms of violence, some form of dirty tricks, tactical ambushes, etc. In the early 1980s, one Ugandan political group boasted that it had 99 "tricks" for capturing and/or staying in power. Aspects of politics by other means were practised in 1966, 1971–9, 1980 and 1981–6. The insecurity, mistrust, frustrations and reactions generated by such practices greatly undermine the rule of law and safeguards for the promotion of human rights.

THE RISE OF THE NATIONAL RESISTANCE MOVEMENT (NRM)

The NRM/NRA assumption of power in Uganda on 25/26 January 1986 was not the usual *coup d'état* by the established military. Rather, it was a take-over with unique features. In term of the rule of law and protection of human rights, there are a number of significant elements in the NRM's antecedents, theory and practice that we need to record.

(a) *The armed-cum-political struggle* The NRM had waged an active armed-cum-political struggle for five years in an essentially rural arena acting amongst peasants. The armed struggle was backed and buttressed by political conscientization and enlightenment. The success of this struggle has great precedential value for alternatives to putting up with violations of human rights and breaches of the rule of law.

(b) *The 10-Point Programme of the NRM* This programme strongly underlines the need to restore the rule of law and respect for human rights in Uganda and also outlines some practical steps to achieve these. The first three years of the NRM administration provide reasonable practice and experience for assessment.

(c) *The NRA Code of Conduct* For the first time in the history of Uganda, it is intended to subject the official army to a strict and people-centred Code of Conduct. This is a serious proposition whose full implementation would change the character of Uganda's politics.

(d) *Cessation of state-inspired murder and terror* The NRM has so far managed to silence *most* of the guns of Kampala and to marginalize state-inspired murder and terrors. The real challenge is to ensure that this success becomes a permanent feature of life in Uganda. One would also wish to see a cessation of detention of civilians in military barracks and more

219

confidence placed in the ordinary court system.

There has also been some criticism to the effect that the conduct of government troops in the areas of insurgency in the north and east of Uganda has left much to be desired. War situations are, by definition, complicated and one needs to resort to the provisions of the Geneva Conventions 1949 and the Protocols Additional to the Geneva Conventions 1977 for a realistic assessment. It is clear, however, that the NRM has not endorsed or condoned breaches of the rule of law and violations of human rights in the areas of insurgency.

(e) *Resistance councils and committees*   The establishment of RCs from grassroots through districts and to national level has significant implications for the rule of law and the promotion of human rights. The powerlessness of ordinary people was a major characteristic of public life in Uganda before 1986. The attempt to re-empower ordinary people through the RC system should give them more control over their own affairs and destiny, and marginalize breaches of the rule of law and violations of human rights.

(f) *The Human Rights Commission*   By Legal Notice No. 5 of 1986, the NRM set up a Commission of Enquiry into Violations of Human Rights from the period 9 October 1962 to the 25 January 1986. The Commission was generally to inquire into all aspects of violations of human rights, breaches of the rule of law and excessive abuse of powers perpetrated by various arms of government and agents. It is also to inquire into the causes of these matters with a view to making recommendations as to how their recurrence might be prevented.

The Commission has been taking evidence in public since December 1986. A good many facts concerning violations of human rights and breaches of the rule of law have emerged. Human rights watchers both in Uganda and elsewhere are waiting for the Commission's report with great interest. Meanwhile, the very setting up of the Commission raises the hope that the goings-on in the offices of the powerful and the influential may, in the long run, be subjected to public scrutiny.

(g) *The Inspector-General of Government*   (IGG) This office has been established by the Inspector General of Government Statute 1987 (Statute No. 2 of 1988). The IGG is generally charged with the duty of protecting and promoting the protection of human rights and the rule of law in Uganda and eliminating and fostering the elimination of corruption and abuse of public offices. The setting-up of the IGG is a serious commitment on the part of the NRM to protect and ensure the rule of law and Human Rights. There have been long-standing calls for government to establish such an office (Mubiru Musoke, 1971; Khiddu-Makubuya, 1984). One expects that the IGG will have properly trained staff in adequate numbers. The office should also open grassroots branches to make its services available to as many people as possible. The need for adequate budget

220

The rule of law and human rights in Uganda: the missing link
and facilities cannot be over-emphasized. Corruption and misuse of public funds upon which the IGG has so far concentrated are serious matters. But one hopes that the IGG will focus on rule of law and human rights issues in the not-too-distant future.

(h) *Control of the intelligence community* Intelligence agencies and paramilitary organizations have played a major role in violations of human rights and breaches of the rule of law in post-independence Uganda. They have always seemed to be above the law or indeed a law unto themselves. In the past there has been some dishonesty and pretense in this matter. The NRM has honestly come out with the Security Organisations Statute 1987 (Statute No. 10 of 1987). This has given the intelligence community a statutory basis for the first time. It is now officially known who controls the intelligence services, and the extent of their powers has also been spelt out.

(i) *Ministry of Constitutional Affairs/Uganda Constitutional Commission* The setting-up of these institutions gives the people of Uganda an opportunity to re-examine the entire constitutional history of the country and to come up with a constitutional framework that promotes and protects the rule of law and human rights.

The foregoing shows that the NRM is committed to and serious about the rule of law and human rights. It is also evident that a good deal more still needs to be done. By Legal Notice 6 of 1986, the NRM government gave itself statutory immunity against all claims arising out of violations of human rights by previous regimes. This immunity even affected claims that had already crystallized into court judgment. In *E.F. Ssempebwa* v. *Attorney General* (High Court Constitutional Case No. 1 of 1986) the High Court struck those provisions down for being unconstitutional. The NRM Government promptly and legislatively overruled the High Court and re-enacted the offending provisions in Legal Notice No. 1 of 1987. The government action may be defensible in economic and financial terms. But it is hard to deny that it was essentially contrary to the rule of law and amounted to a breach of basic human rights.

The continued application of the Public Order and Security Act, 1967 (Act 20 of 1967) under the NRM administration is another disturbing and disappointing development. The detention of persons without trial is simply a violation of the rule of law that one had hoped would not occur under the NRM administration. Act 20 of 1967 should be repealed and never replaced.

THE FUTURE OF THE RULE OF LAW AND HUMAN RIGHTS
The need to focus on the future of the rule of law and human rights partly stems from the realization that negative performance in these two areas tends to coincide with negative performance in the economy and in other areas.

221

The constitutional bases of revolutionary change

Arguments about cause and effect can often become involved and circular. The short point here is that the national economy performed very badly amidst widespread violations of human rights and breaches of the rule of law. It is for this reason that we consider that the rule of law and human rights constitute the missing link in post-independence Uganda, resulting in underperformance in practically all sectors of public life.

With the coming of the NRM, many people thought that fundamental change had finally arrived and that no more action was necessary to protect the rule of law and to promote and ensure human rights. This kind of naive optimism is one of Uganda's great problems. Many people tend to relax too easily and leave the real hard work to a few.

The apparent causes of breaches of the rule of law and violations of human rights are, essentially, still very much around. One would not be serious to imagine that they will just go away. Against this background the propensity of any people-oriented arrangements to breakdown is high indeed. The need for eternal vigilance and actual efforts to overcome those problems cannot be over-emphasized.

The process of evolving a new constitution is already under way. It only remains to point out the necessity of embedding both the rule of law and the idea of human rights in the proposed constitution. In this regard, various themes will have to be considered.

(a) *Abolition of coup d'état*   It is instructive to begin with the Constitution of the Federal Republic of Nigeria 1979. This specifically outlawed a takeover of government 'except in accordance with the provisions of this Constitution.' Less than five years later, however, some of the very military officers who had sanctioned the inclusion of this provision overthrew the Nigerian government. In Uganda one will have to contend with *Uganda* v. *Commissioner of Prisons ex parte Matovu (1966)* E.A. 514 (U) and *Andrew Lutakome Kayira and others* v. *Edward Rugumayo and others* (Uganda High Court Constitutional Case No. 1 of 1979). Does it make sense to write constitutional provisions against irregular takeover? Or should the Constitution invest the power to take over governments with specific groups, e.g., the army, the workers, the students etc?

(b) *Bill of rights*   Because of the problems raised in (a) above, some people argue that human rights should not be part of the constitution because, if they are, then they are subject to all the vicissitudes envisaged in (a) above. Where there is a written constitution, it is imperative that a bill of rights should be part of it. But in Uganda, it is necessary to eliminate the usual exceptions and qualifications that greatly water down the substantive provisions of such a bill.

(c) *Independence of the judiciary*   This is a fundamental requirement of the rule of law and the present Uganda Constitutional Commission is required to address itself specifically to it. Independence will be ensured

222

and guaranteed by training, personal integrity, facilities, tenure security, and public supervision. Independence may be promoted by the importation of foreign judges. But this is likely to be a short-term interim solution.

(d) *Discrimination on grounds of sex* This is an aspect of legal life in Uganda that has persisted despite propaganda to the contrary. In short the constitutional definition of discrimination should include differential treatment purely on account of sex. This is deemed necessary to incorporate women's energy effectively into the mainstream of development.

(e) *Human rights commission* The superintendency of the rule of law and enforcement of human rights should be entrusted to a permanent human rights commission in addition to the role of the courts. It should focus on prevention of breaches of the rule of law, etc. rather than undertaking postmortem exercises after breaches and violations have occurred. It should also be possible for the Commission to evolve an early warning system for human rights disasters.

(f) *Supranational remedies* The Constitution should grant a right of access to international fora to lodge complaints about breaches of the rule of law and violations of human rights. One has in mind the African Commission on Human and Peoples Rights under OAU auspices and the Human Rights Committee set up under the optional protocol to the International Covenant on Civil and Political Rights (1966).

(g) *The military factor* Uganda has had several armed forces since independence. Each of these has been labelled a 'national army' but the brute fact was that they were recruited from limited sections of the population. Certainly, until the advent of the NRM, the army was trained and indeed operated on the basis of sectarian ideology. The army has also tested power and found it sweet. In future a big standing army will be an expensive liability for Uganda. A small, indeed, skeletal standing army would suffice. Even though it will be small, such an army should be recruited on a quota basis from all districts of Uganda from amongst persons with basic education and good character. Moreover, positive political education is necessary for all, including the army, and all able-bodied citizens should be trained in military skills. The standing army must be integrated into the political economy of Uganda and must be subject to the ordinary law, and to democratic and popular control. Moreover, non-Ugandans should be prohibited from joining the army.

As a corollary to this, paramilitary organizations must themselves be few, established pursuant to regular law, and subject to democratic and popular control.

The Constitution cannot execute itself. Consequently, it will need a socio-cultural infrastructure, some of whose elements include a culture of constitutionalism, human rights and peace education; political education; realistic development planning; and equitable distribution of national wealth and resources among citizens and regions.

SIXTEEN
Towards constitutional renovation:
some political considerations

A.G.G. Gingyera-Pinycwa

Uganda's political system for most of the quarter century and more of independence has been an unmitigated disappointment and frustration to its citizens; as well as to the country's friends and admirers elsewhere. It has failed to perform a number of basic social and economic functions and services that have come to be expected from any properly functioning political system in the modern world.

Some Ugandans, faced with this disappointment and frustration, have turned their attention to their country's constitution. They believe that a major cause of the disappointment and frustration is a flawed or faulty constitution and that it should therefore be reviewed or rewritten to enable the political system to perform satisfactorily.

Indeed, one of the major political demands that urgently pressed themselves upon the attention of Yoweri Museveni and the National Resistance Movement (NRM) as their way to power became evidently clear was the demand for a constitutional review. This was a major consideration behind the NRM's appointment of a Commissioner for Constitutional Affairs, as well as the subsequent setting up of the completely new Ministry of Constitutional Affairs, to whose portfolio, perhaps quite appropriately, a lawyer from Buganda has been appointed. Since then, no less a figure than Ronald Mutebi, the son and heir to Sir Edward Mutesa and Head of the Buganda clans; various clan leaders; the Buganda-based conservative party of Joshua Mayanja-Nkangi, Buganda's Katikiro at the time of the 1966 upheavals, and not a small number of intellectuals from Buganda, have taken up their cue behind the agitation for the review of the constitution.

Their efforts have not been without an impact; apart from the setting up of a ministry, above all and most significantly a constitutional commission has been established to study and review the constitution with a view to making proposals for the enactment of a national constitution (see Chapter 14).

But to review or rewrite a constitution is one thing; to live by it is quite another. Nor must it be lightly imagined that once we have a new constitution, then all these things "will be added unto us", if we may

224

Towards constitutional renovation: some political considerations

humbly borrow this apt phraseology from the Holy Bible.

We only need to look at the situation in the north. In August 1986 some defeated Acholi ex-soldiers took to arms, to be followed subsequently by many others in Kitgum, Gulu, Lira, and Apac districts, in Lango, as well as by others in neighbouring districts of the Eastern Region. Although these rebel campaigns have gone beyond the boundaries of Acholi, the fighting still has a clearly sectarian regional-cum-ethnic appearance: Northerners or non-Bantu against southerners or Bantu, by and large. No one has so far bothered to tell us how the constitution was at stake in this wanton blood-letting and/or destructive confrontation.[1]

All in all, it is difficult to avoid the conclusion, whether we confine ourselves to the rebel confrontation with the NRA, that people have *not* been fighting and dying because of the constitution 'per se', or because of differences over its interpretation and application. Other considerations, *not* the constitution, clearly appear to have been more important. The constitutional optimists must bear this, too, in mind. That is why we are sceptical that the bare writing of a constitution would "add unto us" all the things that we as Ugandans have so far had to miss since our independence. Unless this diagnosis is fully appreciated, any rush for a new constitution may not only be a waste of time and money, but it is most likely to lead us into a situation where we will have to work with a constitution that not only does not enjoy the respect and esteem befitting it but whose future, depending on the concatenation of political forces within the country, may always remain uncertain.[2]

Those who might be thinking of taking up the cudgels during the contemplated review in terms of issues that were familiar in 1960–1 might do well to pause for thought, as should supporters of the 1967 constitution. The issues need not be necessarily the time-worn ones of 1960–1: monarchism, federalism, the position of Buganda, who will be head of state, who will take precedence over whom, the so-called lost counties, and so on. Nor need they be only those that inspired the framers of the 1967 constitution, which gave to the centre a highly concentrated power whose benefits have been hard to discern; indeed its abuses have been abundantly in evidence in the years since the enactment of that constitution.

The commission into the affairs of local government was able to get away from the quagmire of the old issues that animated the makers of both constitutions by identifying for itself in the context of local government very clear strategic goals for the country's future. These were, (see particularly paragraphs 14 and 18) a more or less even pattern of social and economic development under an overall developmental framework that would counter centrifugal tendencies in the political economy; a local set-up that would make possible local initiatives that could be

225

The constitutional bases of revolutionary change

realized in the context of the overall developmental framework; and viable and representative or democratic local authorities. The task of our constitutional reviewers will be much facilitated if broad political strategies of this kind are clarified and agreed before the technicalities that are bound to arise in handling individual issues come in to cloud their minds. But what under the present circumstances might qualify to be included within this category of broad political strategies for Uganda?

Behind the lavish pluralism of the 1962 constitution lay the issue of the position of Buganda in an independent Uganda, an issue nourished not only by Buganda's history of special relationship as a 'Treaty' state with Britain, but also by its need to preserve its monarchy, under the *Kabaka*. The two gave rise together on the eve of independence to the issue of a federal relationship for Buganda, failing which another vexing issue of secession was raised to provide an alternative political stance for Buganda. These were issues that were very vigorously and hotly debated in their day. In the event, Uganda must consider itself lucky, despite all the misfortunes that have befallen it since independence, to have survived them as a political entity.

Are we likely to see a return to the theme of secession as we review the constitution? We should not in the light of the broad strategy on national unity and integrity. That strategy is even strengthened by the fact that a lot of water has flowed under the bridge of political life since 1960–1. In particular, Buganda since the coming to power of the NRM enjoys a political position in the affairs of Uganda such that it should be able to secure its interests without having to resort to secessionist tactics. Since it is not as politically isolated as it was in the 1960s, Buganda should be able to fight for its demands, including an appropriate and politically equitable position for various districts bordering on other parts of the country. It is worth noting in this context that even the people of the north and the northeast who have been fighting against the central government have not threatened secession.

The issues of the monarchy for Buganda and federalism are more sensitive, considering what has been heard about them since the NRM came to power. Federalism, in particular, has cropped up every now and then, being an issue people are much less inhibited in talking about under the present circumstance than monarchism.[3] So, let us dispose of it first. The greatest flaw of the 1962 constitution lay in its provisions for federalism. For it did not dispense federalism in an equitable manner to the then existing political units in Uganda.

The notion of *inequity* in connection with that constitution is emphasized advisedly. The country should derive an important lesson from it, particularly as it gropes toward another constitution. Even the die-hard opponents of the 1967 constitution will have to accept that any constitution that enshrines political inequity is not sound and is not readily

226

Towards constitutional renovation: some political considerations

compatible either with the demands of democracy or more generally with the needs and the demands of modern times. Equal treatment for all parts of Uganda within the constitution should therefore be the maxim to guide us this time. If it must be federalism, then it must be federalism for all the conceivable units. About this there should be little controversy, although we may still have to argue about what might constitute suitable units for a federal constitution, a matter about which I feel so strongly that I should perhaps say a few words on it.

While, as we have hinted above, it should no longer matter much whether we have a federal or unitary constitution, as long as there is equity or parity of treatment for all the units involved, Ugandans should think carefully about the basic political and administrative unit below the national state level, especially in the light of broad strategies of economic and social progress for all. Here, of course, economists will not be wanting who will wish to lecture us on the advantages of large units, using concepts like the economy of scale and others about which we have heard so much, but without much concrete result in Africa, where the presence and the involvement of the state in economic and social development is so vital. The latter observation, in particular, must make us doubly wary about large political/administrative units. They simply do not seem to have delivered the economic and social development goods, particularly in Uganda.

Units of governance below the national state level must be small enough to be meaningful units for the rural peasants, who are the group most in need of socio-economic uplift. More precisely, it may be submitted that the present 33 districts are very plausible political administrative units if our goal is indeed social and economic development, rather than the kind of political aggrandizement in the name of large units that permits the so-called economy of scale, which they have never done, but which some people might be craving for; and which, if adopted, will not take long to divert attention into political bickerings within them, as well as across their frontiers. Let us repeat, then, that within the limits of these reservations, it should not really matter much whether the country opts for federalism or unitarism.

What, then, of monarchism? This will, of course, be an important issue to some, particularly in Buganda. But it is not likely to command the enthusiastic support it enjoyed before independence. This is definitely the case outside Buganda where the very idea appears to have become a relic of the past; while even in Buganda surprises about the level of support for it may not be ruled out. To be sure, there will be old guards who support the idea of restoration. But the youth within Buganda cannot be said to be overwhelmingly in favour of restoration. The ideological climate among the youth has undergone a change, not only outside Buganda but even within it; unlike in the years before and

227

shortly after independence, it is now easy to find leftists or progressives who will not easily subscribe to the idea of an institution like monarchism.

In addition, monarchists will have to reckon with the NRM's position on this matter. The NRM has certainly not expressed any open support for restoration, preferring to maintain relative silence over the matter, although a few monarchical fanatics in Buganda have been itching for some official indication of official support. All in all, advocates of the restoration of monarchies should expect an uphill task in the review exercise.[4]

Uganda has experienced many years of army rule, and continues to be ruled by a regime that is in practice an army regime. Nor can we rule out future experience of army regimes, even if the NRM completes the process of converting its regime into a completely civilian one. What this means is that the army has become, for better or for worse, too important in our polity to be mentioned only incidentally in relation to other institutions in our constitution. For example, too many uncertainties about what is right and not right for it to do have emerged in regard to its role vis-à-vis civilians, the police, and so on, all of which doubts should be clarified in the constitution in order to combat the excessive human rights anxieties that Uganda has experienced over the years.

Finally let us deal with the executive or presidency. Simply too much power was heaped upon this institution by the 1967 constitution, a good portion of which could safely have been lodged elsewhere in the interest of democracy and efficiency. We shall however draw attention only to one aspect. This is the very extensive power of appointment to public offices that the presidency now enjoys. This is not to take issue with the manner of the appointment of such public officers as ministers, permanent secretaries, judges and so on. Rather, we are concerned that the presidential hand of appointment seems to be reaching down to even the pettiest of appointments. Too much power is being left in the hands of a single individual, something that cannot be regarded as healthy in a political system where so many people must, as is the case at the moment, look to the state and to the public sector controlled by the state for patronage, appointment, and employment. It is perhaps not surprising, therefore, that accusations about tribalism, nepotism, etc., have been so rampant in the country. As much as possible, the power of appointment should be diffused widely to permit a variety of influences, rather than the discretion of one individual, to come to bear on appointments.

As a further way of cutting the presidency down to a size more compatible with the democratic operation of the state machinery, the constitutional review commission should consider the term of tenure of that office. The open-ended system of tenure we currently have is politically

Towards constitutional renovation: some political considerations

unhealthy. It permits the incumbent to claim (as Amin did) that he is president for life. But that was perhaps because Amin did not have much familiarity with the philosophy of Nicolo Machiavelli as expressed in his book *The Prince*. For those who do, the existing system permits them to claim that they will depart or will organize elections to legitimize their tenure, while being all along set or determined in their mind to remain in office as long as the spark of life continues to flicker within their breasts. Now unduly long tenure of this important public office can have extremely bad consequences for the state, to say the least. Among other things it leads to abuse of power, and to impatience on the part of others who are then forced to make their way to the office by means of violence. Both of these tendencies would tend to be checked in a system of tenure of this office that is specifically and irrevocably limited in time, as, for example, is the American system in which the president may post for only two terms of four years each.

In the circumstances of African politics, where leaders hold such overwhelming powers and patronage in their hands, the sad fact is that even where constitutional provisions to restrain them exist the question of who is to apply them still remains difficult to answer. But in this may lie a useful clue to our own constitutional reviewers. That clue lies in the need to pare down the powers of leaders, so that such leaders are amenable to challenges from other quarters within the polity. Constitutional devices of restraint, such as the American system of checks and balances, as well as that of impeachment of the chief executive deserve serious examination in the constitutional review exercise in Uganda.

Notes

---

1. The character of the NRA, it is only fair to add, has changed considerably since Yoweri Museveni and the NRM got into power. In terms of regionalism/sectarianism, the composition of the force is now much more mixed than was the case initially.
2. This paper is being written at a time when rebellion in the north and northeast cannot yet be said to have been completely quashed. The failure to grip this point is, in part, one reason why the 1966 and the 1967 constitutions are unpopular in Buganda which at the time of their enactments was very much subdued and hence grossly dissatisfied with its political lot.
3. See, for example, *New Vision*, Friday, 22 January 1988, p. 5, 'Opinion: Federation is workable', by Silver Kungu Atenyi.
4. For President Museveni's views on monarchy, see *New Vision*, September 1988.

PART SIX
REBUILDING POLITICAL INSTITUTIONS

SEVENTEEN
Institution-building:
the case of the NRM and the military in Uganda 1986-9

Dan M. Mudoola

The NRM is not a military government. We are freedom fighters who took up the gun as a last resort to fight against dictatorship.

Yoweri Museveni

In the Ugandan political process, as we have argued elsewhere, political actors have failed to regularize power in such a way that conflicts are resolved short of use of physical military force; this may be attributed to failure to build political institutions enjoying a wide degree of acceptability among significant socio-political forces.[1] The Ugandan military, built in response to internal political-cum-military crises, has assumed naked political activist roles, sometimes at the service of individuals or groups wishing to dictate their own political terms or at times on its own terms.

An activist military has characterized Ugandan politics since 1966 when Milton Obote, backed by the military, abrogated the 1962 independence constitution and dictated his own, and ruled until he was overthrown in 1971 by his army commander, Idi Amin, who, in turn, was removed by a combination of the Tanzanian army and exiled Ugandan groups. Yusufu Lule then tenuously held on to presidential power for 68 days until he was removed by the National Consultative Council, supported by the Uganda National Liberation Army, with the benevolent connivance of the Tanzania Peoples' Defence Force.[2] The successive regimes of Godfrey Binaisa, Muwanga, Obote and the Okellos had either the military behind them or, as in the case of the Okellos, the kingmakers assumed the throne in their own right.

It was in response to this politico-military state of affairs that groups feeling politically and militarily marginalized took up arms and waged guerrilla war against the Obote regime immediately after the controversial December 1980 elections. The most prominent and successful of these was Yoweri Museveni's National Resistance Movement and its military wing, the National Resistance Army. Under harassment from the National Resistance Army, the pro-Obote UNLA revolted and overthrew him. The National Resistance Army, for some five months, fought

230

a combination of 'allied' armies and finally defeated them in the battle for Kampala on 25 January 1986.

The NRM assumed power as a result of a successful armed uprising. In this chapter we argue that the military remained a political actor in Ugandan political processes even after the NRM victory. Domestication of the military will depend on the extent to which the NRM administration builds political institutions that enjoy a wide degree of political acceptability among significant socio-political groupings, and the extent to which the military is positively integrated into politico-administrative and economic institutions. In the early stages of its assumption and regularization of power, it is not out of the ordinary for the NRM to use the military because in the final analysis, as Leon Trótsky is reported to have said, all political systems are established by force. The issue is thus how the military can be domesticated and integrated.

It may be relevant, for the purposes of this chapter, to offer some operational definitions of such terms as 'domestication' and 'integration'. Domestication is the process whereby the military may be subjected to civilian control mechanisms and persuaded to accept civilian institutional structures as legitimate channels through which to articulate its interests. Integration is a process whereby the military plays an active part in the legitimately established politico-administrative and economic institutions through generally accepted procedures in society. Through this process, the military is not restricted purely to the exercise of the martial arts, but there are legitimate provisions for horizontal or vertical mobility as and when opportunities arise.

There are examples of successful domestication and integration of the military in 'developed' political systems and, to some limited extent, in 'developing' political systems. In the Soviet system recent studies have demonstrated that the Soviet military is a distinct interest group, but is subject to institutional control mechanisms through organs of the Communist Party through which it too articulates its interests.[3] In Anglo-American political systems, political institutional control of the military is long established. Nearer home, in Tanzania, there is evidence that the Tanzania Peoples' Defence Force is domesticated and well-integrated into the Tanzanian political system.

This was well demonstrated during the 'Kagera War' between Uganda and Tanzania in 1978–9. The CCM, the ruling party, was very much in control throughout the war – matters of high military policy were discussed in the organs of the party; the party was the ultimate authority in issues related to grand strategy; the postwar demobilization process was the responsibility of the CCM Party Secretary-General, Pius Msekwa.[4]

In the Ugandan case, instances of an undomesticated and unintegrated military abound. Since 1966, even behind facades of civilian

231

control, the military has virtually dictated policy, as is evidenced by the overprotectiveness of the military from 1966 up to 1971 and its high visibility. From 1971 to 1979 policy was subjected to the whims of the military; and during the later regimes of Yusufu Lule, Godfrey Binaisa, Muwanga and Obote 2 the military had the power of veto. Dismissals or transfers of high-ranking officers had political overtones and were regarded in punitive terms.[5]

A visible political activist role by the military can best be neutralized not by totally insulating it from legitimate and regular political processes, but by creating conditions in which it cannot be activist on terms dictated by itself, or by some faction supported by it. Before the ascendancy of the National Resistance Movement, Ugandan attitudes towards the military oscillated between fear and over-ingratiation. In the former case these degenerate into 'who will bell the cat'[6] attitudes and render the military more vicious and predatory; in the latter case they generate in the military mind a sense of indispensability. Such attitudes hinder the processes of domesticating and integrating the military in society.

In this chapter we examine the politico-military conditions prevailing on Museveni's assumption of power; the steps he has taken to regularize power and rebuild a new army and institutional control mechanisms; the challenges of the northern and northeastern rebellions, in so far as they have affected the institution-building processes, and the politico-military consequences arising out of Museveni's attempts to regularize power, rebuild a new army and its attendant institutional control mechanisms, and the north and north-eastern uprisings.

REGULARIZING POWER

In establishing institutional structures for regularization of power, the NRM's pace has been conditioned by the external and internal environment. Externally, rise to power attracted suspicion and potential hostility. To the major Western powers he was associated with Marxist rhetoric. President Moi of Kenya was the self-appointed patron of the Ugandan leaders making a bid for power in Uganda. Having been the chairman of the Nairobi peace talks, Moi did not take kindly to Museveni's capture of power since he had not adhered to the Peace Accord timetable. Moi has still not quite reconciled himself to Museveni and the NRM ruling in Uganda and continues to believe there is a power vacuum there. Combined hostility from the Western powers could easily have strangled the NRM at birth. To allay external fears, Museveni's steps to regularize power were therefore a mixture of diplomatic caution and calculated boldness. Caution, in the sense that he went out of his way to reassure potentially hostile external forces that he was not the 'Marxist' they thought him to be. Calculated boldness, in the sense that slowly but surely he introduced his institutional structures.

Institution-building: the case of the NRM and the military 1986–9

Internally, before the NRM entered, Kampala had been in a state of anarchy, the 'allied armies' in complete disarray and incapable of maintaining law and order. The city had been partitoned into war zones supposedly controlled by UNLA, UNRF, FUNA and UFM. For all their numerical strength and sophisticated military equipment they were badly led and divided, and were no match for the NRA. Within 12 hours their armies were routed and melted away, some fleeing north and northeast, the rest waiting to join the victor. The general politico-military state of affairs in January 1986 was a blessing in disguise for the NRM and its military wing. There was no coherent politico-military force to challenge them. The southern areas were generally at peace. It took some eight months for the opposition in the north and northeast to regroup. There was the immediate need to regularize power for purposes of legitimacy, maintenance of law and order, and day-to-day administration.

There is no evidence that there was any very well publicized NRM blueprint for the administration of the country. True, there was the *10-Point Programme*[7] but this does not spell out the institutional frameworks through which the NRM's programme was to be implemented. True, during the five years of struggle a rudimentary framework for administration had evolved, but this appears to have been dictated by the crises of war. The politico-civilian wing of the movement, whose functions had been basically diplomatic and fund-raising, was external. Such institutional frameworks as the movement had within Uganda were basically military and for working out military policy, strategy, mobilization, collection of military intelligence, collection of war supplies, and general welfare for the military and the displaced. In this sense, institutionally the military wing of the NRM was relatively more developed than its political wing in January 1986.

In its immediate politico-administrative and military tasks, the NRM had another advantage in that it consisted of a minority who had been forged in the circumstances of war. In the NRA the movement had a reliable instrument to carry out its will. There was the National Resistance Council with its committees – the political and diplomatic committee, finance and supply committee, external committee – and the high command. In addition, the NRM had the institutions of resistance councils and committees and political cadres and mobilizers. It relied on these institutions to regularize power. In the early days the NRM had to fall back on the familiar. While we have yet to learn which decisions were made where, in the early critical days of their assumption of power sovereignty lay in any of these top organs – National Resistance Council, the army council, high command or political organ.

Initially, political institutions, as in many other revolutionary situations, were established extra-legally. A secretariat was established, headed by the National Political Commissar; the National Resistance

Council was expanded to include the newly appointed ministers and deputy ministers; special district administrators were appointed to replace the district commissioners, who became executive secretaries; an inspector-general of government was appointed; a hierarchy of resistance councils and committees was established through a system of indirect elections for villages, parishes, sub-counties, districts, the city of Kampala, municipalities, post-secondary institutions and trading centres. Some of these bodies were later established by law. Legal Notice No. 1, (Amendment Statute) 1989[8] provided for the composition of the National Resistance Council and its standing committee, the National Executive Committee; modes of electing or removing a president; war powers of the councils; and eligibility and procedures for electing council members. The statute provides for representation of various socio-political forces by members of the NRC prior to the statute; the national political commissar, administrative secretary of the NRM and the director of legal services of the NRM; a representative from each county, division from the city of Kampala, each municipality; ten members from the NRA; a woman from each district; five youth representatives elected by a national youth organization; three workers' representatives and 20 representatives appointed by the President on the recommendation of the National Resistance Council.

The Inspector-General of Government Statute, 1987[9] provides for an office and composition of inspector-general of government with powers 'to conduct an enquiry or investigation into an allegation of violation of human rights, breach of rule of law . . . to require a public officer to answer questions concerning his duties or those of another person . . . to require any person in charge of a public office to produce or furnish any document . . . which is in his possession'. The Resistance Councils and Committees Statute, 1987[10] established the district administrations, and the composition, powers and functions of resistance councils and committees. The Resistance Committees (Judicial Powers) Statute, 1987 established resistance committee courts, and their composition, and defined their jurisdiction.

Some of the above institutional frameworks have been established successfully, especially in southern Uganda and West Nile, where there were no outbreaks of rebellion.[11] The frameworks have also taken care of the immediate needs of the moment. But in establishing them, the NRM has made it quite clear where sovereignty, (that is, the ultimate power to make binding decisions,) lies for the moment. At the same time, however, the frameworks serve the functions of legitimization, and maintenance of law and order, and promote political participation.

The NRM administration, like the early UNLF administrations, is a coalition of strange political bedfellows. The enemies of yesterday are today's allies. But the NRM, unlike the UNLF, has not only managed

234

to survive, but has taken care to leave to itself a reservoir of power to ensure that the democratization process does not lead to political normlessness. Of course searching for where sovereignty lies in the NRM may be somewhat difficult, but it is clear that it does not lie in those newly created institutional frameworks. Sovereignty lies with such relatively politically cohesive organs as the NRM secretariat, the high command and the army council. These organs are manned mainly by those who have spent a relatively long incubation period in their struggle for power and have therefore acquired a similar view on a number of political issues.

The legitimization process has not been easy in a political terrain that is so highly polarized. To allay fears of an NRM monopoly of power and dictatorship, the NRM announced that its government would be interim, lasting for four years. As part of the legitimization and democratization process there have been elections to the hierarchy of resistance councils from the village up to the National Resistance Council and its organ, the National Executive Committee. All sorts of socio-political forces, representing a mosaic of political opinions, took part. The elections were relatively uneventful but there were no serious suggestions of massive riggings.

Even in areas where rebellions had not broken out, there were problems of maintenance of law and order in the early days. Initially, law and order was largely the responsibility of NRA personnel and a very numerically weak and demoralized police force. By creating a hierarchy of resistance councils and committees, the NRM, for purposes of communication and maintenance of law and order, successfully penetrated the countryside in the southern areas and in West Nile. The defeat of the Lakwena Holy Spirit Movement in Busoga may also be partly attributed to a very good system of resistance councils and committees in that area.

Institutional frameworks such as the National Resistance Council, the National Executive Committee and the resistance councils and committee system provide channels for interest articulation and political participation by groups that would otherwise be marginalized. In these participatory organs the NRM is involved in a balancing act to ensure that no single political force has an overwhelming upper hand.

In outlining the institutional framework, and their functions, there may be dangers of indulging in 'Webbism' or 'formalism', whereby formalities may be mistaken for realities. The effectiveness of these institutional frameworks has yet to be proven. At the operational level there are also problems of competing political formulae, and institutional 'immobilisme'.

All competing political groups are agreed that democracy is the ultimate desired end, but are not agreed on a political formula through which it should be operationalized. There are still such issues as the role of political parties, modes and procedures for elections, and the role of traditional institutions. Groups that embrace such issues are so uncompromising that, if given a chance, they would dictate terms at the possible political expense of other socio-political forces. These institutional frameworks have so far survived simply because the NRM has a sufficient reservoir of power to keep the system going.

Operationally, the institutional representative structures and executive structures serve as arenas for groups and individuals to propagate their competing hidden political agendas, for political bargaining, for access to political and material rewards, and the advancement of particularistic interests. In normally balanced political systems, these functions are part of the raw material of politics, but in Uganda, where politics are highly polarized, they can lead to a situation in which a system may become paralysed and unable to perform normal politico-administrative functions. The National Resistance Council consists of more than 250 members, a Cabinet of more than 50 ministers, and a National Executive Committee of more than 70 members, so it is extremely difficult to transact high policy business. The problem is compounded when those bodies are made up of members representing socio-political forces that are also antagonistic. Through political schools, the NRM has tried to provide ideological bases for the movement and has passed the Anti-Sectarian Bill,[12] but these actions have yet to be internalized.

REBUILDING THE ARMY

Like previous armies, the National Resistance Army was and is being built in response to internal politico-military crises. A 'bush army' was organized to remove Obote and the Okellos, but six months after the NRM victory there were rebellions in the north and northeast. All these in themselves called for hard thinking about rebuilding the military. Immediately upon their assumption of power, the NRM leadership made its thinking clear about the Ugandan military in the making. They drew the attention of Ugandans to the character of the old armies, which they regarded as instruments of repression, in the service of factions, and highly undisciplined and predatory. The leadership regarded the military as one of the critical instruments to attain its objectives. On the Second Anniversary of the NRM victory, President Museveni said of the NRA:

> the other distinguishing character of the NRA is that it is committed to the NRM Political Programme of eliminating economic and social backwardness in Uganda, guaranteeing National Independence and always putting the interest of the population ahead of everything else . . . We shall continue to strengthen and improve the quality of the NRA because it is the most advanced element in the process of struggle for progress.[13]

236

Institution-building: the case of the NRM and the military 1986-9

But the NRM leadership was very apprehensive about the victorious NRA. The guerrilla army had successfully held together in the bush and had defeated its enemies. There was no telling what character it would take on within a few days of its victory. Besides, there were immediate and long-term tasks for which it would have to be prepared. The leadership immediately took steps to work out and implement policies for controlling it and absorbing elements from the defeated armies, expanding it, and redefining its roles and functions, 'demystification of the gun', and integrating the military into politico-administrative structures.

Compared with its predecessors, Museveni's 'bush army' was, in terms of discipline, puritanical and ascetic. It was a proud army in rags. But after a few months in power there were isolated cases of indiscipline, including robberies and petty thefts. In March 1986, informed that two senior army officers had been arrested 'in connection with motor-vehicle robberies', Museveni commented, 'I am as happy as when we captured the Pakwach Bridge. The fact that we are arresting and punishing soldiers within our army is in itself a healthy attitude. The past regimes never dared punish a soldier.'[14] During their march into the north whence the Okello soldiers had fled, Museveni 'called on his troops to regard the people of northern Uganda as their parents, brothers and sisters'.[15]

It is worth noting that since the 'Kagera War' the military had been a subject of debate. Lule had made tentative efforts to inaugurate policies for its control but he burnt his fingers and lost the presidency.[16] The NRM leadership, however, felt confident enough to introduce policies for its domestication mainly because the NRA was its own creation. The leadership also did not hesitate to announce these policies to the public. Under earlier regimes in Uganda military policies had been a closed book to the public.

The mechanisms of control of the army are internal and external to the military. The internal mechanisms of control are those peculiar to the NRM as well as those traditionally associated with the military as an institution anywhere in the world. The internal mechanisms included the NRA code of conduct and the system of political commissars, military tribunals and military police. The external mechanisms of control included the resistance council system, the public, the press, and the human rights organizations.

In February 1986 the Ugandan public came to learn that the National Resistance Army was governed by a strict code of conduct when it was published in the press.[17] This was later proclaimed as Legal Notice No. 1 of 1986 (Amendment). This code of conduct defines relations between the military and the public, relations among soldiers, defines the organs for administration of justice should the Code be violated, and the offences and accompanying punishments.

237

Rebuilding political institutions

The code of conduct was not conjured up when the NRM assumed leadership. It was drawn up in 1982 in the bush. The code had been drawn up to forge a powerful military instrument capable of defeating the Obote forces in the field. It was formulated in response to the crisis situation that Museveni's army faced in the bush, to the very bad previous history of relations between the military and civilians and in response to the generally bad performance of Ugandan armies before the enemy. During the years of struggle and thereafter, the code governing relations between the NRA and civilians was clearly meant to win civilian confidence and support. The code governing relations among soldiers was also meant to generate an *esprit de corps*, a quality no previous armies had comfortably boasted of.

Punishment for breach of the code of conduct ranges from 'fatigue, corporal punishment, suspension, demotion, dismissal with disgrace' to 'death'.[18] The past four years have shown that this code of conduct is not simply a paper one. The Ugandan press is full of reports of officers and men who have been punished for violating some aspect of it. Officers have been punished for murder, robberies, indiscipline and mistreatment of members of the public.[19]

A system of military tribunals was also established and the military police strengthened. These control mechanisms are common to all armies. Interestingly the military tribunals are open to the press, who freely report on the proceedings. Here the idea is to show the public that justice *is* meted out.

The external control mechanisms – the judiciary, public opinion, the press and human rights organizations – can be said to be effective because of the general relaxed political atmosphere, especially in the southern areas. The resistance council committee officials have assisted in the curbing of indiscipline by soldiers. If a soldier misbehaves in public where there is no immediate military authority, the nearest authority to report to is the RC official, especially the secretary for defence in the area. Soldiers have been arrested by the RCs and handed over to the appropriate military authority or the police. However, public opinion, the press and human rights mechanisms have not been deliberately set up as mechanisms of control by the government. But the NRM leadership *has* taken care not to interfere with any complaints about the military by the press and the public. Indiscipline by soldiers is freely reported in the press and there have been many instances when the authorities have taken action against indiscipline, acting on press reports or public outcries.

On their assumption of power, the NRM leadership made it clear that the armies they had fought had been defeated and that that there was no question of 'power sharing' with them. In response to claims by the Uganda Freedom Army and FEDEMU to the liberation of the country,

Institution-building: the case of the NRM and the military 1986–9

Museveni retorted: 'Their only contribution we know was to fight us. But we are not bitter with them. We are in fact ready to work with the good ones among them'.[20] By February 1986, plans were already under way for the reabsorption of members of the defeated armies. This was in face of opposition by public opinion *against* absorption of the old armies. The NRA headquarters issued a statement:

> In the spirit of national unity, NRA is willing to absorb members of such defunct forces as long as they qualify to clearly laid down criteria, e.g. discipline, past history, qualifications, age, etc. This we regard as yet another phase in our struggle. However, members of the defunct armies, i.e. UNLA, FDA, FEDEMO, FUNA and UNRF who are now in or may join later NRA will be screened to weed out bad elements. It is our long term plan to screen the entire army to sort out especially opportunists and criminals who joined as the war gained momentum.[21]

In their days of struggle and even in the first year of their assumption of power, the NRM absorbed elements from opposing armies. They continue to do so even with elements from the defeated armies from the north and northeast. Familiar as we are with the official reasons for reconciliation, what other possible reasons could have prompted the NRA to reabsorb their former opponents? The NRM was acting in character with other revolutionary movements. At the height of the civil war in Russia, Commissar for War, Trotsky, in the teeth of opposition from his colleagues but with the active support of Lenin, recruited Tsarist officers and men to fight the White and Allied armies; in China during the Communist revolution, the Kuomintang army was one of Mao Tse-tung's recruitment grounds for his Peoples' Liberation Army. Nearer home, Mugabe and his ZANLA reabsorbed elements of the former colonial army, including its commanding officer, Peter Walls, and soldiers from Nkomo's Zimbabwe Peoples' Revolutionary Army. The NRM could, Amin-style, have carried out general massacres, but in 1986 this was no longer logistically and politically tenable. Fanning out into the countryside looking for 'enemies' to 'massacre', the NRA would also have dissipated its meagre resources. Anyway, Museveni had assumed power on a ticket against 'state-inspired violence'. General massacres would have undermined the *raison d'être* of the NRM. In addition, there were politico-military and techno-functional reasons. Reabsorption is also a control mechanism. A defeated demoralized soldier will more easily obey the victor if there are good political reasons for doing so.

A potential opponent in one's ranks may be safer than one far out in the bush. The NRM may also have realized that in building up a technologically equipped army, it needed the knowhow of some elements from the defeated armies.

239

Rebuilding political institutions

Expansion of the army has involved reabsorption of elements from the defeated armies and general recruitment throughout the country from all ethnic groups. Some reservations have been expressed as to whether there is a need for a big army establishment in Uganda.[22] But the NRM has opted for a big army. In response to criticisms, Mr Kategaya, then Minister of State in the Prime Minister's office, said:

> There is a misconception that a big army is difficult. And arguments that a large army is expensive to maintain are baseless . . . The army is a cohesive institution that can be used easily to introduce new ideas, like large-scale agriculture, cottage industry and construction. The army could foot its own maintenance costs, and even produce surplus for export. A small army is easy to manipulate politically to carry out a coup.[23]

These views were echoed, some two years-later, by Colonel Chihandea, chief of training and recruitment. Chihandea argued that armies are small in the past because they were used to protect minority interests. The new national expanded army was to protect the state from external and internal threats and to produce its own food. It had, therefore, to attract a broad base of skilled manpower.[24]

In advancing its reasons for expanding the army, the NRM leadership has acted in response to hard politico-military, geopolitical and economic realities. Hitherto the Uganda military had been a small elite organization confined to the socio-political forces that happened to be in power. Ironically, whenever tensions arose within this small elite group, it was relatively easy for it to disrupt political life. This problem had been long predicted by Ali Kisekka.[25]

Geopolitically, Uganda is a small country surrounded by volatile neighbours. In the past, there have been instances of internal upheavals in neighbouring countries spilling over into it. Take, for example, the civil wars in the Congo (Zaire) during the 1960s, in Rwanda, and in Sudan. To build a *cordon sanitaire* around Uganda's borders and at the same time to contain internal fluid situations would overstrain a small military establishment. The recent events in the southern Sudan were not so keenly felt to start with . With a small military establishment, northern Uganda, ungarrisoned, might easily have proved a good rear base for the SPLA. In the event of a general military conflagration along its borders, Uganda would be forced to fight on five fronts – the Rwandese, the Zairean, Sudanese, Kenyan and Tanzanian borders. This inevitably calls for a big army. Such general massive recruitment must also have had a sobering impact on Kenya's apparent hostile intentions in recent years.

With an expanded military, inevitably redefinition of its functions is required. In the past, the functions of the Ugandan military have been relatively simple, defined by whoever had the politico-military upper hand. Officially it was to protect the territorial integrity of the state from internal and external threats. But it responded more to internal than external crises, and that turned it into an instrument of repression and predation. The NRM has redefined the functions of the army beyond the simple requirements of law and order and guarding Ugandan borders. Museveni regards the NRA as 'the most advanced element in the struggle for progress'. In this sense it is a political socializing agency. The political schools that have been established are manned by the military, and cadres and mobilizers are given political education courses there besides instruction in the martial arts. Production units have also been established; the army has to build its own barracks and general military infrastructures. Of the productive role of the army, Museveni said:

> It is our commitment that we develop an army that is capable not only to protect the integrity and tranquillity of the state but an army that is capable of engaging in diverse productive efforts. It is the NRA's firm policy to actively participate in the development of this country. For example, the army has already harvested a total 184,500 kgs of sorted cotton at Kiryandongo and Kasese – 720,000 kgs of maize at Kasese and Kiryandongo. Apart from these main crops, the army also grows vegetables, onions and keeps poultry on a non-commercial basis. Ultimately, it is our aim to make the army self sufficient. To this end we have created the National Enterprise Corporation – controlled and managed as a self-sustaining, self-generating commercial entity.
>
> The Corporation will train, organize and utilize army personnel to develop and carry out scientific, technological, industrial construction and contracted service activities on a commercial basis.[26]

Another stated policy of the NRM leadership is 'demystification of the gun'. To some extent, with or without this policy, for the last 25 years Ugandans have been socialized into learning how to live with the gun. In the hands of the few, the gun had been an instrument of terror. We can argue that the past upheavals in the country have themselves demystified the gun since large sections of the population (especially in the southern areas) have had access to the gun. The guerrilla wars further demystified it. In guerrilla-controlled areas there emerged a symbiotic relationship between the gun and the armed population, with the gun being increasingly regarded as an instrument of politico-military liberation. As a policy, the NRM leadership has taken steps to ensure that the use of the gun is henceforth not the monopoly of any particular social force. The past dictatorships particularly thrived on the 'doctrine of ethno-functionalism'.[27] Demystification of the gun has entailed building a large multiethnic and multifunctional army, and military training for cadres and political mobilizers, civil servants, and local defence units.

By the very nature of its mission, a guerrilla army cannot build itself

241

up into a regular army until it has captured state power. This is because, even at the best of times, it has limited resources and therefore thrives on improvization, and because it cannot create conditions where it is easily identified by the enemy. Thus, it may not have uniforms because it has to merge with its environment. It cannot have a rigidified system of ranks because these may be sources of internal tensions; guerrillas cannot have physically permanent barracks because these will render them excellent targets for the enemy. There is no established system of renumeration because resources are hard to come by.

After its victory the NRM took steps to build a regular army characterized by establishment of a bureaucracy, introduction of uniforms, regimental colours, launching of training programmes, introduction of ranks, and a system of regular pay and associated privileges.

Some of these steps were a matter of routine and we need only consider briefly the rationale for establishment of a bureaucracy, training programmes and ranks. There has been a need for a bureaucracy because the NRA in power has to carry out complex tasks of administering the army. The guerrilla leaders realized that the guerrilla skills that win a war may not necessarily be enough to fight a conventional war. Programmes for training have therefore been launched within the country and some guerrilla leaders have been sent abroad for retraining.

Two years after the assumption of power, new ranks were also introduced into the NRA. Hitherto there had been only five ranks – Provisional Junior Officer II, Junior Officer II, Junior Officer I, Senior Officer I and Member of the High Command.

In everyday nomenclature, anyone in a command position had been referred to as 'Commander'. Museveni justified introduction of more differentiated ranks because 'as the army grew it was necessary to bring in ranks and standardize it with other armies in the world . . . The only way soldiers could identify officers was by knowing them physically. And yet there were too many soldiers crowding around five ranks'. Museveni himself was promoted to the rank of Lieutenant-General by the High Command. There were also posthumous and honorary promotions for others.[28]

The process of integration of the military into politico-administrative structures may arise as a result of reabsorption, expansion, redefinition of its functions as well as 'demystification' of the gun. If these processes are successful, the narrow, elitist and functionalistic attributes of the military may disappear. As part of the integrational process, members of the military have been recruited into politico-administrative structures. As an interest group they are represented, as we have already seen, in the National Resistance Council and the National Executive Committee, and some serve as district administrators, ministers and in other areas of socio-economic life too.

Institution-building: the case of the NRM and the military 1986–9

True, even under military juntas, soldiers may serve outside the army. The qualitative difference with the NRM is that there has been an attempt to fuse the politico-administrative and military institutions with a view to creating an identity of interests between the civilian and the military. In past regimes in Uganda, there had been a kind of politico-military proprietary interest in military positions. In the late 1960s, when Amin was 'promoted' from Commander of the army to Chief of Defence Forces, this was construed as a 'demotion' and had political repercussions, ultimately leading to the 1971 coup; Oyite-Ojok, when Commander of the UNLA, turned down an ambassadorship to Algeria, regarding the appointment as a dismissal. Through the Military Commission, he staged a *coup d'état*. In the NRM administration, officers have been moved horizontally or vertically without any political tremors being felt so far.

In the context of our argument about building viable political institutions and domesticating and integrating the military, what possible problems may arise from instituting mechanisms of military control, reabsorbing elements from the defeated armies, military expansion, redefinition of its functions, 'demystification of the gun', and building a regular army and integrating it into politico-administrative structures? Problems undermining the process of domestication and integration may arise from the heterogeneity of the military, its *relative* level of institutionalization *vis-à-vis* civilian institutions, spillover effects from the highly polarized Ugandan socio-political forces and the weak socio-economic base of the Ugandan state.

Today the Ugandan military is made up of the 'historic' NRA, elements from the defeated armies, and those recruited in the course of the general expansion programmes. We have pointed out that there were good politico-military reasons for the reabsorption and expansion policies. But the NRA today is different from the 'historic' NRA. For all the mechanisms of control and efforts made to politicize it, one cannot rule out the danger that the 'historic' NRA will be physically swallowed, along with the ideals it stands for. Fears have been expressed that faced with defeat, elements have entered the NRA to use it as a Trojan Horse.

Although the NRA is admittedly heterogeneous in relation to civilian political institutions, it has a relatively higher level of institutionalization. With the advantage of resources that may accrue to it and its historic role in the political processes, the NRA may eventually acquire such a visibility that civilian political institutions may turn out to be poor cousins. In that instance, the NRA would not be *one* of the actors, but the *major* actor – a situation that may not be different from the politics of the past.

The Ugandan military may well be affected by the political environment outside it because it is part of this environment. The more civilian

243

politics are polarized, the more may be the dangers of the NRA being similarly affected. The relative cohesiveness of the NRA today speaks for the NRM leadership's capacity for political organization. A situation could, however, arise in which the civilian institutional frameworks were so polarized that Museveni and his followers might have to fall back on the NRA as a critical power constituency. This would adversely affect the democratization process.

Political and military institutions are also being built in a situation of extreme scarcity of resources. Because of this scarcity, corruption is rampant. The military has been inevitably affected by it. The NRA leadership has tried to combat it but one reads of complaints about 'supply of air'. The cohesiveness of the military will particularly depend on how effectively utilized are the scarce resources available to it.

THE NORTHERN AND NORTHEASTERN REBELLIONS

We shall not go into detail about the origins and causes of the rebellions in the north and northeast. We shall confine ourselves to discussing how they have adversely affected institution-building processes. When the army of the Okellos was defeated in the battle for Kampala, they simply fled to the north and northeast. The NRA pursued them and succeeded in occupying the towns and trading centres. Within seven months, the NRM leadership was saddled with rebellions in Gulu and Kitgum, spilling over into Lango and Teso districts. The Karamojong took advantage of the fluid situation to carry out raids for cattle in neigbouring districts.

The NRM leadership found itself in a relatively weak position to combat the rebellion – numerically, logistically and technologically. Numerically, the NRA found itself too weak on the ground. To offset this it embarked on a programme of general recruitment. Logistically, it was still an army on foot and yet had to operate in an area about half the size of the country. Technologically, it took some time to acquire weapons and the skills to use them. For some time the NRA had to fall back upon bluff. The rebels then embarked on a campaign of killing the RC leaders in these areas and destroying socio-economic infrastructures.

The rebellions were a strain on the government's meagre resources and this inevitably affected their overall programme; the rebellion somewhat dented the claims to legitimacy of the NRM and gave the military too wide a visibility. Resources that could have been used elsewhere, at least to stabilize the regime, were diverted to fight the rebellion. The opposition took advantage of events in the north and northeast to call for 'peace talks', probably Nairobi-style. The NRM leadership opted for a politico-military solution. Politically they left the door ajar by the proclamation of a presidential amnesty, applicable to those who voluntarily surrendered and had not committed any crimes. The chief of combat operations, then Major-General Salim Saleh, sought to parley with a faction of the rebels; the result was the Gulu Accord of June 1988, signed by the NRA and the Uganda Peoples Democratic Army.[29]

The NRA, however, continued to meet force with force and launched general offensives in Kitgum, Gulu and Teso. To a great extent the 'pacification' of the north has been an NRA show and this in itself has given it wide visibility. If the rebellion in the north and northeast had not broken out, the process of domesticating and integrating the military would have been much faster.

CONCLUSION

We have argued that the Ugandan military will remain a political actor in Ugandan political processes but that it may be domesticated if the NRM builds viable political institutions that enjoy a reasonable degree of acceptability among significant socio-political forces, and if the military itself can be integrated into politico-administrative institutions. We have examined the steps the NRM has taken to regularize power by establishing political representative institutional frameworks. We have outlined their politico-administrative functions and their limitations. To avoid UNLF-like political instability, the NRM leadership has taken care to reserve for itself some of the sovereignty in its strategic politico-military organs.

We have also noted the steps the NRM has taken to rebuild the military through a system of control mechanisms, reabsorption of elements from the defeated armies, expansion of the military, redefinition of its functions, 'demystification of the gun', building a regular army, and integrating the military into politico-administrative structures. The ideal situation would be where there is a 'normal balance' of forces, in which there are residual institutional mechanisms for resolving conflict and no single political force has the upper hand. The limitation to this, however, lies in the fact that the NRM has a power reservoir that it has to use in a potentially polarized political situation. The critical difference between the present-day 'imbalance of forces' and that in the past is that the present situation is the result of an armed uprising involving the strategic heartland in the south. For this reason there is a chance that the NRM may play an historic role, working out political formulae that, with time, may come to form the core of political values in a future integrated Ugandan political system.

Acknowledgement

I have greatly benefited from the discussions I have had with Dr Francis Kidubuka, Department of Literature, Makerere, and Mr Patrick Kiggundu, of its Faculty of Law.

Notes

1. Mudoola, 1987, 1988, 1989.
2. For details on the removal of Lule, see Mudoola, 1988.
3. Huntington, 1964, 1968; Finer, 1962.
4. On the role of the CCM in the demobilization process of the TPDF, see *Daily News* (Tanzania), June–September 1979. On the role of the party in the Kagera War generally, see Avirgan and Avirgan, 1982.
5. Demotion, transfers and promotions in the Uganda military have been interpreted in political terms.
6. See the story in a colonial elementary English reader, *Oxford English for Africa*, Book II.
7. Museveni, 1985b.
8. Legal Notice No 1 of 1986 (Amendment) Statute, 1989.
9. Inspector-General of Government Statute, 1987.
10. The Resistance Councils and Committees Statute, 1987, Government Printer, Entebbe.
11. In Kitgum, Acholi, Kumi and Soroti districts, RC officials were the first target of the rebels.
12. Anti-Sectarian Statute, 1988.
13. *New Vision*, 29 January 1988, President Museveni's speech.
14. *The Star*, 18 March 1986.
15. *ibid.*
16. See Mudoola, 1988.
17. *Weekly Topic*, 20 February 1986. See 'June Code of Conduct of the NRA'. Also see Legal Notice I of 1986 (Amendment), Government Printer, Entebbe.
18. *ibid.*
19. Cases of soldiers appearing in Court or Military Tribunals are numerous – see *New Vision* 11 July 1986, 12 September 1986, 2nd April 1986, 14th April 1987, 3rd February 1987, 2 October 1987, 8 February 1988, 10 February 1988, 17 June 1988.
20. *Weekly Topic*, 3 February 1986.
21. *Weekly Topic*, 13 August 1986.
22. *Weekly Topic*, 17 April 1986.
23. *New Vision*, 24 June 1986.
24. An interview given by Colonel Chihandea, from an unquotable source.
25. Mudoola, 1987, quoting Ali Kisekka.
26. *New Vision*, 13 October 1988.
27. For an elaboration of this concept, see Mudoola, 1988.
28. *New Vision*, 8 February 1988.
29. *New Vision*, 8 June 1988 gives details of the Gulu Accord.

EIGHTEEN
The Ugandan elections of 1989:
power, populism and democratization

Nelson Kasfir

In February 1989 the National Resistance Movement (NRM) organized nationwide elections at all levels in Uganda, including the national parliament, now called the National Resistance Council (NRC)[1]. How far towards democratization did these elections carry Uganda? They cannot be considered fully democratic, because they did not provide an opportunity to replace the ruling government. But neither were they simply a façade for dictatorship, because once the rules were set the government did not intervene in the voting. Popular governing assemblies were given an appreciable degree of free choice. Several ministers who were important members of the NRM lost their elections. Well-known members of the party against whom the NRM had fought a violent war were not prevented from occupying lower-level and NRC seats that they had won in the elections.

The election process produced some democratization; the question is how much? This is not an easy issue to analyse for several reasons. Democratization is not an easily measured unilinear or irreversible dimension. It is not clear at the time of writing (August 1990) whether democratic government can succeed in Uganda. And serious questions have been raised about the commitment of the present government to pursue *full* democratization. Nonetheless, the NRM had endorsed and practised democracy before it came to power. Despite a three-year delay in what was to be only a four-year interim period, it organized this novel mass exercise in which all legislative positions in all the newly created assemblies in the state were openly contested.

Meaningful democratization, that is, the movement from authoritarian rule to democracy, is a social process that requires time, strategy and some unusual alliances (O'Donnell, Schmitter & Whitehead, 1986). It does not suddenly materialize simply because an election is held. Democratization is achieved when people in general are assured that they can organize and discuss political issues openly; they can vote freely; the election will put the government of the day genuinely at risk; and the government can be expected to shape its policies in response to the election (Dahl, 1971, pp. 2–3). An extended, more contested notion of

247

democratization requires dominant social groups, and not just ruling political organizations, to accept the risk of losing power (Laclau, 1977). On that extended basis few countries in the world can claim to have achieved a full measure of democratization. Nevertheless, the NRM came to power supporting some elements of this more dramatic definition.

Furthermore, democratization necessarily depends on choices for organizing democratic institutions. Multiparty representative democracy and populist democracy present two contrasting approaches to these choices. The first emphasizes institutional guarantees protecting the opportunities for individuals to formulate preferences, to organize with others, and to have their preferences count equally (Dahl, 1971, pp. 2–3; Schumpeter, 1950, pp. 269, 270–1). The second rests on the claim that the 'people' be directly involved in governing themselves (Worsley, 1969, pp. 244–7). The creation of a popular culture stressing norms of democratic participation, egalitarian social relations, and organizations representing collective interests are significant objectives (Lobel, 1988, pp. 877, 879).

Genuine democratization necessarily changes the relations of power, though not always quickly, and not always dramatically. If outsiders have no opportunity to weaken the position of rulers, democratization is not occurring. But, rulers can often democratize a little without risking their positions. Policies that recognize and incorporate democratic norms, even without meeting any of the criteria mentioned above, can represent perceptible movement toward democracy. At the same time, however, policies that consolidate the position of rulers by freeing them from previously accepted democratic norms are reversals of democratization.

Thus, the process of democratization is a process of struggle, between social classes or between political organizations and individuals from the same class. Analysis of events in that struggle provides insight into the motivations and commitments of the political actors. Elections are particularly useful as barometers of the democratic intentions of the government that organizes them. The structure of the elections – that is, the rules governing how electoral contests will be defined and how open participation can be – tells the observer a great deal about the fears as well as the hopes of rulers. In addition the level of satisfaction of individuals and social groups with the elections, particularly their judgment of its fairness, indicates whether they are a step towards greater democratization or are rejected as a deception perpetrated by government.

Generally speaking, though with some notable exceptions, Ugandans considered the February 1989 elections to be fair and democratic – indeed the first general elections in the country's history since independence to receive widespread approval. At first blush it is unclear whether that fact should be thought remarkable or not. There is only one other case of independent Ugandan national general elections available for comparison, the almost certainly rigged elections of 1980 that made the Uganda People's Congress (UPC) the governing party for the second time ('A Local Observer', 1988). Yet, just holding national elections that were to some degree genuinely responsive to the democratic norm – after a quarter century of trying – does seem an achievement worthy of note and analysis.

Early in its five-year guerrilla struggle against the UPC government, the NRM firmly committed itself to democratization through mass popular involvement in governance. However, this populist approach replaced the NRM's original support for a return to multiparty representative democracy.[2] Before it took power in January 1986, the NRM had already introduced a novel system of popular assemblies in all villages and indirectly elected assemblies at higher levels, called resistance councils (RCs), in order to establish a new organizational form through which democracy might finally succeed in taking root in Uganda.[3]

During its first two years in power the government invested much time and energy in elections to these assemblies. By the time the 1989 elections were held all Ugandans living outside the war zones in the north and east had had the opportunity to participate in electing some of the officials governing them, and the opportunity to recall some of them in the event of misconduct. The populist character of the NRM regime was strengthened by these elective structures.[4] In addition, by the time the elections were held the government had also passed legislation creating a commission to draft a new national constitution, giving it guidelines that most Ugandans as well as most foreign analysts would regard as firm support for introducing a democratic system. Nevertheless, the organization and conduct of the 1989 elections raise important questions about their democratic nature – whether they should be considered a step toward genuine democratization, or a step towards further consolidation in power of a government that, on its own admission, had reached power prematurely. They demonstrate the narrow line the government walked in restricting unpalatable outcomes in advance, while not interfering in the voting.

The elections were called suddenly, and surprised almost everybody. Electorate, candidates and even the administrators who managed the process were given only a few weeks of preparation. Legislation had to be rushed through the NRC only days before the first round of elections. There was no registration of voters. Voting was carried out by public queueing. Parties were not permitted to take an active role. Campaigning was forbidden. Above the village level, all elections were indirect and the number of electors was small. In addition to the elected members, the government empowered itself to appoint sufficient members to the NRC

Rebuilding political institutions

to guarantee in advance that it would not lose majority control. Finally, the national president and chair of the NRM, Yoweri Museveni, was guaranteed his position no matter what the results were.

The fundamental issue posed by these elections, then, is whether they opened up the political process, moving it towards the point where continuation in office and accountability for policies by leaders will really be dependent on the wishes of the electorate, or were merely a device to shore up an NRM government not yet regarded as a legitimate ruler by many Ugandans. In short, did these elections further the democratization process? A full answer would depend on the extent that social groups participating in these elections felt they had gained some measure of political power by participating in them, and thus would demand, at a minimum, that the government hold them again. Nevertheless, on balance, it is reasonable to conclude that the elections did contribute to democratization. There was widespread and unfettered participation, though only within the narrow confines of rules constructed by a nervous government. What I look at here is the impact of the structure of the elections and general perceptions of popular satisfaction on progress towards democratization.

THE CONTEXT OF THE 1989 ELECTIONS

Answers to three closely interrelated questions provide a basis for situating the 1989 elections. First, did the internecine political competition for control of the state that increasingly characterized Uganda's postcolonial politics make democratization an impossible dream for the time being? Second, did the significant differences in the definitions of democratization adopted by the NRM and its political rivals create new problems for achieving democracy? Third, did uncertainties over the NRM's acceptance by the public at large cause it to undercut or strengthen its commitment to democratization?

Internecine political competition

The obstacles to democratization created by competition for control of the state were especially serious in Uganda. The combination of the opportunities provided by the African state and the pressures for private accumulation of state resources exerted by political notables intensified political competition and dominant class formation (Kasfir, 1984a, 1984b). Although Uganda had long been bedevilled by complex ethnic and religious cleavages, the critical event that decisively transformed the political economy was the expulsion of the Indians ordered by Idi Amin in 1972. At a stroke more than four-fifths of Uganda's commercial and industrial properties were allocated by the state to Ugandan African tenants and in many cases re-allocated when the original client fell out of official favour or when the government was overthrown, as it was in

The Ugandan elections of 1989

1979, 1980, 1985 and 1986 (Kasfir, 1987). Because emergent middle-class elements who controlled commercial and industrial production lacked independent economic roots, their competition for state power took on an unparallelled intensity (Mamdani, 1987, pp. 88–9). At the same time rapid deterioration of the economy led to an unparallelled expansion of state intervention in the economy and the spread of *magendo* (illegal economic activities) as the official economy ceased to function effectively (Kasfir, 1984b). Official salaries of even the highest civil servants ceased to be adequate to maintain a family, and then fell close to the vanishing point. In consequence a variety of corrupt activities became too deeply entrenched for any Ugandan government, including the NRM one, to uproot quickly. Consequently, the historical basis for democratization was at least as unpromising in Uganda as anywhere else in Africa.

Uganda's record of earlier parliamentary elections had been pretty dismal, even including its pre-independence experience. The first 'national' elections in 1958 were marred by the refusal of several local governments to permit participation by their local electorates. The next in 1961 were complicated by a mass boycott of the polls in the kingdom of Buganda, the largest and wealthiest region in Uganda, that resulted – by virtue of the few who voted anyway – in providing the margin of victory (under the British governor) to a party that represented a minority of the electorate there. The 1962 elections, intended to provide a final pre-independence opportunity for voters, involved a mix of coercion and enthusiasm in Buganda that resulted in no party winning a clear majority. As a result Uganda became independent with an improbable and unstable majority that formally broke down two years later. From then until 1980, no further national elections were held. Elections scheduled for 1967 were 'postponed' by Milton Obote's presidential *coup d'état*, and those scheduled for 1971 were cancelled by Idi Amin's military coup. And, as already mentioned, the 1980 elections were widely believed to have been an exercise in force and fraud.

Nonetheless, in Uganda as in many other African countries, there was widespread adherence to the idea of democracy among both rich and poor.[5] An important reason for the enthusiastic reception the NRM received when it took power in 1986 was the popular expectation that it was committed to restoring democracy. The introduction of RCs, though regarded warily as an untried innovation, strengthened this expectation. More so than most regimes, the legitimacy of the NRM depended on its ability to continue to foster this belief, and thus prevent the kind of political competition Ugandans have experienced in the past 25 years.

Firm support by social classes never actively involved in Ugandan politics before would have provided a more reliable base for the NRM

251

Rebuilding political institutions

than the power of this belief. If the NRM managed to gain the backing of peasants, industrial and clerical workers, it would have had some muscle to oppose those members of the Ugandan petit bourgeoise who had dominated politics since the 1950s. In its statement of principles, the *10-Point Programme*, the NRM hinted that it would seek such support by arguing that 'democracy in politics . . . is not possible without a reasonable level of living for all the people of Uganda . . . Therefore, the NRM, after removing Obote, must think of democracy in a total context of real emancipation' (Museveni, 1985, p. 47). As the discussion below makes clear, such suggestions frightened the petit-bourgeois leaders of Uganda's older parties, as well as many supporters of the NRM. After coming to power, the NRM wavered considerably in its commitment to a radical expansion of Ugandan political participation. But its belief in a restructuring of politics to involve underprivileged groups seem to have been an important factor in shaping its view of democratization.

Rival definitions of democratization

Democratization, as the second question implies, can be defined in as many ways as democracy. The NRM, formed in the 1980s, and both the Uganda People's Congress (UPC) and the Democratic Party (DP), which had been organized before independence, had different ideas about how democratic structures should be established. The older parties believed in, though did not always practise, a conventional version of competitive multiparty representative democracy based on institutional guarantees. The NRM, which had come to power through military victory rather than through democratic means, would have been at a clear disadvantage in such a system. It therefore drew on the popular enthusiasm and support it had engendered during the earlier guerrilla war to modify representative democracy with features of populist democracy based on mass participation, decentralization and politicized popular organization.

NRM leaders had already provided substantial evidence of their commitment to democratic norms. In the 1970s Museveni had organized the Front for the National Salvation of Uganda (FRONASA), a guerrilla group dedicated to overthrowing Amin in order to restore democracy. When the factional struggles within the Uganda National Liberation Front (UNLF) government resulted in the sudden decision to organize the 1980 elections on a party basis, the present NRM leaders, together with others, hastily created a political party, the Uganda People's Movement (UPM), wrote a manifesto, and organized campaigns for most of the seats. In its brief existence the UPM followed conventional notions of multiparty representative democracy, probably the only organizational form conceivable for a new party whose organizers were given only seven months' notice that elections would be conducted through

252

multiparty competition. Although they lost badly, the palpable enthusiasm for the party among the youth in Kampala during the 1980 elections showed that it had struck a responsive chord. In protest against the electoral manipulations that put the UPC back into power, though no one in the UPM claimed it would have won even had the elections been fair, a fraction of the leadership went to the bush. In the war zone (the Luwero Triangle) the NRM created the first RCs to enlist popular support, carry out political education, and create structured popular organizations among villagers (Museveni, 1985, p. 47).

This experience, which decisively shaped the NRM's conception of the appropriate mix between populist and representative democracy, was subsequently encapsulated in the first of the ten points of its political programme (Museveni, 1985, pp. 46–8). A 'meaningful' democracy 'must contain three elements: parliamentary democracy, popular democracy and a decent level of living for every Ugandan'. Parliament must be a regularly elected body, but in addition 'there must be people's committees' at the village, parish, subcounty and district levels. 'Above all', these committees 'would be political forums to discuss relevant issues concerning the whole country and act as forums against corruption and misuse of office by government officials . . . They would be a channel of communication between the top and the bottom'. The second point, 'Security', added the idea of a politicized army and police (Museveni, 1985, p. 48). Village RCs were expected to screen applicants.

Though not mentioned in the *10-Point Programme*, the RCs were hierarchically linked so that the villagers at the bottom were only indirectly represented in the councils at higher levels. All adults were automatically members of their village RCs, participated in village policy making and elected a nine-person resistance committee to run village affairs (DIMM, nd, p. 24). Those nine officials joined with members of the committees from all other villages in the parish to form an RC2, and elected nine of their number to form the resistance committee to govern the parish. In turn, the parish officials joined with their counterparts to form an RC3 and elected a nine person committee to run the subcounty. The county level was skipped and the subcounty resistance committees joined together to form an RC5 and elect a resistance committee to govern the district.[6] Until the 1989 elections occurred, no decision had been taken on whether parliamentary representatives would be chosen at RC5 level or from the RC3s.

In the version of democracy the NRM envisaged before it took power, it created RCs to empower ordinary people, but retained parliament as a representative institution. Since its original definition of democratization also included substantial improvement in the quality of life of ordinary people, the process would take many years, and not just the

253

Rebuilding political institutions

four-year interim period for introducing new democratic institutions that the NRM gave itself the day after it took power. Contrary to rhetoric, a considerable degree of centralization was built into the RC councillor hierarchy. An ever smaller number of people had the power to vote as the level of the RC rose in importance and the size of area governed increased. If the people at the bottom had directly elected officials at all levels, instead of delegating that function to their representatives at each level, the RC system would have more closely resembled populist doctrine.

The NRM's approach also sharply diverged from that of the DP and the UPC on the question of parties. The issue here was whether competitive parties or mass mobilization should serve as the frame for democratic elections. If mass mobilization of the population was the key to democracy, then creating cadres and organizations to raise people's consciousness of their real problems was fundamental. But if presenting alternative patterns of policy choice to voters was central to democracy, then allowing parties to organize and campaign was critical. Since the NRM had not yet demonstrated the strength to win a national election, the issue was as much a question of power as it was of principle.

When the NRM seized power, the question of parties was a side issue, because the NRM and the DP were looking for a basis for accommodation, and the UPC leaders were either in exile or in disgrace. In 1986 the DP and NRM set up a joint committee to discuss cooperation, particularly their different ideas about democracy and party activities during the interim period [NEC, DP, 1989a, p. 6]. At first, according to the DP, the committee found the two organizations had a lot in common, but by March 1988, when they met with Museveni, the two sides were in open disagreement over the acceptability of a multiparty system. Museveni insisted that the only compromise the NRM found acceptable was a suspension of party activities for a fixed period of time, after which the question of a multiparty system would be put to a referendum. That put the NRM and its main partner in the government on a collision course.

Uncertainties over political acceptance of the NRM

The NRM sought to widen its political base by accommodating in the government and the army other social forces whose goals contradicted its own. It thus appeared to further democratization by expanding participation and introducing new 'watch-dogs' that could strengthen the accountability of the government. But if the narrow political base with which it came to power and its subsequent accommodation of powerful rivals in government meant that the NRM might be swept from power in democratic elections, would it be tempted to subvert the democratization process in order to protect itself? For the period before the 1989

254

elections there is significant evidence supporting both these points, despite their seeming contradiction. Tension between them was also clearly imprinted on the structure of the elections.

Because the NRM was a relative newcomer to the minefield of Ugandan politics, and had achieved power through guerrilla war rather than the ballot box, its political support had not been tested since it came to power. It earned widespread gratitude in the southern and western parts of the country and, initially at least, tolerance in much of the north. Nevertheless, the limited area in which it had been able to organize itself during the war, and the geographical composition of both its leadership and its army meant that it possessed only a narrow political base when it became the government in 1986. In its earlier manifestation as the hastily organized Uganda People's Movement (UPM), it had generated considerable enthusiasm but few votes in the 1980 elections. The guerrilla struggle that followed the 1980 elections was fought in only two areas – Buganda and the west – though from the start the NRM committed itself to the principle of a 'broad-based government' (*Towards a Free and Democratic Uganda*, nd, p. 4). It also made a conscious effort to include people from other parts of the country in its leadership, welcomed mergers with other guerrilla factions, and even recruited soldiers from the opposing and official Ugandan army during the war.

The broad-based principle was followed so enthusiastically after the NRM took power that its own ideological coherence and the political discipline of its army seemed likely to disappear. Even the notion of preventing a return to the old sectarian politics and casual violations of human rights wilted as political notables of the earlier regimes were invited to join the government. Members of all parties were given significant government positions, as too were leaders of military factions that merged into the NRA (DIMM, nd, pp. 25–6; Mamdani, 1988, pp. 1159–61). The Democratic Party, which possessed the legitimacy of almost certainly having been the actual winner of the 1980 elections, received the largest share of the most important cabinet portfolios.

In addition, to encourage participation by other groups, the NRM set no class or ideological restrictions on elections to RCs. DP officials saw their opportunity to position themselves for subsequent national elections, and by 1987 had probably won the largest share of the first elections to RCs from the village to the district level. In his analysis of 22 of the then 33 districts in the country, the DP's national organizing secretary reported that in these early elections the DP had taken 84 per cent of the RC5 seats, while the UPC and the NRM (including former members of the UPM), had won only 7 per cent each (DP, nd).[7]

Meanwhile the NRM expended little energy or resources in consolidating itself institutionally. The NRM secretariat, which might have been expected to become the voice of the movement, received a small

255

budget, was staffed by few powerful officials, but played only a modest role in setting the direction of government policies. Popular organizations for women, youth and labour were discussed, but nothing was done to form them. Frequently, members of the RCs, particularly those who had not received any political direction from the NRM or NRA, had little conception of what the new councils and committees should do. Considering the amount of energy the struggle for economic survival expended, many officials either resented the time spent on these unpaid positions or tried to take advantage of them for personal gain. Despite valiant efforts, the NRM had few resources to provide political education for these officials, and had no answer, except the slow-moving courts, where resistance committee officials turned out to be corrupt. Nor was there much progress towards a leadership code. Well before taking power, NRM officials had called for leaders to declare their assets and to restrict their business activities during their term in office. But no code had been adopted up to the time of these elections.[8]

Broad-based government nonetheless did not dilute ultimate control by top officials in the NRM and the NRA. Indeed, the movement even expanded its own authority. From the start, the NRA was formally represented in the NRC. Control over the command structure of the NRA was also not weakened by the addition of other military groups. The original NRC was composed entirely of high civilian and military officials in the movement who had been with Museveni during the guerrilla struggle. When the NRC was expanded in 1987 to include all members of the cabinet, it automatically became more broad-based but NRM members still formed a majority. The President appointed his own political agents (including several NRA officers) as district administrators to oversee all districts, instead of relying on the former and supposedly non-political district commissioners. None of the old political parties was allowed to hold rallies or campaign, though each was permitted to maintain its headquarters and publish its views.

As a result, the signals on democratization were ambiguous at the time the NRM decided to call the elections. The NRM had come to power without a sufficient political base to dispense with notables from past regimes, no matter how distasteful their policies might be. The narrowness of its support was made starkly apparent by the revival of civil war in both the north and east only half a year after the NRM became the government. The new wars stemmed in large part from fears by people in those areas that NRM rule would amount to 'domination by southerners'. At the same time, many southerners, while delighted with the return of peace and security, remained sceptical of the NRM's ability to overcome the great unsolved political issues that had plagued Uganda even during the British Protectorate, particularly the relation of Buganda to Uganda. The old parties and rival military factions that joined the

NRM and the NRA also still felt free to promote policies opposed to the goals of the NRM. The movement's willingness to tolerate such open dissent in the face of the resumption of civil war in the north and east was surprising, yet raised genuine hopes for democratization.

What seemed most at risk in the three years of NRM government before the 1989 elections, however, was the populist content of its *10-Point Programme*, particularly the roles to be played in it by popular organizations. What the movement had gained by involving other groups, it seems to have lost in the distinctiveness of its own political identity. The NRM apparently had not made up its mind what form Ugandan democratic institutions should take. Before the elections, no one knew whether the NRM intended to become a party of some sort in competition with the others, or to continue to maintain its rule under a broad-based façade. Despite the incorporation of other groups in the army and the government, the NRM had not relinquished control of critical political and military positions. The NRM had no way to know whether it could survive a fully open electoral test. It therefore responded by suddenly taking the initiative to present the public with a novel design for national elections, and carry them out before its opponents could catch their breath.

THE ELECTORAL STRUCTURE: DESIGN AND CONSEQUENCES
The three questions just discussed demonstrate some of the constraints that affected calculations of risks the NRM was taking by holding elections. Whether control of the state by dominant classes makes full democratizaton impossible was certainly not in the forefront of the minds of government leaders when they designed the rules for these elections. Nevertheless, the political danger to NRM rule posed by democratic elections in which all parties had freedom to nominate and campaign for their own candidates surely reinforced the leadership's view of what was ideologically appropriate with what was prudent. Eager to demonstrate that they enjoyed the political support of a majority, NRM leaders might have been expected to design an election on populist principles in order to empower peasants and workers at the expense of political notables and their parties. In the *10-Point Programme* the NRM had already identified the problem with former Ugandan politics as 'the local elite pandering to the various schemes of the unprincipled factions of the national elite' (Museveni, 1985, p. 47). But no one in Uganda could possibly know whether 'unemancipated' Ugandans felt ready to support the NRM as its new leaders.

In addition, there were perfectly good reasons to think that party leaders, who had earlier manipulated constituency boundaries, altered registration lists, prevented nominations, bribed voters, coerced election officials and committed open fraud in counting votes in the 1980 elections, would take these precautions again, if given the opportunity. The

257

experience of those elections must have left an indelible impression in the minds of those NRM leaders who had been candidates in them. Yet, the same election had also provided the NRM leaders' only test of voting appeal, and Museveni as well as the others had not done very well. All but one UPM candidate lost, most of them by wide margins. Museveni, the party leader, came in third in his constituency, though his particular electoral race was relatively close, if official figures can be believed (*Report of the Electoral Commission 1980*, 1981, p. 149). The only UPM winner benefited from the miscalculation of a UPC candidate, who thought he would win when his DP rival was eliminated before the election. Though this 'test' had occurred under far from ideal circumstances, NRM leaders had no other electoral experience to go on – or any other way of discovering whether their military overthrow of an admittedly unpopular regime, and their ideas for fundamental reform, would now frighten or enthuse a majority of Ugandans. A serious failure at the polls in 1989 – even if caused by the very corruption the NRM wanted to eradicate – would destroy their credibility and thus any possibility of realizing the movement's vision of a new Uganda free from political insecurity and economic deterioration in the future.

Furthermore, the government had neither budgeted any funds for an election, nor any assurance that woefully underpaid civil servants were equal to the task of organizing it, particularly if there had to be a new country-wide voter registration exercise, and acquisition, distribution and protection of ballot boxes and ballots. The time remaining to complete elections within the four-year interim period imposed on itself by the NRM was probably too short to carry out all aspects of an election with conventional safeguards. Much of the energy of government officials during the first three years had been diverted by the unanticipated civil wars, and by the continuing disastrous performance of the economy. On the other hand, completing the four-year period without an election would most probably have profoundly weakened the legitimacy of the government.

All of these factors were apparent to NRM officials in constructing an electoral structure new to Ugandans in 1989. The design they chose protected the NRM's political dominance, relaxed certain electoral rules, denied parties the right to participate, and raised questions about the NRM's ideological commitment. If it amounted to no more than a façade of legitimacy, it would not have contributed to democratization. But that would be to overlook the implementation of the elections, particularly the government's perceived fairness in conducting them, and the widely held belief that voters had a significant impact in the formation of their new assemblies. All these interrelated considerations demonstrate the complexities involved in taking this further step in the democratization process.

The Ugandan elections of 1989

Protection of the NRM's political dominance

The elections were designed to improve the chances of candidates who supported the NRM and to protect the government in case it did not do well. The brief period allowed for candidates to organize worked against the older, better-known political notables in the older parties. The government retained the power to appoint a sizeable fraction of NRC members. The NRM created within the NRC a new standing committee that may turn out to have more power than the NRC itself, and in which the NRM was certain to have a majority. And, a day before the elections, it gave the highest council of the army a new joint role with the NRC to approve the new constitution, to choose or remove the president, and to decide on a state of emergency or a state of war. In addition, as discussed in a later section, the old parties were prohibited from supporting candidates or campaigning for them. Taken together, these moves bespoke great nervousness on the part of the NRM. They also provide evidence that the NRM feared that it still did not have enough support to win the elections itself.

Nothing demonstrates the political uncertainties of the democratization process better than the use of the design and timing of national elections to give an advantage to the government or another contestant. This was certainly the case in Uganda. Though the government had promised to enlarge the NRC for some time, even three weeks before the dates and basic features of the elections were announced their final shape had not been decided. In his 1989 New Year's message Museveni reported that members of RC5s (the district council) would be added to the NRC (*New Vision*, 3 January 1989). Assuming these new members were intended to be elected by each RC5, the indirect representation of the existing system would merely be extended one more level. This would have been the safest course for the regime to take, but would have done the least for building its political base and legitimizing its ambitious plans to reverse Uganda's political and economic decay.

When Museveni announced the elections on 21 January, the design was greatly changed (*New Vision*, 23 January 1989). Fresh elections were to occur in councils at every level following the same indirect arrangements for lower committees to become upper councils up to the RC5 (district councils).[9] Now, however, the RC3s (subcounty councils) were to gather as an electoral college in their respective counties or urban divisions to elect one representative to the NRC, and nine to the RC5. In addition, the RC5s would also elect one NRC member representing the district, but that representative had to be a woman. Candidates could be nominated directly for the NRC even if they had not run in the lower RCs (*New Vision*, 22 February 1989). The sequence of elections necessarily began at the village level and continued to higher levels,

259

followed by a pause to give an opportunity for NRC nominations and elections by RC3s meeting together as an electoral college in their counties or divisions. A second pause was necessary after elections to the RC5 (district council) to permit the RC5 to convene and elect its own resistance committee and its NRC representative.[10]

In his speech on 21 January Museveni set a tight schedule for the entire sequence of elections. The dates for the RC1 and 2 elections were 11 and 12 February, only three weeks from the original announcement. RC3 elections were scheduled for 18 February, RC5 elections after one more week, NRC elections by the RC3s on 28 February, and elections of women representatives by RC5s on 4 March. Despite the difficulties of meeting these deadlines, the actual sequence of elections took slightly less time. County and division elections to the NRC took place on 25 February and elections of both women's NRC representatives and district RC executives occurred on 28 February.

Since preparations for the elections only began with the 21 January announcement, there was an extraordinary flurry of activity. An immediate – and ideologically telling – decision was made to use the Ministry of Local Government rather than the NRM secretariat to administer the elections, though the secretariat also held seminars to explain procedures and supplied some of the election officials. The National Political Commissar, head of the NRM secretariat, and Minister of State in the President's Office, Dr Kiiza Besigye, handled issues that extended beyond the jurisdiction of the Ministry of Local Government, provided political liaison with the President, and settled some of the more sensitive disputes. Legislation needed to make arrangements legal was passed only a few days before the elections began. Nothing had been budgeted for the exercise, but funds were supplied by the President's Office. Some lower officials complained that election expenses were underestimated.

Despite the lack of advance notice, there was intense interest in the elective seats and, despite its prohibition, 'quiet' campaigning appears to have occurred in most constituencies. The turn-out seems to have generally been large, though not for women in rural areas. Elections were held throughout the country except in Gulu district, Usuk county, and Soroti district where they were postponed because of civil war. In other parts of Soroti, Kumi and Apac districts the RC 1 and 2 elections took three days to complete because of attacks by dissidents. The Gulu elections were eventually held in October 1989, though rebels were able to interfere with some of them (*New Vision*, 14 and 17 October 1989).

The decision to call a 'snap election' was surely a tactical manoeuvre intended by the NRM to outflank the old party politicians. Even with the ban on party identification, a long campaign might have permitted the older politicians to revive their networks and raise enough money to defeat the younger, less well known, and less well connected leaders of the NRM. Many candidates thought their chances would improve if they ran at lower levels, even though NRC nominees, unlike all other elected resistance committee officials, did not have to rise by election through the system.[11]

Fourteen ministers and deputy ministers lost elections in county or urban divisional constituencies.[12] Two women defeated male competitors for county NRC seats in addition to the 34 who won the district seats reserved for women. In a few constituencies the UPC successfully canvassed enough support in enough villages to gain control of an entire county at the RC1 level and thus to elect a UPC notable to the NRC. Either through this strategy, or through personal popularity, four important members of Obote's UPC government won seats in county constituencies. These were significant victories, because they were elected from Mbarara, Bushenyi and Kabale districts, the area from which the most important NRM leaders also came. Other former UPC notables who had left the party earlier also won NRC seats from RC3 constituencies. The defeat of NRM ministers and the election of important UPC leaders who were local rivals of top NRM officials were the best indicators that the NRM did not intervene in the elections themselves.

Only well after arrangements for the elections were in place were most of these features made law. The NRC had to enact two statutes, three ordinances and a set of new electoral regulations during the three weeks before elections began. For example, the regulations governing nomination and elections in all RCs, including NRC members, were made law only nine days before the first elections. Fundamental policies, such as the length of the term of the newly elected NRC representatives, had not even been decided before the elections. The government was not sure of its position on so vital a question as the term of the new parliament. At first Dr Besigye announced that it would only be valid until the four-year interim period ended in January 1990 (*New Vision*, 7 February 1989: 8). Just after the elections he shrugged off the question of its life span, leaving it to the newly chosen NRC members to decide when they voted on the new constitution (*New Vision*, 1 March 1989).

But other decisions by the government made it crystal clear that it was not prepared to risk its overall control of affairs on the outcome of this election. Despite its populist inclinations, nearly a quarter of the newly constituted NRC was appointed, not elected. The government decreed that the original 38 NRC members, who had been the core cadre of the movement during the guerrilla war, would hold their seats without facing election. The President was given the right to appoint 20 NRC members; the NRA Council, the highest decision-making body in the army, received authority to choose 10 more.[13] Thus the government started out with the support of 68 votes out of between 279 and 284 seats in the enlarged NRC.[14] However, before these elections, when the NRC contained only the original 38 core NRM cadre and the government ministers, the government had appointed all its members.

Even more telling were three new provisions added only the day before the elections began, when the original proclamation of 1986 was amended to enlarge the NRC. The first created a National Executive Committee (NEC) within the NRC 'to discuss and determine the policies and political direction' of the NRM, and 'monitor and oversee the general performance of the Government' (Legal Notice No. 1 of 1986 (Amendment) Statute, 1989: Section 6).[15] Its membership consisted of the original 38 core, and non-elected, members of the NRM, 10 members of the NRC appointed by the NRM Chair (the President) and 34 chosen by the NRC, one from the elected members from each district.[16] Although the exact role of this committee is not yet clear, it seems designed to ensure that the NRM will have a majority on critical issues that it wants to keep off the agenda of the NRC.

The second and third provisions greatly expanded the political role of the military at the expense of the enlarged NRC. One made the NRA Council, the top policy-making body within the army, a participant with the NRC 'in the discussion, adoption and promulgation of the Constitution' (Legal Notice No. 1 of 1986 (Amendment) Statute, 1989: Section 14B). The other gave the NRC and the NRA Council 'assembling together and jointly' the power to elect or remove the President,[17] to approve a declaration of a state of emergency, to authorize a declaration of war, to regulate the President's operational use of the armed forces, or to determine any other matter either council wanted decided (Legal Notice No. 1 of 1986 (Amendment) Statute, 1989: Section 14C).[18] In Mujuni Stephen's apt phrase, giving the NRA a fundamental role in constitution-making and governance amounted to 'pointing . . . the military finger at the body politic' (*Weekly Topic*, 21 December 1988). In less colourful language, the new parliamentary roles for the NRA Council on top of their 10 appointees to the NRC ensured that the elections could not produce an NRC that could seize political control or direction from the NRM.

Finally, just after the elections were concluded, Museveni made a disturbing observation in the process of rejecting fears that the old politicians would try to manipulate the people. 'If any member of the enlarged house works against [the revolution] . . . he or she will be thrown out . . . this one is a revolution. It is not merely an electioneering exercise' (Radio Uganda, 28 February 1989, reported in FBIS, 3 March 1989, p. 3). From the perspective of a newly elected member, there appeared to be perilous boundaries over which democrats, however well they knew what the people in their constituencies wanted, might not step, at least for the time being.

262

The Ugandan elections of 1989

These features in the design of the 1989 elections were windows into NRM anxieties. The NRM introduced new hope to Uganda; but it had not yet been able to put its programme into place, for reasons that were partly beyond its control. To have lost the elections would have crippled that programme. Nevertheless, in protecting itself the NRM created new obstacles to further democratization. Not only did the legislation introduced restrict the democratic potential of these elections, but much of it will somehow have to be removed if further democratization is to occur.

Relaxation of electoral rules

The question of relaxing electoral rules raises additional worrying issues. The governments of many states whose democratic credentials are far more impregnable than Uganda's have taken measures to give themselves advantages. But changing the rules for conducting elections, even on the basis of 'necessity', creates the prospect of interfering with the free choice of the voter. And in Uganda there was only the smallest gap between prospect and advantage. Ironically, however, reducing formal requirements may have led to a fairer election, at least in the 1989 case, than conventional electoral rules would have produced. There were strong pragmatic arguments for using counties as constituency boundaries, eliminating voter registration, using top NRM officials as election officers, simplifying nomination procedures, relying on indirect representation, and even dropping the secret ballot. Each of these changes in electoral rules responded to blatant violations in the 1980 elections ('A Local Observer', 1988, pp. 84–97). But the opportunities for future misuse created by relaxation in the rules in 1989 are now as a result correspondingly greater.

Because the RC system was a direct democracy only at the village level, never involving more than a few hundred people acting together, and because the government was willing to organize the elections informally – without voting registers, ballot boxes or redrawn constituencies – it was feasible to arrange them quickly and relatively inexpensively. In many respects, the electoral design worked against manipulation and corruption. The well-established county boundaries removed a fertile source for gerrymandering constituencies.[19] Museveni made it clear that the government had this abuse in mind specifically when it designed the new electoral structure.[20] Using villages as sites for the popular elections meant that everyone knew who was a resident and who was not, so voting registers were far less vital, though this argument is harder to make for RCs in urban areas. In the higher RCs all voters had already been identified by virtue of having been elected at the next lower level.

In place of the theoretically neutral Electoral Commission that had organized Uganda's earlier general elections, several members of the existing NRC and of the NRM Secretariat who were not contesting the

263

elections served as election supervisors. District administrators, who reported to the President and whom the government regarded as the political heads of their districts, served as district returning officers.[21] These decisions gave the NRM more potential influence over the elections than a neutral Electoral Commission would have allowed – nonetheless there were only a few accusations that these opportunities were used to affect the results. Election officials who hold powerful positions can be more effective in preventing violations of rules than neutral civil servants, at least where they have no incentive to intervene to help fellow supporters. Having assured themselves they could not lose the elections, NRM officials worked hard to ensure they were run fairly.

Relaxation of the nomination rules for NRC candidates was striking. Each candidate had to fill out two simple forms and gain the support of four members of the electoral college; that is, the assembled members of the RC3s in the county or division (Resistance Councils and Committees (Elections) Regulations, 1989: Section 12). They did not have to win election to lower councils. Candidates did not have to put down a deposit. They did not even have to be residents in their constituencies, so long as they planned to move there within six months of being elected (Legal Notice No. 1 of 1986 (Amendment) Statute, 1989: Section 14D). However, they had to have completed post-primary education or to possess a professional certificate. No political restrictions were placed on any RC candidates (including the NRC), except that they could not have served as members of either Obote's or Amin's intelligence agencies. Given the ease of nomination, it was striking that there were only a handful of candidates for NRC elections in most constituencies. The relatively small number of candidates proposed suggests that some covert organization of the nomination process probably occurred in many localities.

The removal of the secret ballot was probably the most worrisome innovation. As in previous RC elections – at least outside the war zone during the guerrilla struggle – voting in all elections occurred in the open by lining up behind the candidate of choice. Open voting, despite the danger of coercing voters' choices, nonetheless avoided the endemic abuses of ballot boxes carried out behind the cloak of secrecy in the 1980 elections.[22] The NRM defended queuing as an embarrassing necessity. Dr Besigye insisted that 'the government was not opposed to the principle of universal suffrage by the ballot box, but was trying to work out a simple and effective system of representation for today's Uganda' (*New Vision*, 7 February 1989).

Open voting in small electorates made it impossible to hide opposition to the government and thus may have inflated support for the NRM. But the turn-out was generally large, and there were virtually no reports from witnesses that people felt coerced into voting for a candidate they opposed. And even most losers conceded that the votes were counted fairly; that those who had the most supporters queuing behind them were actually declared the winners. Nonetheless, the value of an open vote was increasingly hard to justify for RCs at higher levels, where the political stakes were even greater. Ambitious politicians were likely to have found it extremely difficult to be seen joining the queue behind a candidate of whom the government disapproved. Careerism and uncoerced choice do not easily go together.

Although I have not seen the argument made by the NRM, the populist perspective evident in the design of the RC system and the philosophy of the *10-Point Programme* may have persuaded NRM leaders to accept electoral rules that left procedures more under the control of ordinary voters. The changes in the rules created an informality that could be justified by trusting the voters, acting in their small arenas, to ensure fairness. Substitution of trust in the people for the protection of formal rules is the sort of justification that fits well within populist notions of democracy. But since the argument follows from the populist stress on direct democracy, this claim applies more appropriately to the RC1 in the village than to RCs at higher levels in which 'the people' have only indirectly elected their representatives.

The notion of trusting the people could also help explain the NRM's choice of rules that made nominations easier and banned campaigning. The populist creed frequently claims that political decisions should be based directly on moral considerations felt by ordinary people rather than policies proposed by professional politicians. So long as one accepts the populist premise that real policy choices are simple and easily understood by ordinary people, the position is defensible. Reducing nomination requirements widened the field of candidates for representatives in the RCs, and particularly in the NRC, to people without organization or connections, and thus also exemplified trust in ordinary people.[23] NRM officials often remarked to me that villagers 'know who among them have good and bad character' and thus who should be placed in office. Here, too, the argument is harder to justify for councillors who qualify to vote only because they have been elected several times. The fact that a person's moral character was thought adequate for a position on the committee of an RC1 does not mean that the village voter would have entrusted that person with a higher office.

On balance, relaxation did not much affect the results, because the government tried to observe the rules it set. While that was critical for democratization, it was easier in this case because government leaders knew the elections could not remove them from office. Ease of violation of these rules – despite popular involvement at the lowest level – may provide an irresistible incentive, however, when more is at stake. Thus, rules and practices that served the democratization process at this stage may have to be changed in order to take the next step.

Rebuilding political institutions

Prevention of party competition

The NRM's ban on party competition directly posed the question of what sort of democracy ought to be the goal of the democratization process. Preventing parties from publicizing their platforms, organizing supporters, and campaigning for their candidates, cut the heart out of representative democracy. But in the populist perspective, competitive parties are frequently regarded as a hindrance because they are thought to distort popular choice. In Uganda, this was a matter of more than academic debate, for it brought the opposition between the NRM and the old parties into the open. As with other features of the electoral design, the issue was whether the choice to ban parties could be justified on the basis of moving Uganda closer to a populist form of democratization, or whether it merely propped up a government that could not compete successfully as a party.

The DP and the UPC, the principal parties for the entire period since independence, had successfully opposed an attempt to organize the 1980 elections on a non-party basis. Indeed, it had been the basic reason for the UPC *coup d'état* of 1979 against the Binaisa government. Despite fraud and violence, both parties demonstrated in the 1980 elections that they retained the support of large numbers of voters, even though they had been suppressed during the Amin dictatorship of the 1970s. The social composition of the leadership of both consisted of petit-bourgeois small entrepreneurs and educated professionals similar to party leaders throughout sub-Saharan Africa.

The UPC, however, was in considerable disarray once Obote, its leader, fled to Zambia following the coup of 1985, half a year before the NRM took power. Its members generally did not participate in the RC elections of 1986 and 1987. The DP, on the other hand, had participated in the Okello government, which had staged the coup against the UPC and had then joined the NRM government immediately after it was set up. Though not quite a coalition partner, the DP became the principal reason for considering the NRM government broad-based. As noted already, it had pursued an aggressive but quiet strategy to win as many committee positions as possible in the early RC elections and thus dominated many of the higher RCs before the 1989 elections.

The official leadership of both the DP and the UPC put forward the conventional arguments for a multiparty representative democracy in 1989. The DP's argument for party competition followed the conventional justification that when it functions properly, a multiparty system 'is the best institutional guarantee for orderly and peaceful change of government ... for ensuring public accountability and for promoting individual initiatives for development' (NEC, DP, 1989a: 3). It gives people the choice between different sets of policies or 'blueprints', the

266

opportunity to keep political competition peaceful, and accountability of leaders through opposition in Parliament (NEC, DP, 1989b, pp. 2–4). In Uganda competitive parties were not given a chance to function properly, because 'the system was deliberately undermined through bribery and coercion' by Obote's efforts to establish a one-party system and Amin's military rule (NEC, DP, 1989b, pp. 1–2).

Meanwhile the official UPC leadership in Kampala rejected the elections of 1989 out of hand immediately Museveni announced them. Denouncing the exercise as 'an internal reorganization of the NRM . . . deliberately portrayed as 'The General Elections' to legalise the NRM leadership', the assistant secretary general went on to attack the lack of universal suffrage embodied in the indirect RC electoral scheme and the absence of the opportunity to give Ugandans the choice of 'alternative policy formulations' by denying parties a role (Ogwal, 1989, p. 3). She stressed that such comprehensive formulations were especially important given the economic problems and 'frightful insecurity' afflicting Uganda.

Taking the opposite position, the NRM had insisted in its *10-Point Programme* that party competition harms national unity.[24] Its principal contention was that parties encourage sectarian issues that divide the people, and distract them from considering solutions vital to improving the quality of their lives (Museveni, 1985, pp. 48–50). Indeed, the NRM blamed the DP, and particularly the UPC, for creating the conditions that caused Uganda to slide into dictatorship, corruption and lawlessness. In opposition to sectarianism – 'religion, colour, sex or height' – the NRM stressed they 'consider one's goodness or badness [e.g., corruption] or contribution' when welcoming new members (Museveni, 1985, p. 49). It followed that allowing parties to campaign would work against democratic choice by introducing irrelevant issues and bribery that would distract the electorate from its real concerns.

The electoral arrangements of 1989 adopted the NRM view, though without suggesting (as Museveni had insisted earlier to the DP) that the parties would be suspended only for a fixed period of time after which there would be a referendum (NEC, DP, 1989a, p. 6). Instead, when he announced the elections, Museveni deferred consideration of future party involvement, saying that 'we shall move cautiously step by step', and added a mysterious hint that 'as these elections become more organised, then we shall organise one in a disciplined, but not an opportunistic manner' (*New Vision*, 23 January 1989). In the light of its earlier discussions with the DP, the ban on party competition amounted to a failure by the NRM to find an accommodation with the main party in its government, and thus something of a rejection of the principle of broad-based government. The decision also implied that the NRM did not feel capable of competing effectively against openly organized parties nor, perhaps, of winning a referendum on the issue.

Rebuilding political institutions

However, the ban on the parties had divisive effects on both the UPC and the DP. Several UPC notables ran and won elections despite the boycott demanded by UPC headquarters. Within the DP tension emerged between those who wanted DP ministers to leave the government in order to protect the party, and those who wanted them to continue to cooperate with the NRM despite the ban on party activity. The NRM may thus have gained a tactical advantage by enticing elements of the old parties to seek the rewards of government within the electoral format it had designed.

In practice the ban on campaigning succeeded in greatly reducing the opportunity for politicians to corrupt voters. The regulations strictly forbade all use of party symbols, sectarian appeals, threats of force, the offer of food and drink, or even the display of posters advertising the candidate (Resistance Councils and Committees (Elections) Regulations, 1989: Section 31). Only a brief introduction by the candidate to the RC 'for not more than five minutes' was permitted (Resistance Councils and Committees (Elections) Regulations, 1989: Sections 12(3)). Most Ugandan observers concede that some campaigning, particularly involving food and drink, occurred, but it was very small in scale. On the other hand, because of the small electorates created by the indirect RC system, corruption through campaigning would have had a more serious impact than in larger electorates (*Report of the Commission of Inquiry into the Local Government System*, 1987, p. 31).

The absence of open campaigning made it virtually impossible to discuss policies. Consequently, in virtually all elections, discussion focused on the personal qualities of the candidates – their moral character, honesty and willingness to mix with ordinary people – rather than on the policies they were likely to support. As a commission of inquiry had reminded the government 18 months before the elections, open campaigns were more likely to educate voters about political choices, and restrict voter appeals to those that could withstand public scrutiny (*Report of the Commission of Inquiry into the Local Government System*, 1987, pp. 30–1). But the commission did not say whether it felt parties were essential to achieve these goals. Nevertheless the combination of preventing party campaigns and an emphasis on moral character in these elections tended to shift the opportunity to frame NRC policies to the remaining organized and publicly vocal political body, the unelected NRM leaders at the top.

On the other hand, since both the DP and the UPC were widely identified with specific religious and, to a lesser extent, ethnic affiliations, the ban on party campaigning probably reduced sectarianism, though it certainly did not eliminate it. Whether the sectarian influences reported were the result of the inability to prevent party activity entirely, or simply reflected the beliefs of much of the electorate, cannot be easily

The Ugandan elections of 1989

determined. Religion was frequently reported to have been an important factor in many of the county elections in Bushenyi, Kabale and Mbarara districts. Ethnic concerns were paramount in other areas. Candidates whose families had migrated to the county in which they resided were attacked for not being 'sons of the soil'.[25] On the other hand, the elections of women by the RC5s were thought to be the freest from sectarian influence.

Preventing party competition is not the same as banning open discussion of candidates' policy positions. But during the 1989 elections the two were simply lumped together. The public rationale for the prohibition on campaigning was twofold and negative: to prevent corruption and to prevent sectarianism. The problem with responding to these problems with such blunt tools is the deprivation of informed choice by voters, and, of course, the removal of the main influence voters have on the positions taken by their representatives. Indeed, voters who were not aware of the policy positions of candidates may have felt it safer to vote for those they thought were NRM members.

Banning the parties also sharply raised the stakes in the struggle to stay in power, which meant the next steps in democratization might also be that much more difficult for the NRM. During the debate on extension of the NRM interim regime, many of the newly elected NRC members, including some who had been prominent party notables, rejected the old parties as having caused many of Uganda's political difficulties [*New Vision*, 6 October 1989, pp. 1, 12]. But, as the next section of this chapter indicates, the NRM made only modest efforts to develop a populist rationale for these elections, even though there were some indicators both in doctrine and in electoral design that it took its goal of giving power to the people seriously. Because it did little to justify the ban on parties as a positive contribution to democratization, the NRM appeared to be simply using its ruling position to prolong itself in power, presenting an uncomfortable parallel to the UPC. Though it was important to reduce electoral corruption, if parties were to be banned the NRM needed to provide evidence that it had a democratic justification for doing so. In the last analysis, if this electoral design were to represent the NRM's commitment to democratization, removing sources of past corruption counted for less than creating popular institutions to take their place.

The NRM's ideological commitment

The ideological orientation of the NRM was always ambiguous. The design of the elections did not clearly indicate whether populism or representative democracy was the preferred approach to democratization of NRM leaders. The movement's history, the social background of its leaders and its commitment to broad-based government suggested that when forced to produce a policy the NRM would probably opt for some

269

sort of combination of both approaches. However, such a compromise makes it far harder to justify the 1989 elections as a step towards democratization. A clear choice of a radical and populist definition of democratization would have provided some justification, albeit controversial, for the short period given candidates to prepare, the relaxation of rules and the ban on parties and campaigning in the design of these elections.

The history of the NRM's changing doctrines on its path to power helps to explain its ambiguity towards democratization. It evolved from a tiny military unit dependent on the Tanzanian army during the liberation of Uganda to a hastily organized party for a few months in 1980 and 1981. It then passed through two phases as a guerrilla movement. First, under Lule, it committed itself to restoring multiparty competition and then, under Museveni, to a combination of popular councils and parliament. Finally it became the senior partner, sharing power in a Ugandan government. No wonder the NRM never made a consistent or 'pure' choice of a definition for democracy in Uganda. In addition, the social background of the NRM leadership is as thoroughly middle-class as that of the older parties. In fact the NRM leaders have been more highly educated than their counterparts. If the guerrilla struggle, deprivation of the security of professional careers and relative youth contributed to their sympathy for a radical populist position in 1986, one would expect them to grow increasingly more conservative as they continued in power. Finally, the imperatives of managing a broad-based government with partners all more conservative than the NRM further diluted the NRM's commitment to populism.

If the NRM intended to broaden democratic competition by directly empowering the peasantry – 90 per cent of Uganda's population and the producers of all its foreign exchange – then the monopoly of the old parties, particularly the UPC and the DP, had to be broken. Both of these parties represented fractions of emergent middle classes. Democratization would have had to expand beyond 'the premises shared between the contending parties in Uganda in the post-Amin period' (Mamdani, 1987, p. 93). The NRM could have tried to sink its social roots into the peasantry and become a people's party. During the latter phase of the guerrilla period the NRM leadership seemed to be using the RCs to develop cells of the movement to do just that. But relatively few links were forged between the NRM and the RCs after 1986. Perhaps if the NRM had shared power, rather than winning it outright, it might have put more effort into expanding 'the premises' of Ugandan politics in this way. As with so many other nationalist parties before it, it lost much of its momentum and its coherence when it became the government.

Nevertheless, the most impressive indication of support for populist democratization in the structure of the 1989 elections was the choice of the RCs, the NRM's most significant contribution to Ugandan political institutions, as the framework for the elections. At village level the RCs met any reasonable definition of a genuine populist institution, even though popular control over special interests had not yet been resolved. The reservation of parliamentary seats for women, and for youth and workers through popular organizations, certainly all weak and exploited categories in Uganda, also provided evidence that the NRM designed these elections as a stage in the creation of a Ugandan version of populist democracy. Finally, at least in the context of these features, one might argue that removing formal rules for registration, nomination, voting, or party competition could allow ordinary people more direct access to political decisions.

Nevertheless, the character and implementation of each of these acts raises serious doubts about the depth of the NRM's commitment to populist democratization. The newspaper report of Museveni's original announcement of the elections was striking for the absence of any populist criteria for the exclusion of parties. Without this justification, the ban appears intended more to protect the political dominance of the NRM than to secure better democratization.

The main difficulty the RC system created for populist doctrine was the NRM's reliance on indirect elections for higher councils. A year before the elections, the NRM leadership explicitly rejected a proposal to allow villagers to elect RC members directly at all levels of RCs. Members of a commission of inquiry into local government had agreed with the government on the value of the multiple screening process that the RC system created by having candidates for higher office selected from among those already elected. But, the commissioners added, 'the interests of a consistent democracy demand that the electorate always remain popular, and this can only be guaranteed by direct elections at all levels' (*Report*, 1987: pp. 31–2). They pointed out that this could easily be accomplished by also using the parish as the polling unit for all elections above the RC1 level. The government responded in its white paper that direct elections 'would only provide fertile ground to sectarianism and opportunism' (*Weekly Topic*, 14 December 1988). In other words, the government insisted there must be limits on the trust that could be placed in popular choice, at least in present-day Uganda.

In populist thinking, direct democracy is strengthened if the electorate can secure the accountability of their representatives by having the right to recall them. But the NRM did not create any mechanism through which the people acting in their RC1 assemblies could recall their representatives at any level above RC2. As the commissioners inquiring into local government also pointed out, the indirect nature of the system meant that each RC had the power of recall only from the next higher level. They asked the NRM to provide RC1s with the right to recall their representatives at all levels (*Report*, 1987, pp. 32–3). Here, too, the

271

government rejected the commissioners' proposal. The NRM was not so populist that it was prepared to entrust the power to recall an NRC member, for example, to ordinary people acting in their basic RC1 assemblies.

Finally, there was a curious lack of attention in these elections to popular organizations, frequently a hallmark of populist regimes. If there are groups in society that are weak and exploited, populists argue that special representation may be needed to empower them.[26] The electoral arrangements singled out women, youth and workers as groups to organize. The NRM presumably believed that county constituencies would adequately represent peasants in the NRC. It would take a further inquiry to find out whether, after the elections, peasants felt the same way.

Women were not provided with an organization, but instead one position on each resistance committee at each level of RC was reserved for a woman. This ensured that at least one woman would be a prospective candidate for the next higher RC elections. In addition, a seat representing each county was explicitly reserved for a woman to sit in each RC5 (district council), and so was one seat for each district in the NRC. Thus, women were assured of representation by some women at the highest elected levels, despite the indirect nature of RC elections. By and large, the women elected were not 'ordinary people'. Rather, they were better educated and had more professional experience than even the victorious male candidates. Their social background indicates that they were likely to represent middle-class interests, as well as being articulate speakers for women's issues. Reservation of seats for women created a further dilemma for a populist justification for the elections. Establishing the participation of women in government at all levels, and in noticeable numbers in the national parliament, was a progressive step. But it was contrary to the commonly held belief in Uganda that women should not play an active political role in public life. While it may enhance the prospects of giving political power to women, the policy could therefore only be carried out by ignoring the values of the majority of Ugandans. The same point could be made for youth and workers' organizations.

In his first announcement of the elections, Museveni also said that new popular organizations would be formed to elect youth and worker representatives to the NRC (*New Vision*, 23 January 1989). In order to complete its schedule on time, the government focused all its energies on the RC elections and ignored formation of the popular organizations. More than a year after the 1989 elections the government had still not set up either the youth or workers' popular organizations (Barongo, 1990, p. 18).

The National Organization of Trade Unions [NOTU] complained that the idea of forming a new workers' organization was just a way for the NRM to bypass the trade unions and create a structure to control the workers (*New Vision*, 21 February 1989).

On several counts, the NRM could have defended its commitment to democratization more effectively by reinforcing its populist ideology, even if its motives had been only political. Its failure to launch these popular organizations suggests that it was neither being pressured by a popular thrust from below, nor ready to take the step on its own. Emergent lower-class forces in Uganda gave no indication that they wanted or were ready to sustain popular organizations.[27] The NRM's commitment through these elections to move towards a populist type of democratization was either shallow, or blocked behind the scenes.

CONCLUSION

The design and implementation of the 1989 elections reveals a great deal not only about the extent to which they were democratic, but also about the anxieties of the NRM leadership to maintain power while attempting fundamental change. Much too can be learned about the difficulties of democratization. On the basis of the four criteria for the achievement of democratization posed at the beginning of this chapter, the 1989 elections fare rather poorly. People were not given the freedom to organize and discuss political issues openly. To the extent that open voting inhibited expression of choice, they could not vote freely. The elections did not put the NRM government at risk. And, the prohibition on discussing issues made it difficult for the government to use the elections to learn what the voters wanted.[28] Nor did these elections threaten the position of dominant social groups in Uganda.[29] Consequently, it is difficult to agree with Museveni's suggestion that these were 'one of the freest elections in the world' (Interview in *'Al-Dustur* [London], 19 June 1989, pp. 10–12, tr. from Arabic in FBIS, 23 August 1989: 12).

But the better, if far more difficult, question is not how democratic were they, but did they contribute to democratization? All sorts of policies without much democratic content may make significant contributions to democratization; for example, the establishment of peace and a disciplined army. From this perspective, the 1989 elections are more important for what they tell us about the intentions of the NRM leadership as regards the next step towards democratization, and how far the electorate believes the government intends to proceed with democratization. Such analysis cannot occur in a vacuum. It must take account of the actual possibilities in the Ugandan situation. The earlier history of internecine political conflict, the narrow political base of the NRM, and the additional political issues it created by proposing a new electoral design make democratization problematic. Indeed, questions about the implications of the 1989 elections become all the more troubling in the light of the NRC vote in October 1989 to lengthen the interim period of the NRM, and perhaps the term of NRC legislators, for another five years (*New Vision*, 11 October 1989). Once again, the proposal was a surprise. The government denied the request of some NRC members for a delay in order to consult their constituents. Here again was an issue too fragile and politically explosive to permit widespread involvement of the people.

Some apparently plausible explanations of the contribution of these elections are difficult to justify. In particular, the argument that the NRM intended to adopt a populist path to democratization cannot be supported by inferences from the electoral design and its consequences. At the crucial junctures, most demonstrably in the failure to create the popular organizations needed to complete the elections themselves, the NRM did not act on its populist premises. Nevertheless, the stress on RCs as electoral units, and the populist element in the NRM's heroic past means that a future decision to adopt this approach can never be ruled out.

The notion that relaxing electoral rules would avoid the corruption that had become so blatant in the 1980 elections seemed in general to succeed in the 1989 elections. But the primary reason was that so little seemed to be at stake. The incentive to cheat was much lower than it had been in 1980, when the purpose of the elections was to choose a new government. Still, the NRM was vague about whether there would be another election to choose representatives to debate and adopt a new constitution, as it had once promised. If the present NRC becomes the constituent assembly, the 1989 elections will have had an enormous influence on the definition and prospects for democratization. In addition, managing the next elections without voter registration, secret ballot, open campaigning and participation by parties will raise a storm of controversy by disadvantaged groups that would probably be serious enough to end further progress towards democratization. The suspension of party activities in the 1989 elections introduced a level of intensity that will not be diffused without a new constitution. Since the NRC was expected to play a central role in drafting this constitution, the rules for the 1989 elections could not but help to exacerbate the party issue.

Nonetheless, the elections of 1989 contributed to the democratization process by preparing the way for another. Having held an election that voters felt was basically fair, if limited in what it accomplished, the NRM leaders gained an opportunity to rethink how to organize the next one. There is some evidence to suggest that these elections were an expedient response to a tight political corner into which the NRM had backed, and that the next elections may well be organized differently.

The most likely explanation for the design of the 1989 elections was to provide a temporary solution to the serious problem of legitimation NRM leaders had created for themselves. By decreeing that they would hold national elections within the four-year interim period and then failing to carry them out, they would have risked losing the support they needed to develop a more enduring constitutional framework. The critical point, therefore, was to design elections that would not take away more legitimacy than the NRM would gain by holding them. That meant, above all else, running them fairly once the rules were announced, and accepting all winners and losers. The question of whether it was possible for Ugandans to hold fair elections had not been successfully demonstrated since independence. Perhaps the most important fact to politically conscious Ugandans was the serious attention the government paid to the expression of political choice, even though the choices themselves were severely restricted.

The comparison with election procedures in Kenya is instructive. Through a constitutional amendment, the Kenyan government formally prohibited all parties other than the government party. It also adopted open voting by queuing in primary elections, and other rules that gave an advantage to government candidates. The voting system in Kenya was generally regarded as unfair by both Kenyans and Ugandans, because even with all the advantages ensured by these rules, government officials blatantly manipulated results to ensure that opponents of the government were defeated. Popular opinion in both countries seemed to regard elections as a sort of social contract between citizens and the government that tolerated lopsided rules during the 1980s, so long as they were enforced fairly. The main difference from Kenya appears to have been the widespread belief in Uganda that once the NRM laid out the rules, it insisted on a fair election. For Ugandans, that was a new and valuable experience.

In two of the three reasons he gave for justifying the extension of the NRM interim period, Museveni hinted that the format might be changed in future elections, and that the government was aware of shortcomings in the 1989 design. The extension was needed, he argued, first, for 'the minimum rehabilitation of infrastructure that can support a free and fair general election in the future', and second, 'to put in place the requisite logistical means, e.g. vehicles, ballot boxes, money etc. that would be indispensable in a future democratic exercise . . .' (*New Vision*, 12 October 1989). Both reasons suggest that the NRM leadership felt the 1989 elections were necessary, but temporary, expedients carried out in the absence of the material requirements needed for a fully democratic election with more conventional safeguards.

Because democratization means changing power relationships, it does not proceed in a straightforward manner. The motives of leaders, even when committed to expanding democracy, are complex and tangled. However flawed, the NRM's effort to provide ordinary villagers with more direct access to political choice gave some prospect of escape from the terrible failures of conventional representative democracy in the 1960s and again in the earlier 1980s. By holding the elections, the NRM deepened its commitment to hold others, no trivial matter for a government that came to power by military victory. Nevertheless, the steps the NRM took to ensure that it did not lose control over the electoral process, and its unresolved confrontation with the old parties, ensure that if the process ultimately results in a successful transition to democracy, it will be long and full of surprises.

Notes

---

1. I would like to thank Ken Sharpe for his comments on an earlier draft of this chapter, and a Spoor Grant from the Dartmouth College Rockefeller Center for financing the research. I am responsible for any errors or omissions.
2. The shift coincided with the replacement of the more conservative Yusufu K. Lule, former president of Uganda, with the more radical Yoweri K. Museveni, as chair of the NRM and NRA [National Resistance Army]. It was most likely caused by the NRA's success in organizing village RCs in popular support of its guerrilla struggle. The original approach is presented in an early manifesto, probably written in 1982 *Towards A Free and Democratic Uganda* nd, pp. 16–17).
3. The elected officials form a body which at each level is called a Resistance Committee.
4. For overviews of populism in politics see Laclau, 1977; Canovan, 1981; and Worsley, 1969. Lobel (1988, pp. 838–77) provides an extremely valuable discussion of the compromises in electoral structures that populist regimes are forced by their opponents to adopt.
5. For other examples in Africa see Joseph, 1987, pp. 4–5; Sklar, 1987, p. 706; Hayward, 1988, pp. xv–xvi.
6. The Resistance Councils and Committees Statute (1987) and the Resistance Committees' (Judicial Powers) Statute (1987) codified these arrangements.
7. He claimed that this percentage also reflected party representation in RCs at lower levels. Given the indirect nature of RC elections, this would be likely. Independent observers agreed that the DP had done extremely well in RC elections during the first two years of NRM rule.
8. A code of conduct for the NRA was promulgated before the takeover and reaffirmed by inclusion as a schedule in Legal Notice No. 1 of 1986, the original proclamation validating the authority of the NRA and the NRM.
9. The RC4 level was skipped again.
10. The 211 elected representatives included one for each of the 150 counties, 19 for Kampala and the municipalities, one woman for each of the 34 districts, five chosen by a new youth organization and three by a new workers' organization (Legal Notice No. 1 of 1986 (Amendment) Statute, 1989: Section 1).
11. One male candidate in Kampala, who was rejected for eight of the nine offices on his RC1 executive [the ninth was reserved for a woman], managed to be nominated and won a seat in the NRC (*New Vision*, 27 February 1989).

276

The Ugandan elections of 1989

12. Following a successful court challenge, Jack Maumbe-Mukhwana, a former deputy minister who had been declared the loser in the February elections, regained his seat in a by-election on 3 May 1990 (*New Vision*, 4 May 1990). A minister of state, Semyano Kiyingi, who had been forced to run again by another opponent's challenge, was re-elected in a by-election on the same day.

13. The President used his appointment powers to help maintain the broad-based character of his government. Of his 20 appointments, ten had previously been ministers or deputy ministers – four had been defeated and six had not stood for these elections. Among the four who had lost elections, two reappointed ministers belonged to the old political parties. The NRA Council, chaired by President Museveni, elected ten NRA officers as its appointees. The criteria for election, I was told, were combat experience, good moral character, and regional balance.

14. There has been confusion over how many seats the enlarged NRC contained. *New Vision* reported that there would be 278, a figure frequently repeated (7 February 1989). However, the Ssese Islands were removed from Masaka district to form Kalangala, thus making Uganda's 34th district. The new district was split into two counties, adding one more county constituency. In addition, the legislation enlarging the NRC specified five posts in the NRM automatically carrying NRC membership – the Chairman, the Vice-Chairman, the National Political Commissar, the Administrative Secretary and the Director of Legal Affairs – (Legal Notice No. 1 of 1986 (Amendment) Statute, 1989: Section 1). These posts were held by members of the core NRM cadre who also qualified to sit in the NRC without election. Since these posts will not necessarily be filled with original members of the core cadre, the total number of seats may expand from the present 279 to as many as 284.

15. The language of Section 6(ii)(a) states that the NEC's first function 'shall be to (a) discuss and determine the policies and political direction of the National Resistance Movement'. Why the NRM and not the NRC? Surely the NRM did not intend to have members of the NEC who were not in the NRM tell it what political direction it should take. Presumably this is a typographical error.

16. There was resentment among some of the elected members who preferred to have members from each district choose their representative to the NEC. The selection process chosen protected the NRM by allowing the core cadre and the other appointees to participate in the choice.

17. Section 6 in the original proclamation of 1986 declaring that the President shall be appointed by the NRC was dropped (Legal Notice No. 1 of 1986 (Amendment) Statute, 1989: Section 1(b)).

18. The government had been contemplating the second provision since the debate over the constitutional bill the previous November, so it is unclear whether it was motivated solely by the decision to hold elections.

19. However, because of the uneven distribution of Catholic residents in certain districts, the use of the county as the constituency instead of the RC5 (as originally proposed) was believed by some observers to have helped Protestants at the expense of Catholics and thus to have worked against the DP.

20. 'Counties', he said, 'will be used as constituencies unlike in the past when subcounties were chopped up' (*New Vision*, 23 January 1989).

21. Chiefs and local government employees were appointed presiding officers and enumerators.

22. According to Besigye, the government was not opposed to the ballot box, but needed 'a simple and effective system for today's Uganda, (*New Vision*, 7 February 1989).

23. Contrary to populist doctrine, however, candidates for the NRC had to graduate from some post primary or professional school. Thus, most ordinary villagers were not eligible (Legal Notice. No. 1 of 1986 (Amendment) Statute, 1989: Sec. 14D (b)).

277

Rebuilding political institutions

24. In its earlier manifesto the NRM had accepted the organization of politics through party activity (*Towards a Free and Democratic Uganda*, nd, p. 17).
25. One former MP told me he lost his election primarily for this reason.
26. The NRM's progressive position on women was adopted after it took power. (Kakwenzire, 1990, pp. 3-4). It is an important indication that the NRM still has some potential for radicalism. However, in the face of dire economic conditions it has often refused to take the demands of workers seriously.
27. Populist governments throughout Africa have found it difficult to gain the support of emergent lower-class forces in order to form an effective popular base (Kasfir, 1989).
28. The virtual absence of policy discussions meant that critical issues such as war in the north and east, the economy, and the relation of Buganda to the rest of Uganda could not be openly addressed.
29. A full assessment of the elections would involve research into the political emergence or consolidation of class fractions through a careful study of the social composition of winners and losers and how far their success related to class support despite the ban on campaigning. Such a study would give us some clues to whether the elections expanded 'the premises' of Ugandan politics, or simply put new individuals belonging to the same dominant class fractions back into power.

NINETEEN

Resistance councils and committees: a case study from Makerere

Apolo R. Nsibambi

This chapter seeks to show that the resistance councils and committees (RCs) have created an important structural change in Uganda by enabling the NRM government to penetrate the country, especially the rural areas, in a democratic manner.[1] RCs have also enhanced political participation, political accountability, resolution of social conflict, economic development, security consciousness, and flow of information. However, their efficacy has been reduced by the delay of government and RCs in defining the proper relationship that should exist between RCs and older institutions, such as political parties, the police, and, in the case of the example discussed here – Makerere University – halls of residence and the University Council. Furthermore, many RCs have suffered from lack of economic infrastructure and civic competence, and fragmented and individualistic elites.

THE STRUCTURE OF RCs

When the National Resistance Army (NRA) and the National Resistance Movement (NRM), took over power on 26 January 1986, under the leadership of President Museveni, new structures were introduced in order to promote participatory democracy and enhance socio-economic development from the grass roots. These are the RCs.

The lowest unit of the RC is the village resistance council, which consists of all residents of a village who are at least 18 years old. Displaced persons are also members of the RC but they do not have voting power and may not hold office on the executive committee (The Resistance Councils and Committees Statute, 1987, Section 3 (2)). Each village executive committee consists of a chairman , vice-chairman, secretary, secretary for finance, secretary for security, secretary for youth, secretary for women, secretary for information, and secretary for mobilization and education. These are elected by the village biannually.

The next level of participation is the parish (*muluka*) resistance council (RC2). It consists of all the village executive committees in a particular parish. Their major duty is to discuss, refine and implement the recommendations of RC1s.

279

Rebuilding political institutions

The *gombolola* or sub-county RC3 consists of all *muluka* (parish) resistance executive committees within the sub-county. Each one sits as a college to elect nine members of the sub-county resistance executive committee. Municipalities, town councils, Makerere University, the National Institute of Education, Kyambogo, and Uganda Polytechnic, Kyambogo, have been given *gombolola* status.

For purposes of resistance committees and councils, the county level is skipped. We should note, however, that during the February 1989 elections, counties were recognized as important resistance council structures. Since there is an administrative structure at the county level, this writer considers that it should be accountable to an elected political structure at the county level. For this reason, there should be RCs and committees at the county level. RCs have, however, been formed at the next highest level, the district. This level is known as RC5. In February 1989, elections to the National Resistance Council (NRC), the national legislature, were successfully held.

Makerere University consists of 19 villages (RC1s) of which 10 are halls of residence for students and nine represent residents who are senior academic and administrative members of staff and junior workers. The 19 villages make up four parishes (*miruka*) and one sub-county (*gombolola*).

SOME IMPORTANT CHARACTERISTICS OF THE MAKERERE POPULATION

The ten halls of residence at Makerere display a significant degree of homogeneity. For example, most students stay together in halls of residence, and eat food served from similar kitchens. The students also tend to share aspirations towards improving the quality of the food, accommodation and allowances given to them. They also stay at the university for periods ranging from three to five years, unlike members of staff, who are more permanent. The students are more organized than members of staff. For example, the chairman of all hall students, villages had formed an organization that links them horizontally whereas staff villages were merely talking about doing this. There is more political and - economic heterogeneity among staff and workers than among students. Given the high degree of student homogeneity, we could have used a smaller sample from the ten hall villages. However, we decided to avoid this approach because our academic exercise is the first of its kind and we need as much detailed information as possible.

HYPOTHESES TO BE TESTED

The following hypotheses were tested:

(1) RCs have enhanced community feeling.
(2) The delay in defining clearly the powers and functions of RCs and

how the RCs relate to the existing formal institutions has intensified the struggle for power between the RCs and the existing formal institutions such as the students' guild, the university administration and the police.

(3) RCs are more likely to be accepted as watchdogs if they deny themselves special privileges.

(4) The externalization and distortion of Makerere University conflicts before they had been formally considered by the relevant organs of the university tended to harm the interests of the university.

(5) RCs are more likely to capture the commitment of the people when they portray themselves as organs of the people and not as organs of government.

THE OPERATION AND EFFICACY OF RCs AND COMMITTEES
As already noted, one major indicator of the efficacy of the RCs and committees is an estimation of attendance at village council and executive committee meetings. This measure has quantitative and qualitative dimensions. For example, attendance at meetings where people do not openly discuss major issues and formulate effective policies is an inadequate indicator of efficacy.

According to our findings the average attendance of village councils meetings was as follows:

Zone	*Average percentage attendance*
(1) Dag	20
(2) Northcote	37
(3) Mitchell	32
(4) Lumumba	16
(5) Africa	14
(6) University	8
(7) Zone 3	45
(8) Mary Stuart	7
(9) Nkrumah	13
(10) Livingstone	8
(11) Zone 4	18
(12) Zone 2	4
(13) Zone 5	12
(14) Zone 6A	15
(15) Zone 8	8
(16) Zone 1	10
(17) Zone 7	12

Average percentage attendance of the four parishes was as follows:
(1) Muluka I   31

281

(2) Muluka II	42
(3) Muluka III	40
(4) Muluka IV	Has never met

The average percentage attendance of the RC3 was as follows:

First meeting	47
Second meeting	58
Third meeting	40

Figures on the fourth meeting were not available to the author. The average percentage attendance of the three meetings was 48 per cent.

ANALYSIS OF ATTENDANCE

According to the RC statute, one half of the members of an RC shall form a quorum at any of its meetings and such a quorum shall be maintained throughout the meeting (RC Statute, *op. cit.* Section 7 (8)). If we follow this requirement, most of the RC council meetings have been held without a quorum since 4 September 1987, the date of commencement of the statute. However, this is a legalistic interpretation. It fails to take account of the quality of discussions at these meetings and the fact that despite many economic problems, people find time to attend. One has also to take into account the life span of RCs. When the survey was taken, the RCs were only about a year old at Makerere. Consequently, during this initial stage, people must shape these institutions and the institutions will shape the people later on.

It should also be remembered that some political groups initially resented some leaders of RCs who appeared to be unsympathetic to the problems in the northeast. When the 92 respondents were asked to identify causes of poor attendance, 50 per cent attributed it to the hard economic circumstances, 25 per cent attributed it to poor mobilization of RC members by the executive committees; 10 per cent attributed it to what they called the military suppression of their areas, and 15 per cent attributed it to NRM policy on political parties, which forbade them to organize themselves during the interim period of the NRM government.

THE FREQUENCY OF COUNCIL MEETINGS

According to Section 7(2) of the RC Statute, an RC shall meet at least once in two months. According to the survey, 12 out of 17 RC1 zones had held not less than six council meetings. They had therefore complied with the legal requirements of the statute. Two hall villages had held only one council meeting. One zone had held two council meetings while two zones had held not less than three council meetings. Poor leadership and lack of political consciousness appear to explain the infrequency of the meetings.

282

Resistance councils and committees: a case study from Makerere

FREQUENCY OF MEETINGS AT *MULUKA* LEVEL

While the average percentage attendance appears in some respects to be better at the *muluka* than in some village council meetings, the frequency of meetings is poorer at the *muluka* level than at the *village* level. Indeed, at Muluka IV no meeting had ever been convened! The reason given for this anomaly by the Chairman of the *muluka* was that the problems are solved at the village level. This reason was rejected by the villages in the *muluka*. Indeed, the Muluka II level is the weakest link in the chain of command. Indeed, 58 per cent of the respondents suggested that the RC2 level be abolished at Makerere and that direct links should be made between RC1 and RC3.

MEETINGS AT RC3 LEVEL

The average percentage attendance was higher at the RC3 level than at the *muluka* and village levels, possibly because this level had experienced major confrontations with the administration at Makerere. These confrontations attracted better attendance because each councillor sought to ensure that his views were not ignored in the resolution of controversies. The author noted that whenever major controversies occurred in halls of residence, attendance soared. We should also note that attaining the 50 per cent quorum level is easier at *muluka* and *gombolola* levels where one is handling between 45 and 53 councillors as opposed to villages where councillors range from 161 to over 1000. Council meetings have been held less frequently at RC3 than at village level. This may partly be attributed to the fact that RC2 has been a weak link between RC3 and RC4. Some of the issues raised at RC1 and presented at RC2 were not attended to at this level and thus did not reach RC3 level. The *gombolola* council has shown concern in its meetings for what it called poor attendance and threatened to invoke Section 4 (b) of the statute, which provides that if without reasonable cause or permission of the chairman a member fails to attend two consecutive meetings of the RC, his seat falls vacant. However, some members have retorted that the *gombolola* cannot sack people who were elected by lower levels through an indirect system. The indirect system of electing people from RC2 tends to dilute the democratic principles of allowing people to elect their representatives directly.

ATTENDANCE AT EXECUTIVE COMMITTEE MEETINGS

The survey shows that executive committee meetings were well attended. The statutory requirement that five members shall constitute a quorum has been fulfilled in most cases I studied. The requirement that the committee meets once a month has not, however, been strictly followed. However, in some cases late submission of the data prevented the author from giving the necessary tables and detailed figures.

283

HOW CAN ATTENDANCE OF COUNCIL MEETINGS AT ALL LEVELS BE IMPROVED?

Although we argued that there were understandable reasons for poor attendance at all levels, this phenomenon cannot be condoned. For binding decisions can only be made if the majority of councils participate in making them. Three suggestions have been advanced to alleviate the problem. First, some executive committees have recommended that if a person misses three consecutive meetings of the RC without giving sound reasons that are acceptable to the executive committee, he should be denied essential commodities for specified periods. But now that essential commodities are readily available in shops, RCs cannot use their withdrawal as a sanction. (According to our survey, 58 per cent of the respondents were against the sanctions, 40 per cent were in favour, and 2 per cent were neutral. The author, who was in favour of sanctions, was disappointed by these results.)

Those who opposed the sanctions argued that getting essential commodities was a human basic right, which could not be denied citizens for not attending meetings. They added that it was also against the principles of the NRM to coerce people to attend meetings.

Those who supported sanctions argued that rights must be accompanied with duties and responsibilities. It is interesting to note that while there was no strong correlation between good attendance at meetings and the willingness of the zones to impose sanctions, the executive committees of the two zones that had steady and good attendance had resolved to recommend to the council the imposition of sanctions.

The second solution to non-attendance is to mount political education seminars. We asked 92 respondents whether or not they had attended the RC seminars that were conducted by various institutions such as the NRM Secretariat. Of these, 76 pointed out that they had not. Sixteen respondents were asked to appraise the seminars, and 80 per cent of these pointed out that their political awareness had been greatly enhanced by the seminars. But 20 per cent of the respondents pointed out that they were irritated by the Marxist slogans that were indiscriminately used by some speakers, and 83 per cent of the 76 respondents who had not attended seminars pointed out that they were not particularly keen to attend because they had more knowledge than the official speakers. They also added that since the government had failed to give university employees a living wage, they would rather use their spare time doing odd jobs in order to supplement their meagre incomes. Fourteen respondents pointed out that they resented RC seminars because the NRM had disallowed open organization of political parties. And 19 respondents said that they were hostile to RC seminars because the NRM was militarily 'suppressing' their areas.

Resistance councils and committees: a case study from Makerere

FRAGMENTED AND INDIVIDUALISTIC ELITES

Makerere is in many ways representative of the problems bedevilling the realization of national integration in Uganda. In short, Uganda's elites are highly divided along ethnic, ideological, religious, class and regional lines. Worse still, they have failed to agree on areas of common interest. Consequently, the country has been ruled by shifting minority elites that control the instruments of coercion for limited periods. This problem has enabled domestic marginal groups and external groups to exploit Uganda with impunity. In some respects, Furnivall's description of the conflict model of plural societies (Kuper & Smith, 1969, pp. 10–11) is applicable to Uganda:

> The social basis is a medley of peoples living side by side, but separately within the political unit. It is in the strictest sense a medley of peoples, 'for they mix but do not combine.' Each group holds by its own religion, its own culture and language, its own ideas and ways. As individuals they meet, but only in the market place, in buying and selling. Economic symbiosis and mutual avoidance, cultural diversity and social cleavage, characterize the social basis of the plural society.

In some significant respects, this quotation sums up the problems of national integration in Uganda. For example, we do not even have a widely accepted national language. An upgrading of the language of a particular ethnic group to national status would be associated with giving a higher status to that group. We have presently settled for English, a language of the former colonial masters, as the official language. Problems of this sort are as evident at Makerere University as in Uganda as a whole.

When the Makerere senate set up a committee to co-ordinate the establishment of RCs on the campus it was resisted by various fragmented political groups. The district administrator of Kampala had to intervene in order to solve the conflict. There has been so much individualism at Makerere that even some neighbours do not know each other. They only meet in the marketplaces. Common problems such as roaming animals and poultry have remained unsolved despite several administration circulars banning roaming animals and poultry. It is RCs that have at last seriously addressed themselves to the solution of these problems.

It should not be surprising that attendance at RC meetings has been poor. The rural areas have been much more enthusiastic about RCs since they have filled an authority vacuum in the countryside where police are not readily available. Some chiefs had lost efficacy because they became corrupt. Some were formerly unemployed and others were thieves. And thus they did not command administrative legitimacy, especially in the countryside. This problem became rampant after

285

Rebuilding political institutions

President Obote abrogated the independence constitution and proceeded to rule Uganda by force. He was assisted by partisan and corrupt chiefs. We should, however, make it clear that the institution of a chief is still cherished and respected in Uganda.

Seminars are obviously necessary in order to improve political consciousness and civic competence. However, it is essential to select speakers who have the experience and the sophistication to handle not only the intellectuals but also the non-intellectuals of Makerere University. Two well-organized seminars per year, especially during the vacation, might be enough. There must be time for substantial discussion, and speakers should represent the diverse ideological leanings of Uganda's plural society.

It is sad to note that 60 per cent of the chairmen at all levels have never even glanced at the RC statute because it is not readily available. Vital documents like this should be typed, duplicated and given to RC chairmen to distribute to wide sections of Uganda's literate population. The *gombolola* council should liase with the NRM secretariat and the Ministry of Local Government and the district administrator to solve this problem. The basic philosophy of the documents should be discussed at the seminars.

Some RC chairmen suggested that controversial and cherished items should be put on the agenda in order to induce people to attend meetings. When, for example, the RC1 chairman of Mitchell Hall was sacked by the council because of 'corruption', the incident attracted large audiences. Public accountability was seen to be being openly implemented. It should be remembered, however, that it is not always possible to have controversial and cherished issues on the agenda. However, issues being discussed must be directly relevant to the zone.

WHAT ARE THE MAJOR ACHIEVEMENTS OF RCs?

The first of the achievements of RCs has been to foster greater community feeling. Most people at Makerere did not know each other, especially outside their own departments. Now members of the zone meet at least once every two months to discuss issues of common interest. These have included roaming animals and poultry, security, and cleaning. Professors work with cleaners and messengers in the same zone. In RC1, Zone 3, a colleague's daughter died at the weekend, when it was difficult to get the university administrators to buy a coffin. The zone raised the money and the coffin was bought. Later the administration refunded the colleague the money that the zone had freely given him as commiseration money (*amabugo*). Similar humane practices have been enhanced by RCs in other zones.

Second, RCs have become critical sources of information. Each Chairman has a list of the people in his zone, their occupations and exact

286

Resistance councils and committees: a case study from Makerere

residential location. Researchers have discovered that they get information more readily and accurately from RCs than from some chiefs, who tend to distort information regarding their residents. This has been so because some chiefs hide names of graduated tax payers in order to retain the money. We should point out, however, that there are also corrupt RC members who do such things. We must also add that there are many honest chiefs. However, when RCs become watchdogs of the chiefs, corruption tends to be reduced. Chiefs must be properly remunerated. RCs will increasingly play an important role in improving population census surveys.

Third, RCs have enhanced security consciousness in their zones. Knowledge of the residents of the zone has itself facilitated detection of wrongdoers. All newcomers must bring letters of introduction from their areas of origin. Security consciousness has entailed acting in unison to defend residents from thieves. For example, zones that share borders with slum areas have sometimes been invaded by armed robbers and petty thieves. RCs resolved that a victim should blow a whistle, while the other zone members should raise oral alarms. When armed thieves attacked two colleagues in two zones, most members of the zones raised oral alarms and the armed thieves ran away. The police were contacted and the thieves were arrested. The NRM government has also taken effective measures to reduce armed robbery. These included procuring patrol cars with communication systems.

We should note, however, that in some cases cooperation between RCs and the police has not been forthcoming. This has been so because corrupt policemen have resented RCs that have reported their corruption to higher authorities. In other cases enthusiastic RCs have arrested suspected wrongdoers without adequate reason. When the police have freed the suspects without proper explanation to the RCs, the RCs have become angry and suspicious of the police. Indeed, the struggle for power between RCs, chiefs and the police has in some cases undermined the efficacy of the RCs.

RC activity has also helped restrain abuse of power by the armed forces. For example, when an RC official was coming from a wedding ceremony at 6.00 am, he found a man struggling to free himself from a soldier. He asked the soldier why he was beating the man but the soldier ran away. He was later caught near Makindye Army Barracks by both the RC official and the man whom the soldier had been beating. The soldier was handed over to the army at Makindye Barracks. The soldier tried to distort the story but it was established that the soldier was the aggressor. By Ugandan standards this is a miracle, because in the past a civilian would not have dared to reprimand a soldier for wrongdoing. The civilian would have been killed on the spot. Worse still, the area where the soldier was reprimanded would have been surrounded by

287

other soldiers, and its inhabitants would have been raped, plundered or even murdered. In RC1, Zone 3, a soldier who spent a night at the zone before declaring his presence to the RC officials was reported to the author, who was then chairman of the zone. I reprimanded the soldier, removed his gun, and demanded official documents authorizing him to stay outside the barracks. The soldier apologized. The gun was kept at the Makerere police post. As already noted, civilians had previously lost this kind of authority over soldiers.

We must not give an impression, however, that all soldiers have spontaneously accepted the authority of RCs. For example, Mr Odro Ibrahim Abdulla, the chairman of RC1 Lemule North in Luwero district was flogged by the NRA military police for allegedly being in illegal possession of a gun (*New Vision*, June 24 1989). When the RC secretary for defence tried to intervene, he was also flogged by soldiers. It is our submission that the soldiers had no authority to flog these RC1 officials. They should have taken the matter to the police and eventually to courts of law. The problem is that since 1966, when President Obote ruled the country through naked use of force, the status of civilians in Uganda has been greatly marginalized. The NRM government is now struggling to restore civilian rights but some military personnel find it difficult to accept this change. It is comforting to note that the district administrator of the area intervened in this matter and rectified this mistake. Whenever soldiers misbehave, they are firmly punished by higher authorities. The civilians must also stop paying money to soldiers and misusing them in order to settle their own misunderstandings. This discussion shows that there is a need to create public forums in which RCs, the police, the military and the chiefs meet to coordinate security matters.

Fourth, RCs have in many respects become mediators of social conflict. The Resistance Committees (Judicial Powers) Statute of 1987, gives them authority to settle civil disputes governed by customary law concerning land, the marital status of women, paternity, identity of customary heirs, the impregnation of a girl under 18 years of age, and elopement with a girl under 18 years of age (The Resistance Committees (Judicial Powers) Statute, 1987, second schedule). The RCs also deal with debts, contracts, assault and trespass.

The chairman of an RC committee presides at all sittings of the court and an RC court is constituted by not less than five of the nine members of the committee. People may get a naive impression that academics have fewer social conflicts than other people and that they use their academic training to resolve issues objectively. On the contrary, this training is sometimes used to obstruct and hide issues. The issues tackled by RCs at Makerere have included the following: roaming animals and poultry, which destroy flowers and crops of residents; illegal subletting of garages and rooms to non-university people; fighting between husbands and their wives; petty thefts; illegal selling of university water; and inconsiderate drunkards. Some of these matters go beyond RCs and are considered by the university disciplinary committees.

During RC meetings, resolutions are passed discouraging anti-social behaviour. For example, many RC1s passed a resolution banning roaming poultry and animals. The chairman of RC3 was urged by these RCs to put roaming dogs to sleep using the expertise of the Ministry of Animal Industry. The chairman was reluctant to implement the decision of the village councils because he was exposed to pressure from some selfish dog owners who were against the poisoning of strays. However, after stray dogs had bitten three residents, there was so much outcry that he had to implement the decision of the village councils.

Fifth, RCs have played an important regulatory role in halls of residence and other places. For example, some student common room (SCR) officials in charge of allocating rooms to students used to sell rooms to desperate non-resident students who were frightened of insecurity outside the campus. The RCs tried to deal with this corruption. However, where RCs members tried to use their positions to demand privileges such as single rooms instead of taking shared rooms themselves, the moral standing of RCs was undermined. It will be recalled that we hypothesized that RCs are more likely to attain legitimacy if their members deny themselves special privileges. Available evidence in halls of residence and other zones upholds this hypothesis. For example, in zones where executive committees were allocating themselves more sugar than their colleagues, their moral standing was undermined and they were unable to act as proper watchdogs.

RCs AND ECONOMIC DEVELOPMENT

RCs are expected to spearhead the economic development of their areas. The Resistance Councils and Committees (Amendment) Statute of 1988, which accorded a corporate status to sub-county resistance councils is intended to enable these to embark on viable economic ventures. The RCs will have perpetual succession and a common seal and may purchase, sell, lease or otherwise acquire or dispose of, hold and manage movable and immovable property, and may enter into such contracts as may be necessary (The Resistance Councils and Committees Amendments Statute, 1988, Section 2A). Tractors will be controlled by sub-county RCs. It is hoped that rural people will hire them at reasonable rates and that they will grow food on a large scale. Currently, food is being bartered for essential goods such as sugar and tractors.

Most RCs at Makerere have not, however, been creative in working out projects to generate economic development. Our questionnaire contained specific questions about RCs' plans for economic development. The responses clearly indicated that most RCs were weak on this score.

289

This is sad because RCs pointed out that they lacked basic economic infrastructural support and were unable even to buy duplicating paper and stencils. This problem partly explains why some RCs were unable to type and duplicate the minutes of their village council meetings. Whenever the RCs sold sugar and soap they received a small profit. However, now that these essential goods are available in shops, RCs have lost this source of income.

If zones launched money-making projects they would acquire the necessary administrative and political autonomy and spearhead the interests of the people without being reliant on central government. At the beginning of this account, we stressed the need for RCs to portray themselves as organs of the people and not as organs of the state. Acquiring an independent financial viability would facilitate this.

It is gratifying that some RCs in the countryside have undertaken significant economic projects. For example, the RCs in Kamukuzi in Mbarara district have built housing estates which they are now renting out. The RCs in Kasese district have built dispensaries and roads. In these projects, the RCs have used the free and spontaneous labour of the people. The Uganda Commercial Bank, which started a Farmer's Rural Scheme, uses RCs as guarantors to lend money to the peasants who are encouraged to grow more food or start modest projects entailing dairy farming. We must point out, however, that while many successful farmers' schemes have been reported, there have been also sad cases where RCs have been corrupt.

Since we are talking about economic viability, we should mention that RC officials are not paid a single cent for running these organizations. We believe that the state has no capacity to pay them. We also believe that people should be encouraged to carry out civic duties without being paid. However, those who incur expenses when they travel long distances in order to carry out official RC work should be reimbursed for travel expenses. In December 1987, the head of state directed that executives from RC3 be paid some allowances. The RCs below RC3, where some fundamental and difficult work takes place, will feel that they have been ignored. It is suggested that this matter be put on the agenda of all RCs for special future consideration. Ultimately, the national legislature should resolve the issue by taking into account the fact that our economy is still weak.

AREAS OF CONFLICT BETWEEN RCs AND THE FORMAL ORGANS OF MAKERERE UNIVERSITY

There have been conflicts between the main administration of the university and RC3 and between hall RCs and their SCRs. These conflicts must be briefly discussed, *not least* because some have undermined the efficacy of RCs and university organs. Our contention is that this has

Resistance councils and committees: a case study from Makerere
largely occurred because of failure to define clearly the respective powers and functions of RCs and formal university institutions. This definition must initially be carried out by RCs and the main administration. Where necessary, the district administrator's office, the Ministry of Local Government and the NRM Secretariat should also be consulted. These clarifications should not be concentrated at RC3 level; they must start at RC1. And yet the current trend shows that the clarification of the relationship between the RCs and the university organs has been unduly concentrated at RC3 level. This is partly explained by poor horizontal and vertical channels of communications between RC3, 2 and 1. Moreover the externalization of these conflicts before they were fully tackled by university organs tended to injure the interests of the university.

Example: the Northcote/Mary Stuart/Lumumba halls of residence incident of 2 May 1987
Mary Stuart Hall, which had won the Women's Inter-Hall Games competition, organized a 'Cow Roasting' function on 2 May 1987 in order to celebrate its victory. Mary Stuart, which is nicknamed the 'Box', is geographically close to Lumumba Hall, and has tended to cooperate with Lumumba in many ways. Their cooperation was nicknamed 'Lumbox solidarity'. Historically, Lumumba and Northcote Halls have been great rivals in sports. Mary Stuart planned to march round the Makerere campus while the Prisons Band played the music. They were joined by the Lumumba sympathizers. The Vice-Chancellor, who had agreed to be guest of honour on the occasion, was requested by Mary Stuart to join the march and agreed to do so. When the procession reached New Avenue roundabout and the road that leads to the Makerere swimming pool, it encountered tree branches across the road, which looked like a roadblock. It was manned by a small group of students, some wearing helmets on their heads, some masks and others military-like garments. A person dressed in war-like attire, with a toy pistol, signalled the Vice-Chancellor to stop the marching. He did not succeed. However, as the procession approached Northcote Hall, stones and sticks were thrown at the marching group. Great confusion broke out. The Prisons Band retreated to the roundabout. Injured people included the Vice-President of Makerere Students Guild, and a young girl who sustained a deep wound on her forehead.

Northcote Hall held an Emergency General Assembly and *inter alia* discussed the attack by Lumumbists under the umbrella of 'Lumbox Solidarity'. It resolved (a) that a report addressed to the University Dean be compiled showing their concern about the incident, (b) that papers were to be put in the dining hall for members of Northcote Hall to sign. The letter was signed by 320 students and given to the Dean of Students.

291

It was copied to the Minister of Education, the Vice-Chancellor, the District Administrator of Kampala, and the Guild President. The letter alleged among other things that the attack by Lumumba on Northcote Hall was deliberate. By copying these letters to the Minister and District Administrator, the matter was externalized.

This matter was placed before the Disciplinary Committee, a sub-committee of the University Council. Students were charged with (a) setting up an illegal road block near Northcote Hall, and (b) attacking with sticks and stones a peaceful march of Mary Stuart Hall on their Cow Roasting Day and injuring several people.

The Vice-Chancellor requested his deputy to chair the committee because he had been involved in the episode. The committee instructed that the Secretary for Mobilization, Politicization, Education and Refugees in Northcote Hall should be suspended from the university for his next academic year. Secondly, the Secretary General of RC1 of Northcote Hall Village was declared guilty of carrying dangerous weapons, of throwing them, and of threatening his fellow students. It was recommended that he be suspended pending approval of a recommendation to Council that he be dismissed from the university. Thirdly, the 320 Northcote Hall students who had signed the letter, which was abusive of the Vice-Chancellor, were to be strongly reprimanded and each was to be required to write a letter apologizing to the Vice-Chancellor. They were also fined 150 shillings each. The injured persons were to be paid 500 shillings each out of these fines.

On 28 May 1987, the Inspector General of Government (IGG), received a complaint about the decision of the Disciplinary Committee. Thus the matter was externalized before it was placed before the University Council, the supreme body of the university and matters became more complicated.

On 24 May 1987, the Chairman RC1 of Northcote Hall wrote to the Chairman RC3, Makerere University, outlining his reasons why he believed that the Displinary Committee's decision was unfair and biased. The Chairman RC3 wrote to the Vice-Chancellor and pointed out that the students in Northcote Hall had alleged that the university administration was against RCs. He added that this impression of the conflict between the university administration and the RC was further strengthened by the fact that among those students tried RC leaders were prominent and the two convicted and punished were also RC leaders.

Observations of the Inspector General of Government

The IGG questioned the method of identifying the wrongdoers. He pointed out that Northcoters, though unidentified individually, participated in throwing stones at the procession. He added that the university administration had a right to instil discipline in the university. But he cautioned on the method of identifying wrongdoers. He asserted that the very first punishment be withdrawn because it was unfair. He also pointed out that the punishment in the next case be withdrawn. He questioned the fine of 150 shillings on the basis of collective guilt. The IGG's report appeared in newspapers before it was received by the top university administrators. This incident illustrates the extent to which Makerere matters were externalized before they were fully addressed by the university.

RC3 supported the case of the students. Meanwhile newspapers that supported the students wrote in their favour. For example, *Weekly Topic* of 11 November 1987 wrote in a leading article that RC3, the highest political organ of the university, had supported the students' case. It added that the IGG had pointed out that two students had been unfairly punished to satisfy the ego and dignity of the Vice-Chancellor and to protect the authority of the Disciplinary Committee, which had delivered a wrong judgement. The paper further alleged that the office of the Chancellor (the President of Uganda) had decided to stick to the unjust decision. And finally it said that the IGG's work and effectiveness were at stake.

The Tablet newspaper of 13 November 1987, distorted the issues when it alleged that Mr J. Mayanja-Nkangi, the Minister of Education, who happened to be the Leader of the Conservative Party, feared that RCs might undercut support for his party. The same paper taunted the government by saying that the IGG was stabbed in the back by the government.

Analysis of the basic issues

First, the expelled students appealed directly to the IGG contrary to university regulations.

Second, the IGG in a press release blamed the Vice-Chancellor for trying to satisfy his ego and called for a reversal of the decisions of the Makerere University Disciplinary Committee. Third, although there were disagreements within RC3, this institution supported the students, especially their right to express their feelings. The issues had been so externalized and distorted that the stage was set for an external solution. Meanwhile the RC3 Council summoned the Vice-Chancellor to answer some questions. The action of RC3 raised the following question: Is it the Vice-Chancellor who summons the RC3 members or vice-versa?

Fourth, the independence of the Disciplinary Committee was questioned. Fifth, the independence of Council as a final court of appeal was questioned since so many people who sit on the Committee are also members of the Council. These include the Vice-Chancellor and his Deputy, the Chairman of Council and the Dean of the university who appears in attendance at Council meetings.

Sixth, the RC3 and the main administration of the university failed to find a common ground for resolving the conflict, partly because the role of RCs had not been properly defined with regard to university organs. The organs include the University Council and its sub-committees which include the Finance Committee, Disciplinary Committee, Tender Board, Estates and Works Committee and Students Affairs Committee. We must mention that some members of RC3 were populists who enjoyed taking advantage of the conflict between students and the main administration.

By externalizing and distorting the issues, the affected groups at the university were reduced to the struggle for power between students and RC3 on the one hand, and the Vice-Chancellor and his fellow administrators on the other. That was unfortunate, because the issues did not fit into such simple confrontational terms.

Eventually, the government decided not to interfere with the decisions of the Disciplinary Committee. At this point, the students belatedly decided to appeal to the University Council but their pleas were rejected.

SOME POSSIBLE SOLUTIONS

This episode strained the relations between RCs and the administration and the basic issue of defining the relationship between RCs and university organs was postponed. Later on the RC3 suggested that it should have 50 per cent of the positions on the University Council and its sub-committees. This was an excessive demand. We propose that RCs should send three representative to the university organs. One member should represent RC3, another RC2, and a third one RC1. The RC representatives should be ex-officio members of the university organs. By being ex-officio members, the RCs retain the role of watchdogs. They would also retain the freedom to criticize resolutions of the Councils and its committees.

THE CLASH BETWEEN SCR AND RC1

The body of the Hall of Residence is known as the Students Common room (SCR). RC1 in Halls of Residence overlap in functions and in the geographical location with SCR. It was necessary to address this problem. The RCs should be watchdog while SCR Executive should run Hall affairs. The watchdog role of RCs can be tricky. For example, if they overidentify themselves with the wishes of government or the university administrators, they are regarded as 'spies' or 'bootlickers' of the rulers. For example, when the government accommodated some of its official visitors and guests in Halls of Residence in 1988, it depended on RCs to identify and report students who were staying in halls of residence without permission. The SCR Executive felt marginalized by this measure and tended to tease the RCs that they were 'bootlickers' of government. This role should have been shared by RCs

Resistance councils and committees: a case study from Makerere
and the executive members of the SCR. The RCs must strike a balance between pushing the interests of the students and the interests of the government. What we have so far described endorses the hypothesis stated at the beginning: that RCs are more likely to capture the commitment of the people when they portray themselves as organs of the people and not as organs of government. The vertical link between RC1 and 3 is poor. Since the most important issues are tackled at RC1 level, all chairmen of RC1 should be members of RC2 and RC3. The horizontal link between village councils is also poor. The chairman of all RC1 should meet once every month in order to iron out inter-zone matters such as roaming dogs and poultry.

Some people have suggested that RCs should be watchdogs at places of work, including faculties. Professor Rweyemamu of Tanzania observed that when President Nyerere started workers' councils at places of work, there were strikes, lockouts and downing of tools in public enterprises. The effect was to weaken the power of management of public enterprise *vis-à-vis* the workers. Nyerere had to intervene to restore the power of management (A. Rweyemamu, 1975). Our position is that the role of RCs should be largely residential. However, in places of work the role of RCs should be confined to being ex-officio members of the University Council and its committees.

CONCLUSION

Uganda has lacked adequate consensus concerning the political institutions for resolving political conflict in the past. RCs have so far enabled Uganda to enjoy a political truce by embracing fragmented elites subscribing to conflicting ideologies. Will this truce enable Ugandans to acquire lasting political consensus? The success of RCs in facilitating the realization of political consensus will depend essentially on the following factors. First, we must continue with refining the relationship between the RCs and the old institutions. The initiative here must not be left to the government. Second, we must ensure that we have exemplary, committed, and democratic leadership at all levels. So far the NRM government has been in many ways exemplary. However, it is not yet clear what it means when it says that it wishes to decentralize power. For decentralization can refer to two processes. The first process merely entails delegating functions to a local level but retaining control of these by central government officials (deconcentration). The second process refers to giving meaningful financial, legislative and administrative power to elected local governments (devolution). The author, who was a member of a commission of inquiry into the system of local government in Uganda, was disappointed to note that the majority of his fellow commissioners tended to prefer deconcentration to devolution. The author was forced to write a minority report in which he advocated devolution of

295

Rebuilding political institutions

power (Report of the Commission of Inquiry Into the Local Government System, 1987). RCs must struggle to ensure that genuine power is devolved at a local level and they must use this power to enhance civic competence and self-sustaining economic development. RCs must also remain organs of the people rather than organs of the state.

Note

---

1. This is a revised version of public lecture which the author gave on 'The operation and efficacy of Resistance Councils and Committees at Makerere University' at the Faculty of Agriculture and Forestry, Makerere Lower Lecture Theatre, on 2 February, 1988. The author was Chairman of RC1, Zone 3 at Makerere University, from 1987 to 1989.

TWENTY
Rebuilding survival structures for the poor: organizational options for development in the 1990s

E.A. Brett

In 1966 Uganda's Constitution was torn up, the army moved centre stage and political structures, bureaucracies, parastatals and cooperatives soon became instruments of plunder. By 1986 roads were impassable, hospitals lacked water and drugs, factories stood idle and the countryside was ravaged by war. Uganda had validated Hobbes' prediction – without political order society had become a 'warre of every man against every man' and life 'solitary, poore, nasty, brutish and short'.[1]

Reconstruction now requires institutional reforms that will guarantee personal freedom and autonomy, enforce economic efficiency and impose effective constraints on the use of political and military power. 'Institutional reforms at every level of government' and 'measures to foster private sector and non-governmental organizations' in every sphere are essential, as the government and donors now recognize.[2] Some countries create effective mechanisms to enforce accountability and efficiency, others – like Uganda during the dark years – do not. Institutional reforms incorporate systems of rewards and sanctions that induce their members to behave in certain ways. In Uganda the key institutions in the state and private sector rewarded ruthlessness, misappropriation and nepotism and thus allowed, even encouraged, the transition to the politics of plunder. This must now change.

The past four years have been concerned with pacification, macroeconomic adjustment and rehabilitation, and the prime concern has been to make existing structures work better, liberalize the regulatory system and rationalize prices. This will continue, but now with an increased recognition of the need to reorganize the key structures through which services are delivered and order maintained – political authorities, bureaucracies, firms, and voluntary organizations. A Constitutional Commission is working on political reform, a Public Service Commission is looking at the public sector and also at its relationship to the private sector; an intensive re-evaluation of the regulations and structure of the private sector is taking place. The NRM has restored economic growth and almost eliminated insurgency but has now reached another critical turning point; to consolidate these gains and create a

297

basis for autonomous and self-sustaining growth, it must build an institutional order of a sort that will make a return to the pathological situation of the past impossible.

This chapter will examine that problem and possible solutions to it by looking at the nature of the key institutions through which small farmers gain access to markets and social services. These examples will then be used to illustrate some general arguments about the source of institutional pathologies and possibilities for reform. It will combine case history and theory to explain the failures of the 1960s and early 1970s, show how the dominant institutions were restructured in the crisis of the 1970s and 1980s, and attempt to interpret these problems in the light of recent debates in organization theory. It is based on extensive fieldwork carried out in 1966/7, 1973/4, and between 1988 and 1990.[3]

During the 1960s services in Uganda worked reasonably well, but with hindsight we can see that policy making and administrative control was characterized by fatal flaws. The economic crisis of the early 1970s, which induced the 'economic war' and the expulsion of the Asians in 1972, stemmed from previous policy failure,[4] while the state apparatus inherited by Obote and Amin could easily be used for misappropriation and oppression. Some people would now like to return to what is seen as a 'golden age' that existed in the 1960s by resurrecting the old institutional structure but with a better-trained and more honest cadre to run it. This chapter, however, will not consider how more perfect people can be trained to manage traditional institutions better, but how to create institutions that will bring out the best in the people who are already available. Political theorists are sceptical of attempts to create better people, but seek to build organizations with an internal structure and external relationships that impose honesty and efficiency on ordinary, self-interested individuals.

Uganda will therefore be used as a case study of institutional reform in a context of poverty, instability and decline. But it is also useful as an example not only of failure but also of potential success. Once seen as a 'basket case', it is now moving out of the downward spiral induced by the failure of the institutions inherited from colonialism to guarantee political responsibility or effective service provision. They were imported from countries with high levels of skill, rapid access to information and high levels of organization in civil society, but failed miserably in a poor country where they were absent. Their collapse generated much of the popular support for the NRA campaign, and also led people to devise alternative structures to provide the services that the state system could no longer offer. By examining the reasons for failure and the logic of the new structures, we can extend our understanding of what will or will not work in countries characterized by low resources and environmental stress.

298

CREATING INSTITUTIONAL
ACCOUNTABILITY AND EFFICIENCY

Institutional reform raises all the questions implicit in the current debate on the role of the state and its relationship to private enterprise and the market. Development theory once favoured planning and state provision to eliminate waste and provide the capital required for large scale projects, equating progress with capital-intensive technology. This was reinforced by the paternalism of an expatriate elite that saw central control as the best way to bring 'modernity' to 'traditional' populations. The result was a system dominated by 'statist' structures – departments and parastatals financed at least partly from taxation, allocated monopoly power in their chosen spheres, staffed by tenured officials paid regular salaries, and responsible in the last analysis to the government rather than their consumers or clients through the market.[5]

A private sector existed alongside these state monopolies, dominated by expatriate firms that had enjoyed special privileges in a racially stratified system. Agricultural marketing and processing, retail trade, manufacturing and estate agriculture were all in expatriate hands. African enterprise was confined to small farms and petty trade, and could not penetrate a large-scale sector protected by accumulated wealth and monopoly privileges.[6] Africans thus used political power to Africanize the civil service and to extend further state control by nationalizing private firms and transferring agricultural processing from expatriate monopolies to state-supported cooperatives. These changes were justified using a socialist/populist rhetoric, but they did not redistribute resources downwards. Rather, they expanded the power of an administrative class directly accountable to the political elite. In 1966 Obote severed this elite's links with the electorate and introduced a period of non-accountable government; in 1971 the worst elements in the army took control. After 1979 there seemed some chance that democracy would be restored, but this disappeared with the rigged election of 1980 and the period of systematic political plunder and civil war that followed.

The statist structure was always rigid, hierarchical and non-accountable but the elimination of all democratic controls made it an effective mechanism for repressing dissent, marginalizing autonomous organizations in civil society, and allowing the political elite to plunder the economic surplus. Statism is now blamed for economic failure in the Second and Third Worlds, market freedom for success in Western capitalist countries and the Asian NICs, so state rather than market failure is now seen as the major obstacle to progress. Hence institutional structures are now being sought that will allocate less power and impose more controls on the political and administrative elite.

At present neo-liberal theorists dominate these arguments, claiming that adjustment will only succeed if market disciplines can be imposed on the key producers of goods and services. They now provide a radical critique of the nature of the modern state and the administrative structures that sustain it, based on rational individualism.[7] This view, however, tends to ignore many of the problems associated with market failure in the past, and is highly economistic in its orientation. This chapter will therefore ask whether it does indeed provide us with an adequate understanding of the postcolonial institutional structure in Uganda, and of the objective possibilities that it offers. To do so it will look briefly at the institutional structure inherited from colonialism, at the way it was subsequently modified, and then consider both the potential and the problems implicit in the trend towards liberalization that now dominates the policy debate both there and elsewhere.

THE INSTITUTIONAL INHERITANCE

The colonial economy involved an exchange between small farmers who sold export crops to monopolistic expatriate firms and marketing boards, and less important food crops to competitive African traders. Independence saw the transfer of the assets of the expatriate monopolies to African cooperatives modelled on British 'Rochdale Principles'.[8] They were notionally democratic, but closely controlled by the state, subsidized in many ways and sheltered from competition with the private sector or other cooperatives by the monopolistic nature of the marketing system. Religious institutions – Anglicans, Catholics and to a lesser extend, Islam – exerted a powerful moral influence over rural society and played a key role in service provision. They ran schools and mission hospitals that were complemented by state provision. Fees were paid in mission hospitals and schools, and in state schools but not hospitals. Primary schools and dispensaries were controlled by local authorities, secondary schools and hospitals by central ministries. Local administration used a system of chiefs accountable to a district commissioner in which poor communications gave lower officials some discretion, but effective political control remained at the centre. Local councils were set up at independence but their autonomy was destroyed in 1966; during the colonial period the army and police service was very small but this also changed after 1966.

Here it is important to note, first, that small farmers had relatively little to do with either the market or the state since they sold less than half of their output, only a minority went to school, and few used the dispensaries or hospitals.[9] Secondly, the monopoly controls enforced by the state severely constrained African progress in the money economy. Prices and competition were closely regulated, allowing state enterprise to use capital-intensive and administration-intensive technology in its development of industry and large-scale marketing, thus confining large-scale enterprise to expatriates. Thirdly, development depended on exports produced by small farmers, and thus on their productivity and the size and use of the surpluses extracted from them. Their political isolation, limited capital and poor education allowed the state to marginalize their incomes and activities through taxes, monopoly profits and restrictive practices. But this cut their output and with it exports and taxation, thus producing the balance of payments and fiscal crises that have made adjustment and foreign dependence inevitable.

The relationship between the statist system and the small peasantry has thus been a highly contradictory one. The new political and bureaucratic class used monopoly power to extract resources from small farmers and thus consolidate political control and build up its own personal and business assets[10] at the expense of the productivity of the farmers, whose exports financed the accumulation process and the state system itself. This process must now be reversed by creating structures that will only prosper if they can increase rural productivity and thus base their own wealth on a generalization of prosperity rather than poverty. How, then, did the process of institutional decline proceed?

INSTITUTIONAL TRANSFORMATION AND DECLINE

During the colonial period the exploitation of private and public monopolies had blocked development and reduced equality,[11] but external controls had limited the level of exploitation that had developed. But these controls disappeared at independence, and the new ruling class, recruited from wealthier farmers and chiefly families, used public institutions to enrich itself both as members of the state and as private entrepreneurs. Taxes financed an explosion in state employment; friends, relatives or those prepared to pay secured privileged access to scarce foreign exchange, import quotas or exclusive trading positions; small farmers were exploited by monopolistic cooperatives and marketing boards. Foreign firms exploited development projects that used inappropriate imported technology provided through tied aid and benefited the donors more than the recipients. Resources went from government to government, and were used in public sector activities with a weak budget constraint, leading to enormous irrationalities and waste.[12] This produced a mass of irrational and inequitable rural projects by the mid-1960s.

Mechanization was seen as the only way to modernize agricultural production, so group farms and tractor hire schemes were created. These failed because labour could not be coordinated on the farms and the costs and maintenance of the tractors were not sustainable. In 1971 the average tractor ploughed only 150 acres, by 1974 this had fallen to 55.13 acres. The schemes provided large subsidies, benefited a tiny elite of wealthier farmers, and increased foreign dependence. State farms were also created to introduce 'modern' crops or methods financed by donors – pedigree cattle, irrigation, new citrus varieties – but were run on cost-plus lines and all failed.

Extension workers concentrated on providing elite farmers with information from research stations that were exclusively concerned with cotton and coffee and took little account of the conditions that existed on small farms. They did develop higher-yielding strains of cotton, but there is no evidence that their work had any other impact on practices or output.[14] Similarly, veterinary services went to a tiny minority of 'modern' (i.e. capitalist) dairy farmers and ranchers with aid-subsidized access to land, vulnerable exotic animals and drugs. The monopolistic Milk Marketing Board guaranteed them high returns despite high costs. But the indigenous cattle and small animal sector was neglected, despite its immense size and importance.

After 1962 the cooperative monopolies produced late payments to farmers, and corruption, while democratic control was marginalized by the power of patronage.[15] Fortunately, similar controls did not affect the domestic food market, where low-cost small-sized and medium-sized traders supplied urban markets with great efficiency.[16]

The main marketing boards were run reasonably honestly and efficiently, but price manipulation did not help farmers. Prices paid to them were suppressed in the 1940s to inhibit inflation, and surpluses subsequently used to finance a capital-intensive industrialization strategy using the Uganda Development Corporation, thus reducing rural incentives and investment opportunities. In the 1960s, when the regime was still concerned to maintain rural support, the remaining surpluses were spent to keep prices above world levels, thus concealing the fact that cotton was not an economically viable crop and delaying the search for alternatives. A Produce Marketing Board was set up in the late 1960s to buy 'minor crops' and all private dealers were to be licensed and subject to official supervision. The PMB absorbed subsidies and bought very little. The regulations inhibited the activities of small dealers but fortunately could not be effectively enforced. But for this, competition would have been reduced, the farmer's bargaining position weakened and prices to consumers increased.

Health expenditure was concentrated on modern hospitals at the expense of primary health care. Mulago Hospital in Kampala – a leading teaching hospital and major aid recipient – allegedly absorbed 60 per cent of the health budget in the mid-1960s. Twenty smaller aid-assisted hospitals were then built in the main district centres. Little was done to extend the role of local dispensaries and no interest was taken in improving the performance of traditional healers. Services were free, but facilities were so scarce that few could actually use them. Elite access, on the other hand, was easy and the quality of care its members received very high.

302

Rebuilding survival structures for the poor

Primary and secondary education was extended along traditional lines, and worked reasonably well. Fees rationed places but did not cover full costs. By the late 1960s most children received a few years of primary education, but secondary and tertiary education was confined to the elite. Curriculums had little technical or vocational content and did little to raise the level of agricultural or craft skills.

Elected local authorities existed at the district level until 1966, although they were often split by antagonistic political conflict and allegations of corruption and inefficiency were common. Then democracy was abolished, and a centralized administrative hierarchy stretching from ministry to district commissioner and chiefs became directly responsible for tax collection and services. These operated at the levels achieved during the colonial period, and transport was greatly improved through aid-financed road-building programmes, but there was no accountability to the local populations.

Although gross abuses of power were absent during these years, little was done to raise rural productivity or living standards. The surpluses produced by small farmers went to high-input agriculture and industry that produced low returns, and benefited only the new elite and foreign companies that serviced the aid industry. Central controls were justified by radical theorists who equated market competition with exploitation and large-scale production with efficiency. But the system actually transferred resources from low-cost small farmers with low foreign exchange needs to high-cost monopolists using imported technology and inputs. By 1971 this had lost Obote mass support, and produced a balance of payments and fiscal crisis that prevented his regime from continuing to offer the elite the patronage required to remain in power.[17] Equally important, the system gave Amin every opportunity for political and bureaucratic plunder, as subsequent history quickly demonstrated.

From 1971 a tiny elite maintained power through violence, and rewarded cronies with huge sums extracted through expropriation, price manipulation and corruption. Currency manipulation and marketing monopolies reduced growers' incomes to negligible levels and transferred the surplus to politicians, bureaucrats and their associates. In 1972 one kilogram of cotton was worth 0.46 metres of cloth and one kilogram of coffee 0.44 metres; in 1981 the figures were 0.08 and 0.11; in late 1986, 0.04 and 0.085. Official cotton exports fell from 86,400 tons in 1970 to 1,200 tons in 1981, and were only 6,000 tons in 1986; coffee exports were 237,000 tons in 1973, 123,000 in 1981 and 143,000 in 1986.[18]

Asian business assets were expropriated and allocated to political clients. Payments for official contracts were divided between parties and the work never completed (contracting 'to sell air'). Civil servants ceased to be paid a living wage and tax revenues went uncollected. Free public services had to be illegally paid for, non-essential services were simply

303

not performed and most regulatory controls disappeared or were evaded for a price. Squatters were allowed to invade forest reserves, and members of the elite appropriated large amounts of land and evicted occupants without effective action by the land boards. Military spending escalated, and armed soldiers supplemented their pay by robbery with violence.

The result was impassable roads, unpruned coffee trees, the elimination of cotton as a crop, towns deserted after dark, declining school enrolments, hospitals without water, drugs or equipment, empty shops, hyperinflation and falling real standards of living. Chronic political instability followed, despite the reign of terror – Amin was constantly threatened by dissident officers, and, by eliminating them, destroyed the technical competence of his own army. The Tanzanian invasion was a logical consequence, since the regime had now expropriated everything it could lay its hands on inside the country; the defeat was an equally logical consequence of the purges that destroyed the educated officer corps and the morale of the troops. Under Obote, after a brief period when some improvement seemed possible, the same process began again, lending popular support to the NRA campaign and weakening the capacity of the state apparatus to fight the war.

This history could simply be treated as a cautionary tale demonstrating the wisdom of political theorists from Rousseau to Rawls who claim that political and economic stability can only be built upon institutional arrangements based on agreement, justice and accountability. This message has now been clearly recognized by leading Ugandans, and the reconstruction programme is as a result being based on reconciliation rather than revenge. But our concern is with its implications for more mundane but no less crucial aspects of political and administrative organizations – with the nature of the institutional arrangements that allowed the state to be captured and subverted in this way, and with the lessons to be learnt about institutional reform from examining the survival strategies adopted by people when the official apparatus fell apart around them.

ORGANIZING FOR SURVIVAL: INSTITUTIONAL RESPONSES TO POLITICAL DECAY

By the 1980s popular responses to the failure of formal structures had produced important initiatives that replaced central state provision with private, voluntary or local political agencies, depending on the circumstances. A varied range of organizations had emerged with quite different organizational characteristics, depending on the need they were designed to meet, although all of them are self-financing, accountable to users, and operate on a scale directly related to the nature of the problems involved and the level of skills and capital that exists in the local society. By looking briefly at some of these adaptations we can see how institutional variability and direct accountability are crucial to successful organizational adaption.

Agriculture

Growers responded to exploitation by switching out of traditional crops and selling to private traders. Coffee survived since it had low labour inputs and was smuggled across borders, but long-term maintenance was neglected. Cotton, however was replaced by various food crops that were sold in domestic and regional markets through a complex system of private traders. Thus monopoly had discouraged traditional exports, concealed foreign exchange earnings from the state and strengthened the private marketing system at the expense of the official one. The new private sector is financed out of profits, regulated by the market, small-scale, highly competitive and cost-effective. But it is still constrained by limited skills and capital assets and irrational state interventions. The ability of small farmers to adopt new crops has demonstrated their autonomy, though at some cost, since coffee would, with rational pricing, have produced better results for them and the national economy. Thus farmers and traders have been forced to evade irrational regulations, taxes and controls, and the state has lost revenue and foreign exchange.

Research and extension services collapsed in the late 1970s, but no popular initiatives emerged to restore them because few farmers actually noticed their absence. Here the collapse of a service simply exposed the irrelevance of what was previously on offer. Veterinary services still exist, however, mainly to treat exotic herds and provide inoculations; here it seems probable that semi-privatization has occurred, with payments being made for supposedly free services.

Health

Official 'free' medical services collapsed in the 1970s, and only marginal improvements have been made since. As a result voluntary, private and traditional services have been extended to replace it.

The missions dominate the voluntary sector, providing treatment on a fee-paying but subsidized basis. They raise local and foreign donations and can recruit foreign and domestic personnel with a strong sense of vocation. They are also actively involved, in association with local volunteers and NGOs, in the development of a widespread primary health care movement. Their hospitals and dispensaries are the most successful elements in the 'formal' system. Foreign NGOs like the German Emergency Doctor service and MSF (France) have provided additional limited help.[19] (But see also the comments in Chapter 8 on this issue.)

The collapse of the state system has led to de facto privatization. As a government report points out: 'Private clinics, Medical laboratories, and Pharmacies [have] mushroomed all over the country, involving even the health personnel employed in Government.'[20] Personnel use their official positions to gain access to official drugs and equipment, but sell them through private clinics in which, according to Whyte, competition keeps costs down, consumers accept the need to pay, but prescription is uncontrolled and often irrational or even dangerous.[21]

Most people in fact take their afflictions to herbalists, birth attendants and spirit-mediums on a fee-for-service basis. They also accept orthodox medicine and use both systems, the traditional one in particular for essentially psychic or social ailments such as spirit possession, or 'poisoning'.[22]

Education

Ugandans have devoted great energy to sustaining schools in the face of an almost complete loss of funds and support from government. Private provision has expanded and the churches, which have always played an important role in education, continue to do so. But most interesting here is the development of localized control over state schools through an extension of the role of parent-teacher associations, which have organized a system of additional fees and voluntary work to cover salaries, equipment and extensions. This occurs not only in 'elite' boarding schools supported by the professional class, but also in rudimentary primary schools, where parents make bricks for extensions and pay a large porportion of their incomes in fees.

Complaints about 'exploitation' by PTAs are common, but probably take little account of the real costs of running the schools, which are now being carried by the users. They are dominated by the village elite, but accountability does exist, since they are democratically elected and fees are only paid because services are provided. The victims of this process are poorer children excluded because they are unable to pay. Some efforts are made to provide free access supported by charity but these are of marginal importance. Effective central provision of materials, syllabus reform and general supervision has also been lost, but democratization plus full cost payment has produced a vigorous and expanding service.[23]

Public services

Services like health and education can be sold on the market, with a corresponding direct link between rewards to the provider and the needs of the consumer. But this is impossible for collective services for which users cannot be excluded, such as roads, and law and order, and for access to common assets with finite resources like common grazing land, and fish stocks in lakes and rivers. Here markets cannot be used to ration access, and compulsory taxation and controlled access are essential if the resource is to be paid for or overexploitation controlled.[24]

Here there is no substitute for the state, as the collapse of social regulation and infrastructure during the years of decay in Uganda amply demonstrated. Reform was only possible after the overthrow of a corrupt regime by a new one with a real commitment to change. Institutionally its most difficult problem has been to restructure the traditional civil service, which is incapable of functioning efficiently because of the fiscal crisis and a lack of effective political control. Parastatals, too, continue to operate on their old inefficient monopolistic basis, although discussions about privatization are proceeding.

But improvements have taken place where the government, major donors and external contractors have been involved in rebuilding major assets. There has been an immense improvement in the road system, the Sheraton Hotel, recently a condemned building, now provides good (and very expensive) accommodation, the Jinja power station is being rehabilitated and many other projects are under construction. Not all of these would be classified as 'appropriate', and there is little doubt that 'commissions' have had to be paid by contractors, but projects that previously turned into 'air' are now being completed. The local administration plays little role in this and the foreign input increases indebtedness and dependency, but it is difficult to envisage an alternative approach to the provision of large-scale, capital-intensive works.

At the village level, however, the NRM has been its most significant innovation by attempting to decentralize a wide range of service provision to a complex system of democratic local councils. These, called resistance councils, are directly elected in villages, and indirectly at parish, sub-county, district and national levels. They do not have adequate access to revenue or professional skills but have drawn an immense number of people (more than 350,000 at village level alone) into the political system.[25] They are responsible for law and order, organize some voluntary labour for local works, settle domestic and land disputes, and collaborate with NGOs in service provision. This system is in urgent need of rationalization, but it has created a politically accountable institutional structure that could, with some modification, manage local services and serve as a basis for local political autonomy.

CONCLUSIONS: ACCOUNTABILITY, AUTONOMY AND VARIABILITY IN INSTITUTIONAL REFORM

The preceding analysis confirms much of the validity of the call for a move from state provision to market competition and fee-for-service payment, and most Ugandans, and not just their foreign advisers, now accept this view. But it also suggests that purely market solutions are not enough. The market works well in some sectors but not in others – it is a good servant but a bad master, as Bienefeld suggests.[26] We must therefore examine the requirements of each sector, identify the alternative forms of organization that can operate in each, and then encourage an array of agencies that will maximize choice and accountability to operate.

This means that we must accept the need for institutional variability – a capacity to choose 'horses for courses' on the basis of general theory as well as practical knowledge of particular situations. Liberal economists mainly concerned with prices and markets now dominate the policy debate and do not recognize the contribution of organization theorists such as Ostrom, Buchanan, Tullock, Olsen, Ouchi, Williamson, and Israel.[27] Their work is concerned with accountability, the costs of effective management and decision making, and the wide variety of forms available for service provision. In conclusion we will now consider some of the general implications of their work for the cases already discussed.

There is now general agreement that monopoly power will produce inefficiency and corruption unless effective democratic controls are exerted over those who exercise it. This applies to economic agencies such as marketing boards, and service agencies such as hospitals and schools financed out of taxation. Here much literature emphasizes the need to secure reform by improving skills and managerial structures, but neither will be of any significance unless the actors involved can be made accountable for their performance. This puts market theory on its strongest ground. As we have seen, competitive private traders have been more effective than marketing boards or subsidized cooperatives, private medical services more effective than the public hospital system.

But there are many problems associated with free competition. Small produce buyers cannot finance stocks, guarantee quality, build international markets and cross-subsidize to encourage growers in remote areas. In health, uncontrolled competition can lead to irresponsible prescribing and to dangerous practices. In marketing, the best solution is thus probably not free competition but oligopolistic competition between a few large final buyers; in health, private practice with effective professional regulation.

Fee-for-service payment has emerged in response to the failure of state provision, showing that people recognize that there is no such thing as a free meal and are willing to pay for services that they value. This does guarantee performance, since they only pay for what they get. But it also ignores serious problems of distribution, since fees exclude the very poor and thus lead to cumulative growth in inequality and conflict.

The desire to mitigate these problems has produced voluntary provision through foreign and domestic NGOs, and the emergence of PTAs, which mobilize local money and labour for schools. Here accountability stems from democratic control and dependence on direct contributions. This form of provision is often given higher moral status and support than those operating on purely commercial principles. But this is dangerous – the profit motive often leads to the efficient use of resources, while many voluntary agencies are inefficient, because their resources are free and their budget constraint correspondingly 'soft'. Thus serious attention must be given to the problem of enforcing efficiency in this area and developing evaluation procedures that enable donors to ensure that they are getting value for money.

There are also important areas where access to non-excludable collective goods makes it impossible to use the market and requires 'political' solutions based on monopolistic controls. Here, as Ostrom shows, we do not have to use traditional state systems, since other options exist, some involving competition and privatization.[28] But this does mean that political responsibility is crucial to the adjustment process – privatization and laissez-faire is not a universal panacea. In Uganda rehabilitation could not begin until the NRM took over, and services will not become cost-effective and accountable until democratic control at the centre and in local government can be improved. Hence we must still acknowledge the crucial role played by the state and thus the significance of political and administrative theory for a policy debate still dominated by the atomistic individualism of the economists. In the state, as Hegel says, individuals 'do not live as private persons for their own ends alone' but in a political context in which their activity is also aimed at a 'universal end'.

Hence reform must go beyond simple formulae – whether of the neo-liberal or Weberian variety – and recognize the logic of domestic resource endowments and the varied requirements of different kinds of services. We must have 'horses for courses', and accept that horses bred for Western courses may not survive the harsh conditions found in poor African countries. Finally, let us emphasize again that the successful adaptations described here all depended on some form of direct accountability, whether through markets, voluntary participation, or direct elections. Formal skills and rational systems are important where complex services must be provided, but this study suggests that direct accountability is more so. Without effective *motivation*, agencies will not behave responsibly. Educating the irresponsible simply increases their ability to exploit those who depend upon them.

309

Notes

1. Hobbes, 1981, pp. 185–6.
2. World Bank, 1989, p. 15.
3. The research on agricultural extension and marketing was carried out between 1966 and 1967, and 1973 and 1974 in eastern Uganda and was funded by the Rockefeller Foundation and the Social Science Research Council. My current work on 'service delivery for the rural poor' has taken me to the northwest and to Luwero districts, and is supported by ESCOR.
4. See Brett, 1975.
5. The general implications of this argument for less-developed countries is set out in Brett, 1987.
6. See Brett, 1973, ch. 8.
7. For a general review, see Dearlove, 1987. Leading texts on administration include Niskasnen, 1973; Tullock, 1987. Key economic texts are Bauer, 1972; Little, 1982; Lal, 1983. Toye, 1987 provides a coherent critique.
8. In the 1960s the Uganda Cooperative College still taught cooperative history and principles from the English texts.
9. But this is not to accept Hyden's (1980) characterization of them as an 'uncaptured peasantry', since their cash incomes were indispensable, as was the law and order guaranteed by the colonial state.
10. For these processes, see Brett, 1975, 1987.
11. See, in particular, Brett, 1973; Mamdani, 1976.
12. Burch, 1987.
13. Uganda, 1987c.
14. See, for example, *ibid*. This notes that the second highest ever yield of cotton was achieved in 1938 'when the Department of Agriculture numbered 17 senior . . . and 9 assistant agricultural officers for the whole country' (p. 25).
15. The problem is dealt with in Brett, 1970.
16. The efficiency of this sector is attested to in Uganda/World Bank, 1987, p. 8.
17. I have made this case in Brett, 1975.
18. Uganda, 1987c, p. 18.
19. Allen, 1989, and see Chapter 9 above.
20. Uganda, 1987b, p. xv.
21. Whyte, 1989 and see Chapter 8 above.
22. Allen, 1989.
23. Uganda Government, 1989.
24. These issues are dealt with in the collective choice literature, e.g., Olsen, 1971; Ostrom, 1988a.
25. For a detailed review, see Uganda, 1987a.
26. M. Bienefeld, 1988: 'Karl Polanyi-lessons of history', mimeo.
27. See references in notes 7 and 24; also Buchanan and Tullock, 1962; Williamson, 1979; Israel, 1989.
28. Ostrom, 1988.

PART SEVEN
PROBLEMS OF LANDHOLDING

TWENTY-ONE
Institutional dimensions
of land tenure reform

W. Kisamba-Mugerwa

One of the major issues exercising the minds of most people in Uganda is land tenure reform. The question is – which type of land tenure system will contribute to the economic and social development of agriculture, protect the land rights of the farmers who have no alternative source of income and contribute to the evolution of a single uniform, efficient and equitable tenure system? The evils of land shortage is one issue. Encroachment on natural reserves, excessive subdivision and fragmentation of parcels of land, increasing land disputes arising from evictions of the rural poor, coupled with deteriorating agricultural performance for over two decades; all make land reform a household issue in Uganda.

All those evils are emerging despite government policy interventions. However, the attempt to solve one problem by changing land tenure rules and laws always tends to create new problems. In this paper an attempt is made to present a brief overview of the fundamental historical institutional dimensions of land tenure changes and their consequences. Drawing lessons from recent studies on land tenure, a set of proposals for consideration is advanced as a foundation for a new agenda of land reform. The main thesis of this chapter is that the indigenous land tenure systems are inadequate to cope with the cash economy of a modern society. Underlying the thesis also is the suggestion that land reform in agricultural development strategies is characterized by individual ownership of land and minimal state control.

Land tenure reform means changing the rules by which individuals or groups relate to one another with respect to land. In essence, the rules of land tenure define one's rights and duties with respect to other people concerning the use and transfer of land. According to Bruce (1986), land tenure reform alters the substantive rules and institutional arrangements of indigenous land tenure systems, seeking to induce changes in land use in the interest of productivity, equity, and similar objectives.

A variety of tenure reforms was analysed by Bruce (1986; p. 51) from five perspectives:

Problems of landholding

(1) Individualization of tenure whereby community control over land use and distribution is reduced and the rights of the individual landholder are enhanced.

(2) Cooperativization of production involves government-promoted efforts to institute communal production through new local institutions that are treated as part of the state machinery. Tanzania's *Ujamaa* policy was one example of this.

(3) Re-institutionalizing indigenous land tenure may emphasize building on existing institutional arrangements to the extent that is practicable.

(4) Reforming inheritance, whereby reform is undertaken on the principles of kinship organization and community values.

(5) Nationalization and bureaucratization of land administration.

For our purposes, it is important to note two points. One is that in some types of land reform state control is either promoted or eliminated. Another type promotes individual ownership of land and minimizes communal elements. Where individual rights are promoted and state control is minimized, a comprehensive policy may result, covering ownership and other measures to assist farmers through increased security of tenure, better credit schemes, marketing facilities and effective extension services.

In a World Bank discussion paper on the prospects of land reform by Hans P. Binswanger and Miranda Elgin (1988), a bleak atmosphere was created when they concluded that land reform is unlikely to be a major tool for improving the welfare of the poor in developing countries. This conclusion is based on their observation that even where land reform would make economic sense, it will not happen because the beneficiaries cannot pay for the land reform, implying the need for confiscating appropriations or large tax costs, neither of which is politically palatable. They also observed that other measures have to be devised to improve access of the poor to land or increase incomes from agriculture. They recommended that other measures can help small farmers only if governments abandon policies that favour large farms and put premiums on land prices. They finally call for a stronger commitment from governments and agencies to tackle these policy issues and thereby reduce incentives to accumulate large ownership holdings, increase agricultural production, and ensure greater equity employment and self employment in agriculture.

In Uganda, agriculture is mainly practised on smallholdings that progressively become smaller through subdivision on sale or through inheritance. The second approach, of an integrated and co-ordinated programme, though going beyond the strict domain of land reform, would seem to be the most realistic to pursue in the circumstances of

312

Institutional dimensions of land tenure reform

Uganda. Binswanger and Rosenzweig's theoretical study (1986) discusses in detail the case for smallholdings as more efficient farming units than large farms. We shall consider this later for Uganda as regards progressive farmers. What is important at this stage is to note that the economic development of agriculture is dependent on more than a good land tenure system.

THE EVOLUTION OF UGANDA'S LAND SYSTEM

The precolonial system

The pattern of land tenure in Uganda before 1900 as exemplified by the system in Buganda is well documented by Mukwaya (1953). There were four categories of rights of control over land;

(1) Rights of clans over land (*obutaka*) whereby these rights accrued to heads of clans and sub-clans. The land was viewed as clan ancestral land. By 1911 there were about 522 estates under heads of clans (Roscoe 1911), where land was held by heads of clans rather than collectively, though members of the clan had the usufruct but could not subdivide or sell it. Land under this arrangement was not alienated to strangers.

(2) Rights of the *kabaka* and/or chiefs (*obutongole*). This was where the king (*kabaka*) granted land to chiefs who had only usufruct rights attached to their offices.

(3) Individual hereditary rights. These stemmed from long-undisputed occupation and/or original grant by the king. Through this arrangement, a chief or peasant could have a permanent claim on a parcel of land and royal recognition was granted.

(4) Peasant rights of occupation. This was when an ordinary person acquired a piece of land under a certain chief and occupied it permanently. Such land became inheritable upon the death of the original user. In precolonial Buganda such tenure involved respect to the chief, payment of tribute and occasional work for him.

There was not one pattern of land tenure in Uganda but the system described was common in Buganda and replicated in other kingdoms in Bunyoro, Ankole, Busoga and Toro. The rest of precolonial Uganda was more decentralized, but not without variation in customary tenure from one area to another.

The variations in customary tenure in precolonial Uganda are discussed in detail by Bayer (1958), Makubuya (1981), Edel (1969), and Obol-Ochola (1971). Though details differ to a certain extent, what is clear is that precolonial customary tenure simultaneously recognized individual and collective or communal rights in land. The only difference was that in some respects it only recognized various rights of the

313

individual to possess and use land subject to superintendence by family, clan or community.

Land tenure in colonial times

In conditions of social homogeneity and cultural consensus the precolonial customary land tenure operated efficiently. As these conditions broke down, it became necessary to undertake land tenure reforms. Preservation of customary tenure was a major official policy of British colonial land policy, but in practice tenure was radically transformed.

Among other colonial land arrangements, the Buganda Agreement of 1900 formed the basis of land tenure in Buganda. Under the '*mailo*' tenure, as it came to be called, all the land (900 square miles) was to be divided between the *kabaka*, other notables and the British protectorate government. This enhanced the concept of private ownership of land in Buganda. It has been observed that the right to own land and the conversion of land into a negotiable asset has facilitated investment, created a land market and aided Buganda in its general development. The *mailo* system also put most of the best land into private freehold ownership, thereby breaking the grip of tribal customs and laying the foundation of a sounder future land policy.

The Busulu and Envujo Law (1927), however, ruled that peasant tenants could not be forced off their holdings without a court hearing. Their tenancy could be passed on to the next generation although it could not be divided among heirs and could not be sold. In return the tenant was obliged to pay an annual fee (*busulu*) of UShs 8.50 for the use of the land and tribute on produce (*envujo*) for such crops as cotton and coffee.

The colonial period also witnessed the Crown Land Ordinance of 1903, which gave the British colonial authorities power to alienate land in freehold (Morris and Read 1966). There were, furthermore, native freeholds in Ankole and Toro based on the 1900 and 1901 Agreements whereby chiefs who signed were allocated land. The Ankole Landlord and Tenant Law 1937, together with the Toro Landlord and Tenant Law, also later curtailed powers and rights of the freeholder against tenants on his land.

Freehold titles were also given to Africans in accordance with the Crown Lands (Adjudication) Rules of 1958 which resulted in the Pilot Land Adjudication Schemes of Ankole, Bugisu and Kigezi. Ownership of a parcel was ascertained by an Adjudication Committee and the true owner could, if he wished, obtain a land title for it.

Despite piecemeal land tenure reforms outside the central region, what is clear is that the overall trend was to increase security in land, either by private ownership or the enhancement of individual rights in the possession and use of land.

314

Institutional dimensions of land tenure reform

The post-independence period

The period since independence has been characterized by the Land Reform Decree 1975. This laid down that all land formerly in private individual tenure, such as the *mailo* of the Central Region and freeholds, was supposed to be converted to 99-year leases. In the case of charitable and religious institutions, the freeholds were to be converted to 199-year leases granted by the state, whose executive agency became the Uganda Land Commission. The LRD repealed the Busulu and Envujo Law of 1927 which had provided statutory protection for tenants on former *mailo* and freehold land. These tenancies were converted to customary ones and tenants could be evicted on payment of compensation for improvements if the leaseholder on conversion considered it necessary to develop the land. For the rest of the land outside the former *mailo* and freehold areas, customary tenures continued in force, but are held on sufferance. The state may on six months' notice evict customary holders and lease the land to someone else.

The LRD has never been systematically implemented. In practice the LRD has never really started to be observed in land registry offices. The registry still operates two registers – the leasehold register and the *mailo* register.

POLICY CONSEQUENCES

Having briefly outlined the institutional history of land tenure, it is pertinent to examine its consequences and implications.

During the precolonial period there was a diversity of land tenure systems that varied from one ethnic group to another. They had communal/tribal and clan/family tendencies and to a certain extent there could be individual hereditary rights existing alongside peasants' rights of occupation. The precolonial land tenure system was essentially communal, though strains of individual rights were to a certain extent recognized. The main land tenure institutions were generally centred on tribes and clans and to a certain extent the importance of a family was recognized.

During the colonial period a state emerged when under the Agreement (1900) land was divided between *kabaka*, chiefs and the protectorate government. By establishing freeholds, privatization of land ownership not only became certain but was even safeguarded and protected. When the Busulu and Envujo Law 1927 was also introduced in respect of the *mailo* and freehold tenants, peasant rights in land that had not received recognition in the original *mailo* and freehold arrangements secured recognition. Furthermore, the customary tenure in areas that had not been affected by other elements of colonial land policy also enjoyed fairly comprehensive regulations, as set out in section 24 of the Public Land Act 1969. Under the legislation it was lawful for a person to occupy by

315

customary tenure any rural land not alienated in leasehold or freehold. No land occupied under customary tenure could be given out without the consent of the customary tenant. The trend was generally towards expanding the bundle of individual rights in land. Secondly, the involvement of the state was as a matter of last resort.

It is against this background that the objectives of the Land Reform Decree appear questionable. All the land is vested in the state through the Uganda Lands Commission. The situation of the peasant tenant today is not secure. The Land Reform Decree 1975 abolishes the 1927 Busulu and Envujo Law and appears to favour the development of large-scale holdings by permitting the *mailo* owner to evict tenants on six months' notice with compensation. It involves the state in day-to-day management of land affairs.

BASIC POLICY ALTERNATIVES

Since the Land Reform Decree (1975) has never been systematically enforced, the question arises whether the government should seek to consolidate the leasehold system created by the decree, introduce legal changes to return *mailo* and freehold, or look for a completely new set of land laws.

There are various interpretations of the objectives of the LRD (1975). One interpretation holds that the Land Reform Decree was introduced to make it easier for the *mailo* owner to evict tenants and thus consolidate parcels for large-scale farming. The MISR/LTC field studies (see below), however, indicate that the LRD did not establish who would put *mailo* land to better use, the *mailo* owner or the *mailo* tenant. Instead, it intensified the deadlock and became unworkable. Each party became more suspicious of government. The *mailo* owner has been socially, economically and politically constrained to make full use of the provisions of the LRD section 7 on evictions. On the other hand, the *mailo* tenants are generally not fully aware of the provisions of the LRD. The majority of them feel secure, but they are enjoying a false sense of security. Though socio-cultural ties are still at play in protecting tenants against evictions from land, to a certain extent there is increasing frustration and decline of interest in land occupied by *mailo* tenants since *mailo* owners have not had any socio-economic benefits since 1975.

Whether in respect of a *mailo* tenant or a customary tenant, no eviction should be effected without the consent of the tenants plus six months' notice and compensation. Contrary to that provision of the LRD, leasing land without the knowledge of customary tenants is on the increase, just as sales of land to companies to evict reluctant tenants is also becoming common. Companies tend to have no socio-cultural ties and generally use lawyers to effect their interests. Despite the provision to evict tenants, very often the state interferes with the mechanism of the legal procedure and stops evictions, making the LRD very controversial. Isolated cases are on record where *mailo* owners have evicted tenants, though not without much tension, and colossal legal expense incurred (Nsibambi 1989). However, a landowner who evicts tenants without adequate compensation or notice risks damage to his own property and life from the local residents.

Another interpretation suggests that the main intention of the Land Reform Decree (1975) was not to evict tenants, but to make land available to the majority of Ugandans by converting all land to leasehold on payment of ground rent. The ground rent and development conditions were to stop speculative acquisition of land, and make it expensive to hold large tracts of land. Contrary to that view, others argue that the LRD (1975) was a calculated political move intended to enable government or certain influential people to grab land. There was no proper explanation or consultation made when it was enacted. A study recently conducted by Makerere Institute of Social Research (MISR) and the Land Tenure Center of the University of Wisconsin-Madison (LTC) did not discover any large-scale agricultural projects resulting from evictions inspired by the LRD (1975). Rather, unutilized parcels of leased land are common, especially in cattle-keeping areas.

The MISR/LTC study was undertaken to make recommendations on changes in land tenure policy. It carried out field surveys of sample farmers in Luwero and Masaka districts and conducted Rural Rapid Appraisal (RRA) in Mbale, Mbarara, Bushenyi, Masaka, Luwero, Mubende, Tororo, Iganga and Mukono districts. Farmers studied included *mailo* owners, *mailo* tenants, leaseholders and customary tenants on public land. It revealed that:

(1) The security of farmers on their landholding is closely related to the type of land tenure, but higher levels of security are not positively associated with higher levels of investment on land. In Luwero, customary tenants invested the most but were the least secure in their landholdings. In Masaka *mailo* owners invested most but customary tenants were the most secure.

(2) Progressive farming is not associated with the size of landholding. Most of the progressive farmers were not found to be very large scale farmers. They were, however, found to be full-time farmers. There is also no clear discernible development difference by mode of tenure. It mostly depends on access to capital by virtue of social and professional positions. In Luwero the progressive farmers were customary tenants on public land whereas in Masaka they were *mailo* owners.

(3) The land market plays an important role in agricultural development by providing progressive farmers free access to land. In both Luwero and Masaka, progressive farmers acquired their land through

purchase and less progressive farmers mostly inherited it. The value of land differs widely depending on mode of tenure; *mailo* land is usually the most expensive, followed by leasehold and customary land, though land price is mostly determined by private treaty.

(4) The problem of population pressure on customary land is very acute compared with other types of tenure. Customary landholders have smaller parcels, higher land utilization ratios, and almost all of the available land in Masaka was occupied. With inheritance and consequent subdivision, customary landholding poses a serious development problem.

(5) The Land Reform Decree (1975) was not enforced and hence has not resulted in mass evictions of *mailo* or other tenants except in some livestock-rearing areas. Though the Land Reform Decree altered the fundamental rights of tenants and theoretically exposed them to eviction without compensation, in practice it has for the time being made them more powerful. They no longer make payments to the landlords. The low rate of eviction is also partly attributed to some cultural values, family history and tradition. According to the official records of eviction disputes, tenants are, however, exposed to eviction by *mailo* owners or leaseholders. With the passage of time and commercialization of agriculture, the cultural ties will no longer restrain the *mailo* owners or leaseholders from evicting tenants. This will result in intensification of conflict between *mailo* owners/leaseholders and tenants, with serious socio-political and economic implications.

Based on the above findings, the study team came to the conclusion that any change in the land tenure system in Uganda should pursue the following policy objectives:

(1) A land tenure system should facilitate and be conducive to agricultural development. To achieve this, a land tenure policy should support the emergence and smooth functioning of a free land market to enable progressive farmers to gain access to land for development on a commercial basis.

(2) A land tenure system should protect land rights, particularly those of people who have no other way to earn a reasonable living or even survive. This means that farmers should not be forced off the land before there are alternative opportunities for survival.

(3) A land tenure system should be uniform and land legislation should assist the evolution of a uniform nation-wide system.

The most appropriate form of land tenure for Uganda should meet all the above three goals and with this objective in view the study team made the following proposals:

318

Institutional dimensions of land tenure reform

(1) The Land Reform Decree of 1975 should be repealed. The study team found that:

    (a) The decree violates the principle that a land tenure system should protect people from eviction if there is no other income-earning alternative available in the non-farm sector of the economy.

    (b) The decree vests land in the state; in other words the radical or allodial title is vested in the state. This is tantamount to a state takeover of property without compensation.

    (c) The decree failed decisively to settle the issue of who would put land to better use, the *mailo* owner or the *mailo* tenant. Instead, it intensified the land-use deadlock between the *mailo* owner and the *mailo* tenant and became unworkable.

    (d) The decree also hinders agricultural development because it interferes with the land market, which should ideally allow a progressive farmer easy access to land through purchase. The decree does not carry any provision to enable a *mailo* tenant to purchase his parcel from the *mailo* owner. The *mailo* owner has no legal obligations to sell a parcel to a sitting tenant.

    (e) The decree increases the cost of land administration by requiring periodical renewals of leases and the system of monitoring of leasehold conditions.

(2) All *mailo* land should be converted to freehold. *Mailo* tenants would become freehold owners of their land. *Mailo* owners would have freehold titles to the *mailo* land they own that is not occupied by tenants. The justifications are:

    (a) Freehold is preferable to leasehold because it interferes less with private property rights and involves much less cost to government for administration.

    (b) Freehold gives farmers ownership rights, ability to transfer land through a land market, the greatest possible feeling of security in their land and increased access to bank credit for agricultural development.

    (c) The reality in *mailo* areas is that tenants have had virtual freehold and *mailo* owners have had effective freehold for many years. It is necessary to break the deadlock that existed before 1975 between *mailo* owners and tenants.

(3) *Mailo* owners should receive compensation for the interest in land that they lost from conversion of tenancy land to freehold. This compensation should be provided over a period of years and tenants should share in part of the cost. The *mailo* owner should be compensated for the loss of interest in land. Compensation can be provided partly by the tenant, partly by government and could perhaps be part-financed by international donor agencies. Government should sponsor a study to determine the value of the *mailo* owner's interest in *mailo* occupied

319

by tenants and to cover the whole compensation issue.

(4) Tenants on customary tenure on public land should apply for freehold upon verification of their rights in land by community leaders and under technical supervision. The requirements of a modern cash economy in general and of modern agriculture in particular are likely to be best met by an indigenous customary land tenure system. Land tenure policy should assist in the evolution of a uniform land tenure system by providing security to those who cultivate land or those who wish to register their parcel.

(5) Existing leases on public land should be converted to freehold automatically; the exception would be leases on government-sponsored ranching schemes, and other leases of over 200 acres, which should be reviewed on a case-by-case basis. Conversion to freehold should not be allowed for properties acquired arbitrarily and/or illegally.

(6) No development conditions should be imposed on any freehold, except for land on government-sponsored development projects. Development conditions have been ineffective as stimulants for agricultural development in several African countries where they have been imposed. If an agricultural activity is profitable, farmers will be attracted to undertake it.

(7) A land tax could be adopted as an alternative to development conditions appropriate to leaseholds. If adopted, the tax should be administered at the sub-county level and the revenue should be used at the local level for programmes such as schools. The tax should be based on the productive capacity of the land, with different levels of tax for good, average and poor land. The tax on land will provide an incentive to use land by making it expensive to leave it idle. The land tax could thus provide a source of revenue for local administrations and will relieve fiscal pressure on government. A tax on land will also serve as an inducement for title holders to register transactions, whether sales, succession or partitions at the local land offices.

CONCLUSION

In Uganda the issue of land tenure reform is household talk. Through informal and formal discussions in the National Resistance Council, which is acting as the National Parliament, and in local newspapers, the government is often urged to come up with a land reform policy. This is envisaged to be one of the fundamental changes the National Resistance Movement (NRM) government is likely to undertake in fulfilling its *10-Point Programme*. In this chapter it has been argued that the indigenous land tenure system is inadequate to cope with the cash economy. Secondly, it has been pointed out that until the LRD (1975) was enacted, the trend was to broaden individual rights in land, in other words towards privatization. The LRD (1975) did not resolve the deadlock between the *mailo* owner and the *mailo* tenant; instead it was intensified, making the peasants prone to evictions.

Government interference in the legal proceedings in the implementation of the LRD (1975) is a clear manifestation of its controversial nature. If fully implemented, mass evictions would occur. The magnitude of land disputes would encourage constant intervention by the government, rendering it excessively preoccupied with land issues.

We are seeking a land tenure system that will contribute to the economic and social development of agriculture, protect the land rights of farmers who have no alternative source of income, and contribute to the evolution of a single, uniform, efficient and equitable land tenure system with minimum government interference. Based on findings arising from wide consultation and field studies through sample surveys and RRA techniques, we advocate a freehold land tenure system, whereby the LRD is repealed, *mailo* land is converted to freehold, and *mailo* tenants also become freehold owners of their land with a provision of a compensation scheme for the interests of the *mailo* owner. We advocate that tenants on customary tenure on public land apply for freeholds instead of leaseholds; and also convert leaseholds to freeholds. A land tax ought to be imposed instead of development conditions.

Underlying all those recommendations we emphasize that for a land reform policy to be successful, all other sections and related development institutions must be revived to undertake development in non-farming sectors, create effective government machinery; eliminate encroachment on national reserves and develop new farming systems to minimize excessive land sub-division and fragmentation. We are confident that whatever political system Uganda may eventually decide to adopt, it will be interested in protecting the land rights of the peasants, the economic and social development of agriculture and the evolution of a single, uniform, efficient and equitable tenure system. This is important, because for any land tenure change policy to succeed, values, ideology and political aspirations as well as mere technical factors need to be taken into account.

PART EIGHT
REVOLUTION IN EDUCATION?
TACKLING THE DIPLOMA DISEASE

TWENTY-TWO
Educational reform
during socio-economic crisis

W. Senteza Kajubi

Despite repeated criticisms of the inherited colonial system of education as anachronistic and irrelevant, and the efforts of successive governments to change it, no fundamental transformation has occurred over the years of independence in relating education to the social and cultural realities of Uganda.

Education has not succeeded, for example, in promoting a sense of national unity, economic development, self-reliance, social justice and equity, scientific and technological literacy, cultural values and a sense of mutual responsibility to a degree that society would like to see among the 'educated' class. On the contrary, formal schooling has focused mainly on academic learning for passing examinations *per se* to the neglect of knowledge, skills, values and attitudes needed to function efficiently in the real world of work.

Neither has Uganda been subjected to continuous systematic planning; it has been allowed to develop as a result of uncoordinated responses to social and political demands from time to time. This accounts for the wide disparities not only in the quality of schools, but also between the products of the system and the needs of society.

Governments have each year expended large amounts to educate people who make relatively little contribution to economic and social development. The system provides an expensive and inappropriate education to a select few, while the majority receive little or no formal education. Universal primary education and the elimination of adult illiteracy which were projected by the Addis Ababa Conference of 1961 to be achieved throughout Africa by 1980, remain elusive. While the economy needs teachers, technicians, scientists, and trained workers of all types, the education system is turning out unemployable school leavers and liberal arts graduates.

It was with the foregoing challenges in mind that the Uganda government appointed a commission in July 1987 to review the present education policy, to appraise the current system at all levels and to suggest improvements. This chapter will first assess the dilapidated state into which the educational system has fallen during the recent socio-economic crisis and then give a bird's eye view of the Education Policy Review Commission Report from 1989.

The importance that the government and people of Uganda attach to education as a means of national development cannot be overstressed. Government has in past years spent as much as 20 per cent of its recurrent annual budget on education, and communities contribute materials and labour to build schools. School fees are regarded as a first call on family incomes, and indeed parents sell their livestock and even land to send their children to school and keep them there. Yet, in spite of this public zeal and relatively heavy expenditure, the gap between social demand and public supply is still very wide and in some cases increasing.

SHORTAGES AND SHORTCOMINGS

The civil strife in Uganda over the last two decades or so; external pressures arising from worsening terms of trade; the back-breaking public debt, resulting in the declining value of the Uganda shilling, have combined to strike a heavy blow to the financing of education and other social services. The proportion of government's recurrent budget devoted to education declined from 21 per cent in 1983/84 to as low as 11 per cent in 1986/87, although in 1987/88 and 1988/89 there was a slight rise to 18.2 and 12.2 per cent respectively. At the same time, the proportion of the Ministry of Education's budget devoted to primary education, which is the only formal education most children receive, has not only been small but also declining. What is true of the recurrent budget also applies to capital development expenditure.

There is a critical shortage of teachers at all levels, and there are many untrained/licensed teachers in schools and teachers' colleges. For example, in 1988 56 per cent of the primary school teachers were untrained. The secondary schools had 40 per cent untrained and under-trained teachers and the primary teachers colleges (PTCs) had between 20 and 25 per cent untrained tutors. At Makerere out of a total of 845 established posts only 437 (52 per cent) were filled and 377 (45 per cent) were vacant in March 1990, and 61 per cent of the professorial positions were vacant.

Staff shortages at all levels have been intensified by unattractive salaries and conditions of service. Teachers' salaries, for example, often paid several months in arrears, are abysmally low, as is their morale and efficiency. For example, the starting monthly salary of a primary school teacher in 1988 was just over UShs1,000 (US$3). This is far below the amount an individual would need to survive in Kampala. Under these circumstances teachers cannot be expected to devote their full-time energies to teaching; they have to seek additional employment in order to survive.

While public resources for education have been declining, enrolments in schools and colleges have risen significantly. Enrolment in primary

323

schools doubled between 1980 and 1988, i.e., at an annual growth rate of 9 per cent, and the annual rate of growth at the secondary level was 16 per cent during the same period. The number of educational institutions also increased substantially. For example, the number of government aided secondary schools rose from 120 to over 500, to say nothing of 250 private secondary schools, most of which also sprang up during the same period.

The effect of dwindling public expenditure on the one hand and the growing social demand for education on the other has been deterioration of education. There is an almost total absence of textbooks, equipment and other essential learning materials in the schools. Virtually no new school buildings, particularly laboratories and teachers' houses, have been erected by the government in the last 20 years or so, and 'new' secondary schools and teachers' training colleges have been established merely by converting existing primary school buildings to new uses. Once beautiful and majestic school buildings have been allowed to dilapidate through disrepair. Classrooms are extremely overcrowded, with 100–160 pupils per class in some urban primary schools.

A paradoxical situation exists in that the government has hitherto continued to meet the full boarding and lodging costs, pocket money, transport and dependants' allowances of students in higher education, and 65 per cent of the total boarding expenses in secondary schools, while the basic pedagogical requirements in all educational institutions, including the university, remain unfulfilled.

THE ROLE OF PARENT-TEACHER ASSOCIATIONS (PTA)

Parent-teacher associations (PTAs) have come to play a very important role in the financing and development of education in Uganda. PTAs, which have existed in the Uganda school system for the last 20 years or so, were originally intended to be school welfare associations, concerned mainly with creating a healthy relationship between teachers and parents. The management of schools was entirely the responsibility of the head teacher under the direction of boards of governors or management committees. Of late, however, particularly since about 1980, PTAs have become the major funding bodies of the schools, and have assumed a pivotal role in the development of the education system.

The main function of PTAs now is to raise and in most cases manage funds for the schools. Although official tuition fees are very low, parents' contributions through PTAs are high, and in many cases disproportionately so. Besides tuition fees, parents are variously required to make PTA contributions to such items as school transport, mid-day meals, stationery and other school supplies, textbooks, buildings such as new classrooms, dormitories, and teachers' houses, equipment and animals for school farms, and (even more importantly) to supplement teachers' salaries. The vital role that PTAs have played in sustaining the financing of schools cannot be overstressed. Overall in 1989 PTAs were bearing 70 to 80 per cent of the total recurrent costs of running primary and secondary schools.

Despite the energy and success of the PTAs there is considerable public concern that the dues demanded by them are beyond the means of many parents. On several occasions the Ministry of Education has had to intervene to curb the enthusiasm of PTAs in raising funds. On the other hand, it is difficult to see how parents' contributions can be reduced when PTAs have to meet almost all recurrent and capital costs of running schools. The solution seems to lie in parents being educated to become more actively and democratically involved in the activities of PTAs, particularly the welfare of teachers and pupils.

A conflict of interest also exists in some cases between the PTAs, which raise and control funds, and the boards of governors/management committees, which are the legal owners of the schools. In some cases there are alumni associations that also raise funds and would like to influence the culture of their alma maters.

THE PROBLEM OF EQUITY

A policy of educational financing whereby parents are required to share a much greater burden for basic primary and secondary education, and relatively little or no burden for higher education, raises an equity issue.

Parents who cannot afford to pay fees even at primary level have to withdraw their children from school, only to pay their taxes to support those lucky few who are able to gain admission to the university and other institutions of higher education. Tertiary institutions consume a disproportionately high share of the educational budget. For example the ratio of government spending per capita in tertiary and primary education sectors is the order of 300 : 1. It can be argued that free education, food, accommodation and personal allowances in the tertiary sector are a form of subsidy by the poor to rich parents.

Government decided in 1989 to abolish or reduce some of the allowances and to introduce the concept of cost-sharing. This decision was strongly opposed by the students, leading to the closure of Makerere University between November 1989 and February 1990. It remains to be seen whether government will push the concept of cost-sharing proposed by the Education Policy Review Commission (EPRC) any further.

NOTHING TO READ: THE CRISIS OF INSTRUCTIONAL MATERIALS

It has been suggested that textbooks are the single most important contribution to improved learning in the schools of developing countries. The dearth of instructional materials in Uganda's schools has already been mentioned. Uganda is still at stage 1 of Heyneman's stages of development in school quality, whereby the annual cost per primary school pupil on classroom materials is less than US$1 (ED1 1986, p. 3). It is not unusual to find classes of children and teachers in primary schools with just one or no textbook, no teachers guide and no syllabus either.

The result is that the majority of pupils are drilled on a single reader that may be available; they copy and memorize unsophisticated and poorly digested information from the chalkboard, and leave the seven-year primary school without acquiring permanent functional literacy either in English or in their vernacular languages. The dearth of suitable instructional materials in the classrooms at all levels is at the moment the most serious bottleneck to educational development in Uganda. It is no wonder that standards as judged by students' performances in the examinations administered by the Uganda National Examination Board (UNEB) have dropped considerably in recent years. For example, in 1980 a total of 98,751 candidates took the Primary Leaving Examination (PLE) and 30,011 or 30.4 per cent passed in Grade I. In the years between 1985 and 1989, however, only 11.1 per cent, 13.4 per cent, 13.4 per cent, and 9.4 per cent, respectively, passed. UCE examinations (at the secondary level) show more or less the same trend. Thus while the number of candidates passing UCE Grade I increased from 201 in 1960 to 1,835 in 1989, the percentage of total candidates passing fell from 11.3 per cent to 4.5 per cent.

There is a crying need for locally oriented, culturally and politically acceptable books and other forms of learning materials. Otherwise educational standards will continue to decline. The concept of a book as meaning only commercially and professionally produced material must change. Books locally produced for schools and non-formal education can take the form of low-cost mimeographed materials, including pamphlets adaptable to local needs. With modest inputs of paper, duplicating facilities and teacher motivation, these materials can be produced by teachers, university students, members of the community, and even by school children themselves.

There is need for the National Curriculum Development Centre to be strengthened with qualified staff in different subjects, and provided with adequate physical and financial resources for the production of instructional materials within a reasonable time for the implementation of the new structure of education.

The Uganda government is not unconcerned by the problem of the paucity of materials and declining standards. In addition to the Minister of Education, there is now a Minister of State responsible for Higher Education, and a Minister of State responsible for Primary Education. This arrangement makes it possible for more attention to be devoted to the problems and requirements of each sector.

326

Educational reform during socio-economic crisis

Much of the assistance from the World Bank through the third and fourth IDA Projects has been devoted to the procurement of books for primary schools, and the National Curriculum Development Centre is being strengthened for the purpose of producing manuscripts.

NATIONAL GOALS AND OBJECTIVES

A major problem for educational reform in Uganda is the difficulty of identifying a national ethos that could unite Ugandans into a coherent social order, and whose core values would animate and guide education. Small and compact as it is, Uganda is, as Wrigley (1988, p. 28) rightly observes, 'culturally a heterogeneous and historically shallow collection of people with none of the attributes of a nation'. There are as yet no accepted national political and cultural norms and values that can be internalized by individuals beyond the usual slogans of fighting 'disease, poverty and ignorance'. There is, for example, no common language, let alone a 'we-feeling' of national identity, and ethnic loyalties and religious sectarianism are still much stronger than collective nationalism. Political instability, social and physical insecurity, and blatant violation of human rights have been almost a permanent feature of Uganda life since independence.

Plato suggests in *The Republic* that problems of national unity can be overcome with the right kind of political education. The Education Policy Review Commission accepted this view, and kept Uganda's baffling political and social problems in mind throughout its deliberations. It concluded that national integration is the single greatest challenge and that the type of education provided should have a pivotal role in creating it.

In considering the general problems of '*why*, who, what, and how' to educate, the Commission identified five basic national goals and objectives that should guide and animate the education system:

(1) *The forging of national unity and harmony* This should be attained through pluralistic integration or unity in diversity. Deliberate efforts must be made at every stage to foster among the students and communities an understanding, appreciation and respect for the diverse cultural and social systems of people living in different parts of the country. The concept of pluralistic integration or unity in diversity should, among other things, involve:
   (a) trans-ethnic integration, i.e., an attempt to bring different ethnic groups together to form one nation while allowing cultural diversity to persist and even prosper;
   (b) social integration to reduce the gap between the elites and the masses of the people;
   (c) value integration to evolve national values over local ones;

327

    (d) administrative integration to establish in the people the desire to live together as one nation under a central authority.

(2) *The evolution of grass-roots democratic institutions and practices in all sectors of life* The attainment of national unity and harmony will be impossible without the full participation of the people in initiating, implementing, and evaluating their own socio-economic development programmes. Educational institutions should provide the means by which pupils learn, appreciate and practise the ideals and realities of democracy in order to learn how to lead and how to be led, to rule and how to be ruled so as to become competent, reflective, concerned, and participating citizens.

(3) *A guarantee of fundamental human rights* These should include personal security, property rights and the rule of law. From the visits they made throughout the country, the Commission observed the serious concern of Ugandans that education should foster respect for fundamental human rights, peace and security. Education has to strengthen these aspirations and inspire a desire among the younger generations to work towards their fulfilment.

(4) *The creation of national wealth needed to enhance a better quality of life and self-reliance* The need to resuscitate and sustain Uganda's war-shattered economy also cannot be overstressed. The ultimate aim of building an independent, integrated self-sustaining national economy demands that education must be *applied education* that is oriented towards the development of productive skills with an exposure to new technologies, and must be continuing and life-long in order to enable individuals to upgrade their skills from time to time.

(5) *The promotion of ethical values* Uganda's experience of more than two decades of misrule, violence and unrest has left behind considerable moral degradation and deterioration of ethical values. While every parent would like to teach his or her children social values that will equip them to become competent and responsible citizens, most of the social mores that were the basis of our once well-ordered society are no longer respected. Owing to escalating inflation, for example, the amount of money required for a decent family existence is no longer counted in hundreds or thousands, but in bundles and millions of shillings. Money has to be obtained *anyhow*. The front pages of daily newspapers are full of reports of embezzlement by people in all stations of life 'in order to survive'. Basic individual survival has become generally more important than values of honesty, integrity, justice and equity. In order 'to survive', individuals have to set aside even those principles that they believe are right, and without which our national and community life, let alone our own family life, will disintegrate. 'Our rights', usually claimed through violence, have become more important among the youth than any

Educational reform during socio-economic crisis

consideration of responsibilities or mutual community obligations. The need for moral rehabilitation in Uganda cannot be overstressed, and education has a leading role to play in evolving new generations of Ugandans with new moral and ethical values.

MAJOR RECOMMENDATIONS FOR UGANDA'S
EDUCATIONAL DEVELOPMENT

Based on these broad considerations and bearing the broad national goals in mind, the Commission made recommendations that stressed, among other things, the following:

(1) *The democratization of the education system* In Uganda there are still large disparities in educational provision and participation between different population groups. About 40 per cent of the children of primary school age are still outside the formal school system in some parts of the country. Seventy per cent of the pupils who complete the seven-year primary education cycle then drop out because they are unable to find places in post-primary institutions. The proportion of girls receiving education, particularly at the secondary and higher levels is still very low, and there are yawning gaps in educational provision between urban and rural areas.

The Commission proposes the achievement of universal primary education (UPE) by the year 2000, greater access to higher levels of education and an increase in female participation in order to transform the current pyramidal structure of education to one that could eventually be described as a truncated pyramid.

It is also proposed that during the first four years of the basic cycle the medium of instruction should be a local Ugandan language in order to make learning easier and more meaningful. But others advocate Kiswahili as the national language and medium of instruction although it is not yet widely spoken in Uganda, particularly in rural areas (see Chapter 23).

(2) *A strengthening of the relationship between academic education, vocational education and the world of work* Most parents in Uganda wish their children to enter a 'good' nursery school and end up with a university degree. The curriculum and teaching methods at every level are largely determined by the entrance requirements at the next highest level; the system therefore fails to address the needs of the majority of pupils who will not proceed upwards in this way. The vast majority who drop off at various levels and do not reach the university are regarded as 'failures'.

There is a low regard for technical and commercial studies, and physical work is not necessarily considered as an essential part of education. The general practice is for the 'brighter' pupils to go on

329

and on with theoretical studies, and for the less talented to branch off into technical or vocational courses. Cleverness is still judged only on the basis of ability to memorize and regurgitate theoretical information, and practical people are automatically regarded as less bright. The practice of compartmentalizing general education into academic, technical, commercial and agricultural knowledge and skills reduces the value of general education by divorcing theory from practice and from the understanding of real-life problems. Moreover, little consideration is given to non-formal and out-of-school education, which means that out-of-school youth and adults – the primary producers of wealth – have little opportunity to increase their skills in order to make a bigger contribution to development.

The Commission made recommendations aimed at bridging the gap between academic and vocational education and the world of work through the vocationalization of primary and secondary education, and an increased stress on non-formal education programmes and schemes of community service for school leavers and university students.

The proposed structure also recognizes that vocational and practical education to the highest level possible is as worthy as and more urgently needed than theoretical academic learning. At least one vocational secondary school should be established in each of Uganda's 33 districts, and technical vocational secondary education should not only cease to be terminal but should also provide students with diversified opportunities for further studies in their chosen vocational fields.

(3) *Improvement of the quality of education*   As already pointed out, the quality of Ugandan education has been declining gradually over the last 20 years, mainly because of the shortage of teachers, textbooks and other learning materials in schools and because of a type of examination system that only tests cognitive skills, particularly the memorization of information.

The improvement of the quality of education is considered urgent at all levels and is to be attained through better teacher training, the motivation and retention of teachers, the enhancement of facilities in schools (such as better availability of instructional materials), and improved examination and other evaluation procedures that take account of continuous assessment of pupils' performance in all areas, including practical skills. In other words, the level of a pupil's performance and success in school should not be measured, as is it now, merely in terms of how much theoretical knowledge she/he can reproduce, but also whether she/he has acquired some skills to apply that knowledge to real-life situations.

Educational reform during socio-economic crisis

THE PROPOSED STRUCTURE OF EDUCATION

The present structure of education consists of seven years of primary education (PLE) followed by a secondary cycle (UCE) of four years. This is followed by an upper secondary cycle (UACE) of two years, after which there are three to five years of university studies at Makerere University or the recently opened Mbarara University of Science and Technology.

On successful completion of the primary cycle pupils go either to the four-year academic secondary schools leading to the Uganda Certificate of Education (UCE) or take a three-year crafts course in technical schools (UJTC). However, only about 30 per cent of primary-school leavers are absorbed into these post-primary institutions. The rest either repeat or go out of the system as 'failures'. Those completing UCE have four possible outlets: the two-year Advanced Crafts Course in technical institutes, the two-year Grade III Primary Teachers Certificate Course, a two-year course in commercial schools, or a government department's training programme.

After completing the UACE course, students have a choice of a university course, a two-year course in a National Teachers College, a two-year course in the Uganda Polytechnical College, Kyambogo (PK), a course at the Uganda College of Business Studies, a course at the Institute of Teacher Education, Kyambogo (ITEK) or a two-year government departmental training course.

The proposed structure of education attempts to address some of the above-mentioned issues:

(1) *The basic cycle* There is a widespread feeling that pupils who leave the seven-year primary school at the tender age of 12–13 years are too young to apply what they have learnt at school to any socially or economically productive activity. Since the vast majority of those who see the inside of a school terminate at this level, it was argued that a primary cycle extended to nine or ten years would enable the youth to mature sufficiently to apply their school knowledge and skills to tasks of national development. Although a basic education cycle of nine or ten years would be desirable as a long-term goal, the economic constraints of Uganda dictate otherwise.

The proposed structure, however, lengthens the primary cycle from seven to eight years, which should have two distinct levels:

(a) Lower Primary (P 1 to P 4), where the medium of instruction should be the mother tongue of the child or the dominant local Ugandan language. An important aim of this level would be to impart permanent functional literacy, oracy and numeracy in a Ugandan language.

(b) Upper Primary (P 5 to P 8), where English becomes the medium

331

of instruction and the curriculum aims more at imparting practical skills that would be useful in the area where the school is located.

(2) *The secondary cycle*   At present, secondary education consists of four years of general studies leading to the UCE and two years of the advanced course leading to the UACE. Very little emphasis is placed on practical subjects, and most secondary schools are not even equipped to teach science. Most parents wish their children to go to boarding rather than day secondary schools.

Ideally, a multipurpose comprehensive type of secondary system should be established in Uganda. However, economic limitations and the difficulty of equipping all secondary schools adequately for a comprehensive type of curriculum dictate otherwise. It is proposed instead that:

(a) Ordinary level secondary education should be reduced from four years' to three years' duration and be offered in three types of schools: general secondary, vocational secondary, and comprehensive secondary schools. These would all offer courses leading to the Uganda Certificate of Education UCE (O-level).

(b) Advanced level of secondary education of two years' duration leading to the Uganda Advanced Certificate of Education (UACE).

(c) Vocational secondary education should not only cease to be terminal, but should also provide students with diversified opportunities for further studies leading to the highest possible levels in their chosen vocational fields.

(d) The existing boarding schools should continue, but total boarding costs should be borne by parents and all new government-aided secondary schools should be day schools.

(3) *Higher education*   Higher education is important, not only because of its role in the production of high-level manpower, but also because of its cost and the effect it has on the lower levels of the education system. The admission requirements, and the course structure of the university, for example, greatly determine the popularity and the importance attached to various subjects of study at the secondary level; and primary schools emphasize only what is considered important for admission to secondary school.

CONCLUSION

In conclusion it is necessary to rephrase the challenge: How can the basic needs of the people in a poor country like Uganda be met? How can the productive skills of the people be harnessed and increased through education, and appropriate technology be more effectively brought to rural areas? How can the notions of representative and participatory democracy, the sanctity of human life, the supremacy of law and order, the sanctity of the country's constitution and awareness of the rights and responsibilities of citizens best be taught to the people? And, above all, what is the best way of inspiring love for the country and creating a feeling of national identity among people of diverse ethnic origins who have been brought together only recently by colonial accident? How can limited funds tackle massive problems and make a difference?

We look up to education to provide the answers to these baffling questions. Reforming Uganda's education system significantly will demand not only vast financial resources, both national and international, but also considerable political commitment to ensure the human resources and other inputs needed to change the system. Political decisions will be needed, for example, to devolve certain levels of the education to local responsibility and to institute measures for cost-sharing so as to democratize the system as it changes from the inherited elitist patterns to the new model.

Equally important will be the need for improvement in non-monetary inputs, such as creative planning, efficient administration, creation of a climate of sustained hard work, and the motivation of teachers and other educational workers to dedicate their services to education. A new ethos is also needed among the students to accept responsibility for their own learning so as to be willing to give as well as to receive, instead of expecting to be dependent all the time.

PART NINE
GETTING UGANDANS
TO SPEAK A COMMON LANGUAGE

TWENTY-THREE
Recent developments in the language situation
and prospects for the future

Ruth G. Mukama

Two incidents involving linguistically motivated misunderstandings emerge distinctly in my mind as I write this chapter. One took place in a bus travelling from Kampala to Jinja on 14 October 1988. A dispute ensued over payment of the fare between the bus conductor, who was speaking only Luganda, and a passenger who apparently did not understand that language. The incensed conductor finally pushed the passenger out of the bus shouting: 'Fuluma, tulabye n'Abacholi!' (Get out, we are tired of the Acholi!). The passenger was equally infuriated. He hired a taxi to the next police station to file a case against the 'tribalistic bus conductor'. The bus journey came to an end at the police station as the conductor was escorted to a cell to await the charges.

The second incident occurred on 12 July 1989 in one of the city taxis that commutes between Wandegeya and the city park. The conductor also asked for the fares in Luganda. All the passengers paid except for one in the back seat who simply sat mute, despite the fact that the conductor repeatedly called out to him to pay his fare. He finally responded angrily in Swahili, asking why the conductor should assume that every commuter was Luganda-speaking.

One may wonder if such incidents are merely isolated coincidental reactions rather than symptoms of a linguistic malaise that has become one of the most intractable barriers to national unity and growth. The primary thesis of this chapter is that those and related linguistic contentions are at the heart of the old language problem in Uganda. This characterized official language use and policy at the beginning of the century and is apparently still very live today. It is a problem that has led directly to the continued language policy void in the country. The crux of the language issue is still the problem of the position of Luganda *vis-à-vis* the other indigenous languages on the one hand, and Luganda *vis-à-vis* Swahili on the other. The only historical difference is that the Luganda advancement crusade that was originally led by the European missionaries is now solely spearheaded by Baganda activists themselves.[1] Language policy will therefore have to address the problem of the interrelationship between Luganda and other indigenous languages,

Luganda and Swahili, or even between Luganda and English.

Uganda meanwhile stands out distinctly in East and Central Africa as a country without a common grassroots language for mass inter-ethnic communication. It is also probably alone in Africa in not having a precise language policy. Official communication with the masses is consequently impeded and largely ineffectual. Yet in addition to English, Uganda needs to cultivate a common language for mass communication. After outlining the recent developments in the language situation and analysing the envisaged prospects, this chapter notes some of the undesirable consequences of the imbalances in current language development and use. Finally, some of the misconceptions present in the current language situation are pointed out, and the case for the teaching of Swahili is argued.

RECENT DEVELOPMENTS

English

There is a poignant dearth of research on the use and teaching of English in schools in Uganda. To date, there is no proper English syllabus for secondary schools. The document of reference that serves as the syllabus is still the booklet entitled 'English in Secondary Schools', which was produced by the Ministry of Education Inspectorate in May 1967.[2] This offers advice, but leaves the individual English teacher to establish his own course aims. There is therefore bound to be great variability of aims from school to school, contrary to the usual claim of ministries of education that the aims of education are a national concern.[3]

The variability of teaching aims becomes an even more serious problem considering that in 1971 there were 'still more than 8,000 Grade 1 and unqualified teachers in Uganda'.[4] Thus the majority of teachers who teach English, both in training colleges and in schools, are in fact not qualified to teach it. That is why they simply reproduce verbatim whatever textbook serves as the basis for teaching, thereby behaving like 'technicians' who are 'content to show how rather than explain why'. Certainly, 'this kind of teaching is not producing the type of learning which is so necessary for subject matter mastery, nor can it be said to be serving the purpose of strengthening the use of English'.[5]

Indeed, scholarly acumen was progressively dampened from the early 1970s and was at its nadir in the early 1980s. Yet despite the very serious problems that have decreased the efficiency of teaching English and hindered its use as the major means of instruction in schools, English is the language that has received most official attention from the Ministry of Education. In 1983, for instance, there was an attempt to introduce a proper English syllabus for secondary schools. A document entitled 'The Integrated English Course' was prepared for the purpose and was discussed by teachers and all teaching institutions concerned with the English language. One of the novel elements in the new document was the introduction of the requirement for wider reading. The other was the total elimination of overt linguistic or grammatical explanations in the teaching of English. After preliminary discussions and experimental lessons in some schools the document was shelved indefinitely. But although the attempt was not very successful it showed that the Curriculum Development Centre is at least concerned about the teaching and learning of English. There has in fact been some marked improvement in the last five years. In 1984 Makerere University introduced special BA/BSc with Education programmes designed to speed up the provision of teaching personnel for secondary schools and colleges. On average 60 teachers of English graduate in the BA with Education programme. The number increases when we add about 40 BA graduates who take the diploma course in teaching after successful completion of the general degree programmes. The situation is bound to be even better now that Kyambongo Teacher Training College has also launched a BEd programme for teachers with long teaching experience.

The last two years have also seen an active revival of the involvement of the British Council in efforts to uplift the standard of teaching and use of English. Expatriate teachers of English are in schools in substantial numbers again and experienced trainers of teachers of English are now available to the teacher training colleges and Makerere University on either direct British Council sponsorship or through programmes arranged by it. It has also started funding in-service courses for teachers of English.

Swahili

Swahili has also persisted on the language scene. A situation in which a language that is banned from schools is examined both at ordinary and advanced levels of formal education may seem unimaginable, but this is the case in Uganda with regard to Swahili.[6] There is as yet no definite official policy on the language and one wonders why it is still examined. Every year between three and six private candidates register and sit the examinations, only to get below-average grades. The poor examination results are to be expected since the candidates have to teach themselves, and there is not a single bookshop in the country that stocks Kiswahili books. However, since 1986 there have been semi-official and unofficial overtures towards the language.

From 11–13 July 1986 President Museveni paid a three-day state visit to Tanzania. And on 13 July 1986, both Radio Uganda and Uganda Television reported in their news bulletins that among the items included in the joint communiqué issued by Presidents Mwinyi and Museveni was 'cooperation in the promotion of the Swahili language'. It now appears

Recent developments in the language situation

that the main evidence for this professed 'cooperation' is that Swahili is once again being formally taught by 'Tanzanian instructors' in army and police training camps, and in political schools, although it is not examined at the end of courses.[7] The other sign was the announcement by the Speaker of the National Resistance Council that Swahili was to be used alongside English in council discussions.[8]

Another notable development is the revival of the hitherto moribund Chama cha Kiswahili Uganda (Chaku – Uganda Swahili Association) which was founded in December 1984. The Association started on an ambitious note and objectives of the Association were high-sounding.[9] However, it soon became clear that the ambitious resolutions could not be carried out because of financial and spatial constraints. The Association gradually became inactive. Four years later, in December 1988, a general meeting of adherents of Kiswahili decided to reactivate it under a new executive committee that is promising to do wonders. In April 1989 a branch of the Association was opened in Makerere University, and in May a delegation of four top members of the executive was sponsored by an unnamed benefactor on a three-week visit to Tanzania to consult with institutions and bodies concerned with the development or teaching of Swahili.[10] The delegation returned home with a large consignment of books for use in the voluntary Swahili classes that were planned to begin in August 1989. And with due commendation to the seriousness of Chaku, the voluntary classes did start with 48 students: 45 Ugandans and 3 foreign diplomats.

The composition of the Ugandan learners is of considerable interest. It includes university lecturers, medical doctors, lawyers, business entrepreneurs, civil servants, clerical staff and other workers. The learners are divided into beginners' and intermediate groups. Chaku's long-term plan is to start such classes in different workplaces in Kampala and possibly throughout the country.[11] The lessons are not free of charge, so numbers of learners are bound to remain small.

Luganda

The team that researched the language situation in Uganda between 1968 and 1970 concluded that 39 per cent of Ugandans could hold a conversation in Luganda. Of these, 16 per cent are native speakers, and 23 per cent speak Luganda as a second language.[12] Compared with English, which is spoken by 21 per cent, and Swahili, spoken by 35 per cent,[13] Luganda is certainly understood by more people. The predominance of Luganda has been explained in terms of economic and political factors.

As Gertzel has pointed out: 'Uganda's historically determined uneven development', which placed Buganda in a very advantageous position, is well known. 'Uganda's economic heartland' is the 'axial belt from

Iganga to Masaka' in the south. 'It was in that region, and above all in Buganda, that the greatest economic activity in the modern sector had developed by the early 1960s.' Further, 'the capitalist class was concentrated in the early sixties in the south and especially in Buganda'.[14] Nsibambi has noted in addition that historically, 'the economic and educational opportunities . . . were concentrated in Buganda'.[15] As a result, the Buganda region attracted many itinerant workers from all over Uganda who learnt Luganda in the process.

And with regard to political power, it has been explained that Buganda's favourable position 'may be traced to the domination of Baganda evangelists and government agents during the early years of this century'.[16] The British rulers depended greatly on Baganda agents to administer other parts of Uganda.

This led to the imposition of Luganda on the Eastern Province and Ankole. Parts of those areas still speak Luganda as a second language and use Luganda Bibles and prayerbooks although the language is no longer taught there as a subject as it was throughout the colonial period. Since the abolition of Buganda's political hegemony and special position in 1967,[17] the teaching and learning of Luganda as a subject have been confined to the Buganda region.

Nevertheless Luganda is still in a favourable position since it is the only indigenous language that is being developed and promoted at both an ethnic and a national level. A large number of Luganda teachers are now on the government payroll, since they are fully qualified as national teachers. All teacher training colleges and nearly all secondary schools in the Buganda region, both private and government ones, offer the language as a subject. In the past two to three years, the computer lists of applicants wishing to come to Makerere University show that more and more Baganda candidates, including those in science streams, are now coming to university propped up by good GCE grades in Luganda. Of these, 60–70 per cent find their way into the Department of Languages to pursue the degree course in Luganda. The latest development in the strategy to promote Luganda has been the formation of a 'Special Sub-Committee' of the Luganda Society 'to assist the graduates of the Luganda language to get jobs.'[18] And Luganda is the only Ugandan language that has a Language Panel at the Curriculum Development Centre in the Ministry of Education.

It would thus appear that the promoters of the Luganda language have a definite language planning scheme that has been married very well with an equally definite cultural planning framework.[19] Indeed, the two Luganda language clubs – the Luganda Language Society and the Luganda Academy – are doing very well in encouraging publication and research, now that they have found a home on William Street in Kampala.[20] The Luganda dictionary project is now in its final stages.

338

Recent developments in the language situation

And K.B. Kiingi, a renowned scholar, has spent the last ten years working on a project on 'the expansion and formation of scientific and technological terminology in Luganda.[21] Luganda is also very well placed in terms of mass media, Kampala being the seat of the national radio and TV stations and of the printing presses of all the newspapers. As is to be expected, Luganda still has the lion's share of radio time, just as was the case at independence in 1962.[22] In addition to Luganda dominance of news bulletins and government announcements, the Luganda Society also seems to have what amounts to an exclusive press unit within Radio Uganda, judging from the outsized coverage accorded to all its activities.

And there has been a marked increase in the number of Luganda singing groups put on the air, be they children's groups, choirs or traditional performers. At Easter and Christmas, for example, most of the carols are rendered in Luganda. The same applies to radio and TV theatre. And as far as 'personal announcements' are concerned one could easily assume that Radio Uganda is actually *Radio Buganda*. As one observer put it, 'the Baganda feel that they have to announce on radio even news about a hen which has laid an egg since the service is so easily accessible to them.' Further, five or so Luganda newspapers are now in circulation in Buganda. Luganda language activity is also booming in the performing arts. There are numerous musical and drama groups whose sole or main medium is the Luganda language. Even in the English-medium newspapers it is usual to find headings like: 'Ndere troupe takes off'; 'Omusajja Gyagenda' (where the man is going); 'Ndabye' (I have suffered) on 'Sports/Arts' or 'Theatre Review' pages. This is a clear sign that most theatre activity is now produced in the Luganda language, a view supported by the fact that the last three years have seen the mushrooming of three more theatres in Kampala alone, built by different Baganda musical/drama groups. Even the 'national theatre' in Kampala is dominated by the same performing groups. Upcountry performers find it very difficult to secure a booking at the theatre.[24]

Some agencies and some influential individuals have started working closely with the Luganda Language Society and Academy to spearhead the development of the language. The Cultural Foundation Agency in Kampala has donated equipment to the societies in the last three years. The Summer Institute of Linguistics based in Nairobi has also kept up active support. Executive members are invited to participate in workshops organized by the Institute every year and the Society is also given funds to hold at least two conferences/seminars every year. The UNESCO office in Kampala has also recently started throwing its weight on the side of Luganda. The project on 'the promotion and expansion of the activities of the Luganda language' submitted to the UNESCO workshop of May 1988 was highly recommended by the acting secretary-general and equally positive support was promised by the 'cultural expert'

Getting Ugandans to speak a common language

from UNESCO Headquarters in Paris.[25] The Swahili Association sought similar support from the office soon after its revival but was bluntly informed by the acting secretary-general herself that the Swahili language is 'repugnant' to the office and that UNESCO would have nothing to do with the activities of the Association.[26] Given this sort of background it is understandable that whenever a call is made for the adoption of a 'common indigenous' language it is Luganda that is being alluded to. For instance, at a workshop organized by the NRM Secretariat for church leaders in the first week of July 1989 one of the resolutions passed by the leaders was that 'an *indigenous* language should be one of the national languages of Uganda'. And while opening the Luganda Academy seminar on 20 August 1987, the Minister of Information, Abu Mayanja, said that 'lack of an indigenous *common* language has been cited as one of the major causes of backwardness and sectarianism.' Earlier the same year the Minister of Education, Mayanja-Nkangi, had made a similar allusion while opening a language seminar in Makerere University: 'Do Ugandans who are attending a football match, a wedding, or are sipping a beer in a bar, or etcetera have to speak to each other in English (Cases of sharing or knowing a *common indigenous* language excepted)?'[27]

Other languages

Among other languages that have featured markedly in recent developments is the group normally referred to as 'the Western-Bantu': Runyoro, Rutooro, Runyankore and Rukiga. In mid-1988 two members of staff of the Department of Language, Makerere University, went on a fact-finding tour to assess the viability, in terms of availability of teaching material, of starting a degree programme in these languages. They reported that there was a great deal of material being written by individual scholars who, however, felt that their work might 'not measure up to university standards'. It was also discovered that a number of schools and colleges in the region were teaching the languages, although these were not examined by the Uganda National Examinations Board (UNEB).[28] On the strength of the report the Department of Language went ahead and presented a proposal to the University Senate that a degree course in the languages should be started; this was duly approved.

French and German have also done very well in the last couple of years. French is offered by many schools all over the country. In addition to Makerere University and the Institute of Public Administration, Kampala, several teacher training and secretarial colleges also have French programmes. German is still restricted to the Buganda region. Besides the brisk degree and voluntary programmes at Makerere University, four other schools now offer the language.[29]

Recent developments in the language situation

Russian has also gained ground in recent years. The Russian Cultural Centre, Buganda Road, Kampala, is one of the busiest language teaching centres in the country.[30] Arabic has reappeared on the Ugandan language scene after a moribund period following the removal of Idi Amin from power. One school now has it on the curriculum and the Islamic University in Mbale offers courses. Moreover, UHEB has already entered it among the subjects examined by the Board.

COMMENTARY

None of the recent language activity discussed above is overtly fortified by a government policy statement. One may therefore wonder whether there is any likelihood that it can be sustained. Assuming that it can, the nature of its sustenance will be equally important.

Most activity will probably be restricted to Kampala in particular and the Buganda region in general, thus reinforcing the existing unevenness. Moreover, most Ugandans at the grass-roots level are likeliest to respond to matters that they consider to have been endorsed by the government. Any attempt to take a language to the people will therefore not go far without government backing.

Only the state machinery can adopt and implement a language policy that is functionally efficient and culturally integrative in a situation of an otherwise unmanageable diversity of languages, all serving minorities. And only the state machinery can ensure a reasonable degree of evenness in the teaching and use of the adopted language(s). For if one language group that is well placed with regard to economic and state amenities is left to advance itself along sectarian lines with its language as one of the key tools, then other groups will begin to see the policy of non-intervention as a way of advancing or maintaining the economic, social or political power of one group, rather than as an impartial strategy of national development.

THE FUTURE OF THE LANGUAGES

English

By virtue of its special position as the language of the former rulers, English enjoys the privilege of being the only 'foreign' language used officially in educational institutions and administrative transactions as well as in informal domains patronized by the educated elite. In terms of internationality and 'in the process of modernisation', English has no rival in our context. We need it to put us 'in contact with the world's technical and scientific information and knowledge which is so essential for economic development'.[31] And, as Khubchandani adds, by the time vernaculars have struggled towards acquiring the credibility of 'developed' languages, languages like English 'will have moved higher

341

with additional honours, such as usability with computers, or space satellites, and so on'.[32] And even on the social prestige front, the indigenous languages do not compete with English. For, as Todd remarks: 'The vernaculars . . . are used and loved and clung to, but French, English . . . are admired and respected. For most . . . parents and teachers they have a prestige which the vernaculars lack.'[33]

The main problems with English in our context are pedagogical. Among the issues we have to address is whether the school system can teach it well enough to sustain reasonable standards of mutual intelligibility. An even more serious question concerns its teachability to people outside schools to the extent of having the majority of nationals using it for national concerns. In short, although English will undoubtedly remain the paramount official language, Uganda, like most other African states, will find it difficult to pronounce it the national language. For as Ki-Zerbo notes, by using European languages we may be weakening our own, and 'to accept the death of African languages is to commit cultural suicide'.[34] Harries makes much the same observation with regard to Kenya.[35]

Swahili

The future of Swahili in Uganda is, to say the least, dim. It is unlikely that it will ever get back into schools without decisive government backing. Yet the school would be the ideal place for many Ugandans to be exposed to standard Swahili. It would also be learnt faster were it to be used as a medium of instruction, for it is a pedagogical truism that a language is most naturally acquired and developed when used as a medium for the study of other subjects. Club activity alone, even when backed by a powerful non-governmental sponsor, is bound to be ineffectual.[36] For, as Khubchandani notes; 'Isolated "language development" agencies cannot do justice to the complex needs of various speech communities.'[37]

Thus far the Uganda Swahili Association is not backed by any donor, so it is doubly disadvantaged. And the Tanzanian Bakita, with which the Association signed an agreement to co-operate, is just as short of money and manpower, so only moral support is to be expected from it. As far as university teachers are concerned, there is a tendency for Tanzanian and Ugandan Swahili specialists to go for the oil dollar by teaching Swahili in Arab countries, especially Libya and Egypt. Others are finding their way into the service of foreign radio stations all over the world. Rwanda also had to agree to top up in dollars salaries of Tanzanian teachers attached to its teacher training colleges. It is therefore unlikely that Uganda, which will not be prepared to part with inducement allowances in convertible currency for teaching Swahili, will attract any teachers. As a result, even the prospects of its continuing to be taught at university level are uncertain.[38]

Recent developments in the language situation

The use of Swahili alongside English in the National Resistance Council is also bound to be ineffective since members cannot be expected to use or comprehend a language they have never been given the chance to learn formally. And if we continue teaching Swahili only to the armed forces we will perpetuate institutional segregationism stemming from the use of different languages: standard Swahili for the forces, English for the elitist institutions, pidgin Swahili for group employees and traders, and the indigenous languages for the peasants. Mutual distrust amongst all groups is therefore certain to continue unabated.

Luganda

By contrast with the situation of Swahili, all is presently auguring well for the unlimited prosperity of Luganda culturally, educationally and for general use in the Buganda region. One might ask what is behind the recent impetus to propel Luganda upwards. A possible interpretation is that language is being 'utilised as a weapon in the power struggle'[39] that has characterized Ugandan politics since the mid-1960s. Because Baganda activists feel threatened economically and politically, it is likely that they are seeking, through their cultural and language campaigns, to consolidate and sustain their historical status and position. The other most likely cherished aim of the activists is to present Luganda as a fully fledged candidate for national language status. But it is highly doubtful whether the attempts to get Luganda accepted by all the regional language groups as a common language will ever be successful.[40] The underlying reasons for this are both sentimental and instrumental. Mayanja-Nkangi once equated the acceptability of a Ugandan language for a common language to other national commodities like wheat: 'We Ugandans will just have to learn not to reject Sebei wheat, for example for baking our loaves in preference for Kenyan wheat merely because the Sebei will feel transported and proud if other Ugandans eat Sebei bread.'[41] However, the reality is that as carriers of culture, languages are often deeply rooted in ethnic or social communities and cannot, therefore, be simply equated with other national commodities that have few or no emotive ties and can be distributed and received purely mechanically. As Finsman notes: 'Language planning is more difficult because it more centrally impinges upon human values, emotions and habits than does planning with respect to the production of tangible economic goods.'[42]

The various language groups are likely to resist the dominance and imposition of Luganda.[43] This, they feel, is certain to affect adversely the interests of their own languages. They also feel that this would give native speakers of Luganda even more educational, economic and political advantages over native speakers of other languages than they have already.[44]

343

Other languages

French, German, Russian and Arabic will continue to have unlimited prospects of expansion as long as they are fully backed by interested foreign governments. But if left to fend for themselves they will suffer the same neglect as most of the other languages. For as Finsman has also observed, many government plans 'are more declarations of government goals, intended to inspire or motivate internally and to attract foreign financial assistance, than they are strategies for actions.'[45]

The Western-Bantu languages will certainly need all the assistance in their uphill rise to full appreciation and recognition. Otherwise, they will not get far.

THE LOGICAL SEQUEL

Thus far the structural adjustment programme has not produced a language policy. But then, as Cooper has commented, 'language planning, like any national planning, rarely operates on the basis of rational considerations alone.'[46] Besides, as Kennedy advises, in the evaluation of language planning 'it is important to distinguish between real and stated goals. Quite often the policy-makers mask what their real goals are for quite obvious political reasons.'[47]

In our case the task is made simpler by there being no 'stated goals' to be distinguished from 'real' ones. But how does one begin to work out 'real' goals when there is almost no official language activity? All we can do is to make some assumptions. We assume, for instance, that English will remain the paramount official language since none of the indigenous languages has been encouraged to a level where it could successfully dislodge English either for international communication or for educational purposes at higher levels. The indigenous languages, which are the sole guardians of indigenous cultures, will also remain indispensable in that respect. And pidgin Swahili will continue to be loosely used as an urban and group employees' lingua franca. Finally, the foreign languages will always be welcome so as to attract the aid that follows linguistic accords.

Uganda may therefore never have a national language unless there is a real revolutionary change in the language situation. Lack of interest in language development is obviously a key factor in determining the flowering of some languages and the dwarfing of others. In the absence of a central language planning and development agency, only the economically powerful indigenous groups can afford to promote their own languages. The languages of the relatively poor ethnic groups are in turn doomed to remain at the rudimentary level, even if they are labelled 'official'. The other languages that are likely to flourish are those that come in the same packages with external funding.

344

Recent developments in the language situation

Left to this sort of fight-it-out-state of affairs, the situation will be most certainly rife with competitition among languages and rivalries among the users of the different languages. Further, the continued linguistic tussle will also lead to the perpetuation of communication gaps among different social groups: the English-speaking elite, deemed to be 'the custodians of language for development' will remain 'far removed from the common man's speech',[48] on the one hand, and on the other the English-speaking elitist professionals will remain above the Swahili-speaking group employees. Then the Swahili-speaking armed forces will always stay apart from the entire civilian population, which speaks diverse languages.

LANGUAGE USE: IMBALANCES AND UNEVEN ACHIEVEMENTS

Education: an epitomic example

The lists of admissions into Makerere University in the five years up to 1989 show that, on average, more than 60 per cent are speakers of Luganda as a first language, while speakers of the four major languages of the Western Region – Runyankore/Rukiga, Runyoro/Rutooro – as first languages normally make up more than 30 per cent. Speakers of the rest of the indigenous languages claim only 5–10 per cent of the intake.[49]

Obviously, since entry into good schools is still largely dependent on the economic and/or political power of one's parents, the politico-economic factor could be paramount in determining the educational dominance of Buganda, especially as some of the best schools are situated there.

However, the linguistic factor should also not be minimized. Luganda's literary tradition is impressive compared with that of other indigenous languages. For by 1929, Daudi Chwa was in a position to boast that 'the Luganda language has now developed'.[50] Ladefoged also notes that apart from English, 'Luganda is taught in more schools than any other language'.[51] The favourable teaching and learning situation for Luganda is no doubt helping Luganda-speakers to start their education on a firm footing in a mother tongue that is taught well and applied satisfactorily to the learning of other subjects. For the point that 'optimal development of talent' is 'latent through the full use of a mother tongue'[52] is quite pertinent. And, as Nadkarni further observes: 'The success of the educational system depends to a considerable extent on the efficiency of its language teaching programmes.'[53]

The grim reality of language neglect

Clearly the politico-economic sphere and the educational system should be among the priorities on any structural adjustment list. But, as shown, the neglected language factor could feature prominently in determining their progress, just as it can undermine many other well-intentioned reconstruction programmes.

Khubchandani cautions against the neglect of 'linguistic minorities':

> Failure to or slowness in responding to the sensitivities of linguistic minorities, possibly because these minorities' representation in regional politics tends to be relatively low, and also their socio-economic development has been slower than that of the dominant groups, can lead to gross inequalities in national development.[54]

And 'gross inequalities in national development' in turn lead a nation into 'serious problems in relation to national integration',[55] particularly when the 'minorities' form the majority in sum total. We might succeed in restructuring the economic, educational as well as the political systems, but we have to realize that such restructuring will be only a small part of the push towards national unity. Language is, and will remain, the major weapon.

WILL LINGUISTIC ILLUSIONS AND UNCERTAINTIES CONTINUE?

Deciding on a language policy in conflict-prone Uganda is proving to be very difficult and precarious. For the delicate balance between stability and instability can easily deteriorate into ethnic strife if an unfavourable language policy is imposed. But while the warring situation may be endemic to Uganda the problem of language diversity is pandemic.

And Uganda might derive some comfort from Wallwork's observation:

> There can be no 'normal' solution to any nation's language planning difficulties; each county has to make decisions based on its own circumstances, and no decision is going to be 'right' for every individual in that country; the best that can be hoped for is to ameliorate, so far as possible, the difficulties for as many individuals as possible.[56]

The language situation in Uganda may then be left as it is: chaotically uneven with its attendant 'crisis of uneven development'. But we must clarify what is meant by 'leaving the situation as it is'.

The Report of the Education Policy Review Commission, for instance, refers endlessly to 'the area Ugandan language(s)', which are to be taught at all levels of education.[57] It is quite improbable that any of the commissioners ever queried what is actually meant by 'area language' in Uganda. Of course one may easily say that the term refers to those indigenous languages that are specified as media of instruction in the primary schools: Luganda, Akarimojong/Ateso, Lugbara, Lwo, Runyoro/Rutooro, and Runyankore/Rukiga.[58] Maybe with the exception of Runyoro/Rutooro and Runyankore/Rukiga, which are deemed

346

to have been one language before political events put them apart,[59] the other 'area' languages bore no known historical affinity to the languages over which they were 'imposed'. For instance, the linkage between Akarimojong and Ateso is quite incomprehensible. Does it really mean that there is a possibility of choosing to use either of these languages throughout the Teso and Karamoja area? The realities certainly militate against the conjecture. And historically, Luganda was the 'area' language of the rest of the Eastern Region. But now there is no single school that uses Luganda as a medium of instruction or teaches Luganda as a subject in Bugisu or Bukedi districts. Possibly some schools in Busoga may still be using Luganda, but a number of language societies have also recently sprung up with the aim of developing the Lusoga language.[60] So Luganda is no longer an area language, as was the case in the past. As for Lwo, it simply does not exist as a language. Our investigations have shown that the Acholi use different textbooks from those used by the Langi. The Alur have also started writing their own.[61] And what books will the Kumam use if they do not write their own? And is Lugbara in effective use in the rest of the West Nile district when the Kakwa claim that 'the majority of them do not understand Lugbara'?[62] It is clear that most of the reputed area languages are in reality not in effective use in the respective prescribed zones while others simply do not exist as linguistic systems.

Language policy makers in Uganda should therefore take note that the historical phenomenon dubbed 'area language' does not actually exist in Uganda today. A good indicator is the number of languages that are broadcast on radio – they are now 25 out of the 30 distinct languages.[63] Educational planners should therefore realistically budget for the development of most of the indigenous languages for use at the 'lower primary state . . . P1 to P4 grades'.[64] Where that is not possible the recourse would have to be English or Swahili.

The other point that language policy makers in Uganda have to bear in mind is that the Ugandan cultural/linguistic situation simply cannot be compared to largely unilingual situations such as those in the Netherlands, Lesotho, Botswana, Swaziland, Rwanda, Somalia, Egypt and so on, or even to the situation in countries such as Zimbabwe which have at least one indigenous language as the mother tongue of the majority of the population. Those countries have no problem in developing their God-given and government-endorsed national languages. 'Uganda . . . is a nation of minorities.'[65] It has no one indigenous language that is naturally spoken by a clear majority of the population. In the circumstances, the imposition of one minority language over the other minorities is bound to aggravate the resultant perpetually seething animosities.

Looking at all available language options in Uganda today, Swahili is then the only logical proposition for a lingua franca for grassroots inter-ethnic communication. And policy makers would be well advised to make provisions to start developing and promoting it for this purpose immediately. In this regard, the 1952 policy decision by the Ministry of Education to exclude Swahili from Uganda schools should be reversed so that schools may resume teaching it.[66] Uganda definitely needs the language, not only for mass inter-ethnic communication but also for regional harmony. Besides, it is a human right for the Ugandan population to be given the opportunity and the facilities to learn a language spoken by the majority of their neighbours.

Finally, the crucial point to note is that language development is inevitably an aspect of social change. And as social change is centrally organized and controlled, language change should also be similarly exposed to organized efforts.[67]

Notes

---

1. For details regarding the missionary factor and the Luganda syndrome in the quest for a language policy in Uganda see Hansen, 1984, chs 21, 22; Lulua, 1976, p. 7, and chs 6, 7. Refer also to the debates in mass media and radio on Luganda versus Swahili, which preceded Amin's national language decree of 7 August 1973.
2. See 'English in Secondary Schools', p. 1.
3. Ladefoged *et al.*, 1971, p. 96.
4. *ibid.*, p. 142.
5. *ibid.*, p. 105.
6. The ban was enacted in an 'important language policy decision of 1952' by which it was announced that 'Swahili was no longer a recognized vernacular in Uganda schools, with the exception of the schools for police and their children' (Ladefoged *et al.*, 1971, p. 9). Naturally the police force also could not maintain a language that was banned from other schools. The recommendation which was later made by the East Africa Commission Report of 1953–5 was subsequently adopted:

   > The last thing that is desirable is a police force using a language different from the people among whom it works. We think that the language of instruction in the police schools should be assimilated to that taught in other schools' (Quoted in Lulua, 1976, ch. 14, p. 11)

7. Personal consultations with those who have passed out of the schools.
8. *Star* newspaper (Kampala), 22 January 1988.
9. *Chama cha Kiswahili Uganda*, first draft constitution, 1984.
10. *Daily News* newspaper (Dar es Salaam), 20 May 1989.
11. Informal conversation with the Secretary of the revived Association, an official at the Directorate of Cultural Affairs, National Resistance Movement Secretariat. I have also paid several visits to the premises where the classes are conducted.

12. Ladefoged *et al.* 1971, pp. 24–5.
13. *ibid.*
14. Gertzel, 1988, pp. 4–5.
15. Nsibambi, 1969, p. 200.
16. Lulua, 1976, ch. 17, p. 12.
17. Nsibambi, 1969, p. 201.
18. An item in the news bulletin on Radio Uganda on 30 July 1989, following the meeting held at Makerere University on 29 July 1989 by the Executive Committee of the Luganda Society for the undergraduates and graduates of the Luganda language.
19. 'Language planning has been defined as the organised pursuit of solutions to language problems' (Cooper, 1983, quoting Jernudd and Das Gupta, 1971, and Finsman, 1973.) And 'cultural planning deals with publications, works of art, scientific and scholarly inquiry, musical productions, theatrical production, film production and radio/TV production' (Finsman, 1983)
20. From 'a press release' of the Luganda Society, 25 July 1989, p. 1.
21. As of 1982–4 he was registered for a PhD. programme at the University of Nairobi, working on 'The expansion and formation of scientific terminology in Luganda', while teaching German at Goethe Institute, Nairobi (*Mwamko*, Journal of the Kiswahili Association of the University of Nairobi, Issue No. 2, May 1984, p. 85).
22. Dinwiddy, 1979, p. 3. observes that, 'At the time of Independence (1962) Uganda Radio broadcast in English and in four African languages of which Luganda was given more programme hours than any of the other languages, including English.'
23. *Ndere* is a name of a type of musical instrument in Luganda.
24. An official from the Ministry of Culture presented a write-up to the UNESCO projects workshop which was held in May 1988 seeking a fund to assist upcountry performing groups to raise their standards and to be able to maintain themselves in Kampala while awaiting their turns in the National Theatre.
25. Information obtained through personal participation in the workshop.
26. Personal interview with the Secretary, Uganda Swahili Association, 18 July 1989.
27. The report of the language seminar which took place 16–20 March 1987 in the Department of Languages, Makerere University, p. 15. Emphasis added.
28. Reported by Dr O. Ndoleriire and Mrs S. Byakutaga.
29. News bulletin, Uganda Television, 2 July 1989.
30. From a letter dated 15 July 1989, from the office of the Commercial Counsellor, Embassy of USSR in Uganda.
31. Nadkarni, 1983, p. 153.
32. Khubchandani, 1983, p. 99.
33. Tedd, 1983, p. 170.
34. Ki-Zerbo, 1982, p. 67.
35. 'The political decision to opt for English as the national language would be tantamount to making a public declaration in favour of what is foreign . . . To make Swahili the national language is to make a political declaration in favour of what is African . . .' (Harries, 1983, p. 120).
36. The Kenya Kiswahili Association, for example, is supported generously by the Goethe Institute and that is how it has been able to produce some publications and to host Kiswahili International Conferences every four years. Yet the activities of the Association by themselves would not have gone far into promoting the use and teaching of Swahili in Kenya if the politicians and the Ministry of Education had not also joined in the endeavour.
37. Khubchandani, 1983, p. 107
38. Information obtained in the course of our vain effort to recruit some lecturers in Swahili for the Department of Languages, Makerere University, since 1988.
39. Khubchandani, 1983, p. 102.

40. One of the findings registered by Ladefoged *et al.* (1971, p. 29) is that 'it was clear that people living outside Buganda would be most unwilling to have Luganda as a national language'.
41. Nkangi, p. 15.
42. Finsman, 1983, p. 49.
43. As argued in Mukama, 1987, 1988, 1989.
44. Contributions from the floor to a public lecture on the National Language Issue given on 16 March 1988 at the Police Officers' Mess, Kampala.
45. Finsman, 1983, p. 52.
46. Cooper, 1983, p. 19.
47. Kennedy, 1983, p. 8.
48. Harries, 1983, p. 108.
49. Informal consultations with the Senior Assistant Registrar, Admissions, 20th July 1989.
50. In the Memorandum which was published in *Uganda News* on 22 February 1929 by Mr Stirman.
51. Ladefoged *et al.*, p. 97
52. Khubchandani, 1984, p. 102.
53. Nadkarni, 1983, p. 153.
54. Khubchandani, 1984, p. 103.
55. *ibid.*, p. 106.
56. Wallwork, 1978, p. 157.
57. Ministry of Education, January 1989.
58. Ministry of Education, 1963, 1965.
59. Ndoleriire, November 1987.
60. For instance The Lusoga Language Society, based in Iganga, and the *Abasoga Baino* Cultural Society ('Your Fellow Basoga' Cultural Society).
61. Students' comparative projects, Department of Languages, Makerere University.
62. Nsibambi, 1969, p. 196.
63. Ladefoged, *et al.*, 1971, pp. 16, 83, estimate that there are 30 distinct languages.
64. Education Report, 1989, p. 23.
65. Hooper & Pirouet, 1989, p. 3.
66. See Ladefoged *et al.*, 1971, p. 91.
67. Finsman, 1983, p. 43.

PART TEN

PROBLEMS OF GENDER AND INCULTURATION WITHIN A WIDER CONTEXT

TWENTY-FOUR
Privatization versus the market: cultural contradictions in structural adjustment

Ali A. Mazrui

By 1990 more than 30 African countries had submitted to structural adjustment, usually under pressure from the International Monetary Fund (IMF) and the World Bank.[1] In the 1980s Africa had become particularly fragile and subject to pressure. A number of relevant commodity markets – such as coffee, copper and cocoa – had virtually collapsed. Oil prices were causing disruptions, both when they were high and when there was an oil glut. Access to foreign exchange had declined dramatically for Africa. Population growth was at an all-time high, and food production was nowhere near keeping pace. Africa entered the 1990s with very limited options.

And now options for African governments have narrowed further because donors coordinate with each other much better than they used to. Africa used to be able to play one rich country against another. This has become extremely difficult now because there is considerable concentration and coordination among the rich. One widespread worry about the rapprochement between the Soviet Union and the USA is that this will have an adverse impact on options for the Third World. While rapprochement between the Soviet Union and the USA is good news for peace, it may be bad news for important areas of North–South relations, including the economic domain. Resources may be diverted within the Western world more and more towards the *Second* World. Herr Genscher's call for a Marshall Plan for socialist countries may be just the first clarion call. People are getting bored with aiding Africa and are being inspired afresh by opportunities of aiding Eastern Europe.

The socialist countries themselves in turn are more likely to address domestic problems with their resources than aid liberation movements in distant Southern Africa. Soviet resources may increasingly move towards Soviet Asia rather than towards supporting Third World causes. The impact of the rapprochement between East and West in the economic field is initially bound to be at the expense of the Third World.

The structural adjustment demands are made worse by the debt trap. Now Africa owes more than US$230 billion, 40 per cent of which has nothing to do with what Africa borrowed in the first place. The burden

351

has risen because of changes in exchange rates, rising interest rates, etc. And country by country Africa has turned to structural adjustment in pursuit of balanced budgets, balanced terms of trade, making imports more expensive, making exports less expensive, reducing budgets for welfare and social services, reducing the heavy weight of the bureaucracy, responding to the price mechanism more efficiently, motivating producers etc. These, as elements in the definition of structural adjustment, affect not just Uganda, but of course all African countries.

On top of all these burdens, most of the debates about African policy options fail to draw a simple distinction between restoring African economies to market forces and entrusting them to private ownership and private control. It is true that liberal doctrine, at least since Adam Smith, has tended to assume that the market comes into relatively independent play when the pursuit of wealth is left to private initiative. What we now call *privatization* was deemed to be the only viable approach to the triumph of the market. Privatization was the means; *marketization* was the end.

But in reality an economy could be in private hands and not be subject to the free market. Or it could be under state-ownership and still respond to market forces and to the laws of supply and demand. This chapter will address these particular contradictions.

The imperatives of restructuring African economies have all too often assumed that the only route to the free market is through privatization. Indeed, economic reformers concerned with Africa have equated privatization with marketization. Is it time to take another look? In this chapter we examine Uganda as part of the wider experience of sub-Saharan Africa as a whole. Our agenda is about how privatization can often clash with the market. What are the implications of that particular clash?

THE PROFIT MOTIVE VS. THE PRESTIGE MOTIVE

The free market in Africa can be constrained or inhibited by a number of factors that have very little to do with the state *per se*. A notorious inhibition on the free market in Africa is the simple fact that the whole market can be cornered or monopolized by an ethnic group. Africa has not yet discovered 'ethnic Anti-Trust Laws' to prevent or break-up 'tribal monopolies' in certain key industries. Nigeria underwent the trauma of a civil war partly because the Igbo had been perceived in the North as monopolizing certain areas of economic activity – and the nation had no 'anti-Trust legislation' for dealing with ethnic specialization and monopoly.

In Uganda Idi Amin in 1972 tried to break Asian commercial monopolies by expelling the Asians completely. But Amin replaced Asian nepotism with Nubi nepotism in the economy. Other ethnic groups in Uganda have similarly distorted the market in a nepotistic way.

352

Privatization versus the market

Unfortunately neither ethnic specialization nor counter-ethnic resentment have ended in either Uganda or Nigeria. The ethnicized market is the rule. Certain entrepreneurial groups in both countries are a little too visible for their own safety in certain areas of trade and industry.

Since the mid-1970s in Nigeria there has been more recognition of the need for ethnic 'anti-Trust legislation' to prevent or to break up 'tribal monopolies'. Sometimes the euphemism for this discrimination in favour of the disadvantaged is called 'the federal character of Nigeria'. This is Nigeria's nearest equivalent to the principle of affirmative action in the USA. But in both countries the restoration of ethnic balance is rather haphazard and sometimes in conflict with other democratic values.

Plateau State in Nigeria built what was reputed to be the largest marketing structure in Black Africa. The head of state came to open it. Yet for a long time the building was left hauntingly empty in a desperate struggle to ensure that when it was indeed finally utilized the majority of the owners of stalls and the merchants would be 'indigenes' of Plateau State (and not 'immigrants' from other parts of Nigeria). The precautions to prevent a 'southern monopoly' of the market were successful at the beginning. But, as so often happens, the process of a southern 'take-over' through deepening penetration has since got under way.

But is not Igbo success in certain economic activities or Ganda success in Ugandan trade a case of the free market finding its own equilibrium of efficiency? This would partly depend upon whether Igbo or Baganda preponderance is due to the unencumbered free play of relevant market factors. But in reality there is devout ethnic solidarity and nepotism at play, and these ensure the success of some fellow ethnic entrepreneurs and severely handicap the efforts of others. The considerations of Igbo monopoly in the trade in car parts and other spare parts are not all rational elements of Igbo efficiency. Baganda success in Uganda includes as one of its pillars Baganda nepotism. The same is true of Kikuyu success in Kenya in the late 1960s and 1970s.

In addition to ethnic nepotism as a constraint on the market in spite of privatization, there is also the all-pervasive constraint of the prestige motive in Africa's economic behaviour. Traditional Western liberal doctrine had often taken for granted the psychology of the profit motive (what was later identified as the maximization of returns). African economic behaviour, on the other hand, is more often inspired by the pursuit of prestige than by the quest for profit. Precisely because African cultures are more collectivist, members of the society are more sensitive to the approval and disapproval of the collectivity.

On the positive side, the prestige motive serves as a device of income distribution. Those who are financially successful often desire renown for generosity. Obligations towards wider and wider circles of kinsfolk are fulfilled. Word gets around to relatives far and wide – 'Our son has

353

killed an elephant. There is more than enough meat for us all to chop'. Those who succeed share their rewards with many others.

Kenya has also used the prestige motive to encourage competitive philanthropy. Funds are raised publicly under the slogan of *Harambee* ('Let us pull together'). The funds are raised for such charitable causes as building new schools and clinics. Citizens announce their contributions with a flourish and ostentation. Rich politicians try to outdo each other in philanthropic performance. Competitive and ostentatious philanthropy takes other forms in Uganda.

On the negative side, the prestige motive in African economic behavior encourages ostentatious consumption and self-indulgent exhibitionism. The Mercedes-Benz has become the symbol of Africa's ostentatious indulgence – but the expensive fleet of cars in Nigeria often goes with a palace or two, sometimes a private plane and a helicopter, and a loud way of life, all for a single family!

While the profit motive in classical economic theory was supposed to lean towards greater production, the prestige motive in contemporary African economic behaviour leans towards greater consumption.

What is more, the consumer products commanding the most prestige are often imported and require foreign exchange. Privatization on its own does not make an African economy produce more. The prestige motive operates both privately and at the state level, ominously eating away at the resources of the country. Structural adjustment is severely constrained by cultural forces.

When Westerners call upon African countries to privatize, they are expecting the profit motive to be given free play. But in fact in most of Africa the problem is not simply how to liberate and activate the profit motive, but also how to control and restrain the prestige motive. Arguably the latter crusade is more urgent than the former even in impoverished Uganda.

Indeed the ultimate crusade may well turn out to be how to tap the prestige motive in such a way that it serves the goals of production and not merely the appetites of consumption. Can we make creativity more prestigious than acquisition? Can we make production more prestigious than possession? Should we take a closer look at the problem of incentives in Uganda? How can we be more precisely sensitized to the Ugandan equilibrium between prestige and profit?

A third major private constraint on the market (after ethnic nepotism and the prestige motive) is the general problem of bribery and corruption prevalent in postcolonial Uganda and elsewhere. Corruption can clog up procedures and substantially paralyse production and distribution. Again corruption can be both in the public sector and in the private; it can be bureaucratic or omnipresent. Privatization of the economy may simply mean the privatization of corruption – and sometimes this is

354

more contagious in the wider society than the corruption of officials and bureaucrats.

In order to combat elitism on one side and corruption on the other, Julius K. Nyerere attempted to control both the prestige motive and the profit motive in postcolonial Tanzania. The Arusha Declaration of 1967 was in part a proclamation of a code of conduct. The Leadership Code restrained office holders in government or party from owning more than one house, or having more than one livelihood.

The President himself played down the grandeur of his office. Nyerere retained the affectionate title of *Mwalimu* (or 'Teacher') and preferred the alternative title of *Ndugu* ('Brother') rather than the presidential 'His Excellency' used elsewhere in Africa. There was less pomp and ceremony about the head of state in Tanzania than almost anywhere else in the world. And there was certainly less of a personality cult in Dar es Salaam than in any other African capital.

Under both Nyerere and his successor, Ali Hassan Mwinyi, there is more personal humility in Tanzanian political culture than the average on the African continent. The traditional prestige motive has been restrained from exploding into excessive postcolonial ostentation. The very term *wabenzi* (the tribe of the Mercedes-Benz) was invented in Tanzania as an expression of social criticism at the expense of Africa's new elites.

On the other hand, the profit motive was struggling to assert itself in the country, partly under the demonstration impact of neighbouring Kenya, and partly under the wider stimulus of international capitalism at large. The legacy of Nyerere was triumphant in disciplining the prestige motive but seemed unable to stifle the profit urge.

Tanzania's struggle against the prestige motive has been helped by its language policy. Tanzania is one of the handful of African countries that decided to use an indigenous language as the main medium of national business. Elsewhere in Africa the prestige motive has often found fulfillment in a display of European oratory. Ostentatious command of European languages has often been one route towards political prominence or social status.

Nyerere's Tanzania decided to promote Kiswahili as the national language instead. Eloquence in an African language was given value and social importance. Opportunities for exhibitionism in the use of the English language were far fewer in Tanzania than in neighbouring Uganda and Kenya. The total effect in Tanzania was a significantly reduced arena for the gratification of the prestige motive. The symbols of imperial status have still played less of a role in the ranking order of Tanzania than they have in most other parts of the postcolonial world.

Perhaps the most flamboyant manifestations of the prestige motive in Africa are to be found in Nigeria. Pronounced consciousness of status has often resulted in the ostentatious display of educational attainments as well as in elaborate exhibitions of high consumption patterns. There was a catastrophic depletion of Nigeria's oil wealth in the decade 1973 to 1983 (from the rise of the Organization of Petroleum Exporting Countries to the fall of President Al-Haji Shehu Shagari). The two principle causes were rampant corruption and unrestrained consumption.

And yet one of Nigeria's most fascinating paradoxes has been its capacity to produce relatively self-denying and often self-effacing heads of government and heads of state. This most flamboyant of all African countries has produced perhaps the most humble of all African heads of state – Yakubu Gowon, Nigeria's equivalent of Abraham Lincoln. Gowon saved the union after the agony of a civil war (1967–70). He showed immense magnanimity towards the defeated Biafran leaders after the war. It is true that although Gowon himself was not corrupt, he was too tolerant of corrupt subordinates.

What is more significant from the point of view of his humility was what happened after he was overthrown by his fellow soldiers in 1975. This former head of state of Africa's most populous (and most important) country decided to go back to school as an undergraduate. The idea of their former leader standing in line in a college cafeteria so outraged many Nigerians that they regarded Gowon's decision to attend a provincial British university as an insult to the national dignity of Nigeria. But Yakubu Gowon persevered as an undergraduate when only a few years previously he was being honoured by such a distinguished institution as Cambridge University in England with an honorary doctorate.

Nor did Gowon stop at the bachelor's degree. He struggled his way upwards towards a regular doctorate in political science from Warwick University. History may well decide that this modest Nigerian had two 'finest hours'. The first was when, as head of state, he was magnanimous towards his defeated Igbo compatriots after the Nigerian civil war. Gowon's second 'finest hour' was when, as a deposed head of state, he was humble enough to go back to school as an undergraduate. In Yakubu Gowon Africa's prestige motive had found its most restrained and disciplined exponent.

But Gowon was not the only self-effacing head of state or head of government that independent Nigeria has had. The first prime minister, Abubakar Tafawa Balewa, was also a man of relative humility. The last civilian president, Al-Haji Shehu Shagari, was similarly a modest leader in that flamboyant society.

As for the military heads of state since Gowon, Murtala Muhammed was by no means self-effacing. He was tough and charismatic. He waged a war against the rampant indulgence of the prestige motive and initiated a major crusade against corruption. However, Murtala did not last long.

He was assassinated after little more than six months of assuming power. His successor, Olusegun Obasanjo, was self-denying by Nigerian standards and apparently incorruptible. But he was not self-effacing.

General Muhammed Buhari, who captured power from Shagari, and General Ibrahim Babangida, who captured the reins from Buhari, followed in the tradition of relative honesty and disciplined lifestyle in a society still extraordinarily ostentatious and unruly. The prestige motive in Nigeria continues to be restrained in the lifestyle of the top man – but abundantly triumphant in most of the rest of the population.

Even in religiously conscious Uganda and Nigeria, capitalism has come without the Protestant ethic of work and frugality. Economically Protestantism was not against the acquisitive instinct; it was distrustful of the instinct to consume, especially indulgently. As a Puritan saying put it at the time of the Reformation, 'You may labour to be rich for God, though not for the flesh and sin'. Wealth was regarded as unethical only insofar as it was a temptation to idleness and sinful indulgence. The acquisition of wealth was only dangerous if it eroded the twin disciplines of work and frugality in the name of God.

Capitalism arrived in Uganda, Nigeria and elsewhere with the imperative of acquisition but without the discipline of work and frugality. The white man in Africa himself generally set a dangerous example. He never washed his own clothes, cooked his own food, polished his own shoes, made his own bed, cleaned his own room, washed his own dishes or even poured his own gin and tonic! The luxurious aristocratic life of white immigrants as they played masters to African servants was detrimental to the spirit of the capitalism the white man himself had arrived with. Africa's own prestige motive – which had been sociable in its original indigenous versions – was now transformed by the aristocratic lifestyles imported by the white man. Africa's prestige motive was given the colonial incarnation of expensive European consumer culture complete with huge houses, domestic servants and 'garden boys'.

If entrepreneurship simply meant acquisitiveness, this has now arrived in a big way in much of Africa. Indeed, those who do not take advantage of their opportunities to become wealthy, and to help their kinfolk, are sometimes despised.

The challenge is partly about the means used to acquire wealth. Is the wealth created, or simply obtained? Acquiring wealth from a prosperous farm is a creative process. Acquiring wealth as either a middleman on behalf of external interests or through corruption may not be creative at all. Can we transform the acquisitive instinct in Africa into something more directly productive? Yoweri Museveni has been worried about how to achieve such a transformation of skills in Uganda.

But if the means of acquiring wealth need to be creative, the ends of acquiring wealth also need to be healthy. Ostentatious consumption is not usually among the healthier ends of economic success. In short, African entrepreneurship needs a fundamental reform of both the means and the ends of the pursuit of wealth in society.

Until that happens, privatization of African economies – far from being the best way of achieving a healthy and free market – may itself be detrimental to the marketplace. For those who are sufficiently attentive, the African experience demonstrates that privatization is not necessarily the best protection for the free market in all cultures.

GENDER VERSUS THE MARKET

But so far perhaps the most private of all factors affecting production in Africa has been the role of women in society. Almost all governments on the continent have tried to steer clear of the sensitive issue of Africa's sexual division of labour. Perhaps only the regime of Siad Barre of Somalia was foolhardy enough to confront the cultural trustees of Somali Islam on the question of women's rights. So threatened was the regime by the conservative reaction of the religious leaders on that question that Siad Barre executed several of the mullahs, thus deepening the regime's own alienation from the people as a whole.

And yet in that very tragedy in Somalia lay one moral. Only the state in Africa is – when all is said and done – strong enough to make the necessary cultural readjustment on the gender question. Only the state can enable the market to benefit from fuller female participation in the economy. In Muslim Africa, Somalia is one of the places where progress has gone furthest in improving female participation even in the military. In Algeria – where state socialism has also been attempted with the strong hand of government power – women's rights have fallen short of the expectations of the revolution, but are still substantial in terms of public participation. Algeria even has women airplane pilots – a rather unusual situation in the Muslim world.

At the global level it may also be true that left-wing state intervention has done more to promote female participation in the economy than has privatization. Socialist countries in the northern hemisphere may not have achieved much more than capitalist ones in raising women to the pinnacles of power. Indeed, there is as yet no Communist equivalent of Margaret Thatcher or Golda Meir. But communist countries may have done more than capitalist ones to make women more economically active and productive. Command economies are managed by men as disproportionately as are economies under private ownership. But command economies are more evenly worked by both men and women at the level of ordinary proletarian roles. Moreover, state ownership in command economies reduces the disparities in property between men and women.

The three roles involved are, working the economy (operational), managing the economy (supervisory), and owning the economy

358

Privatization versus the market

(proprietary). Until recently in the West women's operational share (working the economy) was the smallest; their proprietary share (of ownership) was in some Western countries substantial. Their managerial share in the economy (supervisory) was somewhere in-between.

In Africa women's operational share (as workers of the agricultural economy) is in many countries greater than that of men. Women's managerial share (in terms of supervision and decision making) is high when the men have to go to towns or mines for wage labour. But women's share in ownership is perhaps the least developed outside Muslim Africa. Islam in Africa has tended to reduce the operational role of women (as workers) while increasing their proprietary role (as owners) under the *Shari'a*.

On the other hand, Westernization under the colonial impact has introduced its own changes affecting the role of women. Cultural traditions in matters of gender are among the most obstinate and impervious to change in any case. But blind social change when it does occur has its own hazards and unintended consequences. Privatization without state intervention can once again be detrimental to the workings of the market. After all, a true free market ought to be an androgynized market – a market not too severely encumbered by sexist discrimination.

In classical liberal doctrine the state is supposed to be a referee or arbiter rather than a player in the economic game. But does the gender question require so much state intervention that the distinction between refereeing and actual playing disappears? The road towards creating female entrepreneurs may not be through privatization but through intensive and purposeful state intervention. Cultural adjustment is not simply a case of changing the old order. It is also a case of being selective about the new economic and cultural order. Some new trends need to be arrested; others promoted. It is these wider issues of gender roles and cultural adjustment that we must now add.

In much of Black Africa – and most impressively in West Africa – women have traditionally been almost natural entrepreneurs. In addition to their triple trusteeship of catering, water supply and subsistence cultivation, women have also entered the arena of trade and marketing.

But more recently African women are becoming less and less entrepreneurial in response to four wider processes of social change. These processes are the enlargement of the scale of African economies, the internationalization of those economies, the mechanization of production, and the Westernization of supportive values and roles.

Ethno-economies and sub-regional marketing still allow considerable room for women. But as African patterns of production and exchange have become more integrated into national economies, the role of women in them has narrowed.

An even more marginalizing factor for the economic role of women has

359

been the internationalization of African trade and investment patterns. In spite of the new activism of Ugandan women in trading with Arabian Gulf countries, citizens who deal with transnational corporations are more likely to be men than women. Ugandans who sit on boards of directors or who manage international subsidiaries are more likely to be men than women. The same applies to Ugandans who control the Central Bank or who become advisers to the World Bank or the International Monetary Fund. Production of food crops for local markets still leaves women in control in many parts of Uganda. Production of cash crops for export tends to increase male dominance.

Advancing technology and complex organization in African economies are also likely to favour men. There is a cultural presumption against women as technicians or engineers. Women may be extensively involved in a tea plantation in picking the leaves, but not in planning the original planting of the bushes or handling the tractor.

As for the Westernization of supportive values, these range from rules of credit to the language of economic discourse. The problem is not simply whether a Ugandan man is more likely to get credit from a bank than a Ugandan woman. At least as basic is the fact that a Westernized Ugandan woman is much more likely to get credit than a non-Westernized female.

Let us look more closely at the cultural and historical background to this trend of declining female entrepreneurship.

GENDER ROLES IN TRANSITION

Africa since the colonial period has witnessed significant changes in the roles and functions of men and women in Africa. In many traditional cultures there has been a belief that God made woman the custodian of fire, water, and earth. God himself took charge of the fourth element of the universe – the omnipresent air.

Custody of fire entailed responsibility for making energy available. And the greatest source of energy in rural Africa is firewood. The African woman became disproportionately responsible for finding and carrying huge bundles of firewood, though quite often it was men who chopped down the big trees initially.

Custody of water involved a liquid that was a symbol of both survival and cleanliness. The African woman became responsible for ensuring that this critical substance was available for the family. She has trekked long distances to fetch water. But where a well needed to be dug, it was often the man who did the digging.

The custody of earth has been part of a doctrine of dual fertility. Woman ensures the survival of this generation by maintaining a central role in cultivation – and preserving the fertility of the soil. Woman ensures the arrival of the next generation in her role as mother – the fertility of the womb. Dual fertility becomes an aspect of the triple custodial role of African womanhood, though always in partnership with the African man.[2]

What has happened to this doctrine of triple custody in the period since 1935? Different elements of the colonial experience affected the roles of men and women in Africa in different ways.

Among the factors that increased the woman's role on the land was wage labour for the men. Faced with an African population reluctant to work for low wages for somebody else, colonial rulers had already experimented with both forced labour and taxation as a way of inducing Africans (especially men) to join the colonial work force.

According to Margaret Jean Hay, it took some time before wage labour for men began to affect women's role on the land. Hay's own work was among Luo women in Kenya:

> By 1930 a large number of men had left Kowe at least once for outside employment . . . More than half of this group stayed away for periods of fifteen years or more . . . This growing export of labor from the province might be thought to have increased the burden of agricultural work for women . . . As early as 1910, administrators lamented the fact that Nyanza was becoming the labor pool of the entire colony . . . Yet the short-term migrants of the 1920s were usually unmarried youths, who played a relatively minor role in the local economy beyond occasional herding and the conquest of cattle in war. Furthermore, the short-term labor migrants could and often did arrange to be away during the slack periods in the agriculture cycle . . . Thus labor migration in the period before 1930 actually removed little labor from the local economy and did not significantly alter the sexual division of labor.[3]

But Hay goes on to demonstrate how the Great Depression and the Second World War changed the situation as migrant labour and conscription of males took a bigger and bigger proportion of them away from the land. This was compounded by the growth of mining industries like the gold mining at Kowe from 1934 onwards:

> The long-term absence of men had an impact on the sexual division of labor, with women and children assuming a greater share of agricultural work than ever before . . . The thirties represent a transition with regard to the sexual division of labor, and it was clearly the women who bore the burden of the transition in rural areas.[4]

Women in this period, from the 1930s onwards, became more deeply involved as 'custodians of earth'. In Southern Africa the migrations of men to the mines became even more dramatic. By the 1950s a remarkable bifurcation was taking place in some Southern African societies – a division between a male proletariat (industrial working class) and a female peasantry. South Africa's regulations against families joining

361

their husbands on the mines exacerbated this tendency towards gender-apartheid, the segregation of the sexes. Many women in the frontline states had to fulfil their triple custodial role of fire, water, and earth in greater isolation than ever.

The wars of liberation in Southern Africa from the 1960s took their own toll on family stability and the traditional sexual division of labour. Some of the fighters did have their wives with them. Indeed, liberation armies like ZANLA and ZIPRA in Zimbabwe and Frelimo in Mozambique included a few female fighters. But on the whole the impact of the wars was disruptive of family life and of the traditional sexual division of labour.

After independence there were counter-revolutionary wars among some of the frontline states. The most artificial of the postcolonial wars was that initiated in Mozambique by the so-called Mozambique National Resistance (MNR or Renamo). The movement was originally created by reactionary white Rhodesians to punish Samora Machel for his support for Robert Mugabe's forces in Zimbabwe. After Zimbabwe's independence the Mozambique National Resistance became a surrogate army for reactionary whites in the Republic of South Africa – committing a variety of acts of sabotage against the fragile postcolonial economy of Mozambique.

Again, there have been implications for relations between the genders. In addition to the usual disruptive consequences of war for the family, by the mid-1980s the MNR had inflicted so much damage on the infrastructure in Mozambique that many migrant workers never got home to their families in between their contracts with the South African mines. The miners often remained on the border between South Africa and Mozambique, waiting for their next opportunity to go to the mines, without ever having found the transportation to get to their families in distant villages of Mozambique.

It is not completely clear how this situation has affected the doctrine of 'dual fertility' in relation to the role of the African woman. One possibility is that the extra long absences of the husbands have reduced fertility rates in some communities like Mozambique. The other scenario is that the pattern of migrant labour in Southern Africa generally has initiated a tendency towards *de facto* polyandry. The woman who is left behind acquires over time a *de facto* extra husband. The two husbands take their turn over time with the woman. The migrant labourer from the mines has conjugal priority between mining contracts if he does manage to get to the village. He also has prior claim to the new babies unless agreed otherwise.[5]

If the more widespread pattern is that of declining fertility as a result of extra long absences of husbands, the principle of 'dual fertility' has reduced the social functions of the fertility of the womb and increased the

362

woman's involvement in matters pertaining to the fertility of the soil.

On the other hand, if the more significant tendency in mining communities in Southern Africa is towards *de facto* polyandry, a whole new nexus of social relationships may be in the making in Southern Africa.[6]

THE GENDER OF TECHNOLOGY

Other changes in Africa during this period that affected relationships between men and women included the impact of new technologies on gender roles. Cultivation with the hoe still left the African woman centrally involved in agriculture. But cultivation with the tractor was often a prescription for male dominance.

When you see a farmer
On bended knee
Tilling land
For the family
The chances are
It is a *she*

When you see tractor
Passing by
And the driver
Waves you "Hi"
The chances are
It is a *he*![7]

Mechanization of agriculture in Africa has tended to marginalize women. Their role as 'custodians of earth' is threatened by male prerogatives in new and more advanced technologies. It is true that greater male involvement in agriculture could help reduce the heavy burdens of work undertaken by women on the land. On the other hand, there is no reason why this relief in work load for women should not come through better technology. Tractors were not invented to be driven solely by men.

Another threat to the central role of the African woman in the economy in this period has come from the nature of Western education. It is true that the Westernized African woman is usually more mobile and has more freedom for her own interests than her traditional sister. But a transition from custodian of fire, water, and earth to keeper of the typewriter is definitely a form of marginalization for African womanhood. Typing is less fundamental for survival than cultivation. The Westernized African woman in the second half of the twentieth century has tended to be more free but less important for African economies than the traditional woman in rural areas.

The third threat to the role of the African woman in this period came with the internationalization of African economies. When economic activity in Africa was more localized, women had a decisive role in local markets and as traders. But the colonial and postcolonial tendencies towards enlargement of economic scale have increasingly pushed the women to the side in international decision making. It is true that Nigerian women especially have refused to be completely marginalized even in international trade. But on the whole the Africans who deal with international markets and sit on the boards of transnational corporations are men. At the meetings of the Organization of Petroleum Exporting Countries – where Muslims predominate – there are additional inhibitions about having even Nigeria represented by a female delegate.

POLICY IMPLICATIONS FOR WOMEN ENTREPRENEURS

What are the policy implications of all these trends? One central imperative is indeed to arrest the marginalization of women and to cultivate further their entrepreneurial potential. Cultural adjustment is the imperative.

Women as custodians of earth had traditionally emphasized food cultivation. But from now on greater involvement of women in the production of cash crops for export is one way of linking tradition to modernity – and preventing Africa's economic internationalization resulting in the marginalization of African women.

But support for traditional market women in food production and local trade need not suffer as a result of the new androgynization of cash-crop production. Credit facilities should be made available in such a way that there is equity not only between men and women but also between Westernized and non-Westernized females. As matters now stand, traditionalist non-Westernized women are often at a disadvantage when assessed for creditworthiness.

On the other hand, a higher proportion of non-Westernized women are involved in agricultural production than are their Westernized sisters. Indeed, cultural Westernization of women – though improving their creditworthiness – tends to decrease women's direct economic productivity. A balance has to be struck between the two categories of women (Westernized and non-Westernized) in relation to both credit and production.

Preventing technology from marginalizing women is yet another imperative. Special programmes for women in technical training – from driving tractors to repairing lorry engines – should be inaugurated. It will not happen on its own. Such shifts in the cultural aspects of technology need to be addressed purposefully. Effective participation of women in the world of economic entrepreneurship requires their upliftment in the world of technical and mechanical skills as well.

Women as custodians of fire make them the greatest users of firewood in the continent. But shouldn't women also be centrally involved in forest management and reforestation? Wood should increasingly be approached as an integrated industry, sensitized to the needs of environmental protection and ecological balance. Women as the greatest users of firewood should also become among the leading planters of trees for reforestation.

This would not be incompatible with their involvement in the commercial aspects of wood more generally. Carpentry and furniture making are crafts that cry out for much greater female involvement than has been achieved so far. Culturally women are often the selectors of furniture and the trustees of the domestic infrastructure of the family. And yet it is an anomaly that African women have played such a limited role in designing furniture or making it. This is an area of entrepreneurship that beckons the female participant to become more involved.

As traditional custodians of water, do women have any special role in this era of faucets and dams? Africa's women, as we indicated, still trek long distances in rural areas for their water. But water-related industries are surprisingly still male-dominated. This includes the whole infrastructure of water supply in urban areas. Even commercialized laundry and dry cleaning for the elite and for foreigners in African towns is still usually owned and managed by men, even when women do most of the washing and ironing. The soap manufacturing industry is also male-owned and male-managed, even when the consumers are overwhelmingly women. One question that arises is whether these water-related industries are appropriate areas of linking tradition to modernity in Africa's gender roles.

What is at stake is the tapping of female talent where it was previously underutilized. What is at stake is also the androgynization of entrepreneurship. Once again the imperative is cultural adjustment.

Can the traditional custodian of fire be the innovative consumer of hydroelectric power? Can the traditional trustee of water be the new creative user of the high dam? Can the traditional trustee of earth take control of a new (and more creative) green revolution?

The future of the continent depends upon a new sexual equation in the whole economic process. The future of the continent depends more fundamentally on a cultural than on a structural adjustment.

But none of those measures of culture adjustment regarding gender would be feasible without a pronounced role for the state. Classical privatization and laissez-faire would simply permit worsening conditions of marginalization for women. Progress towards female entrepreneurialization would be aborted or retarded.

This is one reason why the cause of androgynous entrepreneurship in Africa needs an activist and enlightened state. The economy under such intervention would become less private – but the market could be released from some of the shackles of tradition and cultural prejudice.

What all these tensions of gender, ethnicity and the prestige motive have illustrated is that the state is not always the most severe constraint on the market. Privatization can imprison rather than release market forces. But if there can be private ownership of the means of production without a free market, can there be a free market without private ownership of the means of production?

In this latter regard the classic illustration is the principle of market socialism, originally tried out in Yugoslavia in the post-war period and probably destined to be repeated under the Gorbachev version of structural adjustment in the USSR, *perestroika*. The guiding principle of market socialism is not privatization but decentralization of the means of production, distribution and exchange. Profitability and inducements are made respectable. It is even possible to permit or encourage competition between socialist cooperatives or state-owned farms. The laws of supply and demand are permitted to seek out an equilibrium between public enterprises.

It is true that the economy of Yugoslavia is currently in severe straits. But is that really an argument against market socialism? After all, for much of the twentieth century the economy of Italy was in shambles, including the years from the end of the Second World War until about 1975. And yet the ailing economy of Italy was not by itself conclusive proof that the private enterprise system was inherently flawed and chaotic.

Market socialism has had few laboratories so far – few countries where it has been tried out. The essential characteristics are ownership by socialist cooperatives or by the state on the one side, and the legitimation of market forces, profit, decentralization, worker inducements and genuine competition on the other.

Partly because there have not been many experiments with market socialism, the model is essentially still virgin. It has yet to be fully explored. One big question is whether it is a relevant model for at least some African countries.

Prospects for the model in Africa are tied up with prospects for socialism more generally. The version of state socialism that was developed among the members of the Warsaw Pact faces an unlikely future within Africa. Even the Cuban model cannot easily be transplanted to Africa. Some conditions in Africa are congenial to the socialist paradigm; others are decidedly inimical. Let us therefore examine these prospects for socialism in Africa more generally before we return to the chances of evolving market socialism *per se*.

SOCIALISM: GOOD CLIMATE, BAD SOIL

As a generalization, we might say that the intellectual climate for socialism in Africa is quite good, but the sociological and material soil is not fertile enough. Let us explore this twin proposition more fully.

Privatization versus the market

As to the reasons why the intellectual climate for socialism in Africa is good, these reasons include basic historical continuities and discontinuities. For one thing, many Africans both north and south of the Sahara have conceptually come to associate capitalism with imperialism. In reality, you can have socialism accompanied by imperialism, and the Chinese under Mao Tse-tung could soon equip you with the necessary vocabulary concerning 'social imperialism' and 'Soviet hegemony'. It is also possible to be a capitalist country without being an imperialist country – Switzerland and Sweden might be considered by some as good illustrations of non-imperialist capitalism.

But in Africa's historical experience it is indeed true that modern capitalism came with imperialism. The enemy of imperialism is nationalism; the enemy of capitalism is socialism. If there is indeed an alliance between capitalism and imperialism, why should there not be an alliance between African nationalism and socialism? Such a paradigm of intellectual and ideological convergence has been found attractive in many parts of Africa.

A second consideration that has contributed to the favourable intellectual climate for socialism in Africa concerns the whole accumulation of frustrations with efforts to develop Africa through Western patterns of economic growth. Many Africans are seeking alternative strategies of social and economic improvement out of a sheer sense of desperation at the inadequacies of the first decades of independence. In reality, socialist experiments in postcolonial Africa have so far not yielded any greater improvement for the masses than other experiments. On the contrary, sometimes the social costs of socialism in Africa have been rather high. It is arguable that while there are relatively successful petty capitalist experiments in places like Kenya, Malawi, Tunisia and Côte d'Ivoire, Africa has yet to produce a significant improvement in the material conditions within which the masses live. The nearest socialist success story is perhaps Algeria – and that needed the sale of oil and natural gas to the capitalist world to buttress it.

In spite of these contradictions, however, many Africans are so disenchanted with the first two decades of independence that they would not mind experimenting with socialist approaches to social transformation.

The third factor that predisposes many Africans in favour of socialism is the rampant corruption among the immediate postcolonial rulers of the continent, all the way from Egypt to the so-called 'homelands' of South Africa. Again, corruption is by no means a peculiarity of capitalism, as many of those who have travelled in, let alone lived in, socialist countries will testify. But there is no doubt that social discipline can at times be more difficult to uphold in conditions of laissez-faire economic behaviour than in conditions of relatively centralized planning and supervision. On balance, it is indeed arguable that the socialist ethic

367

is, almost by definition, more opposed to 'kick-backs, good-will bribery', and even profit itself, than the ethic of acquisitive individualism.

The fourth factor that has contributed to the favourable intellectual climate for socialism in Africa is the widespread belief that traditional African culture was basically collectivist, and 'therefore' socialist. We have already heard claims by such leaders as Julius Nyerere and Tom Mboya that the morality of sharing in traditional Africa, the ethic of responsibility for the young, the old, and the disabled, the imperative of collective ethnic welfare, were essentially a distributive ethic akin to socialism.

Because of this broadly favourable intellectual climate, most African governments soon after independence paid some kind of lip service to socialism. Even regimes like that of Jomo Kenyatta and Léopold Senghor managed to adopt in the initial years of independence a partly socialist rhetoric. Milton Obote in Uganda also attempted a belated 'Move to the Left' in his first administration.

Regimes that planned to take the one-party state route were particularly tantalized by socialist symbolism. After all, the presumed centralizing tendencies of socialism could help justify a one-party monopoly of power. Prospects for socialism in the first decade of African independence did seem to be congenial. Gamel Abdel Nasser, Kwame Nkrumah, Sékou Touré, Julius Nyerere, Houari Boumedienne and the earlier Milton Obote were seen as architects of a new socialist Africa.

What then went wrong? This is what brings us to the barrenness of the sociological soil; in spite of the favourableness of the intellectual climate. One obstinate sociological factor was simply the primacy of ethnicity in Africa as against class-consciousness. Most Africans are members of their ethnic group first and members of a particular social class second. When the chips are down, Banyoro peasants are more likely to identify with the Banyoro bourgeoisie than they are with fellow peasants in Acholi. Jaramogi Oginga Odinga in Kenya attempted to form a radical socialist party. He soon discovered that his supporters were almost exclusively Luo. The late Chief Obafemi Awolowo invoked socialist rhetoric in both the First and the Second Republics of Nigeria. He soon discovered that he was a hero not of the working class of Nigeria as a whole but of all classes of Yorubaland. On balance, it can be legitimately argued that whenever there has been a neat confrontation and competition between the forces of ethnicity on one side and the forces of class-consciousness on the other side, ethnicity has almost invariably triumphed in Africa. This is one primary factor behind the infertility of the sociological soil for an ideology like socialism.

A related factor is the strength of elites in Africa as against social classes as such. The new elites especially have emerged out of the womb of Western imperial acculturation. It has not necessarily been the

368

possession of wealth that opened the doors to influence and power but initially the possession of Western education and verbal skills. As I have indicated in a variety of places elsewhere, the initial political establishment of postcolonial Africa was disproportionately comprised of a Westernized and semi-Westernized core. This galaxy of Westernized stars has included names like Nkrumah, Nyerere, Senghor, Kenneth Kaunda, Ferhat Abbas, Obote, Félix Houphouët-Boigny, Benedicto Kiwanuka, Hastings Banda, Habib Bourguiba, Robert Mugabe, Joshua Nkomo, Sadiq al-Mahdi, Samora Machel, Agostinho Neto, Yusufu Lule and others.

This created a basic sociological ambivalence on the African scene. On the one hand it seemed that the groups most opposed to imperialism rhetorically, and the ones most likely to link it to capitalism, were precisely the elites produced by the West's cultural imperialism in Africa. Even when these elements became truly revolutionary there was a basic contradiction. After all, Karl Marx had expected the most revolutionary class to be the least advantaged class in the most advanced societies. This was deemed to be the proletariat in industrial Western society.

But when you look at revolutionary leaders in Angola, Tanzania and Guinea, and examine the Western credentials of the leaders, you may be inclined to conclude that the most revolutionary of all classes in those societies were the best advantaged. In other words, Westernized Third World radicals were the most likely to produce the dream of socialist transformation. Therefore it is not the least advantaged social class in the most advanced society (the proletariat in the West) but the best advantaged social group in the least advanced societies (the Western bourgeoisie in Third World countries) who are the true agents of revolution in the last quarter of the twentieth century.

It is indeed a sociolinguistic impossibility for an African to be a sophisticated Marxist without being at the same time substantially Westernized. This is partly because the process of becoming a sophisticated Marxist requires considerable exposure to Marxist literature, both primary and secondary. Access to that literature for the time being is only minimally possible through indigenous African languages like Kiswahili, or Yoruba, or Amharic. Even in Arabic, Marxist literature is relatively limited. An African who wants to read many of the works of Marx, Engels and Lenin has to have been substantially initiated into the literary culture of the West.

Even Africans who go to China or to the Soviet Union need to have been previously Europeanized. Scholarships to China and the Soviet Union are not normally offered to rural rustics untouched by Western schools or their equivalents. The nature of elite formation in Africa can therefore be counted definitely as an aspect of the uncongenial

369

sociological soil that socialism has to confront in African conditions.

A third factor of this barrenness of the soil concerns Africa's organizational capabilities in the present historical phase. Many hastily assume that a tradition of collectivism in a traditional setting is a relevant preparation for organized collective efforts in a modern setting. Unfortunately, much of the evidence points the other way. Collective effort based on custom and tradition and kinship ties leaves Africa unprepared for the kind of organized collectivism that needs to be based on command rather than ritual. If socialism requires a rational, efficient command structure that is not based on custom, ethnic empathy or ritual, the present stage of social change in the African experience is still inhospitable to socialist transformation.

TOWARDS MARKET SOCIALISM

The fourth aspect of the infertility of Africa's sociological soil would take us back to issues of historical continuity. Many African economies have already been deeply integrated into a world economy ideologically committed to the market and dominated by the West. African countries that go socialist domestically find that they are still integrated in the world capitalist system. The rules of that system are overwhelmingly derived from market principles evolved in the history of capitalism. In international trade countries respond to supply and demand, and seek to maximize their returns and acquire profit. The rules of business and exchange at the international level, the banking system that underpins those exchanges, the actual currencies used in money markets and in meeting balances of payments, are all products of the capitalist experience. Countries like Vietnam, Angola, and even Cuba discover soon enough that their best economic salvation is to gain international legitimacy by Western standards. Vietnam and Cuba may fail in gaining that legitimacy, but it is part of their ambition to begin receiving Western benefaction and to have easy access to Western markets for their goods, and Western currency markets as well.

What all this once again means is that Third World countries can make their internal domestic arrangements 'socialist' (in the usual command economy sense) while at the same time remaining deeply integrated in the international capitalist system. That is one of the shocks experienced by Milton Obote after his 'Move to the Left'.

Perhaps it is in this last African contradiction that we may have to seek the paradoxical solution of market socialism for at least some African countries. Command economies have a favourable normative climate but a barren sociological soil. Many Africans have socialist dreams but are confronted by capitalist realities. One compromise is a mating of the distributive virtues of socialism with the productive power of the market.

Market socialism will not work in every African country. It almost certainly will *not* work in Nigeria, but may work in Tanzania, and even Mozambique, and could stand a chance in a less militarized Ethiopia. Socialist equity could at last be married to market effectiveness and to the lure of profitability. Is Uganda under Yoweri Museveni preparing the ground for eventual realization of market socialism?

The continent is in search of new models of development and change. Purposeful market socialism is one option on the horizon for Africa's ideological transition. After all, the market is too important to be always left to the vagaries of privatization. Museveni may be fully aware of that particular dialectic.

What the world has been witnessing in the 1980s has been systemic convergence – from marketization in fits and starts in China to *glasnost* and *perestroika* in the Soviet Union. As we indicated, Yugoslavia started earlier with market socialism in the 1960s, reducing the administrative controls of the state and substituting some fiscal controls on the economy.

Indeed, Yugoslavia has been a case of systemic convergence ever since it combined its own version of *glasnost* under Tito with Marxist political economy. There have been times when the growth rate of the Yugoslav economy has been as high as seven per cent. Support from the International Monetary Fund came early in support of Yugoslavia's earlier experiments in systemic convergence. More recent experience in Yugoslavia has been difficult both economically and politically. But if the country's political crisis is not necessarily due to its liberalization of Marxism, its economic problems are not necessarily the consequence of the market socialism either.

Nor is systemic convergence only on the side of Marxist states. Capitalist countries, especially in Western Europe, have long moved in the direction of the welfare state and greater state manipulation of the economy through fiscal and tariff controls.

Yet another case of systemic convergence is the distinctive model of people's capitalism, which is the other side of the coin of market socialism. In this model shareholding and property-owning are distributed more widely in the population. Prime Minister Margaret Thatcher of the United Kingdom called her own concept 'popular capitalism', which is indeed in this tradition of people's capitalism. In the process of privatizing some of the state-owned enterprises, she had made shares available on a much more open market than previously experienced in the United Kingdom. In some cases as many as two million applications for shares were then received, a staggering spread of shareholding culture in the population.

Although Museveni himself may prefer market socialism, is Uganda, in fact, congenial to genuine people's capitalism, complete with widespread entrepreneurial activity and popular investment? People's capitalism there could stand a better chance than market socialism. The latter

371

would require more discipline than Uganda can as yet extract from its population. But even people's capitalism in ethnic-ridden and prestige-conscious Uganda would severely strain market forces.

The informal sector thrives better than the formal in postcolonial Africa, and can be cultivated as part of people's capitalism. The informal sector is also less dependent on political stability. In Uganda since Idi Amin captured power the informal sector has often merged with the illicit economy (*magendo*), and the two have thrived, surrounded by anarchy and carnage. Was the *magendo* economy a preparatory lesson for people's capitalism?

Under normal circumstances market socialism responds to market considerations more efficiently than people's capitalism. Popular capitalism needs privatization, but in Africa this has often been at the expense of the market. Market socialism seeks marketization, but its socialist ethos has militated against privatization.

In the final analysis, marketization is still the end. Privatization has often been the means. But in Africa there remains a mismatch. The means of privatization are not always the best for realizing the goal of market efficiency.

If the market is too valuable to be sacrificed to the goddess of private ownership, it is also too precious to be entrusted to the custody of capitalism alone. That is the lesson that Africa and the world have barely begun to learn.

BETWEEN STRUCTURAL AND CULTURAL TRANSFORMATION
Let us once again return to the primacy of the prestige motive in Africa's economic behaviour. This primacy of prestige distorts the balance between supply and demand, and Africa is on the demand side of prestigious goods. We tend, as has often been repeated, to consume what we do not produce, and in order to get the foreign exchange for such prestigious consumption patterns we tend to produce what we do not consume. Traditional Western liberal doctrine has often taken for granted the psychology of the profit motive and maximization of returns. It has also been taken for granted that if the state left people alone, individuals would productively pursue profit, and Adam Smith's invisible hand would guide individual interests towards the shared common good. Profit in Western terms is calculated as a return beyond capital, skill and labour, and the Western pursuit of profit has therefore often resulted in expanding productivity.

In Africa, however, prestige reduces the inclination to re-invest. Money made rapidly becomes money spent rapidly. What is more, the consumer seeks products that command not only more prestige, but prestige rooted in their alien origin, and therefore prestige costs foreign exchange. Of course in reality prestige does not have to be tied to consumption; Mahatma Gandhi acquired prestige through self-denial rather than self-indulgence. And although postcolonial India is often as ostentatious as postcolonial Africa there is a theme in Hindu culture that accords prestige to frugality and abstinence, perhaps greater than is evident in most African cultures.

Precolonial Africa was distinctive in a remarkable way. It had too little greed. I raised that point with the Uganda ministers and permanent secretaries in August 1989 in Kampala; that precolonial Africa had too little greed and that deficit greed was a problem. Many agreed that stifled greed inhibited certain forms of development. Bertrand Russell used to argue that civilization was born out of the pursuit of luxury, 'that little extra'. Adam Smith argued that the wealth of nations was acquired through the pursuit of profit, 'that little extra'. Karl Marx argued that history was propelled by the pursuit of surplus, 'that little extra'. Precolonial Africa outside the Nile Valley and North Africa did not pursue luxury enough, did not pursue profit enough, did not pursue surplus enough to produce the Palace of Versailles in Africa or Hampton Court or the Taj Mahal in Africa. There were exceptions in Zimbabwe and of course in Ethiopia and Egypt, but on the whole precolonial Africans were not mesmerized enough by luxury, profit or surplus. Hence the limited nature of monumental development. So precolonial Africa was inadequately acquisitive and its structure of greed and incentives was therefore underdeveloped.

Postcolonial Africa on the other hand has been busy making up. The structure of greed has rapidly become overdeveloped, and has redefined the concept of prestige. Ostentatious consumption, sometimes combined with ostentatious generosity, has taken its toll. We mentioned that Kenya uses the prestige motive to encourage competitive philanthropy, so funds are raised publicly under the slogan of *Harambee*. Rich politicians try to outdo each other in philanthropic performance. Ostentatious generosity is usually a safety valve to defend and protect the greed of the ostentatious consumers daily. Against this background, when Westerners call upon Africa to privatize, and they are expecting the profit motive to be given free play, they may just be wrong! The problem is not simply how to liberate and activate the profit motive in Africa but how to control and restrain the prestige motive. And arguably the latter crusade of controlling the prestige motive is more urgent.

Can the prestige motive be made to serve better purposes? Can we tap it to improve production? Can we make productivity more prestigious? Can we make creativity more prestigious? Is there a way of dealing with that dilemma in Uganda by a restructuring of incentives? Is there a crisis of incentives in Uganda, and do we need to find a new equilibrium between prestige and profit? I am sure that those issues will have to be confronted sooner or later.

Problems of gender and inculturation

The second major private theme inhibiting market forces is, as we demonstrated, ethnicity. An even more fundamental constraint on the market can be the political ethnic group; Africa does not have ethnic anti-trust laws to break tribal monopolies. Ethnic nepotism and ethnic monopolies may indeed be a form of love, but what Lord Acton said of power is also true of love: love also corrupts. And absolute love can corrupt absolutely.

In the 1960s there were three formative years that shaped the future of ethnicity in Uganda, each year was separately fundamental. These were not chronological years. The first was obviously 1962: Independence. The British left; Nkrumah's dictum: 'Seek ye first the political kingdom and all else will be added unto it' had been realized for Uganda. We had sought the political kingdom. But the end of the British Empire was in fact the end of the British umpire, the referee. In future years Uganda experienced so much tension one wondered if Nkrumah should have said: 'Seek ye first the political kingdom and all else will be subtracted from it'.

The second formative year for Uganda was 1966. Two events in that year created a special dialectic for structural adjustment. One was the attack on the Kabaka's palace, the Lubiri, which created an entirely new kind of militarized ethnicity in Uganda. The other event was the creation of the Bank of Uganda, a central bank aspiring to become a symbol of economic stability. The Bank sought fiscal sovereignty, very often in vain. The first governor paid the supreme price. Joseph Mubiru was killed, apparently on the order of Idi Amin. The dialectic between militarized politics and structural adjustment through fiscal adjustment was set in motion. That was 1966.

The third formative year of the 1960s was 1969. Did we have in 1969 the death of a king, the attempted assassination of a president and the hesitant birth of an ideological move to the left? The death of Mutesa marked the end of a royalist era, going back centuries. The move to the left, which was to mature in 1970, promised a new structural era. The attempted assassination of the head of state, Milton Obote, escalated the level of political violence in Uganda, and prepared the way for Idi Amin's coup in January 1971. The attempted presidential assassination in 1969 made Obote realize that time might not be on his side. I would suggest that Obote's confrontation with death was a radicalizing experience within the limits of his own intellectual growth that played midwife to his dream about a move to the left. That was a dream about structural adjustment from the left.

The death of Mutesa, on the other hand, was an opportunity for cultural adjustment. In postcolonial Africa incumbents are more fundamental than institutions. In 1967 Obote abolished the institution of the monarchy, but for as long as Mutesa was alive the abolition of royalty

374

stood a chance of being reversed, depending upon who next held power in Uganda. But when Mutesa himself died, that was a qualitative difference to the republican design. It was a more important nail in Uganda's royalist coffin, more important than Obote's formal abolition of the monarchy in the 1967 constitution. The death in 1969 of the king constituted the end of the old rightist order. The attempted assassination of the president constituted the dream of a new leftist order, especially if you accept my thesis that confrontation with death in 1969 was part of the genesis of Obote's radicalization. The death of the king was an opportunity for cultural adjustment, and Obote's move to the left was an ambition for a structural change.

The death of Mutesa also initiated the national integration of Buganda. The new incorporation of the Baganda into the Ugandan body politic was in a sense very different from anything that had happened before. On the other hand, Obote's move to the left tried to achieve integration of minority ethnic groups, the incorporation of small units like the Langi into the Uganda body politic. Idi Amin's coup in 1971 facilitated one process and frustrated the other. Although Amin's group, the Kakwa, were a minority, the total impact of his eight years in power was to make the Baganda more national. The Baganda in the 1970s learnt the art of building coalitions and moderated their tendency towards ethnic exclusivity. Amin remained a hero among the Baganda, partly because of the tendency towards coalition building. But while Amin was nationalizing the Baganda, he was marginalizing the northern groups, the Acholi and the Langi most directly.

In many ways the total impact of Idi Amin on Uganda's equilibrium was to weaken the north and by implication strengthen the south. By weakening the Acholi and the Langi and fraternizing more deeply with the Baganda, Amin turned out to be an ally of the south in the Ugandan equation, and changed the nature of Ugandan politics fundamentally. It is very curious that in precolonial terms, Idi Amin's group the Kakwa and Obote's group the Langi and the Acholi were stateless, and yet in postcolonial terms these groups were precisely the main champions of state leadership. Both Obote administrations were heavily statist. And the Nubi and the Kakwa, traditionally egalitarian internally, became state-conscious under Amin. That pursuit of state power made ethnic monopolies difficult for a while, but only for a while. Idi Amin expelled the Asians ostensibly to end their racially exclusive monopolies of the market, but he inaugurated less-productive ethnic monopolies of his own. That then is the other major area to look at when we are trying to assess what private forces inhibit the market.

The third area we have touched on concerns the market versus the sexual division of labour. Are there gender relations in the economy that are in fact a negation of the free play of the market? In traditional culture

375

the role of the African woman was conceived according to some religious beliefs as custodian of fire, and fire is a symbol of warmth and light. Woman was custodian of water, and water was a symbol of survival and cleanliness. Woman was custodian of earth, and earth was a symbol of production and identity. And God took charge of the fourth element of nature, the omnipresent air.

Which ideology in postcolonial Africa is likely to enhance the position of women in the continent? If we look at the rest of the world, at the global level, it looks as if socialism creates more women workers than capitalism but, almost by definition, socialism creates fewer women owners than capitalism. As for women managers, this seems to vary by culture rather than ideology. What about managing the state itself? On balance if we look comparatively at the world, capitalism has been more successful in producing female rulers in our day. The socialist world has not yet produced the equivalent of Margaret Thatcher, for better or for worse. Scandinavian liberal democracies are beginning to produce politically powerful women, and Scandinavian capitalism is part of that foundation. South Asia and South East Asia have produced female managers of the state. They include Mrs Bandaranaike of Sri Lanka, the first woman prime minister in the twentieth century, Indira Gandhi of India, Mrs Corazon Aquino of the Philippines, Ms Benazir Bhutto of Pakistan. Prospective women rulers include probably Begum Hasina and Begum Khalida Zia of Bangladesh.

Apart from being Asian and being women, what do the societies they belong to have in common? They are capitalist, including India. There has been no female ruler yet in Asian socialist countries, such as China, Vietnam, North Korea, Cambodia. The most powerful female socialist in Asia may be Japanese, another capitalist country. The Japanese woman leader heads a Socialist Movement but in a capitalist country. If we are looking at comparative insights as to which ideology is more likely to produce female involvement in labour and work, the answer is probably socialism. In terms of the rights to own, socialism distrusts private property anyhow, so capitalism produces more female owners. In terms of managers it is unclear. As for the control of the state almost all the cases we have of women attaining supreme power, including Estella Isabella Perón in Argentina, have been in capitalist countries.

CONCLUSION

My presentation has mainly addressed one particular theme, and that is privatization. Yes, it is taken too much for granted that in order to restore the economy to market forces we need to restore it to private ownership. There is a tendency to equate privatization with marketization. Putting economic forces of production into private ownership is supposed to make market forces freer. But we have shown that in Africa it may not

376

be just the state that inhibits market forces. There are private social forces that can create, at times, greater impediments to the market than the state. These private social forces at war with the market include the sexual division of labour, ethnic monopolies in certain sectors of the economy, and the primacy of the prestige motive as against the profit motive as a determinant of African economic behaviour.

The genius of capitalism is, in the final analysis, not gender equality but production. The genius of socialism is distribution. Can Uganda unite the distributive virtues of socialism with the productive power of the market? Is market socialism possible? Yes, it has indeed been tried in Yugoslavia, initially with some success, more recently with a good deal of difficulty. On the other hand, it is possible that the entire socialist world is moving towards the Yugoslav paradigm in the economic domain. Is *perestroika* something that ultimately bears the stamp of Marshal Tito? Is market socialism the answer for Uganda? What does it involve? More decentralization. It involves a greater inclination to allow market consideration to prevail. It promotes the legitimization of profit, while retaining a considerable role by the state operating through fiscal mechanisms.

The other hybrid solution is people's capitalism, distinct from market socialism. As we indicated, Margaret Thatcher calls it popular capitalism. And she has privatized some of the state-owned enterprises in a manner that has made the shares available on a much wider scale than previously experienced in the United Kingdom. A staggering spread of shareholder culture. For Uganda Yoweri Museveni may prefer market socialism for the country. This would not be *perestroika*, not exactly the Yugoslav model, but something that retains some kind of egalitarian principle operating within the economy.

Is Uganda up to it? There is a lot of popular suspicion of socialism of any kind in Uganda. And one of the pragmatic tendencies that have manifested themselves in Museveni is his eagerness to tone down the socialist rhetoric since he came to power. I had an interesting evening with him in 1988. He accused me of having moved to the left and I accused him of having moved to the right. But what was important in the discussion was how much he emphasized the power of technology as the prerequisite of development rather than the technique of ideology as a basis of transformation. He is now much more sensitive to the technological imperative within development than to an ideological blueprint. Does he still want market socialism? He may not call it that, but I suspect that it is his preference. But because of Uganda's inbuilt suspicion of socialist rhetoric I believe Museveni may have to settle at best for people's capitalism. This is one scenario that might emerge, and the *magendo* experience was a preparation for it. The informal sector within the economy diffuses the acquisitive instinct in the society as a whole. But

Problems of gender and inculturation

the state, whether under Museveni or anybody else, will still be needed, not to chain the market but to liberate it from some of the shackles that have their origins in the domains of ethnicity and the prestige motive, in sexual division of labour, in the corrupting power of love, and the continuing lure of privatization in an age of structural adjustment.

Notes

---

1. This paper is based on a position document originally presented to the Council of African Advisors, The World Bank, Washington D.C., 1988, before further discussion at Lyngby Landbrugsskole in 1989.
2. I am indebted to the late Okot p'Bitek, the Ugandan anthropologist and poet, for stimulation and information about myths of womanhood in northern Uganda. Okot and I also discussed similarities and differences between African concepts of matter and the ideas of Empedocles, the Greek philosopher of the 5th century BC. Consult also Okot p'Bitek, 1971.
3. Hay, 1976, pp. 98–9. For a feminist perspective consult also Cutrufelli, 1983.
4. Hay, 1976, p. 105.
5. There is no doubt such arrangements occur in Mozambique. What is not clear is how widespread *de facto* polyandry is becoming in Southern Africa.
6. I am indebted to the field research and interviews in Southern Africa which accompanied the BBC/WETA television project, 'The Africans: A Triple Heritage' (1985-6). I am also grateful to the work associated with Vol. VIII of the UNESCO General History of Africa (edited by Ali A. Mazrui – forthcoming).
7. Ali A. Mazrui.

Bibliography

'A Local Observer', 1988, 'The rigged 1980 Uganda general elections', in *The Roots of Instability in* Uganda (ed. S.R. Karugire)

Abrahams, R., 1985, 'A modern witch-hunt among the Lango of Uganda', *Cambridge Anthropology*, 10 (1)

Addison, T. and Demery, L., 1987, *Monetary Control in Developing Countries*, London

Alland, A., 1970, *Adaptation in Cultural Evolution*, New York

Allen, T., 1989, 'Understanding Alice: spirit mediums, violence and change in northern Uganda', unpublished paper

Amnesty International, 1985, *Uganda: Six Years after Amin*, London

Amnesty International, 1989, *Uganda: The Human Rights Record 1986–1989*, London

Amnesty International, 1990, *Uganda: Death in the Countryside: Killings of Civilians by the Army in 1990*, London

Atwaru, D.O., 1987, 'Need for functional literacy', paper given at the National Operational seminar on the Evaluation, Programming and Implementation of Literacy and Post-literacy Programmes in Uganda (held at IPA, Kampala, 5–15 July)

Avirgan, T. and Avirgan, M., 1982, *War in Uganda*, London

Banugire, F.R., 1987, 'The impact of the economic crisis on fixed-income earners', in Wiebe and Dodge (eds), 1987

Banugire, F.R., 1989, 'Uneven and unbalanced development: development strategies and conflict', in Rupesinghe (ed.)

Barongo, Y.R., 1990, 'The impact of NRM's programme of fundamental change at the local level: a study of performance of the resistance councils system in Hoima District', paper given at Uganda Workshop, Dartmouth College, Hanover, NH

Bauer, P.T., 1972, *Dissent on Development*, London

Belshaw, D., 1988, 'Agriculture-led recovery in post-Amin Uganda', in Hansen and Twaddle (eds)

Bennett, F.J., 1989, 'The dilemma of essential drugs in primary health care', *Social Science and Medicine*, 28(10)

Binswanger, H.P. and Elgin, M., 1978, *What Prospects for Land Reform?*

Binswanger, H.P. and Rosenzwieg, M.R., 1986, 'Behavioural and material determinants of production relations in agriculture', *Journal of Development Studies*, April

Bjoern, C., 1988, *Det Danske Landbrug Historie*, Vol. 2

Bledsloe, C.H. and Goubaud, M., 1988, 'The reinterpretation and distribution of western pharmaceuticals: an example from the Mende of Sierra Leone', in van der Geest and Whyte (eds)

Bond, C.G. and Vincent, J., 1988, 'AIDS in Uganda in the context of cultural pluralism', paper given to the Seminar on Cultural Pluralism, Columbia University

Boyd, R.E., 1989, 'Empowerment of women in Uganda: real or symbolic?', *Review of African Political Economy*, 45–6

Brett, E.A., 1970, 'Problems of cooperative development in Uganda', in *Rural Cooperatives and Planned Change in Africa*, Vol. 4 (R. Apthorpe, ed.), Geneva

379

Bibliography

Brett, E.A., 1973, *Colonialism and Underdevelopment in East Africa*, London

Brett, E.A., 1975, 'The political economy of General Amin', *IDS Bulletin*, 7(1)

Brett, E.A., 1987, 'States, markets and private power in the developing world', *IDS Bulletin*, 17(3)

Bruce, J.W., 1986, *Land Tenure Issues in Project Design and Strategies for Agricultural Development in Sub-Saharan Africa*, Madison, Land Tenure Center, University of Wisconsin

Bruner, E.M., 1986, 'Experience and its expression', in *The Anthropology of Experience*, (V. Turner and E.M. Bruner, eds), Chicago

Buchanan, J. and Tullock, G., 1962, *The Calculus of Consent*, Ann Arbor, Michigan

Burch, D., 1987, *Overseas Aid and the Transfer of Technology*, Aldershot, UK

Canovan, M., 1981, *Populism*, New York

Caputo, R., 1988, 'Uganda, land beyond sorrow', *National Geographic Magazine*, 173

Castle, E.B., 1966, *Growing up in East Africa*, London

Chai Hon Chan, 1971, *Planning Education for a Plural Society*, Paris

Chai Hon Chan, 1972, *Education and Nation Building in Plural Societies: The West Malaysian Experience*, Canberra

Chazan, N., 1988, 'State and society in Africa: images and challenges', in *The Precarious Balance: State and Society in Africa* (D. Rothchild and N. Chazan, eds), Boulder, Colorado and London

Clay, J.W., 1984, *The Eviction of the Banyaruanda*, Cambridge, Massachussets

Commins, S.K. *et al.*, 1986, *Africa's Agrarian Crisis: The Roots of Famine*, Boulder, Colorado

Commonwealth Observer Group, 1980, *Uganda Elections December, 1980: The Report of the Commonwealth Observer Group*, London

Commonwealth Secretariat, 1979, *The Rehabilitation of the Economy of Uganda* (2 vols), London

Commonwealth Secretariat, 1987, *Persistent Indebtedness: The Need for Further Action*, London

Cooper, R.L., 1983, 'Language planning, language spread and language change', in Kennedy (ed.)

Copeland, J., nd, 'In whose interest: structural adjustment and underdevelopment in Africa', unpublished paper

Cutrufelli, M.R., 1983, *Women of Africa: Roots of Oppression*, London

Dahl, R.A., 1971, *Polyarchy, Participation and Opposition*, New Haven, Connecticut

Dearlove, J., 1987, 'Economists on the state', *IDS Bulletin*, 18(3)

Dell, S., 1981, 'On being grandmotherly: the evolution of IMF conditionality', *Essays in International Finance*, No. 144, Princeton, New Jersey

DIMM (Department of Information and Mass Mobilisation, NRM Secretariat), nd, *Political Programme of NRM: Two Years of Action*, Kampala

Dinwiddy, H., nd, 'The use of English in East Africa: colonial perspectives and African comment', unpublished paper

Dodge, C.P., 1987, 'Rehabilitation or redefinition of health services', in Wiebe and Dodge (eds)

Dodge, C.P. and Wiebe, P.D. (eds), 1985, *Crisis in Uganda. The Breakdown of Health Services*, Oxford

DP (Democratic Party), nd, 'Analysis of the five political parties' performance in RC V elections in 22 districts', mimeographed document, Kampala

Edel, M., 1969, *The Chiga of Western Uganda*, London

Edmonds, K., 1988, 'Crisis management: the lessons for Africa from Obote's second term', in Hansen and Twaddle (eds), London

Ehrlich, C., 1965, 'The Ugandan economy, 1903–1945', in *History of East Africa*, vol 2 (V. Harlow, E.M. Chilver and A. Smith, eds), Oxford

Elkan, W., 1960, *Migrants and Proletarians: Urban Labour in the Economic Development of Uganda*, London

Enloe, C., 1970, *Multi-ethnic Politics: The Case of Malaysia*, Berkeley, California

Bibliography

Fallers, L.A. (ed.), 1964, *The King's Men*, London

FBIS (Foreign Broadcast Information Service), various dates, *Daily Report. Sub-Saharan Africa*, US Government, National Technical Information Service

Finer, S.E., 1962, *Man on Horseback*, London

Finsman, J.A., 1983, 'Language modernization and planning in comparison with other types of national modernization and planning', in Kennedy (ed.)

Forster, S. and Furley, K., 1988, 'Public awareness survey on AIDS and condoms in Uganda', unpublished ms

Furley, O.W., 1989, 'Britain and Uganda: from Amin to Museveni', in Rupesinghe (ed.)

Furley, O.W. and May, R.A., 1989, 'Tanzania's military intervention in Uganda', paper presented at Uganda Conference, Roskilde, Denmark, 1989

Gertzel, C., 1988, 'The politics of uneven development: the case of Uganda', paper presented at the Makerere Institute for Social Research Academic Forum Seminar, 25 March

Ghai, D.P. (ed.), 1965, *Portrait of a Minority: Asians in East Africa*, Nairobi

Gingyera-Pinycwa, A.G.G., 1989, 'Is there a northern question?', in Rupesinghe (ed.)

Girling, F.K., 1960, *The Acholi of Uganda*, London

Green, R.H., 1981, 'Magendo in the political economy of Uganda: pathology, parallel system or dominant sub-mode of production?', discussion paper no. 164, Institute of Development Studies, University of Sussex

Hansen, H.B., 1984, *Mission, Church and State in a Colonial Setting. Uganda 1890–1925*, London

Hansen, H.B. and Twaddle, M. (eds), 1988, *Uganda Now: Between Decay and Development*, London

Harrell-Bond, B.E., 1986, *Imposing Aid: Emergency Assistance to Refugees*, Oxford

Harries, L., 1983, 'The nationalization of Swahili in Kenya', in Kennedy (ed.)

Harris, N., 1986, *The End of the Third World*, London

Hay, M.J., 1976, 'Luo women and economic change during the colonial period', in *Women in Africa* (N.G. Hafkin and E.G. Bay, eds), Stanford, California

Hayward, F., 1988, 'Preface', in *Elections in Independent Africa* (F. Hayward, ed.), Boulder, Colorado

Hein, C.T., 1983, *Progress in Literacy: An Unfinished Task*, Nairobi

Helleiner, G., 1983, 'The IMF and Africa in the 1980s', *Essays in International Finance*, No. 152, Princeton, NJ

Hobbes, T., 1981, *Leviathan*, Harmondsworth (Penguin edition)

Hodd, M., forthcoming, 'Prices, money and output in Uganda, 1966–1988'

Hooper, E., 1987, 'AIDS in Uganda', *African Affairs* , 86

Hooper, E. and L. Pirouet, 1989, *Uganda*, Minority Rights Group, report No. 66, London

Huntington, S.P., 1964, *The Soldier and the State*, New York

Huntington, S.P., 1968, *Political Order in Changing Societies*, New Haven

Hyden, G., 1980, *Beyond Ujamaa in Tanzania*, Berkeley, California

IDRC (International Development Centre), 1988, *Economic Adjustment and Long Term Development in Uganda*, Ottawa

IMF, 1989, *International Financial Statistics, 1989*, Washington, DC

International Commission of Jurists, 1977, *Uganda and Human Rights: Reports to the UN Commission on Human Rights*, Geneva

Israel, A., 1989, *Institutional Development: Incentives to Performance*, Baltimore, Maryland

Jaenson, C., Harmsworth, J., Kabwegyere, T. and Muzaale, P., *The Uganda Social and Institutional Profile*, mimeograph report prepared for USAID/Uganda

Jamal, V., 1976a, 'Asians in Uganda, 1880–1972: inequality and expulsion', *Economic History Review*, 19(4)

Jamal, V., 1976b, 'The role of cotton and coffee in Uganda's economic development', PhD dissertation, Stanford University, California

381

Bibliography

Jamal, V., 1978, 'Taxation and inequality in Uganda, 1900–1964' *Journal of Economic History*, 38(2)

Jamal, V., 1985, 'Structural adjustment and food security in Uganda', *WEP Research Working Paper* (ILO), Geneva

Jamal, V., 1988, 'Coping under crisis in Uganda', *International Labour Review*, 128(6)

Jamal, V. and Weeks, J., 1988, 'The vanishing rural – urban gap in sub-Saharan Africa', *International Labour review*, 127(3)

Jewsiewicki, B., and D. Newbury, 1986, *African Historiographies: What History for Which Africa?*, Beverly Hills, California

Joseph, R.A., 1987, *Democracy and Prebendal Politics in Nigeria*, Cambridge

Kakwenzire, J., 1990, 'Women and change under the National Resistance Movement government: focus on discriminatory laws of Uganda', paper presented at Uganda Workshop, Dartmouth College, Hanover, NH

Kasfir, N., 1984a, 'Introduction: relating class to state in Africa', in *State and Class in Africa* (N. Kasfir, ed.), London

Kasfir, N., 1984b, 'The state and the magendo economy in Uganda', in *State and Class in Africa* (N. Kasfir, ed.), London

Kasfir, N., 1987, 'Class, political domination and the African state', in *The African State in Transition* (Z. Ergas, ed.), London

Kasfir, N., 1989, 'Some obstacles that progressive populist governments must overcome', in *Governance in Africa* (R Joseph, ed.), Carter Center, Emory University, Atlanta

Kasozi, A.B.K., 1989, 'The impact of violence on Uganda society, 1966 – present', paper presented at Uganda Conference, Roskilde, Denmark

Kasozi, A.B.K., 1990, Book review, *Canadian Journal of African Studies*, 24

Kelsman, H.C., 1971, 'Language as an aid and barrier to involvement in the national system', in Rubin and Jernudd (eds), 1971a

Kennedy, C. (ed.), 1983, *Language Planning and Language Education*, London

Kenya, Government of, 1985, *Report of the Committee on African Wages*, Nairobi

Khiddu-Makubuya, E., 1984, 'Ombudsman for Uganda', *Uganda Law Society Journal*, 1(1)

Khiddu-Makubuya, E., 1989, 'Paramilitarism and human rights', in Rupesinghe (ed.)

Khubchandani, L.M., 1983, 'Language planning processes for pluralistic societies', in Kennedy (ed.)

Ki-Zerbo, J., 1982, 'Education and African culture', *Présence Africaine*, 10(38)

Kibedi, W., 1988, 'Uganda and the fight against AIDS', Statement to the US House of Representatives Select Committee on Hunger, 30 June

Killick, T., 1981, 'The IMF and economic management in Kenya', Overseas Development Institute Working Paper No. 4, London

Kinuka, R. *et al.*, 1985, *Essential Drugs Management Programme. Base-line Survey for Public Education Programme*, Kampala

Kironde, E., 1985, 'A village perspective of health services in Buganda', in Dodge and Wiebe (eds)

Knight, J.B., 1967, 'The determination of wages and salaries in Uganda', *Bulletin of Oxford University Institute of Economics and Statistics*, 29(3)

Kotey, F.A. and Der-Houssikian, H. (eds), 1977, *Language and Linguistic Problems in Africa*, New York

Kuper, L. and Smith, M.G. (eds), 1969, *Pluralism in Africa*, Los Angeles

Laclau, E., 1977, *Politics and Ideology in Marxist Theory*, London

Ladefoged, Glick and Criper (eds), 1971, *Language in Uganda*, Nairobi

Lal, D., 1983, *The Poverty of 'Development Economics'*, London

Lancaster, C., 1985, 'Africa's development changes', *Current History*, 84(501)

Lancaster, C., 1989 'How the IMF and the World Bank affect African decision-making', *CSIS African Notes*, No. 97, Washington, DC

Lawry, S. and Bruce, J., 1987, 'The role of resource tenure in the management of natural

Bibliography

resources in Africa', paper for African Bureau Agency for International Development, Land Tenure Center, University of Wisconsin, Madison

Lewis, I.M., 1986, *Religion in Context*, Cambridge

Lipton, M., 1977, *Why Poor People Stay Poor: A Study of Urban Bias in World Development*, London

Little, I.M., 1982, *Economic Development*, New York

Lobel, J., 1988, 'The meaning of democracy: representative and participatory democracy in the new Nicaraguan constitution', *University of Pittsburgh Law Review*, 49(3)

Lofchie, M.F., 1986, 'Africa's agricultural crisis: an overview', in Commins *et al.*

Low, D.A. and Cranford Pratt, R., 1960, *Buganda and British Overrule*, London.

Loxley, J., 1989, 'The IMF, the World Bank and reconstruction in Uganda', in *Structural Adjustment in Africa* (B.K. Campbell and J. Loxley, eds), Basingstoke, UK

Lulua, A., 1976, 'Origins and development of Kiswahili in Uganda: with special reference to the question of national language', unpublished, Makerere University Library

MacGaffey, W., 1986, *Religion and Society in Central Africa*, Chicago

Mamdani, M., 1987, 'Contradictory class perspectives on the question of democracy: the case of Uganda', in *Popular Struggles for Democracy in Africa* (P.A. Nyong'o, ed.), London

Mamdani, M., 1988, 'Uganda in transition: two years of the NRA/NRM', *Third World Quarterly*, 10(3)

Mamdani, M., 1989, 'A critical analysis of the IMF programme in Uganda', paper presented at Makerere University, 10 March 1989

Mamdani, M., 1990a, 'The social basis of constitutionalism in Africa', *Journal of Modern African Studies*, 28(3)

Mamdani, M., 1990b, 'Uganda: contradictions of the IMF programme and perspective', *Development and Change*, 21

Mann, I.M., Chin, J., Piot, P., Quin, T., 1988, 'The international epidemiology of AIDS', *Scientific American*, 259

Marks, S., 1986, 'The historiography of South Africa: recent developments', in Jewsiewicki and Newbury (eds)

Mburu, F., 1985, 'Evaluation of government rural health centres and UNICEF essential drug inputs', in Dodge and Wiebe (eds)

Meagher, K., 1990, 'The hidden economy: informal and parallel trade in northwestern Uganda', *Review of African Political Economy*, 47

Middleton, J., 1963, 'Witchcraft and sorcery in Lugbara', in *Witchcraft and Sorcery in East Africa* (J. Middleton and E.H. Winters, eds), London

Minde, K.K. and Kalyesubula, I., 1985, 'The delivery of primary health care in Uganda today: some problems and opportunities', in Dodge and Wiebe (eds)

Ministry of Education, 1963, *Castle Report*, Kampala

Ministry of Education, 1965, *Education Report*, Kampala

MISR/LTC, 1989, *Land Tenure and Agricultural Development in Uganda*, Kampala

Moore, B., Jr, 1966, *Social Origins of Dictatorship and Democracy: Lord and Peasant in the Making of the Modern World*, London

Morris, H.F. and Read, J.S., 1966, *Uganda: The Development of its Laws and Constitution*, London

Mubiru Musoke, G., 1971, 'Uganda needs an ombudsman', *Makerere Law Journal*

Mudoola, D., 1987, 'The problem of institution-building: the Uganda case', in Wiebe and Dodge (eds)

Mudoola, D., 1988 'Political transitions since Idi Amin', in Hansen and Twaddle (eds)

Mukama, R.G., 1986, 'The viability of the indigenous languages in the Ugandan context', *Mawazo*, 6(3)

Mukama, R.G., 1987, 'Linguistics for national development: the case of Uganda', paper presented at Linguistics Association for SADCC Universities Conference/Workshop, Harare, 2–5 September

Bibliography

Mukama, R.G., 1988, 'Uganda's quest for a national language', public lecture, Kampala, 16 March

Mukama, R.G., 1988, 'Uganda's quest for national identity: the linguistic bottleneck to ethnic cooperation towards nation building', paper presented at the Professors Peace Academy (Kenya) Ltd Regional Conference, Mombasa, 15–18 September

Mukama, R.G., 1989, 'The linguistic dimension of ethnic conflict', in Rupesinghe (ed.)

Mukwaya, A.B., 1953, *Land Tenure in Buganda*, Nairobi

Museveni, Y., 1985a, *Selected Articles on the Uganda Resistance War*, Nairobi

Museveni, Y., 1985b, 'The 10-Point Programme', in Museveni 1985a

Museveni, Y., 1989, Interview in *'Al-Dustur*, London, 19 June, English tr. in FBIS, 23 August

Nabudere, D.W., 1980, *The Obote Election Fraud and the New Fascism in Uganda*, mimeo

Nadkarni, M.V., 1983, 'Cultural pluralism as a national resource: strategies for language education', in Kennedy (ed.)

Ndoleriire, O., 1987, 'The Kitara empire', paper presented at staff/student seminar, Makerere University

NEC, DP (National Executive Committee, Democratic Party), 1989a, 'A circular to all DP leaders and supporters throughout Uganda', Circular No 1, mimeographed, 15 June

NEC, DP, 1989b, 'The rationale for a multi-party state in Uganda', Circular No 2, mimeographed, 28 June

Nida, E., 1971, 'Communication roles of language in multilingual societies', in *Language Structure and Translation*, (A. Dil, ed.), Stanford, California

Niskasnen, W., 1973, *Bureaucracy: Servant or Master?*, London

Nkamuhayo, P. and Seidel, G., 1989, 'The context of human rights in Uganda today', *Review of African Political Economy*, 45–6

Nsibambi, A., 1969, 'Some political problems of linguistic communication in Uganda', in *Communications in East Africa* (J.P.B.M. Ouma, ed.), Kampala (Proceedings of the Seventh Symposium of the East African Academy)

Ochieng, E.O., 1985, 'The Uganda government measures to rehabilitate and revive the Uganda economy', in *Development Options for Africa in the 1980s and Beyond* (P. Ndegwa, L.P. Mureithi and R.H. Green, eds), Nairobi

Obol-Ochol, Y.Y., 1971, 'Customary land law and economic development in Uganda', LLM dissertation, University of Dar es Salaam

O'Donnell, G., Schmitter, P.C., Whitehead, L. (eds), 1986, *Transitions from Authoritarian Rule: Prospects for Democracy*, Baltimore, Maryland

Odurkene, J.N., 1988, 'Final report on "Evaluation of Uganda Red Cross Society's 'Public Education Programme' on essential drugs management", from July 1986 to July 1987, in three districts of Uganda', unpublished

Ogwal, C., 1989, 'Open letter: elections in Uganda', Kampala: Uganda Peoples Congress, 30 January, mimeographed

Okech, A., 1987, 'Overview of adult literacy and education programmes', paper presented at National Operational Seminar on the Evaluation, Programming and Implementation of Literacy and Post-literacy Programmes in Uganda, IPA, Kampala, 5–15 July

Okot p'Bitek, 1971, *African Religions and Western Scholarship*, Nairobi

Okot p'Bitek, 1978, *Religion of the Central Luo*, Nairobi

Olsen, M., 1971, *The Logic of Collective Action*, Cambridge, Massachussets

Omara-Otunnu, 1987, *Politics and the Military in Uganda, 1980–1985*, London

Ostrom, E., 1988, 'Institutional arrangements and the commons dilemma', in V. Ostrom *et al.*, *Rethinking Institutional Analysis and Development*, San Francisco

Owor, R., 1987, 'Report and recommendations of the Health Policy Review Commission under the chairmanship of Professor Raphael Owor', unpublished

Paulston, C.B., 1983, 'Language planning' in Kennedy (ed.)

Peagram, R.C., 1961, *Uganda Legislative Council Elections 1961*, Entebbe

Bibliography

Peagram, R.C., 1961, *Uganda National Assembly Elections 1962*, Entebbe

Pirouet, L., 1988, 'Refugees in and from Uganda in the post-independence period', in Hansen and Twaddle (eds)

Powesland, P.G., 1959, *Economic Policy and Labour: A Study in Uganda's Economic History*, Kampala

Pradervand, P., 1985, ' "Tupaye": a medical wonder', *HAI News*, 21

Report on Adult Education Experience in Tanzania, 1987, Dar es Salaam

Richards, A.I., 1956, 'The travel routes and the travellers', in A.I. Richards, *Economic Development and Tribal Change*, Cambridge

Rigby, P. and Lule, F., 1970, *Divination and Healing in Peri-urban Kampala*, Kampala

Roscoe, J., 1911, *The Baganda*, Cambridge

Rubin, J., 1983, 'Bilingual education and language planning', in Kennedy (ed.)

Rubin, J. and Jernudd, B.H. (eds), 1975, *Can Language be Planned?*, Honolulu

Rupesinghe, K., 1989, (ed.), *Conflict Resolution in Uganda*, London

Rweyemamu, A., (1975), 'The predicament of managers of public enterprises in Tanzania', *African Review*, 5

Sathyamurthy, T.V., 1986, *The Political Development of Uganda, 1900–1986*, Aldershot, UK

Scheyer, S. and Dunlop, D., 1985, 'Health services and development in Uganda', in Dodge and Wiebe (eds)

Schumpeter, J.A., 1950, *Capitalism, Socialism and Democracy*, New York

Scotton, J.F., 1970, 'Judicial independence and political expression – two colonial legacies', *East Africa Law Journal*, March

Serwadda, D., Sewankamba, N.K., Carswell, J.W. *et al.*, 1985, 'Slim disease: a new disease in Uganda and its association with HTLV-III infection', *The Lancet*, 19 October

Sklar, R.L., 1987, 'Developmental democracy', *Comparative Studies in Society and History*, 29(4)

Southall, A.W., 1980, 'Social disorganization in Uganda: before, during and after Amin', *Journal of Modern African Studies*, 28

Stock, R., 1985, 'Drugs and underdevelopment: a case study of Kano State, Nigeria', in *The Impact of Development and Modern Technologies in Third World Health*, Williamsburg, Va

Taylor, L., 1987, 'IMF conditionality: incomplete theory, policy malpractice', in *The Political Morality of the IMF* (R. Mayers, ed.), New York

Thomas, H.B. and Scott, R., 1935, *Uganda*, London

Todd, L., 1983, 'Language options for education in a multilingual society: Cameroun', in Kennedy (ed.)

Towards a Free and Democratic Uganda, nd (probably 1982), Kampala

Toye, J., 1987, *Dilemmas of Development*, Oxford

Tullock, G., 1987, *The Politics of Bureaucracy*, New York

Tumusiime-Mutebile, E., 1990, *A Critique of Professor Mamdani's 'Uganda: Contradictions of the IMF Programme and Perspective'*, Ministry of Planning and Economic Development, Kampala

Twaddle, M. (ed.), 1975, *Expulsion of a Minority: Essays on Ugandan Asians*, London

Twaddle, M., 1986, 'Decolonization in Africa: a new British historiographical debate?', in Jewsiewicki and Newbury (eds)

Twaddle, M., 1988, 'Museveni's Uganda: notes towards an analysis', in Hansen and Twaddle (eds)

Uganda Essential Drugs Management Programme, Findings 1986–89, Danish Red Cross

Uganda Government, 1967, *The Uganda Constitution, 1967*, Entebbe

Uganda Government, 1982a, *Background to the Budget, 1982–83*, Kampala

Uganda Government, 1982b, *Report of the Public Service Salaries Review Commission, 1980–82*, Kampala: Ministry of Public Service and Cabinet Affairs

Uganda Government, 1984, *Revised Recovery Programme*, Entebbe

Bibliography

Uganda Government, 1987a, *Report of the Commission of Inquiry into the Local Government System*, Entebbe

Uganda Government, 1987b, *The Resistance Councils and Committees Statute 1987*, Entebbe

Uganda Government, 1987c, *Ministry of Planning, Agricultural Policy Committee Final Summary Report*, Kampala

Uganda Government, 1988, *The Resistance Councils and Committees (Amendment Statute, 1988)*, Entebbe

Uganda Government, 1989, *Education Policy Review Commission Report 1989*, Entebbe

Uganda Government, various years, *Statistical Abstract*, Entebbe

van der Geest, S., 1988, 'The articulation of formal and informal medicine distribution in South Cameroon', in van der Geest and Whyte (eds)

van der Geest, S. and Whyte, S.R. (eds), 1988, *The Context of Medicines in Developing Countries. Studies in Pharmaceutical Anthropology*, Dordrecht, Boston and London

Wallwork, J.F., 1978, *Language and People*, London

Watson, J.K.P., 1983, 'Cultural pluralism, nation-building and education in Peninsular Malaysia', in Kennedy (ed.)

Weeks, J.F., 1971, 'Wage policy and the colonial legacy – a comparative study', *Journal of Modern African Studies*, 9(3)

West, H.W., 1972, *Land Policy in Buganda*, Cambridge

Whiteley, W.H. (ed.), 1971, *Language Use and Social Change*, London

WHO, 1988, *Estimation of Drug Requirements for the Republic of Uganda*, Geneva

Whyte, M.A., 1988, 'Nyole economic transformation in eastern Uganda', in Hansen and Twaddle (eds)

Whyte, S.R., 1982, 'Penicillin, battery acid and sacrifice. Cures and causes in Yole medicine', *Social Science and Medicine*, 16

Whyte, S.R., in press, 'Knowledge and power in Nyole divination', in *African Systems of Divination: Ways of Knowing* (P. Peek, ed.), Bloomington, Indiana

Wiebe, P.D. and Dodge, C.P. (eds), 1987, *Beyond Crisis: Development Issues in Uganda*, Kampala

Williamson, J., 1987, 'Returning to the IMF: different or better?', in *The Political Morality of the IMF* (R. Mayers, ed.), New York

Williamson, O.E., 1979, 'Transaction-cost economics; the governance of contractual relations', *Journal of Law and Economics*, 22

Woodward, P., 1988, 'Uganda and southern Sudan: peripheral politics and neighbour relations', in Hansen and Twaddle (eds)

World Bank, 1981, *Accelerated Development in Sub-Saharan Africa: An Agenda for Action*, Washington, DC

World Bank, 1982, *Uganda Country Economic Memorandum*, Washington, DC.

World Bank, 1983, *Uganda Country Economic Memorandum* Washington, DC

World Bank, 1984, *Uganda Agricultural Sector Memorandum: The Challenge beyond Rehabilitation.* Report No. 5044–UG. Nairobi: Eastern African Regional Office

World Bank, 1988, *Uganda: Towards Stabilization and Economic Recovery,* Washington, DC

World Bank, 1989, *Sub-Saharan Africa: From Crisis to Sustainable Growth*, Washington, DC

World Bank, 1989, *Successful Development in Africa: Case Studies of Projects, Programmes, and Policies,* Washington, DC

Worsley, P., 1969, 'The concept of populism', in *Populism: Its Meaning and National Characteristics* (G. Ionescu and E. Gellner, eds), New York

Wrigley, C.C., 1959, *Crops and Wealth in Uganda*, Kampala

Wrigley, C.C., 1988, 'Four steps towards disaster', in Hansen and Twaddle (eds)

Index

Abasoga Baino Cultural Society, 350n
Abbas, Ferhat, 369
Abdulla, Odro Ibrahim, 288
ab'epsihyo, 143
abiba, 175
Abrahams, Ray, 159
accountability, 297, 299, 300, 304, 305, 306, 307, 308, 309
Acholi language, 156
Acholi people, 180, 334;
    and *jogi*, 172–5, 177n; and Kakwa people, 178; and Lakwena, 166–7; and Madi people, 160; and NRA, 181; and Teso people, 199, 202; marginalization of, 375; politics and religion, 163; soldiers, 164–5, 176n, 225; sufferings of 205–6; textbooks, 347
Acholiland, 8, 162, 164, 166, 176, 187, 189, 225, 368
Acton, Lord, 374
Addis Ababa agreement (1972), 179
Addis Ababa Conference (1969), 322
Adjumani, 150, 151
adorcism *see* endorcism
Advanced Crafts Course, 331
Africa:
    AIDS, 117; and market socialism, 366, 370–2; and socialism, 366–70, 376; and structural adjustment, 65–8, 76, 351–78; education, 66; Europeans, 357; health care, 66; market economy, 351–78; precolonial period, 373; prestige, 352–8, 372–3, 377; privatization, 351–78; state deterioration, 147; traditional collectivism, 368, 370; women, 358–65, 376
Africa Confidential, 194
African Affairs, 121

African Charter/Commission on Human and People's Rights, 197, 203, 208, 223
Africans: a Triple Heritage (TV project), 378n
Agricultural Census (1982), 115
Agricultural Survey (1962), 116
agriculture, 27–8, 60, 74
    and political decay, 305; development, 311, 318, 320, 321; growth, 31; implements, 94; mechanization, 301, 363; monetary, 58; prices, 88–94, 95, 302; processing, 44, 94; producer prices, 58; research and extension, 302, 305; role of women, 361, 363, 364; share of GDP, 21; small holdings, 312–13; statistics, 59, subsistence, 25; surplus extraction, 78; training, 303; *see also* farmers; land tenure; peasants
Agriculture, Department of, 310n
Agriculture, Minister of, 74
aid, international, 25, 35, 37, 41, 57, 145, 185, 193, 301, 351
AIDS, 6–7, 29, 30, 113–29, 129n, 144, 152, 165, 169
AIDS Control Programme *see* National AIDS Control Programme
ajwaka, 174, 176; *see also ojo*
Akarimojong language, 346, 347
'Al-Dustur, 195
Algeria, 358, 367
Ali, Moses, 182
Alur people, 347
amabugo, 286
Amharic language, 369
Amin, Idi, 167, 170, 196, 267;
    and Asians, 78, 84, 85, 98, 250, 352, 375; and *bayaye*, 112n; and health care, 130; and human rights, 1; and land

387

Index

Amin, Idi (*contd*)
reform, 18; and *mafuta mingi*, 115; and *magendo*, 11; and Museveni, 192; and political parties, 266; and Roman Catholic Church, 127; and Sudan, 179, 180; army, 123, 205, 207, 243, 304; corruption, 303; economy under, 50, 79–81, 96n; fall of, 20, 164, 230, 252, 341; invasion of Tanzania, 122; Libyan aid to, 193; murder of Mubiru, 374; presidency for life (claim), 229; seizure of power, 230, 251, 372, 374, 375
Amnesty International, 2, 3, 181, 198, 199, 202, 203, 204, 207
Anatoli, Brother, 126, 127
Anglican Church, 300
Angola, 369, 370
Animal Industry, Ministry of, 289
Ankole, 313, 314, 338
Ankole Landlord and Tenant Law (1937), 314
Anti-Sectarian Bill, 236
Anya Nya guerrillas, 179
Apac, 225, 260
Aquino, Corazón, 376
Arab Jamahiriya, 194
Arabic language, 341, 344, 369
Arivu, 158
army, 15, 228, 299;
and NRM, 230–46; colonial period, 300; politicization of, 253; power of, 207, 223, 287–8; purges, 304; Swahili language, 343, 345; *see also* name of army, e.g. National Resistance Army
Arua, 149, 150, 158, 159
Arusha, 192
Arusha Declaration (1967), 355
Asia, 376
Asians, Ugandan, 56, 81, 82, 84, 85, 86, 96n, 134, 194, 250, 298, 303, 352, 375
Aswa, River, 171
Ateso language, 346, 347
Atiak, 175
atrocities, 3, 149, 166
Auma, Alice *see* Lakwena, Alice
Australia, 208
Awolowo, Chief Obafemi, 368

Babangida, General Ibrahim, 357
Baganda people, 121, 165, 188, 199, 334, 338, 339, 343, 353, 375
Bahr al-Ghazal, 184

Bakiga people, 121
Bakita, 342
Bakongo, 177n
balance of payments, 25, 26, 48, 50, 59, 64, 67, 69, 71
Balewa, Abubakar Tafawa, 356
banana groves, 123
banana plantain *see* matooke (or *matoke*)
Banda, Hastings, 369
Bandaranaike, Mrs, 376
banditry, 201
Bangladesh, 376
Bank of Uganda, 16, 29, 36, 63, 70, 72, 73, 374
banking sector, 28, 36, 49, 56
Bannakaroli Brothers, 126, 129n
Bantu, 225
Banyankore people, 121
Banyarwanda people, 121
Banyoro *see* Bunyoro
Barre, Siad, 358
bartering, 36, 56
bayaye, 101, 112n
beer industry, 64
Besigye, Dr Kiiza, 260, 261, 264
Bhutto, Benazir, 376
Biafra, 356
bill of rights, 222
Binaisa, Godfrey, 230, 232, 266
Binswanger, Hans P., 312
black market, 188; *see also* exchange, foreign; *magendo*
Bond, Dr George C., 128n
borrowing, government, 44, 58; *see also* debt, international
Botswana, 347
Boumedienne, Houari, 368
bourgeoisie, 252, 266, 369
Bourguiba, Habib, 369
brewing *see* beer industry
Britain, 19, 67, 71, 105, 193, 208, 371, 377
British Council, 336
British Empire, 374
British Protectorate *see* colonial period
bubonic plague, 174
Bugalo, 132
Buganda, 224;
and death of Mutesa, 375; and monarchy, 227; communal labour teams, 108; educational dominance of, 345; elections, 251, 255; land tenure, 313, 314; language, 339, 341, 343,

Index

350n; political discontent, 229n; polygamy, 115; relation to Uganda, 15, 225, 226, 256, 278n, 337–8
Buganda Agreement (1900), 314, 315
Bugisu, 314, 347
Buhari, General Muhammed, 357
Bukedi, 7, 148n, 347
Bukoba, 121
Bunyole, 7, 132, 134, 141, 143, 148n
Bunyoro, 174, 313, 368
burial *see* death customs
burule ulcers, 154
Burundi, 3, 117, 120
Busaba *see* Bugalo
Bushenyi, 18, 261, 269, 317
Busia, 137, 187, 188–90, 192, 195
Busoga, 8, 114, 142, 166, 235, 313
Busolwe, 134, 138, 139
Busolwe Hospital, 132, 133–4, 144
Busulu and Envujo Law (1927), 314, 315, 316
Butaleja Health Centre, 132
Buvuma channel, 189
Buwunga, 121

Cabinet, 236, 256
Cambodia, 376
Cambridge University, 356
campaigning, political, 267, 268, 269
capitalism, 357, 367, 369, 370, 376, 377 people's, 371–2, 377
Caputo, Robert, 121
carpentry, 365
cars, 364, 355
cassava, 150
Catholic Church *see* Roman Catholic Church
cattle raids *see* rustling
CCM Party, 231, 246n
Central Bank, 72, 73, 108, 360
Central Medical Stores, 131, 137
Central Purchasing Agency, 56
Central Region, 315
Chad, 61, 79
Chama cha Kiswahili Uganda (Chaku) *see* Uganda Swahili Association
charity *see* philanthropy
Chartered Institute of Bankers, 108, 112n
chiefs, 173, 174, 285–6, 287, 300, 303, 315; *see also obutongole; opi*
Chihandea, Colonel, 240
children, 108;

abandoned, 124; and poverty, 30; child labour, 110, 125; illegitimate, 115; malnutrition, 151–2; *njua kali* activities, 98–9; street trading, 102, 105; teething, 154; *see also* infant mortality
China, 239, 367, 369, 376
China Sitco, 119
Christianity, 175, 188; *see also* Protestants; Roman Catholic Church
Chwa, Daudi, 345
civil liberties *see* human rights
civil servants, 39, 99, 307; Africanization of, 299; corruption, 99–100, 109–10; demoralization of, 21; inefficiency of, 11; overstaffing, 29–30; private employment, 99; recruitment, 63; wages, 28, 35, 101, 258, 303
clans, 313, 315
class, social, 101–2, 248, 251–2, 270, 278n, 368; *see also* social structure
clinics, private, 134, 135–6, 138–41, 146, 306
clothing industry *see* garment industry
Coast Province, 190–1, 196
cocoa industry, 351
coffee industry, 35, 50, 81, 87; collapse of market, 351; cooperative unions, 73; crop financing, 34, 36; exports, 31, 37, 70, 189, 190, 303; marketing, 27, 29; prices, 71, 84, 91; smuggling, 116–17, 305; taxation, 28
Coffee Marketing Board, 29, 36, 72–3
collectivism, 368, 370
colonial period, 81, 121, 217, 218, 251, 256, 300, 301, 310n, 314, 315
Columbia Presbyterian Medical Center, 128n
commiseration money *see amabugo*
Commission of Enquiry into Violations of Human Rights, 2, 15, 202, 206, 208, 217, 220, 223
Commission of Enquiry into the Local Government System, 271–2, 295–6; *Report*, 268, 296
Committee on African Wages, Report (1955), 84
Commonwealth Prime Ministers' Conference (1987), 189
Commonwealth Secretariat (1979), 96n
communist economies, 358
Communist Party (USSR), 231

389

community health workers, 146
Compensating Financing Facility, 67
conditionality, 67, 72–3, 75
Congo *see* Zaire
Conservative Party, 293
Constitution, 14–15, 211, 214–15,
    216, 222, 224–9, 261, 262, 274, 286,
    297
Constitutional Affairs, Ministry of, 214,
    221, 224
Constitutional Commission, 10, 14, 15,
    210, 215, 221, 222, 223, 224, 228, 249,
    297
construction industry, 58, 109
consumer goods, 94, 95
consumer price index, 46
cooperatives, 300, 302, 310n, 312
copper industry, 351
Corner Kilak, 165, 181
'corridor' businesses *see* kikubo
corruption, 3, 62, 74, 85, 100, 203, 218,
    367–8;
    and privatization, 354–5; army, 244;
    chiefs, 285–6; civil servants, 35,
    99–100, 251; electoral, 212, 258, 263,
    267, 268, 269, 274; government, 197,
    220–1, 253, 303; local authorities, 303;
    Nigeria, 356; RCs, 286, 287, 290;
    university accommodation, 289; *see also*
    political malpractice
cost of living index, 50, 58
cotton industry, 81, 84, 87, 88, 89–94,
    96n, 150, 241, 302, 303
counties, 280
coup d'état, 49, 222, 243, 251, 266, 374,
    375
credit, 34, 48, 50, 56, 59, 60, 63, 73,
    360, 364; *see also* Economic
    Recovery Credit
crop financing *see* coffee industry
Crown Land Ordinance (1903), 314
Crown Lands (Adjudication) Rules
    (1958), 314
Cuba, 193, 366, 370
Cultural Foundation Agency, 339
Culture, Ministry of, 349n
currency conversion, 71
currency devaluations *see* devaluations
Customs Department, 74
customs revenue, 28, 74

daktaris *see* herbalists
DANIDA, 131

Danish Council for Development
    Research, 148n
Danish Red Cross, 131
Dar es Salaam, 355
Dar es Salaam University, 180, 195
Dartmouth College Rockefeller Center,
    276n
death customs, 123–4
debt, international, 18, 25, 37, 56, 60,
    65, 66, 71, 351–2; *see also* borrowing,
    government
decentralization, 295, 307, 366, 377
defence, 35, 60, 188
deficits, budget, 46–8, 49, 52, 58, 59, 64,
    66
deforestation, 29
democracy, 213–14, 235–6, 299, 328
Democratic Party, 4, 252, 254, 255, 258,
    266–7, 268, 270, 276n
democratization, 247–78, 329, 333
demonetization, 53
Denmark, 19
Departed Asians' Property, 56
Depression, 361
detention, 202, 203–4, 205, 219, 221
devaluations, 27, 34, 44, 52, 56, 58, 63,
    68, 71, 72, 78, 94, 95, 98
development, 185, 195, 214, 218,
    297–310, 346;
    agricultural, 311, 318, 320, 321; and
    human rights, 197; and RCs, 289–90;
    and technology, 377; expenditure, 35,
    72; role of education, 323
devolution, 295–6
diarrhoeal diseases, 152
Dinka people, 182
disabled, 30
dispensaries, 130–1, 132, 135, 302,
    305
district administrators, 213, 234, 264,
    285, 286, 288, 291
district commissioners, 213, 234
district committees, 213
district medical officers (DMOs), 135
districts, 280
diviners, 168
doctors, 130–1, 135
    bush, 137
dogs, stray, 289
Dominican Republic, 128n
drug shops, 134, 135–6, 137, 138–41,
    145, 146
drugs *see* medicines

Dubai traders, 105–6
Dufile, 155

East Africa Commission Report (1953–5),
    348n
East African Common Market, 79
East Moyo, 151, 159
Eastern Province, 189, 338
Eastern Region, 225
Economic Commission for Africa *see*
    United Nations
Economic Recovery Credit, 26, 56,
    71
Economic Recovery Programme, 20,
    25–37, 56–7
    performance under, 30–7
economy, national, 328
education, 10, 29, 64, 66, 115, 306;
    and ethical values, 328–9; commercial,
    329, 331; democratization, 329, 333;
    government training course, 331;
    higher, 325, 326, 329, 331, 332;
    instructional materials, 325–7; Moyo,
    150; primary, 303, 322, 323–4, 325,
    326, 329, 331–2, 346, 347; quality of,
    330; reform, 322–3; secondary, 303,
    324, 325, 331, 332, 335; structure of,
    331–2; technical, 329–30; vocational,
    329–30, 332; *see also* schools;
    teachers
Education, Ministry of, 63, 292, 293,
    323, 325, 326, 335, 348
Education Policy Review Commission,
    322, 327, 328, 329, 330
    Report, 323, 325, 346
Egypt, 342, 347, 367, 373
El Wel Best, 170
elders, 155–6
Electoral Commission, 263, 264
    Report (1980), 258
elections, 211–13, 214;
    electoral rules, 263–5, 274; election
    (1980), 4, 198, 263, 264, 266, 274,
    299; election (1989), 4–5, 198, 235,
    247–78, 280
electricity industry, 44, 58, 192
elites, 101, 285–6, 295, 327, 355, 369–70;
    and English language, 341, 345; and
    Obote, 303; army, 240; expatriate,
    299; farmers, 301, 302; land
    appropriation, 304; political, 257;
    regional, 127; strength of, 368–9;
    village, 306

Elgin, Miranda, 312
embezzlement, 328
Emergency Doctor Service, 305
Empedocles, 378n
employment, multiple *see* moonlighting
endorcism, 177n
Engels, 369
English language, 335–6, 339, 340,
    341–2, 344, 347, 349n, 355
enguli, 133
Enhanced Structural Adjustment Facility,
    26, 35, 72–3
Entebbe, 131, 137, 157
environment, 29
Equatoria, 181, 182, 184, 185
erowa dipi see herbalists
Essential Drug Kits, 139
Essential Drugs Management
    Programme, 131, 132–3, 139
Essential Drugs Programme, 131, 134–5
Ethiopia, 3, 178, 371, 373
ethnicity, 13, 113, 162, 217, 269, 327,
    346, 352–3, 368, 374–5, 377
ethno-functionalism, 241
European Economic Community, 71,
    161n
Europeans (in Africa), 357
exchange, foreign, 18, 57, 108–9;
    black market, 12, 64, 109; *see also* black
    market; *magendo*
exchange rates, 16, 17, 27, 29, 34, 48,
    49, 50, 52, 60, 63, 72, 85, 94
executions, 3, 202
executive *see* presidency
expatriate firms, 299, 300, 301
expenditure:
    military, 35, 60, 188; public, 28, 30,
    34, 35, 36, 40, 48
expenses, misuse of, 109
export retention scheme, 27, 35, 73
exports, 25;
    agricultural, 21, 88, 95, 300, 301; and
    devaluation, 68; coffee, 31, 37, 70;
    decline of, 48, 57, 59, 78–81, 87;
    diversification, 41–2; increase of, 56,
    89; non-traditional, 50, 74
eye infections, 152

famine, 184, 202; *see also* malnutrition
farmers, 20, 69, 82, 298, 300–3, 305,
    312; *see also* agriculture; land
    tenure; peasants
Farmers' Rural Scheme, 290

Index

FDA, 239
Federal Democratic Movement, 165, 181,
 199, 200, 238–9
federalism, 226, 227
Finance, Ministry of, 29, 63, 70
finders, 126
firewood, 360, 364–5
fiscal policy, 28, 31, 35, 56, 57
fishing industry, 58
food:
 industry, 58; production, 116, 360,
 364; traders, 102, 103, 105, 107–8, 111
Food and Agriculture Organization, 151
forestry, 29, 58, 364–5
Forster, Sarah, 123
France, 67, 127
Frelimo, 362
French language, 340, 344
Front for the National Salvation of
 Uganda, 252
FUNA, 233, 239
funerals see death customs
Furley, Kemlin, 123
furniture making, 365

Gabon, 96n
Gaddafi, Muammar, 188, 190, 191
Ganda see Baganda
Gandhi, Indira, 376
Gandhi, Mahatma, 373
Garang, John, 180, 182, 183, 184, 186n,
 195
garment industry, 64
Geneva Conventions, 220
Genscher, Hans, 351
German language, 340, 344
gerrymandering, 263
Ghana, 79
glasnost, 371
God see Rubanga
Goethe Institute, 349n
gold, 116
Goma, 118, 119–20, 121
gombolola, 280, 283, 286, 289
gonorrhoea, 141, 142
Gorbachev, Mikhail, 366
government employees see civil servants
Government Health Units see health
 centres
Gowon, Yakubu, 356
Great Britain see Britain
gross domestic product, 21, 26, 30, 35,
 44, 58, 59, 63–4, 66, 79, 81, 82

gross national product, 21
growth, economic, 21, 26, 44, 57, 58, 63,
 71, 81
Guide, 193
Guinea, 369
Gulu, 150, 162, 164, 225;
 AIDS, 165; and human rights, 202,
 204; attack on, 199, 245; capture of
 Gulu Town, 180; election (1989), 260;
 Holy Spirit Army, 183; rebellion, 244;
 resistance to Museveni, 181; Verona
 Fathers, 175
Gulu Accord (1988), 245, 246n

hairdressing salons, 112n
'hang to show' businesses see katimba
Harambee, 354, 373
Harrell-Bond, Barbara, 158
Hasan al-Turabi, 183
Hasina, Begum, 376
Hay, Margaret Jean, 361
healing, traditional, 8, 126, 141–2,
 153–4, 155–6, 160, 168, 169, 172, 302,
 306; see also health care
health care, 6–8, 25, 29, 64, 66, 130–61;
 collapse of services, 206, 305–6;
 expenditure, 302; private sector, 308;
 Roman Catholic Church, 126, 127; see
 also healing, traditional
health centres, 130–1, 132, 133, 134, 135,
 145
Health, Ministry of, 115–16; 133
Health Policy Review Commission Report
 (1987), 130, 134
Hegel, 309
hepatitis, 154
herbalists, 126, 141–2, 153–4, 156, 159
High Court, 221, 222
High Level Manpower Survey (1967),
 101
Higher Education, Minister of, 326
Hindu culture, 373
HIV Center for Clinical and Behavioral
 Studies, 128n
Hobbes, Thomas, 297
hoes see jembe
Hoima, 129n
Holy Spirit Army, 183, 189
Holy Spirit Battalion, 181
Holy Spirit Drug, 169
Holy Spirit Mobile Forces, 164, 165–6,
 167, 171–2, 177n;
 rules, 168–9

Index

Holy Spirit Movement, 6, 8, 151, 160, 162–77, 189, 190, 200, 201, 235
Holy Spirit Safety Precautions, 169, 170
Hong Kong, 68
hospitals, 130, 131, 132, 134, 151, 300, 302, 305
Houphouet-Boigny, Félix, 369
households, rural, 114–16
human rights, 2, 14–15, 69, 194, 197–209, 214, 217–23, 228, 255, 284
Human Rights Activists, 208
Human Rights Commission *see* Commission of Enquiry into Violations of Human Rights
Human Rights Committee, 223
hunting industry, 58
hustlers *see bayaye*

IDA, 26, 56, 327
Idra, 225
Iganga, 137, 317, 338
Igbo people, 352, 353, 356
immunization, 152
impeachment, 229
imperialism, 367, 369
imports, 25, 29, 41, 44, 79–81, 94, 95; and devaluation, 68; and *magendo*, 85; decline of, 48; Dubai traders, 105–6; increase of, 70; no-forex scheme, 31; Open General Licence, 56; stagnation of, 37
income, 26, 81–2, 84–8; fixed, 94; rural, 87–8, 91–4, 95; *see also* wages
Independence, 300, 374
India, 105, 373, 376
Indians *see* Asians, Ugandan
industry, 20, 44–6, 64, 78; capacity utilization, 28; decline of, 72, 81; domestic, 124; growth of, 31, 58, 79; share of GDP, 21; small-scale, 60; transfer to parastatals, 85
infant mortality, 25
inflation, 2, 21, 28, 30–4, 35, 36, 40, 46, 56, 58, 63, 64, 69, 71, 79, 94, 95, 96n, 98, 189; and ethics, 328; and structural adjustment, 17; contributory factors, 57
informal sector *see njua kali* activities
infrastructure, 57, 58, 62, 64, 74, 75, 88, 94, 95, 113, 275; and RCs, 290;

destruction of, 20; social, 25, 26, 37, 41, 223, 244, 307
Ing Chu, 170
inheritance, 312, 313
injections, 143–4
injectors *see ab'epsihyo*
Inspector-General of Government, 202–3, 206, 220–1, 234, 292–3
Inspector-General of Government Statute (1987), 220, 234
Institute of Environment and Natural Resources, 29
Institute of Public Administration, 340
Institute of Teacher Education, 331, 336
institutional reform, 297–310
intelligence agencies, 221, 264
interest rates, 27, 29, 31, 34, 36, 44, 56, 58, 60, 71, 72
International Advisory Group, 128n
International Alert, 2, 202, 203
International Coffee Organization, 31, 50, 57
International Committee of the Red Cross, 203
International Conference Centre, 112n
International Covenant on Civil and Political Rights (1966), 223
International Development Research Council of Canada, 62, 65
International Labour Organization, 96n
International Monetary Fund, 37, 59, 360; and NRM, 49; and structural adjustment, 2, 16, 17, 26, 35, 44, 48, 50, 56, 60–77, 78, 85, 98, 351; and Yugoslavia, 371
interstitial operatives, 100–1, 105, 109
intifada, 179
investment, 27, 31, 41, 44, 66
inyinya, 155, 157–8, 159; *see also* witchcraft
Iraq, 191
Islam, 157, 190, 193, 300, 358, 359
Islamic Development Bank, 193
Islamic fundamentalism, 191, 196
Islamic University, 341
Israel, 194
Italy, 366
Ivory Coast, 367
ivory trade, 174

393

Index

Jakan, 176n
Japan, 376
jembe, 94
Jerusalem, 194
Jim Brickey, 170
Jinja, 96n, 137, 166, 189
Jinja power station, 307
jogi, 168, 172–5, 176, 177n; *see also* spirits
Joint Medical Stores, 131
jok see jogi
Juba, 180, 181
judiciary, 222–3
justice, 213–14

Kabaka, 226, 313, 314, 315, 374
Kabale, 123, 261, 269
Kagera War, 122, 231, 237, 246n
Kakwa people, 178, 182, 347, 375
Kalangala, 277n
Kalisizi, 119, 123
Kampala, 117, 120, 137, 150, 164, 190;
    AIDS, 118, 121, 123; as media centre,
    339; battle of, 180, 199, 231, 244;
    District Administrator, 285, 292;
    election (1980), 253; growth rate, 96n;
    Holy Spirit Mobile Forces, 169;
    language activity, 341; language
    difficulties, 334; National Theatre, 339;
    RCs, 234; sexual mores, 125; state
    terrorism, 219; street traders, 86,
    102–3; Swahili classes, 337
Kamukuzi, 290
kandooya, 200, 201, 204
Kapkwomey, Mr., 292, 293
Karamoja, 137, 181, 347
Karamojong people, 201, 206, 218, 244
Kasensero *see* Goma
Kasese, 241, 290
Kategaya, 240
Katikiro, 224
katimba businesses, 104
Kaunda, Kenneth, 369
Kenya, 119, 355;
    AIDS, 121; Alice Lakwena detained,
    166; and capitalism, 367; and human
    rights, 3; colonial labour policy, 84;
    elections, 4, 275; *Harambee*, 354, 373;
    imports from, 105; Kikuyu, 353;
    language, 342, 349n; parallel market,
    64; press freedom in, 2; relations with
    Uganda, 18, 187–96, 240; smuggling,
    117; support for SPLA, 9; Ugandan
    exports to, 79; women, 361

Kenya African National Union, 188,
    191
Kenya Kiswahili Association, 349n
Kenya Railways, 188, 190
Kenya Revolutionary Movement, 191
Kenyatta, Jomo, 368
kerosene *see* paraffin
Khalida Zia, Begum, 376
Khartoum, 180, 182, 183, 186n
Kibale, 119, 120
kibanda see exchange, foreign
Kibedi, Ambassador Wanume, 119,
    128n
Kibuli, 103
Kigezi, 114, 123, 314
Kiingi, K.B., 339
kikubo businesses, 101, 104
Kikuyu people, 353
King Bruce, 170
kiroga, 165
Kirya, Balaki, 189
Kiryandongo, 241
Kisugu, 103
Kisumu, 119, 189
Kiswahili *see* Swahili
Kiswahili International Conferences,
    349n
Kitaredde, 125, 126
Kitgum, 165, 169, 171, 180, 181, 201,
    225, 244, 245
Kiwanuka, Benedicto, 369
Kiyingi, Semyano, 277n
Kony, Joseph, 164, 166, 167, 169, 170,
    171, 172, 176, 183, 201
Kowe, 361
Kreniske, Dr John, 128n
Kumam people, 347
Kumi, 260
Kuomintang, 239
kwashiorkor, 206
Kyagwe, 112n
Kyambogo, 280
Kyotera, 118, 119, 120, 121, 123

labour:
    communal teams, 108; division of, 81;
    force, 82, 84, 86; forced, 361; migrant,
    120–1, 361, 362
Ladefoged, 345
Lagos Plan of Action, 69
Lakwena, Alice, 6, 8, 162–77, 181, 183,
    189, 190, 200, 201, 206, 235
Lamoghi rebellion, 174

land:
  Adjudication Committees, 314;
  administration, 312, 319; clan rights,
  313, 315; colonial period, 314;
  compensation, 319-20, 321; evictions,
  314, 315, 316-17, 318, 319, 321;
  freehold, 19, 314, 315, 319, 320, 321;
  inheritance, 312, 313; *kabaka* rights,
  313; leasehold, 315, 317, 321; *mailo*
  system, 314-21; *obutaka* rights, 313;
  obutongole rights, 313; peasant rights,
  313, 314, 315-16, 321; precolonial
  period, 313-14, 315; private
  ownership, 314, 315, 320; registry,
  315, 320; state ownership, 319; tax,
  320, 321; tenure, 18-19, 115, 311-21;
  use, 311
Land Reform Decree (1975), 18, 315-17,
  318, 319, 320-1
Langi people, 164, 347, 375
Lango, 189, 225, 244
Lango people, 159
language, 9-10, 285, 327, 329, 331,
  334-50;
  area, 346-7; policy, 334, 341, 343,
  344, 345-6, 347, 348, 348n, 349n, 355
laor, 170
Laropi, 149, 155, 156, 157, 158
laundries, 365
law, rule of, 210-16, 217-23
Law Society of Uganda, 205, 208
laza, 154-5
Lebanon, 128n
Lemule North, 288
Lenin, 239, 369
Lesotho, 347
Lewis, I.M., 177n
Libya, 190, 191, 193-4, 195, 342
Lira, 180
literacy, 322, 326
loading *malaika* ceremony, 167
loboto see yaws
Local Administrations Act, 210
Local Defence Forces, 166
local government, 225-6, 251, 295-6,
  300, 303
Local Government Act, 213
Local Government, Ministry of, 260,
  286, 291
'lodgers', 205
Lokichoggio, 187, 192-3, 194
Lord's Army, 164, 167
lorries *see* trucks and trucking

low-income developing countries, 21, 25
low-income sub-Saharan Africa, 21, 25
Lubiri, 374
Luganda Academy, 338, 339, 340
Luganda language, 334-5, 337-40,
  343, 345, 346, 347, 348n, 349n,
  350n
Luganda Language Society, 338, 339
Luganda Society, 338, 339, 349n
Lugbara language, 346, 347
Lugbara people, 149, 155, 159
Lukoya, Severino, 166, 201
Lule, Yusufu, 230, 232, 237, 270, 276n,
  369
Lunyarwanda-speakers, 9
Luo people, 361, 368
Lusoga language, 347
Lusoga Language Society, 350n
Lutheran World Federation, 161n
Luwero, 288, 310n, 317-18
Luwero Triangle, 2, 123, 183, 205, 206,
  253
Lwo language, 346, 347
Lyngby Landbrugsskole conference,
  Denmark (1985), 1, 6

Machel, Samora, 362, 369
Machiavelli, 229
Madi people, 149-50, 156, 159,
  160
mafuta mingi, 106, 115, 116
magendo, 7, 11, 13, 85-6, 99, 106,
  116-17, 251, 372, 377; *see also* black
  market; exchange, foreign
mailo land tenure system, 18, 314-21
Mainz, 177n
maize, 88, 94, 241
Maji Maji movement, 167, 176n, 201
Major Bianca, 170
Makerere Institute of Social Research,
  161n, 315, 316
Makerere Students' Guild, 291, 292
Makerere University, 29, 162, 169, 331,
  336, 340;
  closure of, 10, 325; Department of
  Languages, 338, 340, 349n;
  Disciplinary Committee, 292, 293, 294;
  Halls of Residence, 279, 280-4, 289,
  291-4; languages spoken, 345;
  Lumumba Hall, 291-2; Mary Stuart
  Hall, 291-4; Northcote Hall, 291-4;
  RCs, S, 279-96; Students' Common
  Room, 294; teacher shortage, 323;

Index

Makerere University (*contd*)
  Uganda Swahili Association, 337;
  University Council, 279, 292, 293,
  294, 295; Vice Chancellor, 291, 292,
  293, 294
Makindye Army Barracks, 287
malaika, 167
Malaba, 190
malaria, 140, 152, 153
Malawi, 367
malnutrition, 108, 151–2, 206; *see also*
  famine
Manchester University, 161n
Mandari people, 182
manufacturing, 46, 58, 64
Mao Tse-tung, 239, 367
marijuana, 112n
market economy, 299–300, 307–8,
  351–78
market gardens, 116; *see also* shambas
market, parallel *see magendo*
market socialism, 366, 370–2, 377
marketing, 27, 29, 49, 88
marketing boards, 302
marketization, 352, 371, 372, 376
markets, 102–3, 137, 298, 353
marriage, 125
Martin, Ian, 203
Marx, Karl, 369, 373
Marxism, 369, 371
Masaka, 114–16, 118, 119, 120, 121,
  122, 123, 128n, 277n, 317–18, 338
massacres, 2, 123, 239
maternity homes, 135, 136
matooke, (or *matoke*) 11, 86, 88, 124, 133
Maumbe-Mukhwana, Jack, 277n
Mayanja, Abu, 340
Mayanja-Nkangi, Joshua, 224, 293, 340,
  343
Mbale, 96n, 134, 137, 317
mbandwa, 174
Mbarara, 18, 261, 269, 290, 317
Mbarara University of Science and
  Technology, 331
Mboya, Tom, 368
Mbuye, 126–7, 129n
measles, 132
Médecins Sans Frontières – MSF
  (France), 151–2, 305
Medical Form Five, 138, 139
medical services *see* health care
medication, self-, 141–5
medicines, 130, 131, 132–3, 134–5,

136–7, 138–45, 146;
  African *see obulesi bw'ehimali*
mediums *see laor; ojo*
Meir, Golda, 358
meningitis, 152
Mercedes-Benz cars, 354, 355
Middleton, John, 155, 157
midwives, 133, 135
Military Commission, 243
military police, 238
Military Tribunals, 238, 246n
Milk Marketing Board, 302
millet, 123
mining industry, 361, 362, 363
Minority Rights Group, 2, 198–9, 207
miruka see muluka
missionaries, 175, 305, 348n
Mobile Institute of Moral Political
  Rehabilitation, 172
Mobutu, President, 9
Moi, President, 190, 191, 192, 232
Mombasa, 106, 117, 190, 195
monarchy, 226, 227–8, 229n, 374–5
monetary policy, 28–9, 31, 56
money supply, 17, 34, 48, 50, 70
moneyed people *see mafuta mingi*
mongoto see trypanosomiasis
monopolies, 13, 299, 300, 301, 302, 303,
  305, 308, 309, 353, 374–5
Monrovia Strategy, 69
moonlighting, 101, 109
mortality rates, 152; *see also* infant
  mortality
Mountains of the Moon, 9
Moyo, 8, 149–61, 195
Moyo Hospital, 151, 153
Mozambique, 362, 371, 378n
Mozambique National Resistance, 362
Msekwa, Pius, 231
MSF (France) *see* Médecins Sans
  Frontières
Mubende, 317
Mubiru, Joseph, 374
Mugabe, Robert, 239, 362, 369
Muhammed, Murtala, 356–7
Mukono, 317
Mulago Hospital, 302
Muliro, Masinde, 191
muluka, 279, 280, 281–2, 283
Museveni, Yoweri, 1, 39, 49, 122, 181,
  189, 216, 230, 239, 256, 270, 279, 357;
  and Alice Lakwena, 165, 166, 167; and
  Constitution, 224; and DP, 254; and

Museveni, Yoweri (*contd*)
economic adjustment, 43; and
FRONASA, 252; and Garang, 182,
195; and human rights, 197–209; and
IDRC, 62–3; and Kenya, 187–8, 190,
191, 192, 194; and Libya, 193; and
market socialism, 371, 377; and Obote,
164; and political parties, 267; and
SPLA, 183; and Sudan, 184; and
Swahili language, 336; appointments
of, 227n; attempts to regularize power,
232, 244; election (1980), 258;
election (1989), 260, 262, 263, 271,
272, 273, 275; guaranteed presidency,
250; military consolidation, 179–80;
on monarchy, 229n; on morality,
7; on NRA, 236, 237, 241, 242;
on RCs, 259; on UFA and
FEDEMU, 239; radicalism of,
276n
Muslims *see* Islam
Mutebi, Ronald, 224
Mutesa, Sir Edward, 224, 374–5
Mutibwa, Professor, 162
Mutukula, 119, 122, 123
Muwanga, 230, 232
Mwakenya, 188, 190, 191
mwalimu, 157
Mwanga, Kabaka, 112n
Mwanza, 189
Mwinyi, Ali Hassan, 336, 355

Nabiganda, 132
Nadkarni, 345
Nagongera, 134
Nairobi, 117, 196, 198, 232, 339
Nairobi University, 349n
Namuwongo, 103
Nasser, Gamal Abdel, 368
National AIDS Control Programme, 118,
119, 125
National Consultative Council, 230
National Curriculum Development
Centre, 326, 327, 336, 338
National Enterprise Corporation, 241
National Executive Committee, 212–13,
234, 235, 236, 242, 262, 277n
National Geographic, 121
National Institute of Education, 280
National Islamic Front, 183
National Organization of Trade Unions,
272–3
National Political Commissar, 260

National Resistance Army, 1, 2, 9, 49,
181, 255, 257;
and Holy Spirit Movement, 8, 166,
168, 169, 170, 171, 172; and human
rights, 201, 202, 204–5, 206–7; and
law enforcement, 235; and Okello, 182;
and RCs, 4, 276n, 279; and UPDA,
183, 184, 206; atrocities, 3, 158;
capture of Kampala, 180, 230–1; Code
of Conduct, 204, 219, 237–8, 276n;
composition of, 229n; control of,
13–14; Council, 261, 262; guerrilla war
against, 164, 165, 189, 190, 195, 225;
membership of NRC, 212, 256;
popular support for, 298, 304; power
of, 233; ranks, 242; rebuilding of,
236–45; 35th Battalion, 199, 200, 204
National Resistance Council, 3, 4, 236,
242, 247, 263–4, 268, 280, 320;
and Constitution, 274; and NRA, 256;
and NRM, 212; and political parties,
269; committees, 233; composition of,
5, 235, 277n; elections to, 249–50,
259–60, 261, 264, 265; expansion of,
211, 215, 233–4, 262; nominations
to, 249–50, 259–60, 261, 264, 265;
Swahili language, 337, 343; vote to
lengthen term, 273–4; women on, 13,
74, 272
National Resistance Movement, 14,
15–16, 49, 279, 297–8;
and army, 228, 230–46; and
Constitution, 224; and decentralization
of power, 295, 307; and DP, 254; and
economic recovery, 20, 26; and human
rights, 14–15, 197–209, 217, 219–21,
222, 223; and Kenya, 187–8, 189, 190,
191, 194, 195; and land reform, 18;
and Libya, 193; and monarchy, 228;
and Obote 2 regime, 122; and political
parties, 254, 256–7, 258, 259, 266–9,
271, 274, 276, 282, 284; and RCs,
279, 284; and revolution, 210–16; and
structural adjustment, 17, 40, 61–77;
and women, 13; election (1989),
247–78; executions, 3; ideology,
269–73; political base, 62, 255, 256,
273; political dominance, 259–63, 309;
populism, 247–78; posts in, 277n;
radicalism of, 278n; Rehabilitation and
Development Plan, 50; rise of, 1–3,
219–21, 226; secretariat, 255–6, 260,
263–4, 284, 286, 291, 340; *10 Point*

National Resistance Movement (*contd*)
  Programme, 2, 4, 14, 61–2, 197, 213,
  214, 216, 219, 233, 252, 253, 257, 265,
  267, 320
National Teachers' College, 331
National Theatre, 349n
nationalism, 210, 219, 327, 333, 367
nationalization, 312
Nebbi, 206
nebis, 176
neocolonialism, 188, 218
nepotism, 352, 353
Netherlands, 67, 347
Neto, Agostinho, 369
New Vision, 159
New York State Psychiatric Institute,
  128n
newspapers *see* press
Ngumba, Andrew, 191
Ng'weno, 189
Niger, 79
Nigeria, 96n, 135, 222, 352, 353, 355–7,
  364, 368, 371
Nile, River, 178
Nimule, 181, 184
njaye see marijuana
Njonjo, 191
njua kali activities, 98–112, 377
njuku see venereal disease
Nkomo, Joshua, 239, 369
Nkrumah, Kwame, 368, 369, 374
no-forex scheme, 33
non-governmental organizations, 29, 30,
  131, 146, 151, 152, 193, 305, 307,
  308–9
Nongqawuse, 201
North Korea, 376
Northern Ireland, 128n
Nubi people, 179, 352, 375
Numeiri, President, 179
nurses, 133
Nyanza, 361
Nyerere, Julius, 191, 207, 295, 355, 368,
  369
Nyoike, Kimani wa, 191

Obasanjo, Olusegun, 357
Obongi, 152
Obote, Milton, 165, 179, 193, 196, 236,
  369;
  abrogation of Constitution, 230, 286;
  and fall of Kampala, 199; and human
  rights, 1; and ICRC, 203; and IMF,
  63; and one-party system, 267; and
  Roman Catholic Church, 127; army,
  123, 164, 183; attempt on life of, 374;
  coup d'état, 251; economic
  mismanagement, 50; flight to Zambia,
  266; left-wing move, 368, 370, 374,
  375; loss of support, 303; non-
  accountable government, 299, 304; rule
  by force, 288
Obote 2 regime, 4, 44, 61, 122–3, 202,
  206, 207, 230, 232;
  and Asian businessmen, 85; and
  structural adjustment, 16, 63, 78; and
  Sudan, 9; corruption, 2; end of, 49;
  external financing, 65; international
  borrowing, 37; Teso militia, 201;
  torture, 200
obulesi bw'ehimali, 142
obutaka, 313
obutongole, 313
Odek, 169
Oder, Judge, 2
Odinga, Jaramogi Oginga, 191, 368
Odinga, Raila, 191
Oil Facility Subsidy Account, 67
oil industry, 351, 356, 367; *see also*
  petroleum industry
ojo, 154, 156–7, 159–60; *see also ajwaka*
Ojok, Oyite, 164, 243
Ojuku, Colonel, 201
Ojuku, Major, 171
Okello, Basilio and Tito, 2, 196, 199,
  230, 236;
  and DP, 266; and human rights, 1;
  and NRA, 180, 182, 206, 244; and
  NRM, 188, 193; and Sudan, 9;
  overthrow of Obote, 164
ombudsman, 203
onzi, 156, 157
Open General Licence, 56, 58, 71, 72
Operation Lifeline Sudan, 184
opi, 150; *see also* chiefs
Organization of African Unity, 197, 203,
  208, 223
Organization of Petroleum Exporting
  Countries, 356, 364
Oris, Juma, 170
Otai, Peter, 3, 202
otontong, 166
Owen Falls dam, 189, 192
Pakistan, 376
paraffin, 116–17
paramilitary organizations, 221, 223

parastatals, 27, 49, 56, 85, 131, 137, 151, 299, 307
parent-teacher associations (PTAs), 306, 308-9, 324-5
Paris Club, 37, 56, 71
parishes *see muluka*
Parliament, 253, 320
parties, political, 254, 256-7, 258, 259, 266-9, 271, 274, 276, 282, 284
patronage, political, 228, 229
p'Bitek, Okot, 378n
peasants, 227, 270, 272, 290, 313, 314, 315-16, 321; *see also* agriculture; farmers; land tenure
People's Liberation Army (China), 239
perestroika, 366, 371, 377
Perón, Estella Isabella, 376
petroleum industry, 27, 28, 34, 56, 70, 106; *see also* oil industry
pharmaceuticals *see* medicines
pharmacies, 135;
    private *see* drug shops
pharmacists, 130-1, 135
philanthropy, 353-4, 373
Philippines, 376
pilgrims, 127
Pilot Land Adjudication Schemes, 314
Planning, Ministry of, 29, 63, 70
plantain *see matooke* (or *matoke*)
Plateau State, 353
Plato, 327
poisoners, 154, 157, 158, 159, 161, 174, 176n
police, 253, 287, 300, 348n
political education seminars, 284, 286
political inequity, 226-7
political institutions, 230-46
political malpractice, 219; *see also* corruption
political underdevelopment, 218-19
polyandry, 362, 363, 378n
polygamy, 115, 125
poor *see* poverty
population growth rates, 96n
populism, 247-78
poverty, 12-13, 30, 218, 297-310, 312
Preferential Trade Area, 294
prescriptions, medical, 138, 140
presidency, 15, 228-9, 234
President's Office, 260
press freedom, 2, 208, 238

prestige motive, 352-8, 372-3, 377
price controls, 27, 44, 49, 50, 52, 63
prices, 41, 46, 52, 56, 71, 72, 88-94, 95; agricultural produce, 58; commodity, 79; petroleum, 34
priests, chiefdom, 173, 174
Primary Education, Minister of, 326
Primary Teachers' Certificate Course, 331
prison *see* detention
private sector, 41, 56, 297, 299, 305
privatization, 44, 130-48, 305-6, 309, 351-78
Produce Marketing Board, 49, 302
production, 68, 69, 89
profit motive, 352-8
Programme for the Alleviation of Poverty and the Social Costs of Adjustment, 12, 30, 40
proletariat, 369
prostitutes, 121, 124, 127
Protestants, 277n, 357
Public Land Act (1969), 315-16
Public Order and Security Act (1967), 221
public sector *see* state
Public Service Commission, 297
Puritans, 357

Rabat Resolutions, 69
radio, 339, 342, 347
Radio Uganda, 336, 339
railways, 28, 188, 190
Rakai, 7, 8, 100, 114-16, 117, 118, 119-23, 124, 125, 126-7, 128-9n
ranching, 302, 320
rebellions, 74, 174, 229n, 234, 235, 236, 244-5
Red Cross *see* Danish Red Cross; International Committee of the Red Cross, Uganda Red Cross
referendums, 267
refugees, 149, 151, 155, 158, 178-9, 182, 184, 189
regional cooperation, 60, 187
regionalism, 113
Rehabilitation and Development Plan, 50
Rehabilitation, Ministry of, 151
religion, 218, 269, 300
Renamo *see* Mozambique National Resistance
Resistance Committees (Judical Powers) Statute (1987), 234, 288

resistance councils/committees, 14, 74, 210, 215, 244, 272; achievements, 286-9; and democracy, 198; and economic development, 289-90; and health care, 133, 146; and Joseph Kony, 172; and NRA, 238; and NRC, 211; and NRM, 233; and PAPSCA, 30; and poisoners, 158, 159, 161; attendance, 282, 283-4, 285; corruption, 256; counties, 280; courts of justice, 214, 234, 288; districts, 280; elections, 235, 249, 254, 255, 259-60, 261, 263, 264, 265, 266, 267, 268, 270-1, 274; executive committees, 283, 284; formation of, 4, 5-6, 213-14, 220, 234, 251, 253; frequency of meetings, 282-3; *gombolola*, 280, 283, 286, 289; Makerere University, 279-96; *muluka*, 279, 280, 281-2, 283; party representation in, 276n; powers of, 100; Roman Catholic members, 127; structure of, 307; village councils, 281-2, 283

Resistance Councils and Committees (Amendment) Statute (1988), 289

Resistance Councils and Committees (Election) Regulations (1989), 264, 268

Resistance Councils and Committees Statute (1987), 234, 279, 286

revenues, government, 28, 29, 34, 35, 74; *see also* customs revenue; taxation

revolution, 210-16

Rhodesia *see* Zimbabwe

Rift Valley Province, 191

roads, 28, 31, 58, 65, 74, 116, 120, 303, 307

robbery, 287, 304

Rochdale Principles, 300

Rockefeller Foundation, 310n

Roman Catholic Church, 8, 125, 126-7, 150, 156, 175, 277n, 300

Rosebery channel, 189

Rubanga, 153

Rubia, Charles, 191

Rukiga language, 340, 345, 346-7

rulers, 13, 218

rum, homemade *see enguli*

Runyankore language, 340, 345, 346-7

Runyoro language, 340, 345, 346-7

Rural Rapid Appraisal, 317, 321

Russell, Bertrand, 373

Russia *see* USSR

Russian Cultural Centre, 341

Russian language, 341, 344

rustling, 187, 195, 201, 244

Rutooro language, 340, 345, 346-7

Ruwenzuru secessionist movement, 9

Ruzindana, A., 292

Rwanda, 3, 9, 106, 117, 120, 121, 127, 196, 240, 342, 347

Rwandan Patriotic Front, 3, 9

Rweyemamu, Professor, 295

Sadiq al-Mahdi, 179, 182, 183, 369

St Anthony's Hospital, 132

salaries *see* wages

Salaries Review Commission, 101

Saleh, Major General Salim, 205, 244

savings, 27, 31, 44

Scandinavia, 376

schistosomiasis, 152

schools, 25, 300, 323, 324-5, 332; *see also* education; teachers

secession, 9, 226

sectarianism, 267, 268-9

Security Organisations Statute (1987), 221

seers, 126, 127, 129n

Seers, Professor Dudley, 96n

Senghor, Léopold, 368, 369

services, public, 306-7

sex discrimination, 223

Shagari, President Al-Haji Shehu, 356

shambas, 86; *see also* market gardens

shareholding, 371, 377

Shari'a law, 359

Sheraton Hotel, 307

Silly Silindi, 170

Silver Coni, 170

Singapore, 68

slave trade, 174, 207-8

sleeping sickness *see* trypanosomiasis

'slim' *see* AIDS

Smith, Adam, 372, 373

smuggling, 48, 85, 116, 131-2, 185, 196, 305

soap industry, 365

social change, 348

Social Dimensions of Adjustment Project, 30

Social Science Research Council, 310n

social services, 12-13, 25, 60, 69, 72, 115-16, 298

social structure, 113-29; *see also* class, social

socialism, 366-70, 376, 377

Index

socialism, market, 366, 370-2, 377
Somalia, 3, 96n, 196, 347, 358
sorcery *see inyinya; kiroga;* witchcraft
Soroti, 3, 165, 260
South Africa, 96n, 171, 197, 361-2, 367
South Ankole, 164
South Korea, 68
Southall, Aidan, 116-17
Soviet Union *see* USSR
Spacioza, 127
Special Programme of Assistance, 26, 37
spirits, 170-1; *see also jogi, mbandwa, tipu*
squatters, 304
Sri Lanka, 376
Ssese Islands, 277n
stabilization, economic, 16, 17, 31-4, 37, 39, 40, 44, 53, 57-8, 65, 71
state:
   administration, 210; and advancement of women, 13, 358, 359, 365;
   deterioration of, 147; intervention of, 40-1, 50, 68, 75-6, 227, 251, 371; land ownership, 319; language policy, 341; role of, 297-310, 378; terrorism of, 219
Stephen, Mujuni, 262
structural adjustment, 13, 16-18, 20-77, 78, 98, 99, 147, 344, 345, 351-78
Structural Adjustment Facility, 26, 35, 37, 56, 71
sub-counties *see gombolola*
subsidies, 44, 60
Sudan, 3, 96n, 117, 152, 167, 171, 195, 199;
   refugee camps, 149, 158; southern, 8-9, 96n, 178-86, 186n, 192, 194, 240
Sudan African National Union, 179
Sudan African Parties, 183
Sudan People's Liberation Army, 8-9, 18, 149, 180, 182, 183, 184-5, 192, 194-5, 240
sugar industry, 117, 188
Summer Institute of Linguistics, 339
Susser, Dr Ida S., 128n
Swahili language, 9-10, 329, 334-5, 336-7, 342-3, 344, 345, 347-8, 348n, 349n, 355, 369
Swaziland, 347
Sweden, 367
Switzerland, 367

Tablet, 293
Taiwan, 68
Tanganyika *see* Tanzania

TANU Youth League, 207
Tanzania, 164, 167, 189, 201, 240;
   AIDS, 120, 121; and market socialism, 371; and Swahili language, 336-7, 342, 355; army, 123, 207, 230; invasion by Amin, 122, 304; leadership, 369; Leadership Code, 355; smuggling, 117, 119; Ugandan exports to, 79; Ujamaa, 312; visit by Museveni, 336; workers' councils, 295
Tanzania People's Defence Force, 207, 230, 231, 246n
taxation, 58, 82-4, 94, 287, 301;
   coffee, 28; colonial, 361; conversion, 53; farm, 89-91; land, 320, 321; reform of, 27
tea industry, 360
teachers, 110-11, 192, 323, 330, 335, 336, 338, 342; *see also* education; schools
technology, 363-4, 377
telephone service, 109-10
television, 339
Telex Budget, 71
terrorism, state, 219
Teso, 114, 244, 245, 347
Teso people, 199, 201-2
textbooks, 325-7
textile industry, 64
Thatcher, Margaret, 358, 371, 376, 377
theatre, 339, 349n
Thika, 166, 190
timber trade, 29
Tipis, Justus ole, 189, 190
tipping, 101-2
tipu, 175, 176
Tito, Marshal, 371, 377
tobacco industry, 64
Toninyira mukange, 102-3, 104, 112n
Toposa people, 182
Toro Landlord and Tenant Law, 314
Tororo, 96n, 100, 130-48, 166, 188, 190, 317
torture, 201, 203; *see also kandooya*
Touré, Sékou, 368
tractors, 301
trade:
   balance *see* balance of payments; controls, 60; internationalization of, 360, 363-4; unions, 273
trading sector, 82
trading, street, 86, 98, 101, 102-8
transport, 28, 57, 64-5, 74, 94, 303

401

tribes, 315
Tripoli, 183
Trotsky, Leon, 231, 239
trucks and trucking, 28, 120, 121
Trust Fund, 67
trypanosomiasis, 132, 152, 153
tuberculosis, 152, 174, 175
Tunisia, 367
Turkana, 187, 192

UFM, 233
Uganda Advanced Certificate of
    Education, 331, 332
Uganda Archives, 157
Uganda Certificate of Education, 326,
    331, 332
Uganda College of Business Studies,
    331
Uganda Commercial Bank, 290
Uganda Constitutional Commission
    Statute, 215
Uganda Cooperative College, 310n
Uganda Development Corporation, 302
Uganda Freedom Army, 181, 238-9
Uganda Hardwares, 49
Uganda Higher Education Board, 341
Uganda Land Commission, 315, 316
Uganda Medical Council, 135
Uganda National Examinations Board,
    326, 340
Uganda National Liberation Army, 149,
    160, 162, 165, 199, 200, 205, 230, 233,
    239, 243
Uganda National Liberation Front, 252
Uganda National Unity Movement, 181
Uganda People's Army, 3
Uganda People's Congress, 4, 249, 252,
    253, 254, 255, 258, 261, 266, 267, 268,
    269, 270
Uganda People's Democratic
    Movement/Army, 160, 162, 165, 166,
    180-1, 182-3, 184, 200, 201, 206, 245
Uganda People's Front, 181
Uganda People's Movement, 252-3, 255,
    258
Uganda Pharmaceutical Board, 135, 137
Uganda Pharmaceuticals Ltd, 131
Uganda Polytechnical College, 280, 331
Uganda Red Cross, 134
Uganda Study Team, 97n
Uganda Swahili Association, 337, 340,
    342
Uganda Television, 336

*Uganda, the Human Rights Record
    1986-1989*, 198, 202
Ujamaa, 312
ulcers, tropical, 152, 154
UNDP, 30
UNESCO, 339-40, 349n
UNICEF, 131
United Kingdom *see* Britain
United Nations, 151;
    Convention against Torture and other
    Cruel, Inhuman or Degrading
    Treatment or Punishment, 203;
    Economic Commission for Africa, 17,
    59, 69; High Commission for
    Refugees, 151, 192
United Salvation Army, 164
United States, 127, 128n, 194, 229, 351,
    353;
    House of Representatives Select
    Committee on Hunger, 119
University of Wisconsin Land Tenure
    Center, 317
UNLF, 234
UNRF, 233, 239
Upper Nile, 182, 184
urbanization, 88, 99
USSR, 231, 239, 351, 367, 369, 371
Usuk, 260

venereal disease, 152, 153
Verona Fathers, 175
veterinary services, 302, 305
Victoria, Lake, 117, 121, 187, 189
Vietnam, 370, 376
village councils *see* resistance
    councils/committees
Vincent, Dr Joan, 128n
Virgin Mary, 127, 156
visions, religious, 126, 127
Vurra, 158, 159

Wabigalo, 103
wage-fixing, 84
wage labour, introduction of, 361
wages, 39, 49, 58, 95;
    and *magendo*, 11; civil servants, 28, 30,
    35, 101; health care workers, 136;
    living wage, 12, 98-112; minimum,
    78, 84, 86; non-African, 82; *see also*
    income
Walls, Peter, 239
Wallwork, 346
Wamwere, Koigi wa, 191

Wandegeya, 334
waragi, 150, 169
wars, 48, 49, 79, 122-3, 149, 164, 202,
  240, 241, 256, 257, 258, 260;
  Kagera War, 122, 231, 237, 246n;
  Nigeria, 352, 356; Rwanda, 240;
  Southern Africa, 362; Sudan, 179, 184,
  196, 240; World War II, 361, 366;
  Zaire, 240
Warsaw Pact, 366
Warwick University, 356
water supply, 360, 365
wealth, acquisition of, 357-8
Webbism, 235
Weekly Review, 187, 189, 190, 192
Weekly Topic, 12, 109, 293
welfare *see* social services
welfare state, 371
West Moyo, 149-61
West Nile, 100, 108, 164, 179, 206, 234,
  235, 347
West Pokot, 187, 192-3
Western Bantu languages, 340, 344
Western Province, 187, 191
Westernization, 360, 363, 634, 369
wheat, 343
witch doctors, 126 *see also ojo*
witchcraft, 163, 165, 167-8, 172, 173,
  174, 176; *see also abiba; inyinya*
women:
  agricultural role, 361, 363, 364; and
  market economy, 358-66, 377; and
  poverty, 30; and state, 13; and
  technology, 363-4; custodial role,
  360-1, 364-5, 376; economic survival
  strategies, 11; entrepreneurial role,
  359-60, 364-6; fertility, 360-1, 362; in
  armed forces, 362; in Holy Spirit
  Movement, 162-3; in politics, 74, 212,
  259, 260, 261, 269, 271, 272; *inyinya*,
  157; myths, 378n; *njua kali* activities,
  98-112; *ojo* 156, 159-60; single-parent
  households, 115; widows, 124
won ngom, 173
wood *see* firewood; timber trade
workers' councils, 295
workers' organizations, 271, 272
World Bank, 7, 36, 59, 65, 79, 312, 360;
  and Economic Recovery Credit, 71;
  and social services, 12, 326-7; and
  structural adjustment, 2, 16, 17, 30,
  72, 78, 98, 351; Council of African
  Advisers, 378n; East Africa
  Department, 42n; Special Programme
  of Assistance, 26
World Development Report, 12
World Health Organization, 117
World War II, 361, 366
worms, intestinal, 143, 152
wounds, infected, 152

Xhosa movement, 201

yaws, 153
Yoruba language, 369
Yorubaland, 368
youth, 112n, 271, 272
Yugoslavia, 366, 371, 377

Zaire, 3, 9, 106, 117, 121, 128n, 151,
  170, 185, 240
Zambia, 96n, 121, 266
ZANLA, 239, 362
Zimbabwe, 347, 362, 373
Zimbabwe People's Revolutionary Army,
  239
ZIPRA, 362